Table Of Contents

Dedication

To the memory of my father, who loved camping, and to my tenderfoot mother, who went along with humor and good grace.

Preface

The bed of pine needles was as fragrant as a Christmas tree, and surprisingly soft as I swizzled into it like a contented spaniel. I was 8 years old, camping with my family in the Adirondacks. My sleeping bag was home-made out of old army blankets. They were scratchy wool that was warm, wore like iron, and was nearly wetproof. My canopy was a pine tree, not far from the canvas tent that smelled of creosote and old campfires, where my parents and brother were making their beds. I was asleep when Dad carried me into the tent, safe from whatever wild creatures were abroad in the mountain night, but I'd drifted off feeling like Sacajawea, a child of the forest and one with the earth.

In our family, camping was not just a cheap way to sleep and eat as we traveled. It was educational, character-building, and a challenge that pitted us and all of our wiles against hunger, cold, heat, wet, voracious bugs, hungry bears and raccoons, getting lost, and all of Nature's other tricks. Turned into a game, camping became fun. Turned into fun, it forged a family bond, teaching us that we could make a safe survival home almost anywhere. It was one of the greatest gifts parents could give a child.

Much has changed since those early camping trips. Gear can be researched on the Internet, and ordered from sophisticated Web sites and catalogs. High-tech

materials last forever, almost never leak, and are fire-proofed at the factory. Complete meals can be picked up at the supermarket, or created from freeze-dried packets that swell into hot, filling meals that taste like real food. Campgrounds offer golf, massages, modems, and cable television hook-ups.

But many of the old ways still apply. I can still make my own sleeping bags as needed depending on whether it's winter or summer. I can improvise a stove out of a tuna can, dig a toilet, and waterproof my boots with natural waxes. I'm not alone. Worldwide, knives are still sharpened with whetstones. Biscuits are still baked with reflector ovens. The old Coleman gasoline stove is still standard issue throughout the planet. And some campsites can still be reached only by those who walk or paddle in.

While it's important to remember and practice the many time-worn skills that still work best in whatever kind of camping we tackle, it's also important to let go of the past. We welcome today's tough, waterproof fabrics, its foolproof fire starters, and the cell phones and other high-tech aids that keep us safer in the outdoors. Most of all, we cherish tomorrow. For all its problems and unknowns, it promises camping pleasures and discoveries yet to come.

–Janet Groene

How To Use This Book

One of the greatest pastimes in the outdoors has always been to sit around the campfire, spinning tales of our triumphs, defeats, and lessons learned. This is the way wisdom has been passed down through the ages, since long before the written word. It's still the way that campers share tips and warnings. Think of this book as a campfire chat with a friend who may not always have the right answers but whose answers are based on firsthand experience and *do* work at least some of the time in some circumstances. Your input is always welcome at: janetgroene@yahoo.com.

This isn't a book to read from start to finish. It's a handbook to keep handy and refer to often. Write notes in the margins. Add your own pages of checklists and recipes. Make it an ever-evolving part of your camping life. You may choose a new tent only once every 10 years. You may winter-camp only once in a blue moon, and you may never canoe camp. However, you'll find useful information everywhere, even in chapters that don't apply to you at this moment. Read the entire book eventually, skipping around according to the campout *du jour*.

PART

1

Get it together

KOA Kampgrounds

What Do You Mean, Camping?

Some campers walk, some drive, some ride horseback or lead pack llamas.

Photo courtesy of Amarillo CVB

In these stressful times, many people treasure the simple pleasures of outdoor lifestyles, says Bill Phillips, president of the Coleman Company. "It comes as no surprise to us that Americans who camp and participate most in outdoor activities say they are the most satisfied with their personal lives," Phillips says.

Coleman's survey showed that, of those who go camping three to five times a year, 80 percent feel satisfied with their personal lives. That's far more than those who do not go camping at all (65 percent are sat-

isfied with their lives) or those who camp only once a year (50 percent express satisfaction with their lives). Americans who say they go camping three to five or more times a year also say that they are more satisfied with their relationships with friends than those who don't camp at all.

When asked what would help them spend more time in outdoor recreation, 44 percent said more time, and only 28 percent said more money. In general, men and boys go camping 2.9 times a year while women and girls go 1.7 times a year. A majority of the men, 66

The good times are out there. Go find them at a beautiful rustic campsite.

percent, said they'd like to go camping more often; 44 percent of the women would also like to camp more.

Coleman asked Americans what words they associated most with camping. Rated highest are peacefulness, adventure, and self-reliance. Words least associated with camping are boredom and stress. On average, women are more likely than men to associate camping with bringing back old memories (5.8 percent vs. 5.2 percent).

As for how time is spent in camp, sharing special times around the campfire with family and friends ranks first with campers, followed by beautiful landscapes and wildlife. Ten percent praised such camping activities as boating, hiking, and fishing. For 9 percent, cooking and eating outside are the most fun of camping, and 6 percent rated sleeping in a tent or under the stars as what they like best about camping. The poll was based on 1,013 interviews done in 2001, Coleman's centennial year.

According to the Travel Industry Association of America, half of all American adults took an adventure travel vacation within the past five years. That's more than 100 million people who are camping, hiking, mountain biking, rafting, off-roading, diving, kayaking, canoeing or all of the above. Half of them take their children; about 10 percent take their parents. They're vacationing –not just overnighting or weekending–for a median price of less than $400 for the entire trip!

They're evenly mixed, 51 percent men and 49 percent women. Most are married and work full-time. The mean age for campers and other soft adventure travelers is 39, but you'll see infants and toddlers in the campground as well as people in their 80s.

If you're new to camping, it begins with choosing the right shelter for your family, climate and terrain.

Canoe camping offers unique pleasures unavailable to walk-in and drive-in campers.

Photo courtesy of Minnesota Office of Tourism

It's the aim of this book that you will find here more than you need to know about camping. We all camp in different regions, using different gear, eating different foods, pursuing different pastimes. Once you've been hooked on camping and the outdoors, however, it's likely you'll try it in many different forms–most of which are described somewhere in these pages.

If you're new to camping, start with the basics of shelter, safety skills, and food. Build a secure foundation of gear, knowledge, and confidence, then gradually add to your repertoire just as a juggler goes from three oranges to six oranges, two spinning plates, and a hula hoop around one ankle. The list of Resources at the end of the book is your lifeline of additional information, providers, outfitters, and sources for more information or buying gear. Within a few months, we hope this will be the most well-thumbed book in your library, with stains on the recipe chapter, notes throughout the Resources section, and entries in the margins of most of the chapters.

Early on, let's agree on unity. We're all campers who love the outdoors and want to preserve it. Before you drive your first tent stake, you'll start worrying that a noisy RV will pull in and "there goes the neighborhood." Or, the tenters next door will turn up their bat-

tery-operated boom box while you'd rather listen to the crickets. Or, a powerful outboard will scream past your lakeside campsite, sending up a cloud of smoke.

Get over it.

It's only human nature to be peeved when others invade our space. My husband I once beat into headwinds for three days and nights to sail to a small, deserted island in the Bahamas, where we had an entire beach all to ourselves until a 1,500-passenger cruise ship dropped anchor and began ferrying people ashore. We've had to move our camp because of noisy teenagers or punky campfires. One could paddle or ski or hike to the end of the world, and someone would arrive in a helicopter or speedboat or snowmobile to ruin the idyll.

In exchange for the bad times, however, you'll spend endless nights with no noises but nature's and no smells except the popcorn and s'mores that are cooking over your own fire. They are there. Go out and find them.

Camping is a big tent with room inside for people of all ages, genders, faiths and colors. There is room in this happy family for you.

Come, join the fun!

CHAPTER

Who's Camping Now?

Camping is one of the most widespread outdoor activities in the world.

Photo courtesy of Gordon Groene

Say hello to the new era in camping! Nuclear families are still around, just as they were in the days of "Leave it to Beaver," but they're outnumbered now by a new society in which single parents, loners, groups of friends, and blended families are discovering the beauties, wonders, and affordability of the outdoors. Our friends Alice in Ohio and Ruth in Florida, both divorced and struggling to raise six and five children respectively, turned to tenting as the only vacations they could afford. The result was a rich bonding and the learning of skills that provided a lifetime of rewards for mothers and kids.

According to the U.S. Census Bureau, about 44 million Americans participate in camping, not counting millions of Canadians and Mexicans who camp in North America plus millions more who camp worldwide.

Most North Americans drive to the campsite in a car or van loaded with a tent, sleeping bags, food, and supplies. Others hike in, pack in on horseback, lead pack mules or llamas, ride in on their bicycles or motorcycles, sail in on a Hobie Cat, paddle in by canoe or kayak, or whoosh in on a whitewater raft. Many families enjoy fly-in camping in private planes, using small

Camping is a happy, bonding activity for families, friends, in-laws, step-parents, half-siblings, adopted grandparents, and everyone in between.

airports that welcome visitors to pitch a tent under a wing.

There's no end to variations on the theme. For instance, your backpack trip might start on a train or bus that takes you across the country to where you hit the trailhead in Colorado or northern Maine. Or, you might fly to the island of St. John in the U.S. Virgin Islands, taking only clothes and a bedroll. A camp and rental gear are available on the spot, and you can shop local markets for the food you'll need. We heard of one loner who, carrying an inflatable boat and a backpack, took a bus to a city upstream and floated down-river for days, camping along the banks.

Most campers go on their own, which is the least expensive way to go, but you can also sign on with an outfitter-guide who will provide all the savvy, most of the gear, and all the grunt work. They range from guides who will simply show you the way to large companies with a major investment in rafts, bush planes, llamas, canoes, kayaks, bicycles, mountaineering gear, dive boats, horses, native porters, Land Rovers, and so on.

Do an Internet search for adventure camping for lists of outfitters in the place and the sport that inter-

Kamping Kabins provide shelter, bunks, and a grill but campers must bring everything else.

Whatever your yen from tame to terrifying; whatever your budget from meager to millionaire, there is a camping scenario that will work for you.

Above: The fastest-growing segment in tent camping is single parents, who find camping to be affordable, bonding, and fun.
At right: Fill your sketchbook with wildflowers

Photo courtesy of Alpen Outdoors

Photo courtesy of Gordon Groene

ests you. Whatever your yen from tame to terrifying; whatever your budget from meager to millionaire, there is a camping scenario that will work for you.

TOP TIP

So you can't afford to buy camping gear? A program at Big Basin Redwoods State Park near Santa Cruz, Calif., is just the ticket for newbies who don't know a tent peg from a pie iron. The Hassle Free Camping program provides a tent cabin in the redwoods, and complete camping gear for four, for as little as $135 plus, if you want it, ingredi-

ents for breakfast the first morning for an additional $8. The package includes a tent cabin, Coleman stove, lantern, fuel, two bundles of campfire wood, pots, pans and utensils, pillows, up to four sleeping bags, and a 60-quart cooler with two bags of ice. For information call (800) 874-8368.

Ohio State Parks have a similar program called Rent-a-Camp in which you get a lodge-style tent and dining canopy, cooler, two cots, sleeping pads, propane stove, lantern, fire ring, and picnic table.

Write the Ohio State Park Information Center, 1952 Belcher Drive, Building C-3, Columbus, OH 43224.

Some people camp to camp. Others camp to have a place to sleep after they fish all day.

Photo courtesy of Gordon Groene

Affordable Options Available

KOA campgrounds offer Kamping Kabins that are cute, little log cabins with a front porch, grill, bunks, and perhaps an air conditioner or heater. It's camping without the tent. Everything must be brought with you. Stop at any KOA to get a free directory of all KOAs in the United States, Canada, and Mexico, or call (406) 248-7444, www.koa.com. Individual KOAs have their own, toll-free phone numbers.

In St. John, the island in the U.S. Virgin Islands that is almost entirely national park land, campsites and gear can be rented near the beach. Maho Bay Camps, built on breezy hills overlooking the beach, is a complete resort where you sleep and cook in canvas cabins that have solar electricity and composting toilets. The resort also has a restaurant, swimming pool, a camp store, lessons in glass blowing and other crafts, and organized nature hikes and ranger talks.

Many state and national parks also offer primitive cabins at affordable rates. Don't confuse them with luxury lodges, also found in some state and national parks, that rent for hundreds of dollars a night. In these cabins, you must bring everything needed for camping except the shelter itself.

For the price, you get a roof over your head and maybe a rough bunk, an outdoor grill or fire pit, and a food cache that's safe from bears. If there are toilets at all, they're primitive and they're probably shared with other campers. Everything, often including water, must brought with you.

CHAPTER

Less than $100 buys a classic, 10-foot by 8-foot dome tent that sleeps up to four people.

Photo courtesy of Coleman

Give Me Shelter
Choosing and Caring For a Tent

A tent is probably the most important piece of gear you'll choose for camping because it is your shelter against cold, rain, harsh sun, bugs, and much more. Ideally, your tent will be as big as a ballroom. It will set up and pack away in seconds, weigh no more than cotton candy, and cost almost nothing. Dream on. To compromise, you need the tent that provides the most and best features for your style of camping, at a realistic price.

Choices range from individual tents for backpackers and bikers to large, multi-room family tents. The marketplace offers every shape under the sun in models that range from free-standing to elaborate lash-ups of frames, ropes, and pegs. My friends who are Civil War re-enactors even have an authentic replica of a wood-frame campaign tent that would have been in use in the 1860s! It takes an army to set it up but it's authentic down to the last stitch and tent peg (although they did cheat by adding an extra room for the Porta-Potti).

Your tent's weight and its size when stowed are among the most important things to consider when you're backpacking, canoeing, kayaking, horseback camping, or traveling by bicycle or motorcycle. In car camping or trekking with pack animals, however, compactness and weight aren't as crucial. In fact, if your camping vehicle is a big van or pickup truck, you may even have room to carry a circus big top and everything that goes with it.

First, think about how many you want the tent to accommodate, not just sleep. For backpacking, it's enough to have a snug, warm place to sleep before returning to the trail. If it's raining or blowing too hard to cook, you can hunker down and chomp gorp. In

Sleep up to three people in a four-season backpacking tent that weighs as little as 10 pounds, 3 ounces. Coleman's Lynx™ is shown with vestibule.

family camping, however, you need enough space for each person to stretch out, move around, stow gear, sit up and read, and change clothes. You may also want two or three separate rooms for privacy, and an attached screen room to act as a living room and dining room.

The Shape of Things

Every design has its compromises. Dome tents have generous floor space and headroom, and are usually freestanding. They erect quickly and can easily be skated around on the ground for a few feet in all directions until you find just the right place to stake down. On the minus side, any free-standing tent can turn into a balloon in high winds. Once it's up or partially up, it can be a bear until you get it fully secured.

Here's what L.L. Bean experts say: "Dome and cabin styles are our most popular designs. With their lower profile, dome tents are more aerodynamic and stand up well to high winds. Higher profile cabin tents are less aerodynamic, but provide more headroom and floor space. Freestanding tents do not need to be staked in order to stand. Non-freestanding tents will not stand without...stakes and guy lines."

L.L. Bean tents are made of polyester, which is UV resistant, tough, and preferable for family camping, or nylon, which they recommend for backpacking because of its light weight. "A breathable inner wall allows condensation to pass through to the outside, creating a drier, more comfortable environment inside," say Bean spokespersons. The company also recommends color-coded pole sleeves or clips to help you set up the tent quickly, rain-fly adjustments that keep the fly taut even in strong winds and driving rain, an extended rain fly for protection against extreme conditions, self-sealing zippers to prevent jamming and freezing, and no-see-um screening to keep out the smallest insects.

Buying a Tent: A Checklist

☐ **Weather Protection.** A tent should be waterproof enough to keep rain out, breathable enough to keep condensation from building up on inside walls, and windproof enough to withstand whatever your campout is subjected to. Look for stitching that won't tear, sewn with thread that won't rot or weaken. Seams should be taped at the factory for extra strength and to make them leakproof. Sun and rain flies can be a flapping menace in high winds and elaborate seaming can invite weak spots and leaks. (Yet both have their merits). The design shouldn't have spots that can sag when filled with rain or snow. This in turn leads to strain on seams and supports, leaks and/or condensation.

☐ **Snow Load** is a consideration for winter camping, so it's best to have a tent with steep, slippery sides. A slick, plastic tarp can be rigged over the tent, but it's best if the tent itself is designed without hollows and flats where snow can build up.

☐ **Interior** space isn't just a matter of cubic footage, but usable space that allows you to sit up and read, stretch, write in your journal, or eat crackers and cheese while you wait out a storm. Know the interior height throughout the tent, not just at the highest point. You need this space to change clothes, wiggle in and out of a sleeping bag, stow a bag or two, and perhaps seek shelter from insects or weather while you eat.

☐ **Tent poles** are available in steel, aluminum or fiberglass, each with their own good points. Fiberglass flexes, which can strain fabric, snap and flap, making for a noisy night in high winds. However, it is a strong, featherweight and rustproof material. Aluminum is light and strong, but can corrode in a saltwater atmosphere. Steel is strongest, but it's heavy and, when the protective coating wears off or is invaded by a scratch, it rusts.

Most tent poles are fitted with shock cord, which can lose its elasticity in freezing weather. In any case, shock cord eventually loses its stretch, so look for poles designed for easy bungee replacement.

☐ **Color** determines whether you blend with the environment or stand out. A dark tent can add to depression during a long, shut-in period, and a red or orange color, while it's easiest to spot from the air if you need rescue, can close in on you. White and light colors are cooler in the tropics; dark colors are warmer in the snow. Color is a minor point, but give it some thought if the manufacturer offers a choice.

☐ **Guarantee.** What is covered and how is warranty work done? If you have to ship the tent to a factory on the other side of the world, then wait months for repairs or replacement, the guarantee loses its luster.

☐ **Fasteners.** Are grommets and snaps solid brass or stainless steel, or are they plated steel that will rust in time? Are zippers a non-corroding material such as solid brass or a good plastic or nylon? Aluminum or plated steel zippers won't last a season if you camp near the ocean. Are zippers configured for the best possible opening and closing? For example, a door might be fitted with a separating zipper that allows complete removal of the entire door. Or, twin zippers meet at the top, bottom, or sides of windows so you don't have to pull one tab all the way around to open or close a window. Or, the tent has a tub-type floor with an all-around zipper that allows the entire floor to be removed for cleaning or replacement.

☐ **Stitching.** Are seams single, double, or triple stitched? Are seams taped? Is the thread UV resistant? Rot-proof? Are the seams also heat sealed or otherwise waterproofed? How generous are reinforcements at strain points such as stake loops? The larger the patch, the larger the area to take the stress. Are reinforcements waterproofed as well as seams?

☐ **Weight.** If the tent weight is not specified in the catalog (and it should be), compare shipping

Continued on **Page 17**

Photo courtesy of Coleman

Coleman's three-room Weathermaster model is constructed for a dry interior, measures 17 x 9 feet, and sleeps 6-8 in three rooms, with 76 inches of headroom at the tallest point. The curved roof is designed to shed rain and withstand winds.

Take your time. Sit down. Relax. Review the instructions. Use the manufacturer's checklist or make your own.

Photo courtesy of Coleman

Coleman's INYO™ backpacking tent can be used with or without a full rainfly. It sells for about $90.

SETTING UP THE TENT

E ven if you have seen the tent set up in a showroom, it's best to make one or two trial runs in your back yard before tackling setup in the campsite. At best, you'll be dealing with unfamiliar terrain. At worst, it will be raining, blowing a gale, dark, buggy, too hot, too cold, or all of the above. The more familiar you are with handling frames, fittings, tent poles, stakes and guy ropes, the faster the job will go. In fact, some families do a trial setup at home at the start of each season–not just to review the drill but to check for damage and to make sure that all the necessary components are still there.

Take your time. Begin by popping the top on a cold drink. Sit down. Relax. Review the instructions and parts list. Use the manufacturer's checklist or make your own checklist, which will probably be longer and more comprehensive, then laminate it for use every time you put up or take down the tent. It's one way to make sure you don't leave something behind.

A new tent may need seam treatment or waterproofing initially or once a season, or a pre-conditioning treatment that involves a thorough wet-down after it's set up for the first time. Instructions are different for every model, size and fabric, so take good care of the manual that comes with your tent. Even if you never have to refer to it again, it will make a resale easier because the new buyer will need it.

The best tent is stressed just taut enough to look shipshape, to shed water, to stand strong against winds, and to allow windows and doors to open and close easily, but not so tightly that strain is put on any part of the entire shebang. With each trip, each campsite and each setup, there are subtle differences as ropes stretch, tent poles sag, seams "give," and fabrics shrink. The tent and its components will also be stiffer or more pliant depending on the temperature.

With luck, you'll soon have a fit as comfortable as an old house slipper – a tent that's easy to put up and take down, tight against the elements, and with just enough "give" in the right places to allow for small differences in temperatures, humidity, and terrain. ◆

weights to get an idea of the overall weight of the tent. Will you be able to carry it on your back or, in drive-in camping, can you load, lift, fold, unfold, and pitch it, wrestle it into its storage bag, and lug it into the basement or attic for storage? A typical, three-season backpacking tent designed for expedition use, Coleman's Exponent™ series Inyo™ model, weighs only four pounds. It can sleep two in a floor measuring 95 x 52 inches. Its four-season Lynx™ tent, also from its Exponent™ series, sleeps up to three and weighs just over 10 pounds while its Weathermaster™ four-sleeper, made for family use in car camping, weighs slightly more than 35 pounds including the steel frame. Note too, whether a tent is designed for winter camping. If you need only a three-season tent, don't carry the extra weight of a four-season tent.

☐ **Maintenance needs.** How big a job will it be to re-waterproof, re-coat, or otherwise treat the tent periodically? How often is this step called for by the manufacturer? What will supplies or materials cost?

☐ **Accessories.** How much paraphernalia goes with the tent? Is the company going to be around when you need a new ridge pole #351AE457XY or when you have to replace oddball poles? Are accessories available from North American sources or do you have to send your credit card number to Outer Mongolia and hope for the best? Does a good carry-bag come with the deal?

☐ **Rip resistant.** Many of the new fabrics and coatings are very hard to penetrate and, if they are cut, won't continue to tear. Is the tent reinforced at stress points?

Sold through major outdoor suppliers, Eureka manufactures an extensive choice of expedition, all-season, backpack, and family tents.

☐ **Ease of use.** It's best if you can put the tent up and down before buying, but that isn't always possible in the real world. The more different parts, the longer it will take to assemble and pitch the tent and stow it again when you break camp. Add rain, high winds or darkness to the job, and you could have a tiger by the tail. For example, some tents have poles that are all the same size; others require a set of hardware bigger than the Legos kit you had as a kid. Keep it simple.

☐ **The floor** should be waterproof, but a coating on the outside can soon wear and leak. A waterproof coating over a coarse, ripstop fabric can also abrade along the high spots, creating leaks. A fine-denier floor with multiple coats of waterproofer is best. Then add a ground cloth, preferably one offered by the tent manufacturer to be used with this model. It's important that it be large enough to protect the entire floor but not so large that it extends past tent edges, where it could collect rain and encourage leaks.

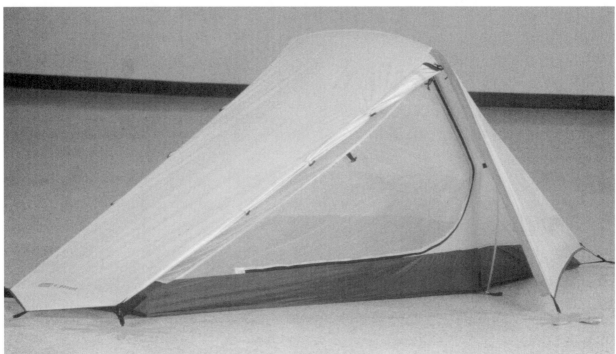

Coleman's INYO™ backpacking tent is shown with a full rainfly.

TENT CARE

The one rule that applies to every tent is to put it away clean and bone dry. Even the most mildew-proof fabrics can host growths if dampness is allowed to remain. At best, a tent that is put away damp will smell dank and discolor. At worst, mildew will eat away thread, destroy seams, weaken fabric, and spread to everything that is stored with or near the tent.

The owner's manual is the best place to look for information on caring for your tent because fabrics and components differ.

Check your instruction manual for:

☐ Zipper care. Marine stores and some camping supply stores sell spray-on or smear-on products that keep zippers zipping.

☐ Instructions on how to fold the tent so it will fit back into the carry bag.

☐ Annual maintenance such as re-waterproofing or seam treatment.

☐ Instructions on how to wash the tent including what soaps or detergents are safe to use without damaging waterproof coatings or flame retardants.

☐ Instructions on how to mend or replace screens or other components that are easily damaged.

A Eureka! tent is set up, ready for camping.

Photo courtesy of Eureka!

It's a wise investment to buy certain spare parts, such as extra tent pegs, matching screening material, or a new carry bag when you purchase the tent. Models change and manufacturers come and go. Factory spares may not be available later. While generic substitutes can be found or improvised, nobody can match your tent better than the manufacturer. Additions and repairs done with factory materials will not only work better but will look better at re-sale time.

The Mantis three-season tent is shown without a fly.

Photo courtesy of Coleman

The same Mantis three-season tent is shown with a fly to protect campers from rain.

Photo courtesy of Coleman

IF YOU CAMP ON THE BEACH

One of the most corrosive substances on earth is sea water. It corrodes aluminum, dulls brass, and rusts steel – sometimes overnight. I once heard of a seagoing canoe camper who found all her canned juice in the bilge on the second day out. A few drops of sea water on aluminum pop-tops was all it took.

TOP TIP When shopping for a tent to use at the seaside, carry a small magnet and check everything for ferrous content. Even an innocent grommet, rivet, or zipper pull could be steel. When it rusts and spreads to nearby fabric, it's ugly at best. In time, rust eats into fabric or stitching. Opt for fiberglass tent poles or frame, plastic or stainless steel tent stakes, and plastic, nylon or brass zippers. For the best holding in beach sand, get stainless steel or heavily chromed, auger-type stakes.

No matter how clean the tent appears to be when you get home from the beach, give it a thorough washdown with fresh water. Then dry it thoroughly, preferably in the sunshine on a day with low humidity. If you don't, salt crystals stay behind in the fabric and it never dries completely because the salt draws moisture out of the air. Even if you camped many yards from the water, the tent probably received a lot of salt spume from the wind or picked up salt from the sand.

Photo courtesy of Eureka!

A Eureka tent is set up for comfortable family camping.

Eureka's Camp Trails tents offer plenty of space.

TENTS: A GLOSSARY

Anti-wicking materials refer to threads, zippers, webbing, and other construction materials that repel water rather than telegraph it into the tent.

D Door is a popular design shaped exactly like a capital letter D, with a straight seam or zipper at the left and a rounded zipper on three sides. Unzip the three sides, roll the fabric aside, and the door is wide open. Other doors are designed in a T, with a center zipper and flaps to both sides. When shopping for a tent, note how easy it is to get in and out of the tent when (1) you want just to scoot in through the flap without admitting mosquitoes and (2) when you want the door wide open to move gear in and out.

Floor protector, often offered by tent makers or as a stand-alone product from outdoors suppliers, is a rugged cloth that is put down before the tent is put up. It saves the tent floor from the abrasion of soil and rocks. It should be slightly smaller than the floor footprint. If it extends beyond the tent, it can collect rain and cause leaks.

Guys or guy lines are ropes that aid the tent poles in keeping the tent up in high winds.

Mallet or a hammer may be needed to pound tent stakes into hard ground. In sandy ground, tent stakes will go in easily, perhaps too easily. For secure holding in terrain that's too soft, you may need longer or auger-type stakes.

No-see-um-mesh is an ultra-fine screening small enough to keep out sandflies, also called no-see-ums.

These tiny, biting insects can fly through regular screening.

Nylon is used for its high tear strength. Its UV resistance depends on the grade and type.

Pockets are often sewn into tent sides to provide storage for small items. Don't forget to empty them completely before storing and folding the tent.

Polyester is a tent material used for its good UV resistance and sag resistance.

Photos courtesy of Coleman

Coleman's Exponent™ line offers the Dakota™ tent to sleep up to six in three rooms. It's shown here with and without fly. It sells for about $300, weighs less than 38 pounds, and stands 6' 3" at its highest point.

Polyurethane coating, rated in millimeters, e.g. 450 mm, is used as a waterproofing on tents. The higher the mm, the better the water resistance. Usually specs are given separately for the tent fabric, the floor, and the tent fly.

Rainfly is the protective awning that provides additional rain protection and also provides insulation against hot sun. A partial rainfly covers doors and windows. A full rainfly covers the entire tent and often forms a vestibule where gear can be stored. A sunfly merely provides shade.

Repair kits are available for most tents and it's wise to get one when you buy the tent. Later, you may not be able to find compatible tapes, materials and adhesives.

Shock cord is also called bungee. It's a stretchy cord that runs through the center of tent poles to keep them connected, making setup easier. Note how it is installed because it has to be replaced periodically.

Taping is a waterproof tape, usually plastic, put over tent seams to cover needle holes.

CHAPTER

A Wake-Up Call

Photo courtesy of Coleman

A good, basic sleeping bag with a nylon cover and cotton flannel liner sells for under $25, weighs about 7 pounds, and is adequate for family camping in moderate weather.

Sleeping Bags

Most articles on sleeping bags focus on wrapping you up like King Tut so you can survive an Arctic winter. However, most camping is done in temperate climates with their highs, lows, and some nights so steamy you could fry an egg on the tent flap. Campers don't necessarily want the "best" sleeping bag as recommended by Indiana Jones. You want the bag(s) that is best for you and the way you camp.

Unless you're taking the kids on an expedition in the Himalayas, discount store sleeping bags are best for them. They'll probably outgrow them before they wear them out. Shop for real sleeping bags, however, and not those cute, thin, sleeping envelopes sold for indoor slumber parties. As long as it's warm, durable, and washable, it will do the job for a season or two.

For adults, the right bag is the one best suited to your outdoor life. If you backpack, ski-camp, bicycle or paddle, light weight and water resistance are important and usually cost goes up for more warmth with less weight. For all kinds of camping, you're looking for warmth, comfort including a good fit for your body, durability, and perhaps additional features such as a removable liner or a double zipper that allows two bags to be zipped together to make a double bag.

Some bags also have an inner layer that allows you to slip in two different ways. In cooler weather, slip into the section that leaves two layers on top; in hot weather, slip into the other slot and you'll have two layers under you and only one on top. Other dual-climate bags made, have a thin side and a thick side. Sleep with the thin side on top in hot weather.

It's an old camping rule that you sleep with as much insulation under you as on top so, in addition to the sleeping bag, you'll need a camping pad that insulates you from the ground's chill and damp and also cushions your bones. More about that later.

Temperature Ratings

Manufacturers rate sleeping bags according to the temperatures they are designed to be used in, usually in 20-degree increments. Coleman, for example, rates its bags Extreme, for temperatures to Minus 5; Moderate, for 20-40 degrees, and Mild, for climates where you don't expect temperatures to fall below 40 degrees F.

If you're one of those people who are always cold, select a bag that is rated 5-10 degrees below the lowest temperature you're likely to encounter in camping. Since a lot of body heat is lost through the head, get a mummy bag that surrounds everything but your face. Or, wear a hat on cold nights. Not everyone agrees on whether it's warmer to sleep in the nude or in clothing. Whatever your choice, Coleman says that clothes damp with perspiration won't keep anyone warm. At bedtime, choose clothing that wicks moisture away from the body. For the warmest sleeping, find a sheltered campsite out of the wind, and out of the lowest-lying areas, where cold settles. Don't forget too that nutrition has a lot to do with sleeping temperature. Get plenty of calories in cold weather.

TOP TIP

REI, which offers a line of women's sleeping bags, points out that women need narrower shoulder space, wider hip space, and more insulation at the head and feet.

The Shape You're In

Sleeping bags come in three basic configurations: rectangle, tapered, and mummy. Rectangular bags are available in many fabrics and warmths, have plenty of foot room, and can usually be zipped together to make a roomy double. Tapered bags are wider at the shoulder and narrower at the foot end, which makes them lighter, more compact to carry and warmer because there is less air inside for your body to keep warm.

The mummy is the high-tech version of the sleeping bag, the warmest for extreme weather conditions because it has so little interior space for your body to keep warm. It is the lightest to carry and its extremely compact size is also a plus when you're sleeping the maximum number of people per square foot of tent space. On the minus side, it's usually the most expensive bag. It's the hardest to get into and out of because of its tight fit. Claustrophobes and people who thrash about in their sleep may find a mummy too confining.

Basic sleeping bags come in children's, regular, and king sizes, but top-of-the-line manufacturers also offer sizes for people who are extra tall or extra wide. Rectangular bags may be insulated for temperatures to as low as 20 degrees, but for really cold conditions, you'll want a bag with a drawstring at the head so only your face is exposed.

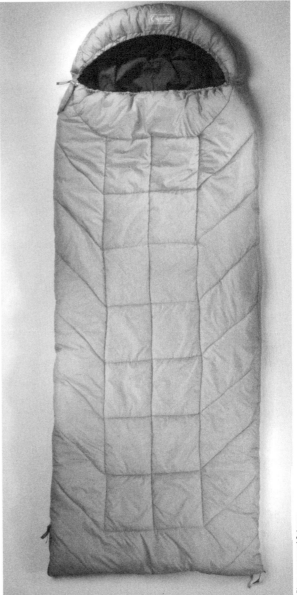

Photo courtesy of Coleman

Coleman's Ontario™ sleeping bag fits most people up to 6' 3" tall, has an orange nylon outside and cotton flannel inside, and is rated for temperatures down to 20 degrees. It sells for about $50.

As you read sleeping bag specs in the store or catalog, look for a materials list for each part of the bag. There should be one for the shell, one for the liner, and perhaps another for an accessory. For the outer shell you're looking for a durable fabric such as Ripstop nylon. For the liner, flannel is soft and fuzzy, warm to the body. Polycotton weighs less and dries more quickly, which makes it cooler in summer because perspiration is wicked away from the skin. Nylon is the lightest, most compact and quickest drying, but it can be hot. If you'll be sleeping on a slippery air mattress or vinyl boat cushion, look too for an outer fabric with some grip to it, not a slick taffeta.

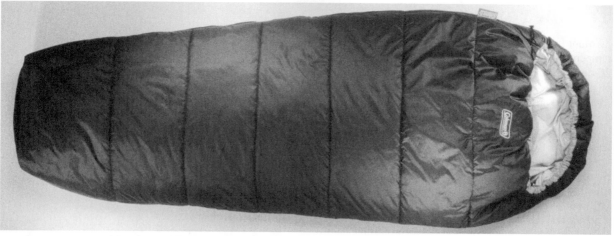

Photo courtesy of Coleman

TOP TIP While it's tempting to get a big, super-size bag you can thrash around in all night, cold weather campers prefer a tighter fit. The more air space inside the bag, the more body heat you must generate to defrost the bag and keep it warm. You can slither into a tight-fitting mummy bag on the frostiest night, pull the drawstring around your head, and have your cocoon toasty warm in minutes. A large, rectangular bag, however, will always be cold at the corners.

Types of insulation used in sleeping bags:

Down is a natural material plucked from ducks and geese, the most warmth you can get for the weight and a luxurious feel. On the down side, pardon the pun, it's expensive to buy and to clean; it can clump and drift if the manufacturer didn't provide the right construction, and some people are allergic to it. "It's the longest lasting of insulations as well as the most compactible and lightest in weight for any comfort rating," say L.L. Bean experts. "Down loses much of its insulating ability when wet. For this reason, most water sports enthusiasts choose sleeping bags with synthetic insulations."

Dupont Hollofil ® is an industry favorite for softness, warmth, low price, and compressability. It comes in three types, listed in order of good, better and best, from the cheapest to the costliest: Hollofil 808, Hollfil 11, and Quallofil.

3M Thinsulate Lite Loft is 3M's brand of a light, efficient, synthetic filler.

Polyguard ® HV is a new version of the time-honored Polarguard, a hollow-fiber filler known for its warmth, softness, and compactness.

Zipper features should include a flap that keeps a cold zipper from connecting with your skin. The zipper should also keep warm air in and cold air out. Look for a zipper that works as smooth as butter, especially around the corners.

Photos courtesy of Coleman

Above: Coleman's inflatable mattress has a flocked finish with the comfort of fabric. It's available in twin, double, queen, and king sizes weighing about 10-14 pounds. King and queen sizes are available with dual chambers, allowing for individual firmness adjustment. **At top:** The mummy-style Quebec™ model is rated to temperatures as low as 15 degrees and fits people up to 6' 2". Nylon inside and out, with a DuPont Hollofil II liner, it sells for about $50.

Sleeping bag construction terms:

Baffle is a barrier, usually a sort of tunnel, that is sewn into down bags to keep all the down from collecting in one spot.

Double Layer, Quilt Offset refers to two quilted layers put together so that the seams in one layer are in a different spot from the seams in the other. That avoids thin spots at seams that would allow cold to seep in.

Quilted is a stitching pattern that keeps loose insulation from drifting around. The closer the quilting, the less likely the insulation will shift during laundering but also the less puffy the insulation will be.

Perimeter Stitching is used with solid fillings that don't have to be tacked down every few inches. It makes for an even heat over and under the entire body.

The Canyon™ sleeping bag at $75 weighs 2 pounds, 9 ounces and is good for temperatures as low as 32 degrees.

Camp Pads

Modern camp pads, also called sleeping pads (the pad that goes under the sleeping bag) form rolls little larger than a bread loaf yet unfold to insulate you from the cold, rough ground underneath. Most are 72-77 inches long, about two feet wide, and 3/8 inch to 2 inches thick. Also available are pads in 3/4 length. They cushion only the area from shoulders to hips, but are much smaller and lighter to carry. REI's Ultralite 3/4 costs about $50, self-inflates, weighs only a pound, packs into a bundle 3.5 by 11 inches, and forms an inch-thick pad 47 inches long by 20 inches wide.

Prices go up with length, width, thickness and features such as covering and thermal protection. The thicker the pad, the more comfortable it will be but also the more unwieldy it will be to carry and store. Most camp pads are made from open-cell foam, which is light and comfortable but can absorb water. Cascade Designs offers its Strata Rest in 1.5- and 2-inch thick-

nesses. A layer of closed-cell foam is bonded between two layers of open-cell foam.

Inflatable mattresses are available in bunk, twin, double, queen, and king sizes, with dual controls available in the larger sizes. They are more durable, and can be patched. "Instant beds" are sold in major discount stores at attractive prices, and they're ideal both for camping and for use at home as a guest bed. Some inflate with a vacuum cleaner or air pump. Others have a built-in electric pump, which adds weight but is handy if you always camp at sites that have electrical hookup. Also available are 12-volt models that work off a vehicle battery.

A compromise is the compact, self-inflating sleeping pad. Self-inflating pillows, and sleeping pads-cum-pillows are also available. Open a valve and the pad plumps itself up. Roll it tightly, and air is forced back out again and it's ready to stow. It's quick and carefree, the best choice for backpackers and others who pack up and move on every day.

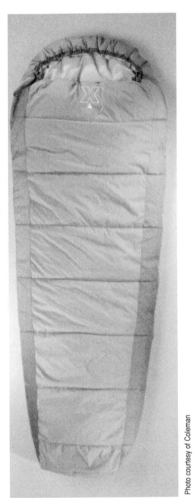

The Northbound™ series from Coleman at prices under $70 provides lightweight warmth and rugged comfort in temperature ratings of down to 25, 15, or 0 degrees.

TOP TIP

A cheap beach float can be inflated by mouth or a tire pump. It serves as an air mattress, takes up no space in storage, and it's usually long enough for kids and short adults. Floats aren't durable, but at the price can be considered almost disposable. Shop at the end of the season when they're half price.

If you're on a really tight budget, just buy "egg crate"-type mattress pads at a discount store. If you measure and cut carefully, you can probably get enough for the whole family out of one or two king-size pads. One layer is nice; two layers are better. These pads aren't very durable or washable, but it takes only minutes to sew up slipcovers for them out of old sheets or bargain fabric. While you're at it, sew up stuff bags to help corral them. They're bulky and unwieldy, but will do until you can afford real camp pads.

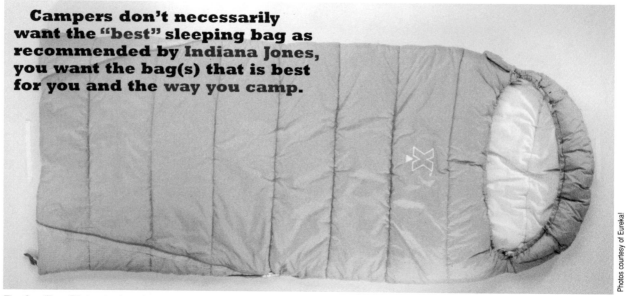

Campers don't necessarily want the "best" sleeping bag as recommended by Indiana Jones, you want the bag(s) that is best for you and the way you camp.

Photos courtesy of Eureka!

The OmniTemp™ sleeping bags have two ratings, one for use as shown and a rating up to 30 degrees colder when the zippers at the bottom end are closed, creating a tighter fit.

Pillow Talk

Pillows are bulky but are also a crucial ingredient in sleeping comfort. Many people never travel without their favorite pillows in the car, on airlines, and everywhere. For camping, bring plenty of extra pillow cases. In hot weather, fresh pillow cases every few nights feel and smell cooler, even if you can't change sheets or wash the whole sleeping bag. In cold weather, slip a pillow case over a hot water bottle and snuggle with it. No room to carry bed pillows? Here are some alternatives:

■ Blow a little air into a heavy duty zip-top bag, enough to make it pillowy but not so much that it's too bouncy, and zip it shut. Slip it into a clean tee shirt.
■ Shop travel and camping supply stores for inflatable and self-inflating pillows.
■ Carry an extra pillow sham and fill it with a rolled-up down jacket or vest.
■ Soft-sided ice chests are often just the right size and softness to use as pillows. Roll tightly. Put one or two inside a fresh pillow case.
Get your toddler a stuffed animal that also serves as a pillow.

Right: A small air compressor inflates beach toys, air mattresses, or soft tires. Camping World's cordless, rechargeable compressor costs less than $50. It can be charged from a vehicle's 12-volt outlet or a 110-volt plug, then carried to where it's needed.

Photo courtesy of Camping World

Pumped

Many campers carry an air pump for many uses, from inflating a boat or beach toys to blowing up an air mattress, beach float, boat, air bed, and even inflatable furniture. Coleman makes a full line of inflatable armchairs and sofas, including a sofa bed. In camp supply stores and catalogs, you'll find a full line of foot pumps, full-size and compact bicycle tire pumps, and electric pumps that operate on D cells, car batteries, or the campsite's electrical outlet.

TOP TIP Beware of nature's padding for use as a filler in a camp pillow or mattress. Pine needles harbor ticks and Spanish moss is probably full of redbugs.

For colder weather, use the same idea with up to five blankets or quilts. Just keep piling and folding, and you'll have as much protection underneath as on top. I've managed with this homemade bed roll for campouts of two and three nights. After that, it starts to drift apart and needs to be re-done, which isn't easy unless you have a large, clean area to spread out the blankets. For short campouts, however, it's a great sleeping bag to assemble on the living room floor.

Make Your Own Sleeping Bag

If you have a tight budget or don't have space to stow a separate sleeping bag, here's how to make a bedroll at home. When you get back from a camping trip, disassemble it and you have sheets or blankets again. You'll need at least three blankets, sheets, or a combination of both. For camping in really steamy climates, make the bag out of sheets only. You'll also need supersize safety pins, the largest you can find. This bag can take a lot of thrashing about without coming apart during the night.

Lay the first sheet or blanket on the floor. Spread the second over half of the first, extending the rest to one side. Spread the third sheet or blanket over the first. Fold the extra half of Blanket # 2 back over half

of Blanket #3, covered by the other half of Blanket #3 and the other half of Blanket #1. Flip about 3-4 inches under at the bottom, and secure with pins.

Fold down the corners of the top just enough to provide an opening to slide into, and secure the rest of the flap with safety pins, rather like buttons down a shirt front. Now, starting at the bottom, roll it up, secure with clothesline or old belts, stuff it into an old pillow case if you like, and it's ready to go.

Made with standard double blankets and sheets, this bed roll won't be long enough for tall people. Do a trial layout and see how it works for you.

Using as many sheets and blankets as needed for expected temperatures, you can make your own sleeping bag out of sheets and blankets.

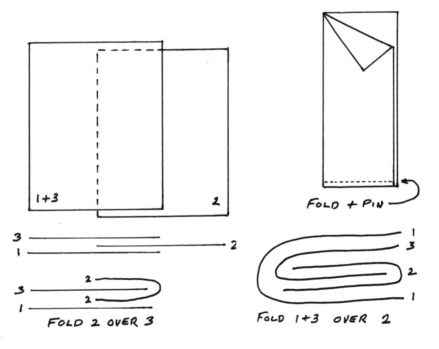

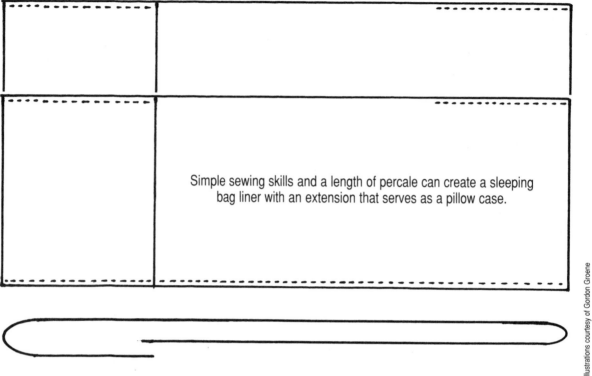

Simple sewing skills and a length of percale can create a sleeping bag liner with an extension that serves as a pillow case.

Make a Sleeping Bag Liner

Even if you're not an experienced tailor, it takes only a few minutes to zip up a percale sleeping bag liner using a sewing machine, all-purpose thread, and sheets or yard goods purchased on sale. To make a single bag, sew two bunk- or single-size sheets together on one side, across the bottom, and about 2/3 up the third side as shown, leaving a generous slit so you can slip in and out. You now have an envelope that is all the covering you need for camping the tropics. Or, use it as a removable liner for your sleeping bag.

To make a double envelope, start with two double or queen-size sheets and stitch across the bottom and 2/3 of the way up both sides. If you'll be using these envelopes as sleeping bag liners, sew Velcro dots into the bag and on the envelope at strategic spots to keep the bag from twisting and bunching.

It takes a little more time to make a sleeping envelope that has its own pillow case, and you'll need to start with yard goods. Here's how. Start with a length of fabric at least 2 ? times the length of your sleeping bag. If your bag is six feet long, you need about five yards of fabric, 36 inches wide. Buy a nice percale, tricot, silk or whatever you prefer for sheeting material, as long as it will wash easily and will feel good next to your skin. Hem both the raw edges at each end. You now have a 15-foot length of material 36 inches wide.

Double one end over for six feet and stitch up one side with a double seam. Sew the other side up about 2/3 of the way, leaving an opening because this is where you'll get into the bag. You've used four yards of the material. Now, double the other end over for about 18 inches to form the pillow case. Double stitch it along both sides. You now have a long envelope with a big pouch in one end for you and a small pouch in the other end for your pillow.

Silk sleeping "bags" are seen in specialty travel catalogs such as Magellan's (see Resources), where they are sold to hotel travelers who want a clean, luxurious sack between themselves and hotel bedding. If you don't want to sew your own, order one and use it alone as a summer sleeping bag or as a liner for your sleeping bag. Sleeping bag liners are also found in catalogs in percale or flannel for $20-$30.

Camp Cots

No matter how comfortable the sleeping pad, some campers prefer to sleep on a cot. For the modest price and small size, cots are a tempting choice for the family that has plenty of room in the trunk or van. The marketplace offers a large choice of folding cots including the bed style with a thin mattress over springs, the cot style in which canvas is stretched over an aluminum frame, and a combination style that can also be used as a chaise lounge.

If you're tall, note cot lengths because there is no standard size. Cots that look much the same may be as short as 69 inches or as long as 84 inches. Widths are usually 25-28 inches.

The timeless camp bed is still a good choice for campers who prefer to sleep on a platform. Cots provide comfort, a secure foundation for a camping pad or airbed, and an under-bed storage area. Both aluminum and wood models fold for easy storage.

Caring For Your Sleeping Bag

■ Save all the papers and labels that come with your sleeping bag. Basic care labels are sewn in, but valuable information may also be contained with the package. The paperwork also contains guarantee and warranty fulfillment information you may need later.

■ If your sleeping bag is washable, it deserves special care. Brush off any loose dirt and pre-treat stains with chemicals suitable for the fabric. Use the machine settings recommended by the manufacturer (e.g. cold water, gentle spin) and invest in a special detergent such as Sport Wash. Cleaning agents for specialty sports materials aren't found in supermarkets; shop sporting goods stores.

■ If possible, wash the bag alone or with a couple of light-colored bath towels to balance the load. Don't risk stains or snags from other items. Top-loading, agitator washers are very hard on sleeping bags. Use a large, commercial, front-loading type or one of the new non-agitator home machines. If it is machine-dryable, put the sleeping bag in the dryer alone until it's fluffed and damp-dry, then dry thoroughly on a rack.

■ Unless the manufacturer recommends otherwise, launder the bag zipped. Unzipped, it may be subjected to undue stress when wet.

■ Don't use an expensive sleeping bag as anything but a sleeping bag.

■ Sleeping bags should be dried and aired every morning as best you can. It isn't always possible when you hit the trail early, but later in the day you may be able to spread the bag in the sun during a lunch break. Fabric freshener sprays come in small bottles. If you have room to carry one, refresh the inside of the sleeping bag often, then dry and air it.

■ Drawstrings have a way of working their way out of a hood. Before they do, make the ends too big to sneak into the gusset by adding decorative beads or knots, a leather thong, or distinctive buttons. With wear, the openings to the gusset will tear or widen.

Inflatable mattresses are found at mass marketers and discount stores.

Keep them tight with a couple of stitches with a strong thread such as button or carpet warp.

■ Manufacturer directions may call for regular use of a zipper lubricant. They're sold in sporting supply stores.

■ Don't subject a sleeping bag to intense heat or sunlight.

■ If serious zipper repairs or replacement are called for, try a marine canvas shop.

■ Using a sleeping bag liner helps keep the interior fresh and you won't have to subject the entire bag to frequent laundering.

On Your Back

Choosing and Cruising the Right Backpack

It's essential to choose a backpack that can organize and carry gear in comfort and safety.

Have a fit with your backback.

"It's a hip belt, not a waist belt," explains Patrick McHugh of MPI Outdoors. "All of our backpacks are meant to be worn low and secured across the hips, not the waist."

Without a frame a backpack is nothing more than a floppy bag, which is fine for small loads. For serious loads, however, a frame is added to distribute the weight over the wearer's body. External frame packs are best for heavy loads in easygoing terrain. They allow the wearer to walk upright with a natural gait. The frame creates an air space between your back and the pack, for cool carrying.

An internal frame is preferred for tougher trails involving climbing narrow passages and slippery surfaces. The pack is held tighter against the body, giving the wearer more freedom of movement and maneuverability. A solid frame is just that. A flexing or suspension frame moves with the body, allowing more flexibility even with a heavy load.

Pack Pointers

Here, from Patrick McHugh of MPI Outdoors, are tips on making the most of your backpack:

• Never pick up a backpack by one shoulder strap. Use both shoulder straps or the "haul loop" on top.

• Don't over-tighten the compression strips. They are meant to stabilize a load once it is packed, not to hold it in place.

• Clean zippers often and lube them occasionally with a silicone spray. Keep frayed fabric trimmed back so it doesn't get caught in zippers.

• When you're not wearing the pack, keep all buckles fastened. This keeps them from being stepped on and broken.

• Before each trip, inspect stress points. Make any necessary repairs, using strong upholstery thread and a heavy-duty needle.

• Pack smart, so sharp objects don't cut or stress fabric. Wrap pointed objects, such as the stove or tree pegs, in clothing.

• Don't overload a backpack, for the sake of the pack and the sake of your back.

•Distribute the load in a fanny pack carefully and evenly so you are not off balance on the trail. Carry weight as low on the hips as is comfortable, keeping the weight off the small of the back and centered on your body frame.

• In shopping for a backpack in summer, keep in mind that you may be wearing it with a heavy jacket in autumn, winter, and fall. Look for extra long webbing on the shoulder belt adjustments and on the hip belt.

• Clean your backpack regularly with a soft brush and mild soap and water. Never use harsh laundry detergents. While cleaning it, inspect for abrasions, tears, and loose threads. Before storing your backpack, open all compartments and make sure it is dry, empty, and well aired. Never store a wet or damp backpack, or it will mildew.

Get the Picture?

Picture yourself living with this pack. Are you hoisting it off and on buses and planes, hitchhiking across Europe this summer and camping the Caribbean next winter? Climbing a mountain? Skiing hut to hut? Tenting at night or just unpacking your sleeping bag in a hostel, outfitter's tent, or shelter? Will you have control of your pack at all times, or will you have to turn it in to baggage handlers on the airline, bus or train? Riding to the trailhead with your buddies, is there room for your pack inside the van or will be riding on the roof in the rain?

In world travel, I find that control of my luggage is sometimes taken away from me despite my best efforts. It's especially a problem for women in countries where we are considered the weaker sex, but my husband and I have also had our bags snatched out of the taxi in Third World countries by porters desperate for a tip. It's all part of the ballet between taxi drivers and skycaps or bellmen, contrived to provide a little more income for native people. To fail to go along with it could be heartless. If you travel internationally, be prepared by (1) having small bills or coins on hand, (2) keeping your valuables on your person and (3) using a protective cover on the backpack.

Coleman's 5-pound Conquer™ weighs 5 pounds, has an aluminum internal frame, and carries 6,000 cubic inches of gear.

Coleman's Lumbar™ Pack carries low and compact, with a capacity of 600 cubic inches for serious day hiking. It weighs only 1.1 pounds and fits waists 26-36 inches.

Picture yourself skiing from hut to hut.

National Publicity Studios

TOP TIP

According to equipment experts at L.L. Bean, a general rule for beginner backpackers is that a man's pack should weigh no more than a third of his body weight; a woman's no more than one-fourth her weight. Start with that, then fine-tune according to your comfort level.

Keep in mind that carry-on rules have changed a lot since September 11, 2001. If you have to check your backpack on an airline, choose a slick profile that won't snag on conveyor belts and luggage handling equipment.

At some airports, private businesses offer a shrink-wrap system for about $10. It protects a bag against wear, wet, and pilfering and, in the case of a backpack, will bind up all the straps and buckles so they can't snag. You can't get into the bag without destroying the shrink wrap, so it's best for a multi-leg flight where you check the pack and don't see it again until you arrive at your destination. You can also ask the airline to put the pack in a protective bag or box and hope that it stays there through all the transfers.

A rain cover for your backpack is good insurance for your gear as well as extra protection for the pack itself. I once looked out from an airport window and saw my pack, which had been checked as required, sitting in a torrential, tropical downpour while waiting to be loaded aboard a bush plane. Another time, while on a bus trip through England, the driver took my pack out of the luggage compartment at my destination and, before I could grab it, plunked it down in a big puddle.

Covers cost about $20 and weigh as little as 4.5 ounces for a small cover to as much as 19-20 ounces for a big cover measuring almost four feet long. On the minus side, you can't get into your pack when it's sealed up in a protector (although some designs come with some external lashings that allow some items to be attached.) Too, a plastic garbage bag large enough to cover the pack provides good temporary rain protection. It weighs almost nothing, and you can always use it as a garbage bag. Some packs, such as Coleman's Rush', come with a rain fly, which is good protection on the trail.

Additional tips on choosing a backpack:

❑ Some backpacks have a detachable fanny pack or day pack, a nice feature for campers who want to leave the big pack in camp, hut or hostel while sightseeing.

❑ Open the pack completely to see how easy it will be to pack and unpack. Some have top access only; others open completely so the entire main compartment lies flat.

❑ Decide whether you want a pack that has a handy pocket for a separate water bottle or canteen, or a built-in hydration chamber with sip tube that is easily accessed on the trail. Water weighs about two pounds per quart, so where you carry that weight can make a difference in the day's fatigue. Built-in hydration chambers are often placed for convenience and comfort, such as cushioning, optimum center of gravity, and ease of getting a drink.

❑ Some backpacks, especially larger ones, offer the same size pack for different waist/hip measurements. REI's CIMA, for example, a $175 pack, is a 3,050 cubic inch pack available in Small for hip/waist measurement of 28-34 inches, Medium for 31-37 inches and Large for 37 inches and more.

❑ Catalogs and Web sites offer the best choice of backpacks but it may be better to shop in person, especially if you're new to backpacking. At a large outdoor supply store that is staffed by knowledgeable experts, you can try on several styles and be fitted with the right pack for your stature, weight, gear requirements, and the type of outdoor activities you'll pursue.

❑ Having a lot of pockets isn't always a plus because it means the extra weight of all those zippers and fabric. It can also be hard to remember where you packed every little thing. Look for a variety of stowage options such as straps for a camp pad or camp shovel, an internal pocket or two for security, and a stretchy mesh outer compartment for a bike helmet or windbreaker.

❑ Larger packs sometimes have a double bottom for added strength and protection. Look at construction features not only from the standpoint of carrying the pack on your back but lifting it when filled and setting it down in camp and on the trail.

❑ Some larger packs have a separate compartment for the sleeping bag, keeping it dry and accessible where you don't have to root through other gear to get at it.

❑ Backpacks usually die of other causes before rust is a problem, but hardware should be considered if you hike and camp in ocean settings. Seaside air is highly corrosive, and brackish water (high salt content) can extend far inland. Nickel- or chrome-plated steel will eventually rust. If you're a beach camper, shop with a small magnet to check all gear for ferrous content. Shop marine chandleries for sprays and protectants for metal zippers. Nylon zippers won't rust or corrode. Brass hardware will corrode and discolor in salt air, but it's hard to beat it for strength. Protective sprays can help keep brass zippers from sticking.

❑ Larger packs have foam-cushioned straps and supports. Look for dual-density foam (usually a blend of open cell and closed cell foams) for durability and comfort.

❑ Color choices are offered by some manufacturers while others make everything in one, practical color such as olive drab or khaki. Once pockets and straps are filled with personal gear, it's unlikely you'll have trouble finding your pack, even in a pile of look-alikes. Still, it's fun to customize a pack with a badge, reflective strip, or a patch of needlework. One of my friends who is a quilter made an intricate piecework design and appliqued it on a daypack, making it truly distinctive.

❑ Never forget that technology is ever-changing, even in a simple piece of gear like a backpack. The more experience you have as a backpacker, the more you'll be able to evaluate the pluses and minuses of new features, fabrics, and construction. Allow too for changes in yourself as years pass: conditioning, total weight gain or loss, loss of bone density, muscle gain or loss, body fat-to-weight ratio, and even a loss of total stature. This year, you may need a new pack that is larger or smaller.

TOP TIP

While most backpacks are unisex in design, some suppliers including L.L. Bean offer women-specific packs that have narrow shoulder straps, a smaller torso height, and smaller waistbelt. The company also offers a real backpack designed for kids with a torso measurement of 11-14 inches.

One Day at a Time

Here are Patrick McHugh's instructions for packing a day pack:

• Layer extra clothing in the bottom of the pack. Carefully folded and stacked, items will be easier to get at when you need them. This also helps cushion other items in the pack and gives you a more flexible base when you set the pack down.

• Place the heaviest gear in the next layer above the clothing. Cushion loose items with clothing or wrap them in plastic bags.

• In the next layer, put food, a rope, and the first aid kit.

• Near the top, keep the rain gear, camera, personal hygiene needs, and a survival kit.

• Keep your water bottle, map, compass, GPS, knife, snack food, and extra fire starter kit in the outside pockets of the pack.

• Don't hang items from the pack or from the shoulder strips. They bounce around, make noise in the wilderness, stress and/or abraid the material, and catch on branches or underbrush. The only exception is wearing bear bells if you're in bear country.

• Position heaviest items toward your center of gravity. For me, says McHugh, it tends to be higher in the pack and forward towards the body. For women, it is lower, towards the center of the pack near the small of the back.

• Wear your day pack as low on your back as is comfortable for you to walk and maneuver. Let the hip belt (it's not a waist belt) secure the majority of the weight on your hips. The shoulder straps should only stabilize and balance the weight, not put it on your neck and shoulder muscles. Let hips, which are the stronger, do the heavy work.

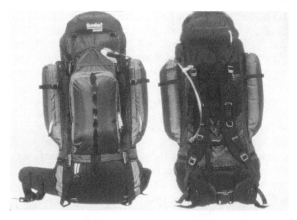

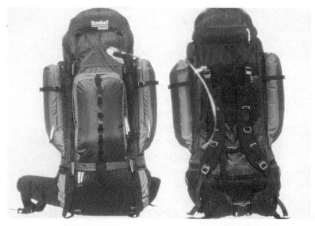

Eureka

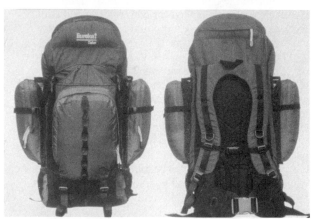

All Packs Alike?

Some of the many variations of backpacks are evident in this collage of Eureka packs. The size and weight of the packs, number of pockets for storage, and special compartments for water bottles, sleeping bags or tents are among factors to consider when buying a pack.

CHAPTER

Just Add Water

Canoe or Kayak Camping

More and more campers go the extra mile to get away from the crowd. If you want a campsite that can't be reached by horseback campers, hikers, bikers, cars, or anything except perhaps a seaplane, paddle in! For starters, the Boundary Waters Canoe Area in Minnesota, Wisconsin, and Canada covers 1.25 million wilderness acres! For paddlers there are also the vast expanses of the Everglades, Washington's San Juan Islands, Intracoastal Waterways east and west, Land Between the Lakes, the 1,000 Islands of the St. Lawrence, the 10,000 Islands of Florida. I've even seen paddlers in the Erie Canal and the Trent-Severn Waterway. Circumnavigate a Caribbean island, or paddle a river all day, sleeping by night on its sandy banks.

In a canoe or kayak, the world's your oyster.

Canoes are the ballet of the camping world. Kayaks are its poetry, and sailboats are a symphony filled with soft passages and crashing crescendoes. Extensive camping expeditions have been dared by small boat sailors – one even crossed the Northwest Passage in a Hobie Cat– but sailing is a specialized art best covered in other books. There are also overnight whitewater expeditions, usually booked with outfitters who provide the rafts, tents, cooking gear, know-how, guides, and cooks. You just go along for the ride.

For now, let's focus on the how-to of lone canoe and kayak camping.

Canoe Definitions

Pick a **recreation canoe** for agility and steadiness.

Pick a **cruising canoe** for efficiency and sporty performance

Pick an **expedition canoe** for more space for gear and for seaworthiness.

Pick a **touring canoe** for some of all three.

Minnesota Office of Tourism

Flee the crowds in a canoe or kayak that can take you to serene, beautiful spots such as Minnesota's endless lakes and waterways.

Choosing Your Canoe

Pick a **recreation canoe** for agility and steadiness.

Pick a **cruising canoe** for efficiency and sporty performance

Pick an **expedition canoe** for more space for gear and for seaworthiness.

Pick a **touring canoe** for some of all three. Canoes have been so popular for so long, choices range from mere beach toys to hand-made, custom canoes costing thousands of dollars. They're made in wood, aluminum, fiberglass, graphite composites, and all sorts of exotic new plastics that could survive a rhino attack. Here are some considerations in choosing and camping with your canoe:

• Weight becomes an increasingly important factor if your trips involve portages. Otherwise, just don't get more canoe than you, or yourself and your crew, can hoist to the top of the car.

• For canoe camping, you're shopping for a touring canoe, which is an all-purpose compromise, or an expedition canoe, designed for a steady ride in a variety of water conditions, with space for gear. That space is best achieved with more length, according to Tom Watson of We-non-nah, rather than increased width or depth, because it will perform better when heavily loaded. A good expedition design, says Watson, will paddle well with little load as well as with full camping gear. Marathon, racing, and whitewater canoes and historic replicas are made for a specific purpose, usually one unsuitable for canoe camping. There are also canoes designed to take an electric or gasoline outboard motor, but this book is about canoe camping under paddle power.

• Canoes are available for solo, tandem, or multiple paddlers. If you get one with a sliding seat, you can use it solo on some trips and take a partner on others.

Canoe Materials

Aluminum is tough, which makes it a good choice for canoe liveries, but metal canoes can be heavy and sluggish. They require specialized maintenance, and can become permanently stained from use in high-acid waters.

Composites consist of layers of such materials as fiberglass, graphite, Kevlar, or Tuf-weave. Extra labor at the manufacturing level adds to their cost but also to durability, versatility, lightness with strength, and paddle-ability. These canoes vary from maker to maker, but are the top of the line.

Polyethylene makes for low cost, durable canoes. They "give" on impact, which is a plus in snag-filled waters, but poly can be heavier than aluminum and awkward to paddle and maneuver. Don't confuse generic polyethylene with high-tech plastics such as Royalex ®. There are rugged and patented materials that have the advantages of plastics without the disadvantages of a cheap, plastic canoe.

Wood is for purists, a work of art that's guaranteed to require a lot of care and maintenance.

Canoeing a spring "run" in Florida is to paddle a tunnel through thick, fragrant jungle.

A Short Course in Canoe Lingo

There is much more to be learned about canoe terminology, but this will get you started if you're ordering from a catalog or Web site. Your best teachers are canoes themselves. Get as much experience as possible with rented and borrowed canoes, and as many paddle styles as possible, so you'll have a better idea of what you want and don't want.

Caddies are wheels to place under a canoe or kayak to help get it from the car to the water and from the beach to your campsite. If you get a collapsible caddy that can be carried in the canoe, you'll always have it with you when beaching each afternoon and launching each morning.

Car Topper Kits make it quick and secure to carry your canoe atop the car or van. It's best to buy your kit from the canoe manufacturer for the best fit. Learn proper knot-tying (or use straps with cam locks) and don't use a rack that attaches with suction cups. Nothing ruins a good canoe faster than a flight from the car roof followed by a collision with the asphalt before an18-wheeler boots it into a roadside ditch.

Chine is the angle where the hull and topsides meet. A round-bottom canoe has no chine at all. Hard chine refers to a sharp angle, usually seen in homemade or inexpensive boats.

Color is more than fashion statement. Hunters prefer green or camouflage canoes. Dark colors also absorb heat better if you're canoeing in frigid waters or if you use a canoe as part of your shelter in canoe camping in a cold climate. Canoe campers can choose a bright color for easy identification, or forest green to blend into the environment. Yellow is the color most easily seen in an air-sea rescue situation, and it absorbs less heat, but it can reflect a lot of glare back at the paddler.

Depth refers to the measurement from the top of the hull to the bottom. Greater depth at the center adds volume and stability. Greater depth at bow and stern helps combat waves and spray. If the canoe is a v-hull or has a keel, catalog dimensions will probably include them in the depth measurement, meaning that the canoe is not functionally as deep as the measurements suggest. The amount of water needed under the hull to keep it afloat is called draft or draught.

Entry line refers to how sharp the bow is as it enters the water, which in turn affects efficiency and tracking. Some materials can be shaped better than others for a sharp entry line.

Flotation should be sufficient to keep the canoe afloat even if filled with water. However, flotation bags are available for whitewater use, where you want the canoe not just to break the surface but to float high enough to avoid rocks.

Freeboard is the amount of hull remaining above the water. The heavier you load the canoe, the more freeboard you lose.

TOP TIP

An excellent reference is the *Beginner's Guide to Canoeing and Kayaking,* which is published annually by Canoe & Kayak magazine.

Keel line is the length of the bottom of the canoe.

Knee pads allow you to paddle on your knees for maximum effort.

Prices range from almost nothing for a used aluminum or poly canoe to thousands of dollars for a handmade, historic reproduction. Plan to pay $1,400-$3,000 for a typical 19-foot, two-person, expedition canoe.

Rocker refers to the way the hull rises from its deepest point to the top of the bow and stern. Picture the rocker on a rocking chair. The more rocker in the hull, the more easily it will turn and the less easily it will track in a straight line. Slalom competitors want canoes with a lot of rocker; canoe campers want little or none.

Shape at the waterline may be different from the shape of the hull above the water. To predict performance, advises Watson, envision the shape of the canoe at the waterline.

Sheer line is the curve of the outer edge of the rail (the top of the hull) from bow to stern. Usually, it's flat or straight. If it's reverse sheer, it's convex. Spelled shear by some manufacturers.

Skid plate is an extra piece at the bow of a canoe to add strength in case of a bow-first collision. It's not usually recommended because it can affect performance, but it's a wise addition for canoeing rapids. Get the right model skid plate for your canoe from the canoe manufacturer.

Stability is usually expressed as primary or initial stability, meaning steadiness when upright, and secondary or final stability, referring to a canoe's ultimate resistance to a capsize. A wide hull may have excellent primary stability (when you're climbing aboard, for example) but poor final stability (when, for example, you are hit with a high wake from a motorboat).

Thwarts are braces or bars that run across the hull. When something rides from front to back or vice versa, it is loaded fore and aft; when its weight is distributed from side to side, it is positioned athwart ship.

Trim is front-to-back balance. Ideally, the canoe will ride level and you can achieve that by moving gear. Since the heaviest thing on board is usually you, here's where sliding seats come in. Good trim is important in all waters and is essential on windy waters because handling is so quickly affected. If, for example, the bow rides high, it has more windage and paddlers have to work harder to maintain course.

Width. The narrower the canoe, the farther it will travel per paddle stroke, but the more tippy it will be. A wider canoe is more stable, but requires more paddle power. You're looking for measurements at the waterline, which is what determines how the canoe will paddle, ride, and recover from motion.

Choosing Your Kayak

According to Brian Henry and the team at Current Designs, here are the elements that go into choosing a kayak.

Length: a longer waterline means a faster kayak and a more streamlined passage through the water.

Width: the wider the kayak, the more stable it is. While a narrow kayak is faster, width makes for more creature comfort and more room to stow camping gear.

Rocker refers to the degree of upward curvature of the hull from bow to stern along the keel line. The more rocker, the more maneuverable the hull, but the less waterline. A compromise has to be made because a kayak with no rocker will track well but will be difficult to maneuver.

Plane view. If you look straight down at a kayak from overhead, you'll see where the widest part of the kayak is. In a "swede form" kayak, the widest part of the vessel is behind the cockpit, which makes for a clean, long, slender entry for easy touring speed and maneuverability. A "fish form" kayak has a more blunt entry, but a more slender exit through the water, which increases track-ability, especially in adverse conditions. The performance of a kayak is determined by the shape of the waterline, not the deck.

Cross section. A round hull is extremely fast, but unstable. A flat hull is stable, but slow. Flared sides give extra stability because of added buoyancy when you are leaning to the side. Current Design's Expedition model has a rounded V, which is fast but more stable when gear is added. The V hull also give structural rigidity to the hull, excellent track, a lively feel, and a comfortable level of stability. A "hard chine" kayak has a well-defined turn where the V comes up the side. It gives good stability, even in a slender craft. The kayak camper settles for less speed in exchange for more stability and more stowage space.

Bow Shape determines how the kayak will meet and slice through waves. This in turn determines how well you'll punch through rough seas and how dry a ride you'll get.

Construction. You're looking for the strongest kayak in the lightest weight. Materials used today range from primitive animal skin and wood canoes shaped by traditionalists such as Inuits and Native Americans who want to keep old skills alive, to high-tech fiberglass, Kevlar, Kevlar Tuff laminate, molded polyethylene, and graphite.

Bulkheads and hatches add structural integrity and keep gear dry. Look for impact-resistant bulkheads that are bonded to the hull, and hatches that seat tightly into a groove that has a gasket. For a watertight seal, the hatch should have a positive lock that compresses the seal.

Seams are formed in many ways according to the construction material. Look for high strength and watertight integrity at seams.

Safety perimeter lines are lacings placed on deck for you to grab onto and right the kayak. They're also a place to tuck a chart and other small items. Look at the fittings for strength and a clean, flush line.

Seats should have proper support for the back, legs, and hips for long hours of paddling. Some models have an adjustable back band for more comfort for the paddler's lower back.

Rudders are available on some kayaks to aid maneuvering and stability in some wind and sea conditions. They're operated by foot pedals and are retractable.

Skeg is a fin that drops down close to the stern of a kayak to increase its tracking ability. When it's up, the kayak is more maneuverable. When it's down, it's easier to maintain a course.

Accessories you may want to add with your kayak include a spray skirt, which fastens around your waist and fastens to the cockpit coaming; a flush-mount deck compass, which is optional from some manufacturers; a bilge pump, and a paddle float. That's a bladder that can be slipped over a paddle, inflated, and used as an outrigger to help stabilize the kayak when you're re-boarding it from the water. You'll need tiedown straps and a cradle to transport the kayak atop a car, and a good life jacket.

Paddles are available in many styles, sizes, colors and materials. For kayak camping, you'll be paddling long hours with a load, so choose a paddle designed for touring, not slalom competition.

Prices for a new kayak start at about $800 and go into the thousands of dollars for a custom design in exotic materials. Paddles start at about $70 for wood, and go to $300 or more for graphite competition models.

The ABCs of PFDs

If your camping takes you on or near water, PFDs (Personal Flotation Devices) are a must for everyone including the family dog. They're available from marine, fishing, and outdoors sources in dozens of styles and in sizes for infants, youths and adults as well as for small, medium, large and extra large dogs weighing 2 to 90 pounds.

If you haven't shopped for a "life vest" lately, you're in for a pleasant surprise. They're now available in so many colors and models that nobody kicks about wearing them. In fact, the new PFDs made for canoeing and kayaking have zippered pockets that are a real plus for stowing small items you want to keep at hand. Special PFDs for women provide flotation without bulk in the wrong places. For hot weather paddling, flotation modules are attached to a mesh vest.

It's just a matter of deciding how much flotation you want. The best ones, but also the bulkiest and most awkward to wear, will right you and keep you afloat even if you fall in head first and are unconscious. At the other end of the scale are simple, smelt harnesses or vests that you hardly know you're wearing. If buoyancy is needed, however, you have to be conscious and able to inflate them with a gas cartridge (which will need to be replaced after use.)

Here, from the Boat U.S. Foundation, are tips on choosing and cruising life jackets.

❏ Stow PFDs where they will get good air circulation. Dry thoroughly before storing.

❏ Don't use PFDs as cushions or fenders.

❏ Don't clean with harsh detergents or solvents, nor dry them in a clothes dryer.

❏ The best place to stow PFDs underway is on yourself and your family. In any case, keep them unwrapped and accessible. In most states, children under age 12 are required to wear life jackets at all times when aboard a boat.

❏ Bright colors, especially orange or yellow, increase your chances of being seen if you fall into the water.

❏ Inflatable life jackets require more attention. Always check the inflator to see if it's properly installed. Check for leaks every two months by inflating the jacket orally, then leave it overnight. Any time a cartridge is used, replace it immediately. Take extra care around sharp objects. Once holed, an inflatable is useless.

❏ The best life jacket, or Type I, is the busty, uncomfortable "Mae West" style. Most people balk at wearing one, but it will turn a wearer face up even if he or she falls into the water head first and unconscious. It will right the wearer and keep the head above water almost indefinitely – a definite plus for swimmers and non-swimmers alike. A Type II or Type V may or may not accomplish this; Type III won't. Some inflatables will also inflate automatically in hitting the water and turn an unconscious wearer upright. Type IV devices are life rings and cushions, which can be tossed to a victim in the water. They are a help but they don't meet U.S. Coast Guard requirements for the number of PFDs that must be carried.

For More Information

In addition to addresses found in this book under Resources, paddle campers should contact:

American Canoe Association, 7432 Alban Station Blvd., Suite B-232, Springfield, VA 22150, tel. (703) 451-0141, e-mail acadirect@aol.com, www.aca-paddler.org.

United States Canoe Association, Inc., 606 Ross St., Middletown, OH 45044, tel. (513) 422-3739, usca-canoe-kayak.org or e-mail uscamack@aol.com.

Read *Canoe and Kayak* magazine, found at newsstands, and get a copy of its annual *Beginner's Guide to Canoeing and Kayaking*. It lists more than 250 paddling clubs throughout North America.

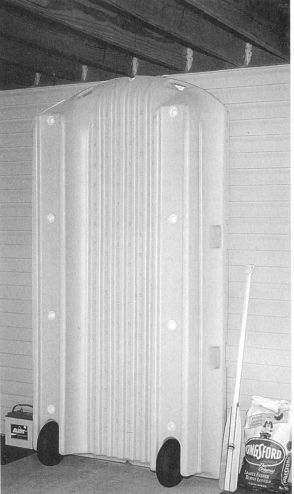

The boat market offers many lightweight, inexpensive fishing boats that store in little space and can be car-topped to the campground for day fishing.

A speedy ski boat can be used for some boat-in campsites (motorboats aren't always allowed) and can also be towed behind your family car, SUV, pickup camper, or van conversion.

Packing For Canoe or Kayak Camping

See Chapter for checklists. You'll need much the same equipment as for backpacking or

tent camping, depending on the carrying capacity of the canoe or kayak. If the trip involves portages, every ounce counts just as it does in backpacking. If not, take whatever the canoe or kayak can safely and comfortably carry. In addition to camping supplies, you'll need some marine items including:

❏ U.S.C.G. approved PFDs for every soul on board including the dog. It's best to wear one at all times, swimmer or no. In an upset, you could be knocked unconscious or the PFD could be swept away in current before you could put it on. In cold water, the struggle of donning a PFD–even if you can find it and get into it–uses up crucial minutes and robs your body core of heat. Besides, wearing a PFD is the most space-efficient way to stow the gol-durn thing and keep it out of the way.

❏ Sun hats and sun block. Except for rivers in deep canyons or narrow streams through the forest, there is no shade at sea.

❏ Easily accessible water bottles for each person on board.

❏ Ropes to serve as docking lines if you'll be at docks or in locks.

❏ An anchor to serve as a lunch hook, emergency brake, and to help secure the boat on shore. (Even when dragged above the water line, a vessel can come adrift if the tide rises or if a passing speedboat sends up a big wake. Run a sturdy line from the bow to an anchor you dig in well up on the beach.)

❏ Marine flares and other signal devices used on the water.

❏ Waterproof flashlights.

❏ Waterproof packs for gear, preferably with flotation in at least some of them.

❏ Repair kit suitable for your vessel's construction.

❏ A marine VHF radio if you're in waters where they are the preferred method of communication. If you're boating in convoy, it's nice to have UHF/FM family radios. Not to be confused with yesterday's toy walkie-talkies, these clear, powerful radios have a two-mile range and sell for under $100 per pair. Weather information is always important in camping but, in paddling large bodies of water, it's crucial to have the latest meteorological information. Consider carrying a weather radio that comes on automatically during alerts, or at least a portable radio that has a 24-hour NOAA band.

❏ According to We-no-nah Canoes, the Red Cross recommends the wearing of a wet suit when canoeing really cold water, where hypothermia is an even greater threat than drowning.

TOP TIP If you camp on or near the water, it's good practice to keep children in PFDs at all times. I once ran into a Swedish couple in the Caribbean whose two little girls were wearing nothing but nut-brown suntans and their life jackets

CHAPTER

Dress The Part

Choose Proper Clothing For The Season

Gone are the days when outdoor activities meant wearing buckskin and denim, and waiting all night for your clothes to dry over the campfire. Today's high-tech fabrics are formulated not just to look great but to keep you warm, cool, dry, and clean. Most of them wash like a compliant puppy. They dry in a wink and shake out, wrinkle free, when you take them out of the dryer, backpack, or duffel.

Here's the latest lingo on the materials you'll find in outdoor supply stores and catalogs. Note that most of these are trademarked names, so names may be different for fabrics that are almost identical.

Activent® is a breathable, water-resistant fabric that also keeps you dry from the inside out. It's made up of two or three layers, one a microporous membrane and others composed of special polymers including a polyester fabric next to the skin to wick perspiration away from the body. It dries very quickly, keeping you cooler in high-energy activities on hot days.

Active Dry® is a fabric used for socks, underwear, bicycle shorts, and other active wear. It moves moisture away from the skin.

CoolMax® is a breathable, silky, comfortable fabric that wicks moisture away from the body, allowing it to dry quickly in the air. It's a good choice for garments for hot weather camping.

Cordura® is Dupont's name for an airy, high-strength nylon. It comes in different weights, expressed as deniers, for light, medium, and heavy duty wear in backpacks, luggage, and hiking boots.

Cover Cloth is Filson's supple, wind- and rain-resistant, 100 percent cotton with an oil finish. It's lighter than Filson's Tin Cloth or **Shelter Cloth**. Lighter still is the company's Safari Cloth, a light, long-staple cotton that is breathable, water repellant, and cool in the tropics.

Down has been proven through the ages, since the first neanderthal plucked a handful of fluff from the feathers of a bird, and stuffed it inside his deerskin vest. It's the lightest insulation you can carry and is a natural powerhouse for warmth. Its density is expressed in Fill Power, which refers to cubic centimeters per ounce of compressed down. The higher the number, usually 500-830, the more insulation you get for the weight of your down jacket or vest.

DriClime® is a two-layer polyester fabric in which the layer next to the skin has a brushed surface that keeps it from clinging to the skin. Sweat is wicked up and moved to the next layer, which spreads and evaporates it.

Dryloft® is another weatherproof, breathable, featherweight fabric that is used in sleeping bags to keep the outside dry and to minimize condensation on the inside.

Duraguard® is a tough, supple, waterproof nylon fabric used in tarps. It's sturdy and abrasion resistant, a good choice for a ground cloth.

Feather Cloth is Filson's lightest cotton, valued in the tropics for absorbency and sun protection.

EPIC® by Nexte encapsulates tightly woven polyester fibers in a thin, durable polymer. The result is a waterproof fabric that is highly breathable.

Fleece, the ultimate in softness, lightweight, and warmth, comes in several names including Polarfleece®, Polartec®, and Synchilla®. They're all polyester.

Gore-Tex® is a synthetic fabric filled with billions of tiny pores per square centimeter. They're sizeable enough to let water (perspiration) escape from the inside, cooling your body, but small enough to keep wind and rain water out. It's commonly used in foul weather suits.

Intelligent Garment Technologies is a North Face company that offers a $500 jacket that has battery-operated heat panels and thermostatic control. Developed for the military, heated garments are now available for civilian purchase.

Intera® is a process used on polyester and nylon that causes moisture to wick away from the body.

Microfiber is a polyester that is woven so tightly that it makes a nice wind break. It's flyweight and durable, ideal for a jacket or the shell of a sleeping bag.

Nycott Oxford is a breathable, tough nylon fabric that resists stains and wrinkling. It washes and dries readily, so it's popular for travel clothing.

Polar-Loft® is a synthetic fabric that copies the long, hollow fibers of polar bear fur.

Polarguard® has been around for generations. It's polyester woven from continuous thread, so it's almost tearproof. Used in a sleeping bag, it can stretch and pull without tearing, which in turn would create cold spots in the bag. It's modestly priced, which makes it a favorite with price-appeal manufacturers. The newest Polarguard HV is lighter and Polardguard 3-D lighter still.

Polartec® is a stretchy polyester fleece, fuzzy on both sides, warm and comfortable for layered clothing. Polartec Power Stretch is fuzzy inside and a sturdy nylon outside for more wind protection and better strength. It's good for winter outerwear. Another version, Polartec 200, is warmer, with a shearling-like surface inside and a dense, velvety finish outside for good wind protection and warmth without weight. There's also a Polartec 300, and Polartec Power Dry with X-static, woven with silver fibers that are said to kill bacteria that cause garments to harbor body odor.

Powershield® is a stretchy nylon face laminated to Polartec fleece, for durability and wet resistance on the outside and a brushed softness next to your skin.

Ripstop is a popular weave for durability because it stops tears in their tracks. It comes in many weights and patterns.

Shelter Cloth is Filson's term for a dense, strong, water-resistant, midweight cotton that may have an oil finish. It's more pliable than Filson's Tin Cloth. (See below.)

Silk underwear isn't as sexy nor as expensive as it sounds. For the outdoors, it provides a featherweight, slippery liner under the clothing, creating extra warmth without binding or weight.

Supplex® is nylon, combining the strength of a synthetic with the softness of cotton. MicroSupplex® is even more drapable.

Taffeta isn't the fabric used in your prom dress, but an industry term used to describe light, nylon materials. It might be coated to make it waterproof for use as tent flies or foul weather gear, but it isn't breathable.

Tencel® is a high-tech rayon, usually used for dressy clothing resembling silk, cotton, or wool.

Tin Cloth is Filson's name for tightly woven, durable cotton fabrics that may have an oil finish.

Thermal underwear can refer to any number of fabrics and weaves. Usually it's cotton or a cotton blend woven with little bumps, pockets or bubbles that trap air, retaining body heat.

Triplepoint Ceramic refers to a coating that contains ceramic dust. Applied to nylon fabrics, it makes a breathable, durable, yet supple waterproof fabric. It comes in different weights and coatings.

WindStopper®, another Gore fabric, isn't totally waterproof but it's more breathable, a good choice for a windbreaker that also wicks perspiration away from the skin so you stay warm and dry.

What's Hot, What's Not

You can't always go by manufacturer claims that a garment or a pair of boots is good for, say, minus 15 degrees. In addition to the best fabrics for the purpose, you also must consider your own physical condition, circulation, metabolism, activity, and how tired or wet you are.

Sunproof Clothing

Fabric can provide shade, but that doesn't mean it offers protection against skin damage caused by ultraviolet rays. You can still burn under an umbrella or a long-sleeve shirt. Clothing with built-in UV protection is available from outdoor clothing specialists (see Resources) and you can also treat your own garments so they allow less UV to pass through. Atsko makes U-V-Block, which is sprayed on.

Rit, the dye company, makes a product that goes into the washing machine with the laundry. It's found in supermarkets in the fabric dyes department for about $3 per regular-size washer load; if yours is an extra-large washer, use two packets. Set aside a load of shirts, hats and other outdoor garments that you want to treat, then just wash them normally in water that is at least 100 degrees F., using a packet or two of Rit's Sun Guard. Set the machine to wash for at least 15 minutes, then rinse and spin as usual. One treatment is said to be good for "repeated" washings unless you use bleach, which can destroy the product's effectiveness.

Filson

The Alaska Guide Shirt by Filson is a popular option with campers who want rugged wear in a shirt that is soft and flexible.

The Ol' Tried and True

The fabrics above are a boon to camping, but wool and cotton still have their place. In fact, treated cottons, natural linens, boiled wool, and unprocessed wool permeated with natural lanolin have made a comeback thanks to a renewed interest in time-proven, natural fabrics.

Here are some words you'll encounter in shopping for outdoor clothing.

Cork has been used as a footbed in boots for centuries. As a natural material, it dissipates sweat, conforms well to the foot, provides support, and soon "imprints" to a custom fit.

Cotton is known by dozens of names that our grandmothers knew from their McGuffy Readers: duck, calico, muslin, balbriggan, flannel, plissé, seersucker, twill, chambray, broadcloth, percale, and many more. Today, cotton is still valued because it is versatile, washable, holds dye well, is cool and absorbent in summer, and can be found in many weights and weaves for home sewing. It isn't used much any more for tents because other fabrics shed water better and can be made more flame resistant.

Cotton is still a popular choice for upscale sportswear that is waxed or oiled. While these garments have to be re-treated from time to time, there is nothing quite like them for dry, warm comfort as well as rakish good looks. Brushed cotton is used for garments, such as heavy duty shirts, that must be durable but must drape well for comfort. When choosing percale for sheets, underwear and lightweight garments, the quality may be expressed in threads, meaning threads per inch. The higher the count, the finer the weave. Better percales start at 220 threads and higher. Other cottons, especially duck or canvas, may be expressed in ounces per square yard to give you an idea of their weight and durability.

Cotton terry is thick, warm and absorbent, a good choice for a robe to wear to campground showers.

Kelly James/Filson Co.

Filson's

Filson's Guide Sweater is made with virgin wool that keeps the wearer warm even when it's wet.

Filson

Filson's interchangeable outfitter coat shell accepts zip-in liners in several weights. The Outfitter System comes with three coat shells in tan cotton duck dry finish, dark green cotton oil finish, and dark tan cotton duck oil finish. Zip-in liners shown here come in moleskin and two weights of virgin wool. Features include hand-warmer pockets, waist bungee, and stand-up collar. The coat shell has a storm flap, lined hand-warmer pockets, sleeve adjusters, and plenty of cargo pockets including a security pocket. The liner vests can be worn alone.

Filson's Jac-Shirt in virgin wool is light and durable for camping in cold weather. It's cut in jacket style for use as an over-garment as well as a shirt.

Filson's

Filson's

Long wool underwear provides serious warmth when it's made from soft, 100 percent Merino wool. Filson's Alaskan Long-Johns come in separates, with a crew or zippered neck, and are machine washable.

Waffle weave cotton is lighter weight, a good choice for the campground bathhouse in summer. Also see Tin Cloth, Shelter Cloth, Safari Cloth, Feather Cloth, and Cover Cloth listed above. Cotton has its minus points. It's slower to dry than synthetics, it has little abrasion resistance, it affords little or no warmth when wet, and it shrinks up to about 3 percent of its original size. And most weaves need ironing.

Cotton may be sold as pre-shrunk or may be blended with synthetics that make it more shrink-resistant, quicker drying, stronger, more dye-stable, stretchier, or more wrinkle-proof. The more cotton, the more softness and absorbency, however. Read labels. Some cotton garments may require dry cleaning.

Linen is sometimes used in high-end garments, in its natural form or with an oil or wax finish. As a natural fabric it's comfortable on the skin, drapes well, and absorbs perspiration, and it wears well. There's nothing better for dish towels, indoors or out, because it mops up water and leaves a shine. On the debit side, linen wrinkles badly, can shrink, is subject to sun fade when dyed (although white and natural linen bleach well in the sun) and it's slow to dry. And, like cotton, it is best for warm climates where you want a lightweight, absorbent garment.

Moleskin is a very soft, very tightly-woven cotton that is as soft and pliable as chamois. It makes a warm, butter-soft lining. It's also sold in drugstores as patches for use on tender spots on the feet, to prevent or protect blisters.

Silk is used mostly for lightweight, insulating underwear that feels comfortable next to the skin. The price has come down in recent years, so it's another choice to consider for underwear, undersocks (socks worn under rough, heavy wool socks to provide a smoother surface next to the skin), and sleeping bag liners. It stows in very little space and dries quickly. It wrinkles, may not hold dyes well, is not the most durable of fabrics, and it should be washed with care.

Wool is still a favorite because it sheds water to some degree – sometimes almost as well as plastic – and it's warm even when wet. In sheep country, freshly shorn sheep can soon be turned back out on the chilly range because of the lanolin that immediately forms on their skin to keep them warm and dry.

Wool has drawbacks that vary depending on how it has been prepared, woven and treated. Generally, it's tricky to wash, expensive if you must dry clean it, scratchy to those with sensitive skin, and it may shrink anywhere from a little bit to a lot. Unlike most other fabrics, which do most of their shrinking the first time they are wet, wool can keep shrinking with each washing. Many a brawny man has put his favorite old wool sweater through a hot water wash and into the dryer and taken it out to find that it's now too small for the family cat.

Boiled wool is almost indestructible, warm when wet, and is past the shrinking stage, but it's too stiff to conform tightly to the body. It's usually found in hats, shoes and shoe liners. Virgin wool is fresh from the sheep, cleaned and perhaps dyed. If it's not 100 percent wool but not virgin wool, that means that the garment may contain factory trimmings. Such garments aren't as supple and strong because suppleness is reduced each time fibers have been cut and rewoven. Reprocessed wool, used in cheap clothing and sometimes in linings or interlinings, may contain all sorts of leftovers, and may be stiff and scratchy. "Nylon for added strength" may mean that it isn't 100 percent virgin wool with its long, strong fibers. Nylon has been added to make up for the lack of virgin wool, and it may also mean less shrinkage, but it also means the garment probably won't be as warm as 100 percent wool.

Merino wool is known for excellent insulation that wicks moisture away from the body. Harvested from Merino sheep, it's often used to make socks and underwear because it's soft and supple, best for wearing next to the skin. Worsted wool is long-fiber wool that has been tightly twisted for a strong, durable finish with a soft touch.

Filson's

Filson's Camp Shoe is especially popular for canoeing and camping because it gives firm support yet it slips off without laces. The removable cork footbed becomes a custom fit as it conforms to the wearer.

His, Hers, and WERS

Look for the term WERS in women's underwear for the outdoors. Picture the fly in men's undershorts. WERS works much the same way but in a different part of the garment. It's a double flap that allows a woman to part the crotch for bathroom breaks without pulling down her knickers.

Another lifesaver for women is WizZip®, a zipper that runs from the waistline in front, down the fly, through the crotch and up the back about as far as the tailbone. Combined with the WERS, it allows women to take a bathroom break without removing slacks or shorts.

Also new on the market is pantyhose for men. Some types offer support and compression for men who are on their feet all day or are under doctor's orders to wear compression stockings to prevent blood clots. Pantyhose offer warmth without weight, and the convenience of an all-in-one garment.

It started with Joe Namath's ad for pantyhose on TV in the 1990s, then many men started wearing them for warmth or comfort – buying them on the sneak because they didn't want to appear effeminate. Clever marketers caught on that there was a huge, untapped market for pantyhose among mainstream men, not just cross-dressers, and it's now easy to find pantyhose with a fly. Other names for them are Waistsock or waist-high legwear, and they are still mostly available only on the Internet because many men are still embarrassed to buy them in person. Among sources for them are www.shapings.com and www.comfilon.com.

Caring for High Performance Fabrics

"Washing high-performance fabrics with ordinary laundry detergents destroys the very properties that you're trying to restore," warns Dan Gutting of Atsko, Inc. Some detergent residue always remains, reveals Gutting, and after about 10 washings it makes up 2 percent of the weight of the fabric. Says Gutting, "It consists of perfume, dyes, salts, surfactants, processing aids, washing machine lubricants, and other muck that clog fabrics that were specifically engineered to keep you warm, cool, or dry. Fabrics stiffen, so you use fabric softener, which just leaves more residue and compounds the problem." Dry cleaning also can leave residues.

The answer, says Gutting, is to use a laundry product such as Sport-Wash or Sensi-Clean that does not leave any residue, leaving the fabric as supple and effective as the manufacturer intended. Fabrics containing Durable Water Repellents (DWR) such as Scotch Guard or Zepel can also be washed in these products to make them last longer. When they finally lose their repellency, they can be retreated with a spray such as Permanent Water-Guard.

TOP TIP "Insulation value is also dependent on fabric care," explains Gutting. "Insulation depends on creating little air pockets. When it mats down and the air pockets are reduced, heat is lost. That's where a no-residue detergent comes in, allowing a sleeping bag or insulated vest to be cleaned without matting. You also need to eliminate residue in high-tech fabrics that wick moisture away from the body. The more the fibers become clogged with what household laundry products leave behind, the less effective they are."

Additional tips on care of high-tech, outdoor fabrics:

• Don't hand wring high-performance fabrics or use a high-speed spin.

• High heat can damage high-tech fabrics or invisibly destroy their high-performance characteristics. Follow label directions.

• Rinsing a garment with a few drops of Sport Wash or Sensi-Clean in the water will leave it with less residue than rinsing in plain water.

• If you have an extensive wardrobe of high-performance clothing, consider getting one of the new, horizontal axis washing machines. The new machines have no agitator, allowing you to machine-wash fabrics that formerly required hand washing.

• Family members who have skin problems will also benefit from low-residue washing products.

• Commercial, front-load washing machines are a must for washing tents, sleeping bags, and other outdoor gear that is too big for a home machine. However, these machines are probably coated with residues from many different detergents. Before trusting a commercial machine with an expensive ski suit or sleeping bag, do a load of towels and other things that aren't as sensitive to laundry abuse.

• Look for a product called N-O-Dor, which is sold at hunting supply stores to remove human odor from clothes and skin so animals can't get your scent. Keep a packet on hand for pet accidents, skunk attacks, and other serious stink problems in camp. Mixed with water, it neutralizes odors rather than covering them up. N-O-DOR II is the same neutralizer in powder form.

Give It the Boot

• Buy waterproof, breathable liners for your hiking boots.

• Use Welt-Seal, a nitrile rubber adhesive, on welts, stitching, and seams of boots that are to be waterproofed. The welt should be clean, free of grease or wax, so use a brush and cleaning solvent if necessary.

• To waterproof boots after treating with Welt-Seal, use a beeswax coating called Sno-Seal if they are smooth, top grain leather. Wash with a soft brush and dishwashing detergent, then dry thoroughly. Sno-Seal can also be used on leather gloves, oiled canvas coats, belts, hats, and any other wearable leather including deck shoes worn in salt water. It's also used for horse harnesses and saddles. If boots are not smooth, top grain leather but are silicone tanned, split, suede, brushed, or napped, waterproof them with Silicone Water-Guard.

• It's expensive to use for this purpose but in a pinch Sno-Seal, which is a natural beeswax, can be used as a fire starter. Smear some on kindling, even wet kindling, and light it. It will burn hot and steady.

Why Buy From Outdoor Outfitters?

Inexpensive imports are pouring into North America, so why pay the high prices charged by major manufacturers of outdoor clothing? Primarily, you're looking for three things: the right fabric for the purpose, personal safety and comfort, construction that will stand up over the long haul, and innovative features. Top sporting wear manufacturers excel in all three, but it's in the small features that you'll probably find the greatest advantage: handwarmer pockets (slits behind regular pockets), a map pocket, a slotted breast pocket for a penlight, pencil, whistle and other gear, vents or plackets in the right places for temperature control, perhaps a security pocket or two for valuables and keys, and a generous cut that allows easy movement even if all the cargo pockets are stuffed with gear.

The proof is in the wearing year in and year out. Try the cheap stuff first and, as you learn more about your needs in the outdoors, invest in the best. It will last your lifetime and beyond.

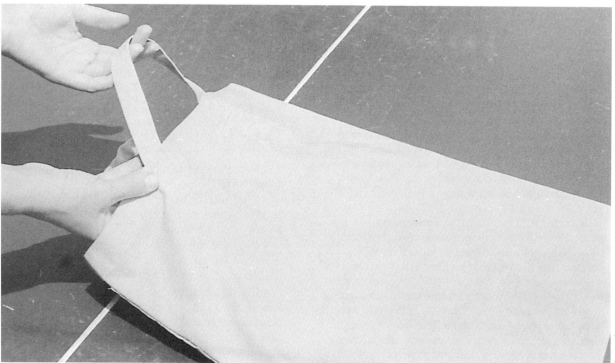

With basic sewing skills and sturdy fabric, sew up shopping bag-size sacks to be used as laundry bags, stuff bags, and for carrying toiletries, a change of clothes, and towel to the shower room.

Gordon Groene

Packing: A Checklist

These are just suggestions, but they should get you started on a personal packing list for your next campout. Much, of course, depends on the season, how long you will be gone, and the activities you plan to take part in. If you'll need a dressy outfit for each family member, add that to the list. (Hint: a night out in a nice restaurant at least once per campout will work wonders for everyone, not just the cook and clean-up crew but for picky eaters who will appreciate a chance to choose from a menu rather than eating camp grub.)

Quantities aren't listed here. Our rule is to have enough changes for three days for a weekend trip, seven or eight days if you'll be camping for a week, and at least four days if you'll be gone a very long time and are willing to do laundry every few days. Children need about a third more changes than adults. In any case, the goal is to carry enough clothes so you don't have to do laundry every day, but not so much that you end up carrying and stowing tons of clean clothes outbound and tons of laundry as the trip progresses.

For everyone, a minimum of:

❑ Underwear, socks for each day plus one extra pair of socks so you'll always have a dry pair. Dry shoes and socks are crucial in maintaining healthy feet.

❑ Tops, one clean for each day.

❑ Bottoms, one to wear and one for a spare. Slacks that turn into shorts when you zip off the legs are a plus.

❑ Shoes, a pair and a spare so you'll always have one dry pair.

❑ One sweater.

❑ One windbreaker or, in colder weather, a parka.

❑ For cold weather camping, a long, wide, fleece scarf. It can be wound around the head and neck, or crossed across the chest to form a warm vest under a windbreaker.

❑ One hat, depending on the season, for protection against sun or cold.

❑ Pajamas (if you wear them).

❑ Robe or other warm cover-up for going to and from the campground showers.

❑ Shower clogs to wear in campground showers as protection against foot injuries and diseases such as athlete's foot.

❑ Seasonal sports wear (swim suits, snowmobile suit, wet suit, hunting orange).

Additional Clothing Checklist Especially for Children:

❑ One extra outfit, carried in a handy day pack, in case clothes need to be changed en route.

Additional Clothing Checklist for Infants:

❑ Diapers, wipes, outfits according to daily needs (take plenty of extras for mishaps).

❑ Bunting or suitable outerwear for extra cold weather.

❑ Bibs.

❑ Plenty of empty plastic bags for dirty diapers.

❑ Changing pad. Get a nice, thick one to keep baby comfortable and clean no matter how rough or dirty the surface available for changing.

❑ Extra outfit handy in a day pack in case a complete change is necessary en route.

More Tips for Choosing and Packing Clothing:

❑ Take extra tee shirts in adult and child sizes that will fit more than one family member. Whoever needs 'em, gets 'em. They're comfortable and practical for outerwear, underwear, and sleepwear. Stock up when you find souvenir tee shirts from your home state on sale, and take them along as your emergency wardrobe or to give away to friends made along the way. They're especially welcome abroad. Even in a backpack, you can find room for two or three new tees to wear or give away.

❑ As you pack shoes, replace any shoelaces that have begun to fray. Take along a spare pair of 42- or 52-inch laces, which can be cut to fit as needed.

❑ Try to manage two swim suits per person so you'll always have a dry suit to put on.

❑ A sarong, also called a pireu or lava-lava is an all-purpose garment that can be worn as a skirt (in Indonesia, it's worn by both men and women), dress, or shawl and it can also be used as a tablecloth or a lightweight bed cover). Buy yours, or make your own by hemming a length of fabric 45 inches wide and about two yards long.

❑ Bring several bandanas, which can be used in many ways: head scarf, sweat band, neckerchief, stuff sack (just tie a knot around a small lunch or a pile of treasures), handkerchief, or table napkin.

❑ Leg warmers, found in dancing and exercise supply stores, provide a lot of extra warmth if the weather turns unexpectedly cold. Slip them on under slacks to warm ankles or knees or under a windbreaker to add extra warmth for arms. Use one to keep a baby's bottle or your thermos warm longer.

❑ Don't buy cuffed shorts or trousers. At best, they pick up chaff and dust that end up in your tent. At worst, they harbor chiggers and ticks that can emerge later to feed on you. Smooth-soled shoes bring less sand and soil into the tent. (Better still, enforce a no-shoes-in-the tent rule).

❑ A belt is more than a fashion accessory in camping. It's the bridle on which you'll hang countless tools and accessories. Choose skirts, slacks and shorts that have belt loops, and never be without one.

❑ In adventure travel with a guide or outfitter, certain clothing may be required or forbidden for a variety of reasons ranging from local cultural taboos to making yourself less visible to wildlife. Respect local customs, whatever they are.

❑ When choosing a fabric that you want to be either "breathable" or windproof, hold it up to your mouth and blow. (We're assuming here that you aren't wearing lipstick or sunscreen and will not soil or damage the garment in any way.) Then note how much air comes through.

CHAPTER

Choosing Your Chuckwagon Gear

Cook in Style in the Great Outdoors

Time was when camping gear, if you could buy it at all, had to be bought from everyday hardware and housewares stores. The rest was cobbled up in a home workshop. However, today's campers hardly have time or a workshop for banging together a waterproof spice rack or a suitcase that unfolds to form an entire kitchen. The good news is that the marketplace offers just about everything you'll need, ready-made, and it's probably cheaper, lighter, and better than anything you could hammer up at home.

For most toting purposes, it's hard to beat plastic milk crates, which sell in discount stores for a dollar or two. In camp, they serve as carriers, drawers, and seats, and two crates side by side form a stable enough grate to stand on while using a solar shower. Water drains through, so you don't end up in mud up to your ankles.

For covered containers, shop discount stores for lidded plastic storage bins in every shape and size from shoe boxes (sewing kit, crackers, first aid kit) to huge boxes that fit the back of a pickup truck. Choose sizes that are small enough for you to lift and move, but large enough to hold the gear and keep it handy. At least some of them need to be waterproof, and a few need to be lockable to keep wildlife out of your food and children from getting into medications or cleaning supplies.

Camp supply stores sell folding stove stands, tables, and chairs in a variety of materials and sizes. You'll find ice chests that double as a fish cleaning station or a camp seat, and endless oddments that will make your job as cook much easier. Some are merely gimmicky,

It's important to choose the right gear depending on whether you'll be cooking on your knees or in a fancy camp kitchen setup.

Gordon Groene

more trouble than they are worth. Others will solve a problem in your camping life. Start out with bare-bone basics, then add gear as your camping skills improve and you can see clearly what you want

Even if you plan to do all your cooking over a campfire, carry at least one campstove, even if it's just a solid fuel pocket stove, to use in case of rain or fire bans.

TOP TIP When choosing your campstove(s), keep in mind that you will probably be using it as an emergency cooker at home too. Many people who never camp keep a camp stove and fuel on hand as a backup. During ice storms, forest fires, floods, and hurricanes, homes can be without utilities for days, sometimes weeks. After Hurricane Andrew, some Miami homes were without power for months.

Hot Stuff: Choosing Your Campstove

Whether you're concerned about light weight for backpacking or kayaking, or you travel by van and have room to carry a deluxe, three-burner campstove, your first choice is to decide what fuel(s) will be best for availability, efficiency, and safety. Your choices include:

• Coleman fuel, which is affordable, available worldwide, hot and quick cooking.

• Kerosene and diesel fuel are also available worldwide. They produce a very hot flame.

and can be purchased in bulk at very low cost, even in Third World countries.

• Dual or multi-fuel stoves. Coleman makes a single burner and two- and three-burner campstove that can be used with Coleman fuel or unleaded gas, and the Exponent™ line offers single-burner stoves that operate on Coleman fuel, unleaded gasoline and, with an optional generator, kerosene. Camping and marine suppliers also offer stoves that can be used with almost anything combustible, from diesel fuel to gasoline.

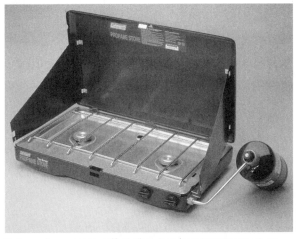

Coleman's compact, self-storing, two-burner propane stove sells for about $45.

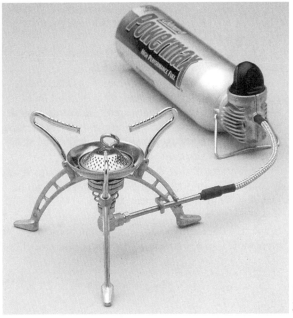

The lightest camp stoves for backpacking are made with a sturdy, but featherweight, magnesium alloy frame. Fueled with PowerMax, this little giant can produce up to 14,000 BTUs.

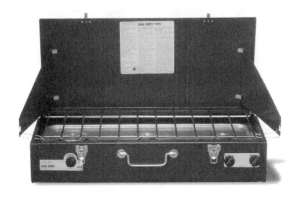

When shopping for camp stove(s), keep in mind that you also may need a backup stove for home use during utility outages.

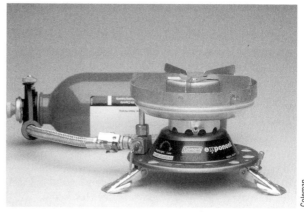

By adding a special generator to a dual-purpose stove, you can use it with three fuels: kerosene, Coleman fuel, and unleaded gas.

They're a good choice for campers in truly remote areas overseas.

• Solar cooking is bulky. You'll need a backup stove for days when the sun doesn't shine.

• Butane stoves use a cartridge or cassette that is easy to carry and change, quick to light, and highly heat efficient. The cartridges aren't as easy to find as propane, and butane won't liquefy in very cold temperatures. Empty cartridges have to be packed out of the wilderness for disposal.

• PowerMax® fuel is a blend of propane and butane. It comes in 6- and 10.6-ounce cartridges that can be recycled (with aluminum cans).

• Propane stoves use (1) a special manufacturer cartridge, (2) the familiar cartridge sold in home improvement stores, or (3) either, depending on the model.

Propane is hot, easy to light, and available at hardware and mass market stores at competitive prices. Note whether the stove can be used with a "bulk" or universal cylinder or requires a cylinder made by the stove manufacturer. Some stoves can use "bulk" cylinders with adapters. Never use a bulk cylinder with a stove that was not designed for it. Propane is hot, easy to light, and it has little odor. On the debit side, cartridges are a disposal problem in primitive camping.

• Do a lot of frying? Coleman makes a propane-fire griddle that can turn out big batches of pancakes, burgers, grilled cheese sandwiches, or French toast.

• Solid fuel is available in many types. The most familiar is Sterno, which is found in most supermarkets. Its disadvantage is an eye-smarting smell. Camp suppliers sell fuel "pills" that are even more compact

Selling for about $40, a stove that will operate on either unleaded gas or Coleman fuel is ideal for expeditions.

A top-of-the-line liquid fuel stove costs under $100 and burns unleaded gas or Coleman fuel, producing 13,500 BTUs on the main burner and 11,000 BTUs on the auxiliary burner.

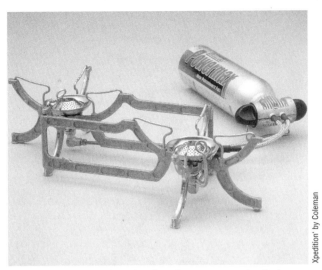

PowerMax provides quick, hot heat from a compact cylinder.

Xpedition¹ by Coleman

Campstove Tips

• Get a carry case for your stove if the manufacturer offers one. It will pay for itself by saving wear and tear on the stove's delicate parts. If a factory case isn't available, use canvas or duck to make one on your home sewing machine, or order one in a heavy fabric such as Sunbrella from a sailmaker.

• Put the stove away clean and dry in a dry environment. Camp stoves are usually steel or have at least some steel parts, and can rust in a damp environment.

• Strictly observe manufacturer directions for setting up, filling, and lighting the stove.

• If you camp at sites that provide a sturdy picnic table, that is the most stable spot to set up your campstove. If not, folding campstove stands and a large choice of folding tables are sold at camping suppliers.

• As every auto owner knows, unleaded gas can vary greatly in quality. Store stove gas in a clean container in a cool place. If the stove continues to be cranky, the generator may have been damaged by bad fuel. Replace it, then refill the stove with fresh gas. Never use kerosene, gasahol, or any leaded gas in a campstove designed to burn unleaded gas or Coleman fuel.

• If a stove develops any leak in a pipe, hose, tank, or fitting, don't attempt to repair it. Replace the gasket, fitting or whatever. We once observed a tragic fire in which a pressure stove erupted in flames because its owner "repaired" a break in a pipe with duct tape!

• Buy the funnel offered by the manufacturer for filling the stove. It probably has features such as a built-in filter and a safety shut-off that are an important part of stove operation.

than Sterno. Even if you carry a full-size stove, it's handy to have an Esbit Solid Fuel Stove, which is no larger than a package of cigarettes yet it forms a burner that can support a pot or kettle. It burns pellets about the size of a large Alka-Seltzer. It can't self-ignite accidentally, has no harmful vapors, is nearly smokeless, and leaves no ash. Each cube burns 12-14 minutes and brings a pint of water to the boil in less than eight minutes. The cubes also make excellent fire starters.

• Alcohol stoves (Britons called them spirit stoves) are popular with people who cook on board small boats because an alcohol fire can be extinguished with water. Marine stores stock one- and two-burner alcohol stoves starting at about $150. Their marine-grade, stainless steel construction is a real plus and non-pressurized alcohol is easy to light and use. Alcohol's drawback is that it delivers less heat for the gallon and for the dollar than almost any other fuel.

• Other fuel choices, of course, are wood and charcoal. There's nothing like the taste of char-grilled hamburgers or the smell of woodsmoke on the morning air, but campfires are slow to start and slow to cook. And, while you can often buy firewood at the campground or find enough dead wood in the forest, there's always the chance that you'll wake up hungry some morning to find that it's pouring rain or is so dry that a "no fires" ban is in effect in the campground that day.

• Portable grills and tripods for use with campfires are available in many shapes and sizes in mass market stores or through camping suppliers.

• Camping World sells propane grills in cast aluminum, stainless steel, cast iron, and steel in several models including a smoker-grill and a stove that has both burners and a grill. For quick grilling, keep one or two disposable charcoal grills on hand. They're a breeze to light, and one grill will cook four hamburgers or fillets, a dozen hot dogs, or a couple of steaks plus a packet of vegetables.

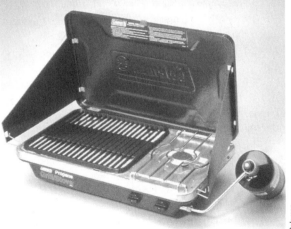

Coleman

Grilling is on everyone's menu, and camp stove manufacturers have responded by designing grill-stoves and small, portable propane grills.

Propane Safety

Propane is one of the hottest, cleanest, and most convenient fuels campers can use. Appliances that take the familiar, one-pound cartridges include radiant heaters for use outdoors, combination cooker-heaters for outdoor use, lanterns, camp stoves, turkey fryers, and two types of indoor heaters. It's a plus to use the fuel that is also used in one or two other camp appliances, so you don't have to carry a variety of spare cartridges and fuels.

The first line of precaution is in the hardware itself. The stove should be kept in good condition, with no loose fittings where gas could leak. Cylinders too should be kept in a dry spot so they don't rust. Inspect them for signs of damage of any kind that could result in a leak or rupture. Propane tends to "pool" in low spots when it leaks, creating spots that you cannot see, although you'll smell it. It's stinky, like skunk cabbage, and just one spark can set off an explosion. Store cylinders where any leaks can flow away harmlessly rather than puddling in, say, a tent floor or the trunk of a car.

If your propane heater is using up all the oxygen in an enclosed space, yawning and sleepiness are usually the first symptoms. You keep yawning more often, a sign that your body is crying out for oxygen. As your anoxia increases, your peripheral vision begins to shrink – a sign that you could be about to lose consciousness. Don't take chances.

Remember that all burning depletes the air of oxygen and produces carbon monoxide. Symptoms of CO poisoning are often mistaken for flu or a migraine. They include headache, dizziness, watery eyes, and fatigue. Depending on the person, CO poisoning can do damage that lasts a lifetime.

Here, from the Coalition for Portable Propane Safety, are tips on using this fuel safely:

❐ Don't cook or use an outdoor heater or cooker-heater inside a tent or any other shelter, and do not sleep with an indoor heater on.

❐ Never use a propane cooker as a heat source.

❐ Always store portable propane cylinders upright. Read manufacturer directions before using.

Coleman provides these additional propane safety tips:

❐ It is unsafe, and illegal in some places, to store or use LP cylinders of greater than 2.5 pound water capacity (about one pound propane) in occupied enclosures.

❐ Camping gear is usually stored in the attic, basement or garage. To avoid an accumulation of dust and cobwebs (spiders love propane), place your camp stove in a plastic bag and seal with a rubber band. Refillable cylinders should be stored outdoors, not in a house, camper or tent.

❐ Never re-fill disposable cylinders. Refillables should be used only with the manufacturer's parts and accessories.

Coleman

Propane produces a very hot cooking flame that is easy to light and adjust. Standard cartridges can often be found on sale.

❐ When setting up the stove, check hoses and fittings with soapy water. If there are any leaks, you'll see a bubble.

❐ Always inspect the propane cylinder and stove propane connections for damage, dirt and debris before attaching the cylinder. Pay special attention to gaskets and O-rings.

❐ Before attaching or detaching a propane cylinder, make sure the stove is cool to the touch and no other flame, spark or pilot lights are operating nearby. Don't forget to replace the protective cap on the cylinder.

❐ Don't use a campstove indoors or in a tent.

❐ Don't store fuel containers where temperatures might rise above 120 degrees. (That includes airplane baggage holds. Don't attempt to take fuel with you on a fly-in trip. If you're taking a stove, make sure its fuel is available where you're going.

❐ Operate any stove on a firm, level surface. Most camp stoves are designed for light weight and compactness, so plan menus that are suitable for the stove's capacities. Don't overload a stovetop with ungainly pots or large amounts of boiling water or food.

❐ Keep the stove away from flammables (clothing, paper towels, cardboard boxes) and never leave it unattended while cooking. Keep stoves out of children's reach.

❐ Don't try to adjust the preset 15 psi regulator that comes with the stove.

❐ If you smell propane in an enclosed place, get out immediately and ventilate the area.

❐ Keep the stove clean. When grease accumulates, it can catch fire.

❐ Lastly, strictly observe manufacturer directions. Every stove has its own, special quirks and precautions.

Tin Pan Alley: Choosing Cookware

In backpacking and bicycle and kayak camping, small size and light weight count more than anything else. Outfitters offer a good choice of nesting cookware with folding handles. An entire mess kit including pot, skillet, cup, soup plate, and eating utensils locks together in one, compact bundle.

In tent camping out of the family car or van, you're concerned about weight too, but it's more important to have pots and pans that clean easily, hold heat when you have to shuffle four pots on two burners, store compactly, and do as many different cooking jobs as possible. For example, a pressure cooker saves fuel, saves time on a hot day, and can cook multiple courses under pressure, and it can also be used without pressure as a big saucepan or (take out the rubber ring) as a stovetop oven. For the space and weight it takes up, few pots do more than a pressure cooker.

Here's a quick course in cookware metallurgy as it applies in the campground.

Aluminum. Second only to copper as a heat conductor, aluminum is ideal for stovetop baking and for low- or no-fat frying over a small flame. Thin, stamped aluminum pans are light to carry and quick to heat. Heat spreads evenly over the bottom of even the thinnest aluminum pan. Treated with a nonstick finish, aluminum is one of the most carefree choices for cookware.

On the minus side, aluminum can warp, distort or even crack from metal fatigue. Don't overheat it or plunge a hot pan into cold water. Don't store foods overnight in aluminum because acids in food react with the metal. Foods could discolor or develop a bad taste, and the pot could be stained or etched. Nonstick finishes are tender, so use and clean them according to manufacturer directions.

Sets of nesting pots and pans are compact and light for camping, but many campers prefer to choose individual pans as needed.

Copper. Chefs and gourmet cooks prefer copper because it reacts fastest to heating and cooling. Yet copper dents easily, corrodes, melts at 450 degrees, and is a cleaning headache. Forget it for camping.

Iron and Steel. Rolled steel is warp-resistant at high temperatures, so it's the best choice for quick, hot cooking in a wok. Cast iron, by contrast, absorbs and distributes heat slowly, so it's good for oven baking, for cooking over a bed of coals, or for deep fat frying with a lot of oil that distributes the heat.

Iron and steel are porous, so they can be "seasoned" to a finish that is almost as nonstick as Teflon. Here's how. When it is new, coat the pan with a light film of vegetable shortening or vegetable oil. Then bake it at 350 degrees for one hour or, if the pan was factory-sea-

A pressure cooker is quick, saves fuel, and does many tasks.

soned with silicone, 250 degrees for 30 minutes. Frying pans can be seasoned atop the stove. Coat the frypan with oil, heat until it smokes, wipe clean, then repeat.

After use, clean iron or steel pans with mild soap or none at all. Detergents dissolve the fat in the pores and destroy the nonstick coating. Once cleaned of its resident fat, the pan has to be re-seasoned. Don't put cast iron in a dishwasher when you get home either, because the strong detergent dissolves the seasoning oils out of the pores and you have to go through the seasoning process again. Oil iron and steel before storing, and re-season from time to time as needed. Because it is troublesome, messy, prone to rust, heavy, and it develops hot spots over a small flame, cast iron isn't recommended for campstove cooking. Try cast aluminum instead. It seasons like cast iron, but creates a more even heat.

Enameled steel pots such as the time-honored blue speckleware have a long history with campers. It's still hard to improve on the folksy, saddle tramp look of an old-fashioned, speckled blue or gray enamel coffee pot on the campfire. Because of the danger of chipping, however, there's no reason to use these pans now that better stuff is available at the same price. Tinned steel is also not recommended for camping. Bakers like it because it cooks more evenly than regular steel, but the coating wears off.

Stainless Steel can take years of knock-about camping because it's so sturdy. The more chrome and nickel, the better the stainless steel (18/8 or 18/10 indicates better qualities, i.e. 18 percent chrome and 8 percent or 10 percent nickel). On the minus side, foods can stick to stainless steel and create dishwashing woes. Stainless, because it is steel, doesn't spread heat well, so that can be a problem if you're using a large-bottomed skillet or pot atop a small flame. A copper or aluminum core or cladding is sometimes incorporated into stainless to solve this problem, but these pans can warp or delaminate if plunged into cold water when hot.

Wish List

A recommended shopping list for basic pots and pans includes:

• A 10-inch, cast aluminum skillet with heavy cover. It serves as a fryer, roaster, griddle, skillet, and Dutch oven.

• A three- or four-quart pressure cooker to speed cooking, save fuel, and double as a saucepan even if pressure isn't needed. Get a pot large enough to hold a meal for your family, but not so large that you or your stove can't handle it. Stainless steel is best for all-around use. Cast aluminum is best for stovetop baking because it spreads heat better. The cooker comes with a rack that you'll also use for cooking, steaming, cooling, baking, and much more.

• Stack Steamer. Better than a double boiler, which is two pots, is a stack consisting of one big pot, a

steamer insert, and a smaller pot insert that can be used as a double boiler or a separate pot. The steamer basket also serves as a colander and strainer; the double boiler can be used to warm rolls or leftovers. The bottom pot is large enough to make a big batch of soup.

• A lightweight nonstick aluminum skillet. It can be used as a saute pan, pan broiler, wok, omelet or crepe pan, and frying pan. Opt for a good brand of nonstick coating. Cheaper coatings work briefly or not at all.

Other pans you may find useful:

• A griddle that covers two burners can mass-produce pancakes, eggs, bacon, toasted sandwiches, French toast, burgers, hot dogs, and chops galore. Griddles are available with or without a nonstick finish.

• A 12-volt coffee pot that plugs into the car's cigarette lighter isn't what your scout leader taught you to use, but sometimes you need a cup of coffee in the morning before you can find the energy to light the stove or campfire. Find coffee makers and other 12-volt appliances at camp supply stores. Just be sure you don't run down the battery so the car won't start.

• A campfire corn popper will provide more food and fun per square inch than any other piece of cooking gear you carry.

• Consider carefully whether electrical appliances should be part of your camping gear. Many tent sites have electric hookup, and many cooks wouldn't dream of going camping without a hotplate or toaster oven. If you take only one appliance, make it an electric hotplate that can be used with your skillet, griddle, coffee pot, wok, Dutch oven, ad inf., providing easy heat and thermostatic control. A toaster oven is also a good choice because it can toast, broil, or bake. Be aware, however, that campground wiring may not be heavy enough for you to run two kitchen appliances at once. Too, kitchen appliances weren't designed for outdoor use and must be protected from wetting and weather.

Soap Stops Soot

A cooking vessel used over a campfire will have an outer coating of soot that will stain everything it touches. While the clean pan is still cold, go over the entire outside with a soft bar soap such as Ivory or Fels-Naptha, coating it thoroughly. When you wash the pot, the soot will come off with the soap.

Slip every pot into its own storage bag, such as an old pillow slip, to protect it from getting banged up and to keep it from soiling nearby gear. If nonstick pans are nested, coatings will be damaged. Line each pan with a coffee filter, then stack.

Lovin' Without An Oven

Stovetop ovens have been around since the days of Great-Granny's kerosene cookstove. In summer when it was too hot to light the coal or wood cookstove, Grandma used a kerosene cooktop for her canning and frying. Realizing that homemakers also wanted to bake in summer, traveling salesmen peddled cast aluminum, "waterless" cookware. It was heavy enough to surround food with even heat, and it got hot enough to bake cakes and pies. Although tin box-type stovetop ovens were also sold for kitchen use, they rusted away while the durable, cast aluminum was handed down through the generations. My friend who grew up in the 1940s learned stovetop baking during summers on an Indiana farm, and told me about it. More about that later.

The familiar tin-box camp oven with a temperature gauge in the door is still available from camping suppliers. On the plus side, it mimics a real oven, surrounding the dish with even, dry heat. Its drawback is that it's hard to keep it up to temperature on a cold, windy day. Most are steel, so they rust away in a few years, and they take up a lot of space.

Solar ovens are available in many sizes, from individual ovens to large, commercial sizes used in group camps. They work, of course, only when the sun is shining, and who feels like cooking and eating before sundown when camping in summer or in the tropics? In any case, solar ovens are best in climates or seasons when you can reasonably expect long hours of sunshine.

Commercially made solar ovens are available from companies including Sun Oven International (see Resources) and from suppliers who specialize in all things solar, such as www.solarcooking.org, but it's

Commercially-made solar ovens provide sturdy construction, efficient cooking at up to 400 degrees F., and instructions for use. Sun Ovens have a built-in thermometer.

also easy and fun to make your own sunshine cooker. An Internet search for the key words solar+oven finds endless designs for homemade solar devices. Most are inexpensive, even disposable, and will have varying degrees of success, but it's fun to experiment with them or to make a family project out of assembling and using a solar cooker. (Have a backup plan for dinner in case it doesn't work out.)

Tips on solar cooking:

• It's essential to capture as much of the sun's heat as possible, so this means cooking during the best hours, usually 10 a.m. to 2 p.m. and re-focusing the oven as the sun moves, usually twice per hour.

• Every time you open the door to check on the cooking, heat is lost. Add about 10-15 minutes to cooking time each time you peek. A well-constructed solar oven has no hotspots, so stirring isn't needed for most recipes.

• Buy cooking pans that fit inside your solar cooker. Dark-colored, thin-walled pans are best. Oven-proof glass casseroles can also be used.

• Use hot mitts to handle cooked foods. The outside of the oven remains fairly cool but you could be burned by the pot inside.

A **reflector oven** can be rigged near the campfire from sheet metal or aluminum foil. A useful addition to the gear box is a hinged, three-sided wind screen that can be set up around the camp stove or camp fire to keep heat focused on one spot. It's also useful as a spatter shield around the frypan when you're cooking bacon or frying chicken. If you can't find one in a housewares department (ask for a spatter shield) or camping supplier (ask for a stove windscreen), make your own with three flat cookie sheets or any other flat, shiny stock that doesn't have sharp edges.

Drill or punch two holes in each flat sheet so they can be held together with rings that act as hinges. Key rings are inexpensive and work well. The three sheets fold flat for storage but can be set up, freestanding, to form a reflector, wind shield, or splash screen wherever you need one. The shinier the metal, the more heat is reflected, so keep it clean and shiny or, if it becomes too sooty or stained to be effective, wrap it in fresh foil as needed.

Stovetop baking. You can also bake on the stovetop in either of two pans that you carry with you anyway, the pressure cooker or the large, cast aluminum skillet that also serves as your frying pan, roaster, and griddle. Here's how.

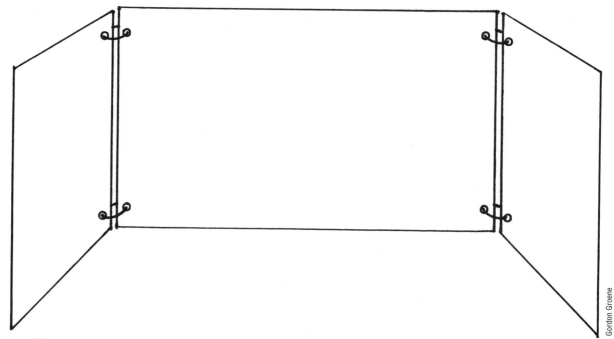

Use any shiny metal stock or three cookie sheets to make reflector/wind screens to use with the camp stove, camp fire, or space heaters.

In both cases, cast aluminum is best – not stamped aluminum, stainless steel, or cast iron. The pan should also have a heavy, tight-fitting lid. The object is to surround the food with a steady, hot, even envelope of heat. Cast iron is fine for the campfire, where you can bury a Dutch oven in hot coals and shovel more on top. For baking on a campstove, however, cast aluminum is best because it spreads heat evenly over the entire bottom and sides of the pot. When using a pressure cooker for baking, remove the rubber gasket and don't use the pressure regulator. Make sure the pan is clean because it will get very hot. Any oily residue will bake on.

It's also helpful to have a flame diffuser, also called a flame tamer or flame spreader. Some stoves have blowtorch burners that can't be turned down low enough for slow, even baking, especially using the direct method. Nonstick coatings aren't recommended for pans used for indirect baking. High temperatures soon destroy the finish.

Indirect method for stovetop baking. Choose a pot as described above and think of it as a small oven. Just as your oven at home has a shelf, this oven needs one too. Place a rack in the bottom of the cold, clean "oven." It can be a pressure cooker rack, a metal rack sold for cooling cookies, or just a thin, level, pile of old nails, nuts and bolts – anything that keeps the baking pan from sitting directly on the "oven" bottom.

Prepare the dough, batter, pie, meatloaf, or whatever you are baking, and place it in a suitable baking pan, which could be washable or disposable. Pre-heat the covered oven over high flame for about 10 minutes. Then quickly remove the cover, place baking pan on the rack and immediately replace the lid, minimizing

heat loss. Bake over medium-high flame for the prescribed time. Don't peek for at least 15 minutes. You do have to eyeball it and test for doneness in due time, but it's important not to peek too often because heat escapes and baking is interrupted. At best, this will waste fuel and prolong cooking time. At worst, your cake could fall.

One advantage to indirect baking is that you remove the baked item when it's done and the "oven" is clean and ready to use for another purpose such as frying the chops or pressure cooking the rice and vegetables. Just let the "oven" cool somewhat because it becomes very

Place small rack in a clean, cast aluminum Dutch oven, heat it over the campstove, and treat it like any other oven.

hot during the baking process. Take all precautions for your own safety as well as the pan's. Adding cold meat or liquid when it's very hot could cause it to warp.

Direct method for stovetop baking. With this method, you are baking directly on the bottom of a heavy, cast aluminum skillet or pressure cooker. The pan will, therefore, have to be washed after cooking. While nonstick pans aren't recommended for indirect baking, they're fine for the direct method. Just don't scratch the coating by, for example, digging pizza out of the pan with a metal spatula.

Start with a clean, cold, greased cooker or skillet and place the batter, dough, or meatloaf and scrubbed potatoes directly on the bottom of the cold pan. Cover, place over medium-low flame, with a flame spreader if necessary, and bake until it's done. One of the most popular dishes for direct cooking is upside down cake. It's also ideal for meatloaf and baked potatoes because bottoms turn a crusty brown. Times and burner settings will depend on outdoor conditions, your stove, your pans, and your recipes, so some eyeballing is necessary.

To make yeast bread using the direct method, use a cast aluminum pressure cooker, rubber gasket removed. Grease the pressure cooker thoroughly, sprinkle it lightly with cornmeal, and shake the pan so it's evenly coated on the bottom and sides with the cornmeal. Dump out excess cornmeal. Then add dough that has been kneaded and raised once, cover, and raise until it's double in bulk, ready to bake.

Then lock the lid in place (without the rubber gasket or pressure regulator) and bake over low-medium flame. A loaf that calls for four cups of flour (one-pound loaf) takes about 40 minutes. With practice, you will be able to sense from the smell of the escaping steam when the bread is the right shade of brown. The top of the loaf will remain white, but you can judge doneness by the springiness of the top. Turn it out on a cutting board and the bottom and sides will be a corn-meal-crusted, golden brown. Like any yeast bread, a pressure cooker-baked loaf cuts better after it cools a little and better still if it's cooled, wrapped, and "seasoned" for a few hours.

To bake biscuits using the direct method, place cut dough on the cold, greased surface of the cast aluminum Dutch oven. Cover, and bake 10 minutes or until one side is light brown. Turn, cover and bake 8-10 minutes more until the other side is golden brown, Turn, cover, and bake again until the first side is golden brown and the biscuit is done through.

To make pizza, press a tube of biscuits into the bottom of a cold, greased skillet to form an even crust. Spread with pizza sauce to within ? inch of the sides, then add your favorite toppings and sprinkle with grated cheese, no closer than ? inch from the sides. Cover and place over medium-low flame for 15 minutes, then check for doneness every five minutes. When it's golden brown around the edges, it's probably done through.

Additional tips on stovetop baking:

• Most camp stoves have one burner that is hotter than the other(s). Don't use the "blowtorch" burner for stovetop baking.

• Never leave a camp stove unattended when it's in use. There are safety considerations and, if wind should blow out a burner, a cake could be ruined before you notice that the oven has gone cold. Cakes, cornbread, and quick breads that rely on baking powder rising are fussy about temperature.

• When shopping for camping gear, have the measurements of your Dutch oven handy so you can buy a rack and baking pans that will fit inside. By using different pans and the indirect method, you can keep the oven going all day to make a cake, then a pie, then a batch of brownies. Square, round, and pie pans can all be found to fit inside. Choose metal pans. Glass bakeware isn't practical for camping anyway, and isn't suitable for stovetop baking. Disposable foil pans and foil packets can also be used for indirect baking.

• Because the oven area is so small relative to the size of the food, a lot of moisture builds up. Don't try meringues or baked-on toppings. To make crisp, brown toppings, brulees, and other finishing touches that require broiler heat, carry a small blowtorch. Simply move it back and forth over the topping until the desired color develops. Tiny propane and butane blowtorches are sold in tool and hobby departments. Yours may also come in handy for soldering, fusing and other repairs, and for starting stubborn campfires.

• Clean tin cans are ideal for stovetop baking in a pressure cooker, which can usually hold three or four 15- or 16-ounce tins. Prepare batter for quick bread, (e.g. banana nut, pumpkin bread), fill greased cans no more than 2/3 full, and bake by the indirect method. When the breads cool, open the bottom end of the tin with a can opener, push it through to remove the bread, and put the cans in the recycle bin. No baking pans to wash! The resulting, round loaves are attractive to look at and easy to slice.

• Pastries are slow to brown in indirect baking. Make pie crust with butter or oleo, which brown faster than shortening. Browning is also aided by brushing a little milk on the top crust.

Coleman

Made especially for camping is a folding table that provides plenty of work and storage space for cooking items.

More Gear for the Portable Pantry

Here are some suggestions that might work for your camping style:

• Barbecue tools: Get a barbecue or pastry brush with natural bristles that can withstand high heat. It's also handy to have long-handled tongs, fork, and spatula for use on a hot barbecue or campfire.

• Unshakable salt. If you find yourself constantly throwing away salt because it clumps up in damp, outdoor air, carry it in liquid form. Make a heavy brine by stirring four tablespoons of salt into a cup of water. Funnel it into a soy sauce bottle and simply shake it onto food at the stove or table. Discard after each campout. Incidentally, you'll find lots of other uses for used soy sauce bottles too. They make good shakers for sherry (use in chowder), vinegar and oil (salads), homemade hot sauce made by soaking dried hot peppers in vinegar, or homemade infused vinegars made by placing sprigs of fresh herbs, such as tarragon or basil in a bottle of vinegar.

• Fireproof fireplace gloves are a real plus for handling hot logs.

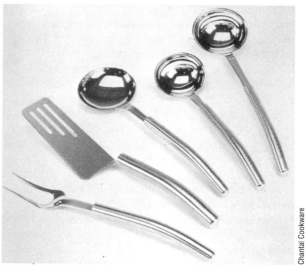

Buy tools and serving pieces in a good quality stainless steel. Plastic and wood handles can melt, split, or burn.

Chantal Cookware

Canned goods are lifesavers in camping. It pays to buy a heavy duty can opener.

Gordon Groene

• A double-gear can opener can open rusted or odd-shaped cans including corned beef cans that have lost their key. Cheaper openers have only one, toothed gear, and are not as effective.

• **Good knives** are a good investment for camping and are safer to use than dull, nicked, kitchen castoffs. Carry knives in holders or sheaths so blades are protected.

• **Square containers** stack and store more efficiently than round ones. Before buying, try them out for ease of opening and closing. Square corners are sometimes hard to seal. In any case, choose storage containers with flat, not domed, lids for easier stacking.

• **Two for the money.** See how clever you can be in finding multi-purpose kitchenware. For example, a set of plastic measuring cups can measure, but the same set in stainless steel can also be used as miniature pans.

• **Set for life.** Don't carry more than you need just because kitchen items come in sets. Where possible, buy only what you need in the sizes you need. If the item is available only in a set, use extras in the kitchen, give them away, or sell them at a yard sale.

• **Paper napkins** flutter and fly away. Instead, carry a roll of paper towels and keep it handy by setting it in an empty tin, such as a shortening can. The hole in the cardboard roll is a good place to carry and stow other items such as a sharp knife. Buy corks that measure a minimum of 1.5 inches and flare to 1.75 inches, put one in each end of the paper towel cardboard, and stash small items inside. There's room for up to four film canisters filled with dried spices, an ice pick, the wood skewers you'll use for kebabs, or a bundle of spaghetti. (Wrap it first in plastic wrap).

A stainless steel cooler costs more than painted steel or plastic, but is a lifetime investment.

The top of a big cooler can also serve as a work surface, seat, or dish drainer.

The Big Chill

Campers can't have too many ice chests. Carry as many as you have room for unless, of course, you camp in places where ice isn't available. You'll need one cooler for fish and bait, so your other supplies don't get smelly, and another just for drinks, so everyone can help themselves without constantly opening the food chest. It's nice to have yet another cooler that's filled with clean ice to use in drinks and perhaps others sealed with frozen food to open later in the trip.

A big ice chest doubles as a seat and work surface. A wheeled ice chest makes the handiest cart for carrying supplies from house to car and car to campsite. A metal ice chest with a locking lid keeps food safe from bugs, rats, and raccoons. Soft coolers are ideal to carry as spares or for shopping trips. When they're not needed, they can be used as extra stuff bags or pillows.

Here's how to manage coolers for the coldest, longest-lasting chill:

• Days before your campout, turn your home freezer to its coldest setting to make ice for your cooler. Freeze ice in clean, food quality containers. When it melts, drink the ice water. Water, milk, or juice jugs are good for this because they pour easily and can be burned or recycled. Better still are bladders saved from wine boxes. Cut off one corner so the bag can be rinsed clean and filled with fresh water. Close the corner with a rubber band, and freeze the bladders in square or rectangu-

Used as a cooler or just as a food cart, a cooler with big wheels can handle sandy or uneven terrain.

Keep one cooler just for ice and water, and you'll always have cold drinks on hand.

When ice chest temperatures fall below 45 degrees F., spoilage speeds up.

An ice chest also makes a warm, windproof place to raise yeast dough or to culture yogurt.

lar containers so they don't form odd-shape blobs. Blocks stow more efficiently. As the ice melts, you can draw the water using the built-in spigot. Best of all, the bag collapses as it empties, so there isn't the wasted space you have when using ice made in milk jugs.

• Don't bother with "blue" ice on a long trip unless you have a way to re-freeze it daily. Once it thaws, it's just dead weight.

• About an hour before filling the cooler, fill it with as much ice as you can spare and let it pre-chill. Then, working quickly, dump out and discard this ice and fill the cooler with fresh ice and pre-chilled drinks, food, and frozen foods.

• Any time you can buy block ice, do so. You can always add a bag or two of ice cubes for convenience, but block ice is best for keeping things coldest, longest.

• Keep a refrigerator thermometer in your food chest. When temperatures fall below 45 degrees, you are inviting spoilage. A good maxim is, "Life begins at 40." At temperatures higher than that, organisms begin to grow in earnest. Another good maxim is, "When in doubt, throw it out." (Or, as the kids like to say, "Better throw it out than throw it up.")

• Frozen meat will last for several days in a pre-chilled cooler. For the best head start, order boneless, skinless, waste-free meat, cut to your order. Ask the meat manager to wrap it in freezer wrap without bulky trays, and freeze it for you. Thin cuts and patties thaw first; a block of ground meat will last two or three days; a whole turkey will keep three to five days in a well-insulated cooler.

• When you shop for fresh supplies during a camping trip, buy pre-chilled sodas and frozen foods where possible, rather than buying the same items off the shelf at room temperature. Why waste ice?

• Discover the new, vac-packed cuts, roasts, and lunch meats. Some are marinated and require cooking;

others are fully cooked. They are freshness-dated and last far longer than other fresh meats. They should, of course, be kept cold and handled with the same safety standards as other meats.

• Buy coolers that are all white and keep them in a cool spot out of the sun and wind. If the cooler is a dark color, throw a white cover over it.

• Be cautious if you use dry ice. It can "scorch" frozen foods, burn bare hands when you touch it, freeze delicate produce, and explode canned or bottled sodas. It is much colder than water ice. Wearing gloves, wrap the ice in several layers of newspaper to keep it from coming into direct contact with foods.

• A cooler can also be used to keep things warm (e.g. raising bread dough or culturing yogurt) or hot (carrying take-out fried chicken, pizza, or a Chinese meal to the campground). For very hot items, line the ice chest with several layers of newspaper to add insulation and to prevent damage to the plastic liner.

• If you camp in areas that have warm days but very cold nights, you can just flip open an ice chest at night and let it cold-soak. Then close the lid in the morning as the sun comes up. It's an ideal way to chill the next day's supplies of canned and bottled drinks. (Don't try it with foods that critters can raid.) Camped next to a very cold stream, you can also chill a cooler filled with drinks. (Tether it so it can't float away). After a couple of hours, fish it out and drain off the water. If the water was polluted, wipe off cans before drinking from them.

Campers can't have too many ice chests. Carry as many as you have room for.

Choosing Food-Quality Plastics

Plastic is plastic, right? Wrong. Many synthetic materials weren't made to tolerate heat, acids, alcohol, or other ingredients in foods. You could endanger yourself and your family by carrying, say, pancake syrup in a squirt bottle that detergent came in or cooking oil in a plastic oilcan sold for the garage. Fortunately, many foods now come in plastic dispensers, and the marketplace offers a wide range of storage containers and dispensers made with food-quality plastics.

Plastics are essential to camping because they are tough and light weight. Begin by buying high quality food containers and take care of them correctly:

* Cool foods before putting in a plastic storage container. (It's better too for your ice chest if you fill it only with pre-chilled or frozen foods.)

• Don't reheat foods in the microwave in non-microware plastics. They could stain or, worse still, melt and contaminate food.

• Don't let plastics stand for long periods before cleaning. Occasionally put camping plastics through the dishwasher at home to remove stubborn stains and odors. Or, dissolve dishwasher detergent in boiling water and give plastics a soak. Keep your hands out of this harsh cleaner. A very hot soak with dishwasher detergent or a bleach solution (don't mix the two) also removes stains and odors from plastic coffee mugs.

• Wash plastic containers that come with cottage cheese, yogurt, margarine, and other foods and fill them with salad, sandwich filling or the foods listed below for a one-way trip to the campground. After one use, put them in the recycle bin.

Top 10 Foods That Stain Food Storage Containers

According to the National Sanitation Federation, an independent public health safety testing facility, here from worst to least are the top 10 items that stain plastic food containers. If you carry them on camping trips, carry them in disposables (such as cottage cheese containers) that can be discarded in the campground's recycle bin.

Pasta Marinara	Chocolate pudding
Vegetable soup	Strawberries
Chili	Cranberry sauce
Salsa	Chicken broth
Carrots	Turkey breast with gravy

Life in a Vacuum

A couple of centuries ago, somebody figured out that food wouldn't spoil for months and even years if it were saved in a vacuum. Tinned foods went to war with Napoleon and came to the New World in ship galleys as early as the late 18th century. Home canning became easier and safer with the invention of the pressure canner. I still "put up" boneless, skinless meats, trimmed of all fat, for camping trips. (While we won't go into home canning here, you can get information from your county extension home economist.)

Not long ago, campers were using primitive ways to suck the air out of bags and packages. Backpackers sealed things in zip-tip bags, leaving just enough space to insert a soda straw to draw out as much air as possi-

Sturdy jerry jugs made from food quality plastics are a must for storing and transporting drinking water.

For about $100 plus the cost of plastic bags, you can preserve food and make it more compact. Cooked foods can be vac-packed in boilable bags, frozen months ahead, then brought along on camping trips. Just heat in a pot of hot water.

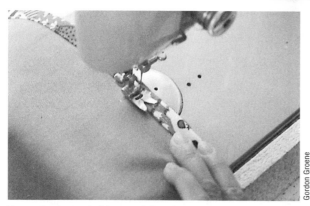

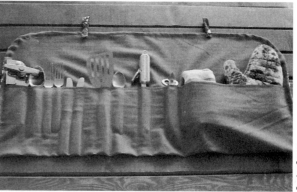

Use a sturdy, washable material such as denim to sew up holders for silverware, utensils and tools. They roll up for carrying and are easily laundered when you get home.

ble before the final closing. It didn't help much with food spoilage, but it did make each packet smaller. Dry foods such as nuts, dried fruits, and pastas could be heated gently in an oven in glass canning jars, then sealed while hot to create at least a partial vacuum to extend food life. Now, thanks to new vacuum packing systems, anyone can vacuum pack any foods from soup to nuts for longer keeping and more compact carrying.

Home vacuum systems don't sterilize food, as canning does. They do, however, extend the life of dry food by removing oxygen, allow you to stow packs of food in smaller spaces, keep dry foods dry and moist foods moist, and let you seal up entire meals in boilable bags that can be rewarmed in camp in a pot of water. Here is a guide to food storage using a vacuum system such as FoodSaver®.

Glue sandpaper to the lid of a jar and you'll have a waterproof carrier with a built-in striking surface.

Save ribbed tops from worn-out socks and draw them over any glass bottles to protect and quiet them. If you like, a draw thread can be used to close the bottom or just use them as sleeves. Ribbing can also be drawn over rolled garments or hats to compress them.

WHAT IS THE SHELF LIFE OF VACUUM PACKAGED FOODS?*

FOOD	WHERE TO STORE	RECOMMENDED FOODSAVER CONTAINER	NORMAL SHELF LIFE	VACUUM PACKAGED SHELF LIFE
Fish	In freezer	VacLoc Bag	6 months	2 years
Large cuts of meat (beef, poultry, lamb and pork)	In freezer	VacLoc Bag	6 months	2-3 years
Ground meat (beef, poultry, lamb and pork)	In freezer	VacLoc Bag	4 months	1 year
Coffee Beans	At room temp.	VacLoc Bag, FoodSaver Canister or mason jar	3 months	1 year
	In freezer	VacLoc Bag	6-9 months	2-3 years
Ground coffee	At room temp.	VacLoc Bag, FoodSaver Canister or mason jar	1 month	5-6 months
	In freezer	VacLoc Bag	6 months	2 years
Berries (strawberries, raspberries, blackberries)	In refrigerator	FoodSaver Canister or mason jar	1-3 days	1 week
Berries (cranberries, huckleberries, blueberries)	In refrigerator	FoodSaver Canister or mason jar	3-6 days	2 weeks
Cheese	In refrigerator	VacLoc Bag	1-2 weeks	4-8 months
Cookies, crackers	At room temp. (periodically opening container)	FoodSaver Canister or mason jar	1-2 weeks	3-6 weeks
Flour, sugar, rice	At room temp.	VacLoc Bag, FoodSaver Canister or mason jar	6 months	1-2 years
Lettuce	In refrigerator	FoodSaver Canister or mason jar	3-6 days	2 weeks
Nuts	At room temp.	FoodSaver Canister or mason jar	6 months	2 years
Oils (with no preservatives), i.e., safflower, canola, corn oil	At room temp.	FoodSaver Canister or mason jar	5-6 months	1-1.5 years
Wine	In refrigerator	FoodSaver Bottle Stopper	1-3 weeks	2-4 months

*Source: Dr. George K. York, Department of Food Science and Technology, University of California, Davis

Chart from Tilia.

Tilia FoodSaver®

CHAPTER

9

For The Health Of It

Prevention is the best medicine for campers

Few outdoor activities are more healthful, safe, and exhilarating than camping in the sweet air of the mountains, deserts, seashore, and forest. Camping is the best medicine of all. Still, precautions and planning can save a lot of problems.

The things most campers fear most are dramatic tragedies such as snake bite, poisonous plants, and attacks by wild animals. The truth is that all these are extremely rare. The biggest camping dangers are the most obvious and the most easily avoided: sunburn, dehydration, heat stroke, hypothermia, and getting lost.

It's easy to pick up a first aid kit at the drug store. The bigger the kit and the higher the cost, the better the first aid, right? Wrong. "Canned" first aid kits are better than none at all. They're available in sizes as small as a cigarette pack to slip on a belt loop and as big a suitcase, and most of them are marked with a big, red cross that makes them easy to find in your pack or tent. They're filled with stuff you need, might need, and will never need in a million years, in quantities that are about right for the average person, not you, and they are not specifically for camping. However, if you make your own first aid kit, you'll have exactly what you need, in the container best suited to your camping style, at the lowest cost.

Camp First Aid Kits

• Select a sturdy, waterproof container that's sized for your campout style. Add basic bandages, triple antibiotic ointment, an Ace bandage, antibacterial cleaning pads, and medications for pain, indigestion, and diarrhea.

• Talk to your doctor and pediatrician about special recommendations for your health needs, and the children's, in the region where you camp.

• Sample sizes are compact, sealed until needed, and allow you to carry a great variety of over-the-counter medications in little space. Buy full sizes only in meds you're likely to need in greater quantities.

• Carry medical insurance cards in your wallet but also carry phone numbers for your doctors, pharmacist, any med-evac insurance, and the national poison control hotline (800-222-1222) in the medical kit. It's also wise to have written copies of prescriptions for medications and eyeglasses. Some prescriptions can't be filled by pharmacies outside your home state. Diabetic supplies require a prescription in some states even if you can buy insulin or syringes at home without one. If you're flying to your camping destination, security personnel will also require proof of need for syringes or other medical paraphernalia. If you are traveling with children that are not your own or you are the non-custodial parent, carry a medical power of attorney in case the child needs treatment while in your care.

• Tweezers are a first aid essential; tweezers with a built-in magnifying glass are a plus. If you fish or are around people who do, carry wire cutters. The best way to remove a fishhook is usually to push it all the way through the skin and cut off the barb.

• A Space® Blanket takes no more room than a few tissues, but can be a lifesaver in weather emergencies.

• Don't forget a dental emergency kit containing dental wax to cushion a rough spot on a broken tooth or broken braces, denture adhesive for temporary replacement of a crown (don't use a permanent adhesive) and topical anesthetics as recommended by your dentist. The old wives' tale about melting an aspirin on an aching tooth is bad advice. It could cause a painful ulcer.

• Instant hot packs and cold packs are available in major drug stores. When you squeeze the packet, two chemicals mix and you have a healing pack that lasts up to a few hours. Read labels and, for camping, make sure you're getting packs that work chemically and don't require a freezer or microwave. Chemical packs are good for only one use, but they are a godsend in the field.

• If you have young children, keep medications in a locked container, just as you keep them in a locked medicine cabinet at home.

• Browse a bookstore for a general or outdoors first aid manual.

Once Burned, Twice Shy

"If you believe that light summer clothes will protect you from the sun, you could get burned," says Dan Gutting of Atsko Sno-Seal. The company makes U-V-Block, a spray-on sun block that can be applied to clothing to keep UVA and UVB from getting through. "A white cotton tee shirt may provide an ultraviolet protection factor (UPF) of only 5, and less when stretched or wet," says Gutting. "A white dress shirt has an SPF of 4-6 dry and 2-5 when wet. Sprayed with U-V-Block, that protection increases to 20-30."

If you're buying clothing for sun protection, the American Society for Testing and Materials (ASTM) has created standards for UV transmission. Tags indicating Good are for garments with a UPF of 15-24, Very Good indicates a UPF of 25-39, and Excellent on the label shows that ASTM has found the shirt, hat or slacks have a UPF of 40-50. An alterative, if you don't find protective clothing in sizes and styles you want, is to spray your clothes with U-V-Block or use a wash-in sun block found in the supermarket and made by Rit.

Here's how to assure that you will never suffer sunburn again:

• Apply sun block first thing in the morning before dressing, preferably after a shower, while you're still damp. The goo will cover more thoroughly, dry quickly, and protect places you usually miss after dressing, such as the back of the neck and the space around your wrist watch.

• Read labels. In addition to different UPFs, some blocks are more waterproof than others. Some call for re-application every 30 minutes when sweating or swimming.

• Consult your pediatrician about products that are safest to use on the very young. Be extra diligent about sun protection for little ones. Sun damage is cumulative for life.

• When swimming, re-apply sun block as necessary.

• When swimming or snorkeling in clear water, where sun penetrates the water and is reflected back from a white sand bottom, wear long-sleeve garments such as light pajamas. You can be burned while in the water.

• Sunburn is almost always a possibility, even on a cloudy day or on a cold day high in ski country. A moisturizer that contains sun block is a good choice in dry climates. Double your vigilance when you're on the water, which reflects the sun and gives you a double dose.

• The shorter your shadow, the greater the danger of sunburn. Stay out of the sun as much as possible between 10 a.m. and 2 p.m. Tropic cultures invented the siesta for good reason.

Critters, Crawlies, and Poison Plants

Millions of people camp their entire lives without so much as seeing a rattlesnake or a black widow spider, so forget the horror movies you've seen. Learn to recognize poison ivy, poison oak, and sumac, and stay away from them. Here are some other hazards to identify:

Elderberry, found along roadsides and railroad tracks throughout most of North America, has a delicious fruit used in jellies and pies. Just stay away from the woody stems. They're toxic, unsuitable for kids making whistles or parents looking for a stick to spear the hot dog or stir the chili.

Manchineel, a tropic tree, is so poisonous that you can get a rash from rain dripping off the tree or go temporarily blind if you're near the smoke from a manchineel fire.

Mushrooms. Even experts get fooled by wild mushrooms. Don't eat them. Besides, foraging is illegal in most parks and campgrounds. Let nature's bounties live on where you find them.

Coral snakes, found in the tropics, are beautifully banded in red, yellow, and black and are often irresistible to little boys. Warn the kids not to disturb snakes, even the pretty ones. If someone is bitten by a snake, get help as quickly as possible, with as little exertion on the part of the victim as possible.

The old tip about cutting an X on the wound and sucking out the poison is no longer recommended for any snakebite, according to the Florida Poison Information Network. Don't apply ice or a tourniquet either. There's no substitute for prompt, professional care, preferably brought to you because exercise speeds the circulation of the venom. Stay quiet, remove jewelry near the bite site, and keep the bitten part at or below heart level. While all snakebites aren't from venomous snakes, all bites should be medically evaluated. Even a bite from a non-poisonous snake can lead to a nasty infection.

TOP TIP Remember that a "dead" snake can still bite due to a reflex reaction.

Fire ants are found in the Southeast and are working their way northward. Their hills are conical white mounds. Most people get into trouble by accidentally standing or sitting on one. You're immediately swarmed by stinging ants, and can do little but dash for the nearest pond. Give any anthills a wide berth.

Bees Wax Protects Skin

Pro-Tech-Skin is a natural, beeswax product that protects skin from drying or windburn. Sport-Wash Hair & Body Soap and Sensi-Clean Shampoo & Body Gel are two bath products that remove soil, body odors, and the residues of other soaps, leaving no perfumes or residues to attract bees or mosquitoes. Both are sold in sporting goods stores and catalogs.

Poisons Lurk in Nature

If there is a chance that a child has tasted a poisonous plant, call the Poison Control Hotline at once, (800) 222-1222. You may note symptoms starting with the child crying and complaining of a burning sensation in the mouth. Other symptoms include headache, nausea, lethargy, and/or a falling heart rate. Onset may not be immediate. Symptoms can occur 6-12 hours after the child has eaten the poison, depending on how much was eaten and what type of plant it was.

The good news is that the majority of harmful plants taste terrible, and kids quit after one bite. Most children who have eaten most plants will be perfectly fine. However, only an expert can advise you, and that's where the hotline comes in.

When you call the center, be prepared with as much information as possible. Explain when the child ate the plant, how much you think was eaten, and which parts of the plant were involved. Some edible plants have poisonous parts; some poisonous plants have harmless parts. Describe what reactions have been observed. If possible, take a sample of the plant with you to help experts identify it.

Pets can eat the wrong plants too. Unlike kids, who often know a yucky substance when they taste it, pets don't know when to quit. If you suspect that a pet has eaten a poison plant, the only solution is to get professional help, taking a sample of the plant if you know what was eaten.

Among plants that are poisonous to people are:

- Angel's trumpet (Brugmansia)
- Azalea
- Carolina jessamine (Gelsemium sempervirens)
- Castor bean (Ricinus communis)
- Cestrum spp.
- Daphne
- Delphinium
- Echium vulgare
- Foxglove
- Heliotrope
- Jimson weed (Datura stramonium)
- Larkspur
- Lily-of-the-valley
- Lobelia
- Lupine
- Meadow saffron (Colchicum autumnale)
- Morning glory (seeds)
- Myoporum
- Nicotiana spp.
- Oleander
- Poison hemlock (Conium maculatum)
- Pregnant onion (Ornithogalum)
- Scilla
- Sweet pea
- Yew (Taxus spp.)

Plants that can also cause problems include:

- Arrowhead plant (Syngonium podophyllum)
- Birch tree (Betula species)
- Bird of paradise (Caesalpinia gilliesii)
- Boston ivy
- Caladium
- Calla lily
- Camphor tree
- Carnation
- Clematis
- Columbine
- Cotoneaster
- Croton
- Cyclamen
- Daffodil
- Dieffenbachia
- Elephant's ear (Alocasia/Colocasia)
- English ivy (Hedera spp.)
- Eucalyptus
- Euonymus
- Euphorbia species
- Four o'clock (Mirabilis jalapa)
- Gladiolus
- Holly (berries)
- Hyacinth
- Hydrangea
- Iris
- Jatropha
- Jerusalem cherry (Solanum pseudocapsicum)
- Kaffir lily (Clivia spp.)
- Love-in-a-mist (Nigella damascena)
- Ming aralia (Polyscias spp.)
- Mistletoe
- Mum
- Narcissus
- Peace lily (Spathiphyllum)
- Philodendron
- Pokeweed (Phytolacca americana)
- Poppy
- Potato (green parts)
- Pothos (Epipremnum aureum)
- Primrose
- Privet (Ligustrum)
- Pyracantha spp.
- Rhubarb (leaves)
- Rubber plant (Ficus spp.)
- Sago palm
- Sansevieria
- Schefflera
- Snowflake (Leucojum spp.)
- Tobacco
- Tomato vines
- Tree tobacco (Nicotiana glauca)
- Tulip
- Umbrella plant (Cyperus alternifolius)
- Wisteria (seeds)
- Yarrow

Make Your Own Trailside Foot Care Kit

Place these items in a small, zip-top bag.

• Moleskin pads

• Antiseptic wipes

• Cushioning pads found in any drug store

• Small scissors (unless you already have some in another kit)

• Foot powder. If you can't carry a full-size container, fill a film canister.

Stop during the day to take off your shoes and air your boots, suggests MPI's Patrick McHugh. "Change socks mid-day if possible," says McHugh, "And you'll be amazed at how good your feet feel."

Dancing with Wolves

Wildlife authorities are increasingly dismayed at the way an unwary public has lost its fear of wild animals. Babies have died horribly, snatched from the arms of mothers who held them out car windows to get a better look at the "honey bear." One Florida ranger rushed into a scene in which a woman was putting a toddler astride an alligator's back so Daddy could get a photograph. A friend of ours was horribly disfigured by a raccoon she picked up and tried to cuddle.

Avoiding injury from wild animals boils down to a few basics:

Animals Are Wild

Movies and TV programs that show people reacting with wild animals are fun to watch, but make sure everyone in your family understands that they are just stories. A wild animal can be expected to act like a wild animal. Even long-time trainers have been mauled and killed by animals they have worked with every day since the animals were kittens or cubs. Instinct trumps training.

TOP TIP Wild creatures instinctively fear people, so don't try to change their minds. Stay away from them, their food, their babies or eggs and their lair or nest.

Respect their habitat. They were here first. Even if you don't look like a threat, you – or your dog or your children – may look like groceries. Keep your pets on a leash and very close to you. We once happened upon a hysterical woman in Alaska who was standing outside her camper when an eagle suddenly swooped down and left with her poodle struggling in its talons. The eagle was simply doing what eagles do. The same can be said of sharks, who are only doing what comes naturally when they take a bite out of you, or alligators, whose modus operandi is to grab a small animal in its mouth, drag it under until it drowns, then dine at its leisure.

Don't Feed The Bears

Don't feed wild animals on purpose or accidentally. Keep your food supplies well out of reach and secure garbage where they can't get into it. Recently Florida passed a law against shark feeding by divers who provide food to attract sharks so they can get a better view. It's already against the law to feed alligators, but well-meaning people continue to do so and then grieve when the gator mistakes a toddler or small dog for a handout. Don't take food into your tent in bear country.

Playing Doctor

It is wrong anywhere, and probably also against the law if you're on government lands, to pick up a wild animal that appears to be injured or to try to "rescue" a baby that appears to be abandoned by its mother. Contrary to popular belief, a bird that falls out of the nest can simply be put back in its nest. If you can't reach the nest, improvise a suitable shelter, put the bird out of harm's way as best you can, and back off. It isn't true that human smell remains on the bird, causing the mother to reject it.

Unless a mother is lying dead beside a fawn or kit, it's likely that she's around somewhere, perhaps even watching the scene and thinking of ways to get you away from her baby – by deadly force if necessary. Wildlife rehabilitators are angels in disguise. They are trained in what to do and what not to do, and they know how to deal with situations that you are not empowered to interfere with. If you find a dead, injured, sick, or seemingly abandoned wild animal, call a ranger or a certified wildlife rehabilitator. To do otherwise could get you bitten, fined, infected with rabies or some other horrible disease, or even sent up the river.

Menasha Ridge Press publishes a series of Dangerous Wildlife books region by region. They're invaluable handbooks that cover everything from identifying harmful plants and critters to first aid. Color illustrations make it easier to make a surefire identification. Each hazard is covered extensively with information on its habitat, season, feeding habits, reproduction cycle and much more of what you need to know to avoid it.

Two excellent books, both from Lyons Press, cover Bear Attacks and Cougar Attacks in extensive detail. (See Recommended Reading in the Appendix.) They're fascinating armchair reading because both are filled with case histories and chilling reports from witnesses and survivors. Your chances of even seeing a wild animal, let along confronting one, are very small. Still, it's smart to take precautions when you are in country where dangerous animals roam, and both books are recommended if you camp in bear or wildcat country.

The chief difference between bears and wildcats is that bears may menace you to get at your food or to protect their territory or their young. Cats, by contrast, look upon you as a food source. It's sometimes recommended that the victim of a bear attack, when all else fails, play dead. However to a cougar, according to author Kathy Etling, that just indicates that you're done for and are ready to be eaten. It may be better to fight back with whatever means possible, with as much ferocity and noise as possible.

Black bear sightings, according to the Connecticut Department of Environmental Protection, are on the increase in the state because of an increasing number of fruit trees, bird feeders, garbage cans, and compost piles around an increasing number of homes. The DEP recommends:

Make your presence known when hiking or camping by making noise and waving your arms. Keep dogs on a leash and under control because a loose dog could be perceived by a bear as a threat to her cubs. If you surprise a bear, walk away slowly.

Don't cook food near the tent or store food inside your tent. Use rope to suspend it from a tree or keep it in a secure vehicle. If a bear is in your area, wait in a vehicle. Don't climb a tree.

It's even more important to separate yourself from food preparation areas if you're in grizzly country. Cook well away from the tent. Don't make camp in known bear feeding areas and don't keep food inside the tent.

Here are just a few of the tips from Cougar Attacks:

To avoid a confront with a cougar, according to author Etling, never hike, jog, or ride a bicycle alone in mountain lion country. Make enough noise so you don't surprise a cougar. Keep children close at hand and under control.

If you smell rotting meat or see an animal carcass, don't move closer. It may be the dinner of an animal that is watching you. Never approach a mountain lion. If you see one, stop and provide it an avenue of escape. Although averting your eyes is wise in a confrontation with a grizzly, do not look away if you lock eyes with a cougar.

Search and Rescue

Lost or hurt in the wilderness? Many rescues still take place the old-fashioned way, but cell phones have revolutionized wilderness emergencies. While dead spots exist and batteries die, a cell phone is still one of your greatest hopes if you're in trouble. A dying mountain climber said goodbye to his wife, who was halfway across the world, by cell phone. A sailor trapped inside the hull of a capsized sailboat in the Southern Ocean called for help by cell phone. Hundreds of cell phone calls were made by those trapped inside the World Trade Center. Cell phone use is soaring, and for good reason.

Every day, the list of dramatic cell phone rescues gets longer. Carrying a cell phone on a camping trip won't win you any popularity contests if it rings all the time or intrudes on the camping experience, but it can be a godsend if you need help. Yet it doesn't replace common sense and all the other precautions you can think of. (Even if you have a cell phone, carry a whistle and supply one for every member of your party.) Check ahead with authorities and with your cell phone company so you'll know how to reach 911 from where you'll be camping. Not all areas are the same.

Even if you have a phone and can reach someone, you still have to tell rescuers where you are. But do you know where you are and can you explain it to others? In most of the country, 911 dispatchers automatically know your location if you're on a hard-wired phone, but systems for locating cell phone callers are not yet in widespread use. In a recent near-tragedy, an elderly woman went off a well-traveled highway into a ditch. She was able to call for help on her cell phone, but it took rescuers days to find her. Fortunately, she survived.

Rescue involves (1) alerting outsiders that you need help and (2) making sure rescuers can find you. The first step, the call for help, could be anything from a phone call to a loud yell, blowing on a whistle, sending up a flare, flicking on an ELT (Emergency Locator Beacon), stomping an SOS in the snow, or simply not showing up at the time you were expected to arrive at a given point. See below for more about that.

One of the first rules of calling for rescue is to know where you are. Ideally, you'll have a GPS and will know your position to the degree, minute, and second.

Many different types of flares are available for use on land and sea.

Lacking that, you could use a compass to take bearings off two distinctive landmarks and report that information to rescuers. In any case, you'll have a good idea of your location if you have kept track of your progress on a map or chart.

It can speed things greatly if you tell rescuers that you're at Site 46 on Loop 3 in the state park, or Marker 17 on the Wilderness Waterway or Campsite 15 on the shore of Lake Catchalot. In canoe or kayak camping, a road map can also be a great help in helping you locate yourself in relation to the roads. On large waterways, rescue could come by boat but on rivers help is more likely to come by road. If you know the location of the nearest road, bridge, marina, boat launch, or other site that has highway access, so much the better.

When You're Lost

Unless a bear is close on your arse, don't start running around when you realize you are lost. There's a good chance that someone is out looking for you (and there will be if you followed instructions above and below). Most greenhorns thrash about and soon learn they have been walking in circles. Save your energy for making or finding shelter, staying warm or cool, conserving or finding portable water (food can wait, water needs are more immediate), and devising ways to signal.

"We search the trails first," say officials at Great Smoky National Park. "If you do get lost, stay calm and do not leave the trail."

In addition, there are many ways to make your position known. Three short blasts on a high, shrill whistle are a recognized distress call. It's easy to attach a small whistle to a zipper tab, and you'll always have it handy. MPI Outdoors makes an emergency strobe light that is only larger than an alkaline D cell yet it sends out a 300,000 candlepower Xenon strobe that is visible for up to three miles day or night. One battery gives up to 60 hours of use, starting with a flash of 50-70 times per minute, which lasts 16 hours. (After that the power diminishes depending on outdoor temperatures and the strength of the battery.)

If your survival kit contains waterproof matches and a solid fuel cube, the type sold for use in pocket stoves, you'll have a fail-safe starter for a signal fire except, of course, in wildfire conditions. (One thing worse than being lost is being lost in the middle of a forest fire.) Fire can also warm you, cook food, and purify water. Three small fires forming a triangle are a universal Mayday signal. During the day, you can add wet brush to create smoke that will be seen more readily.

Skyblazer is best known for its water rescue gear, but the company also makes XLT Wilderness aerial flares for outdoors/camping use. "They are the perfect wilderness signaling device," says company spokesperson Kelly Flory. "Flares shoot high in the air to attract attention but they complete the burn cycle prior to landing." XLTs burn only six seconds to minimize the chance of starting a fire when they land. Shot correctly

When you're lost, think **STOP.** It stands for:

Stop
Think
Observe
Plan

into an unobstructed sky, they reach an average height of 425 feet and are cold before they return to the ground. The company's water rescue flares, by contrast, burn for eight seconds.

Also available, and perhaps a better choice during wildfire season, are Skyblazer's smoke signals. They ignite with a pull on the chain, burn for 45 seconds, are waterproof, and float. However, they can't be held by hand during the burn time, so an area should be cleared before lighting them. If you can't find flares in camp supply sources, try a marine store.

If it's likely that rescuers will search from the air, lay out a signal using colored clothing, rocks, or tracks in the snow. If you see a plane, use a signal mirror. A Space® Emergency Blanket is a reflector that can signal, provide shade, act as a rain catchment for drinking water, or wrap the body to conserve heat, yet it's smaller than a deck of cards. Another product, the Space® All Weather Blanket measures 5 X 7 feet and takes up no more space than a folded shirt. It's made up of a dark blue outer layer to absorb solar heat, a metallic outer layer to reflect heat or light, and inner layers for insulation and strength. It's an ideal, all-purpose blanket for a ground cloth, rain protection, water catchment, wind break, and sun shade.

A third choice, the Space® Emergency Bag carries as a 4 X 3-inch package but expands to envelope 36 X 84 inches. If you're caught in the weather with no other shelter, it will preserve body heat. It can also be slipped on over a sleeping bag for added protection against rain and snow. The same company also makes a Sportsman's Hooded Blanket, which is much like the All Weather Blanket except that it has a hood.

Flight Plans, Float Plans and Hike Plans

Most wilderness areas have a registration procedure that automatically triggers a search if you don't report out within a reasonable time. In boating, it's a float plan. In fly-in camping, it's a flight plan. In addition to whatever backcountry permit or filing is required, leave detailed information with a friend, neighbor or relative who can notify authorities if you don't report in as planned.

The plan should contain:

Number of people, with ages and descriptions including any medical information (heart history, asthma, pregnancy, diabetic) that would be needed by rescue teams.

Description of major gear, such as the canoe color, tent color and type, car license number, and so on.

A detailed outline of the area you plan to cover.

A description of what self-help gear you have with you, e.g. smoke flares, cell phone, whistle, Xenon strobe.

Latest time you expect to report in and, if you're leaving the information with a friend or relative, the phone number of authorities to be contacted if you don't report in.

Bring Water To A Boil

According to Patrick McHugh of MPI Outdoors, stream or river water that you must drink in an emergency situation should be boiled for 10 minutes plus one minute for every 1,000 feet above sea level. Cloudy water can be strained through a piece of fabric, such as a bandana or handkerchief.

In the Drink

It's a necessity for some backcountry camping and wise for other camping to carry a water purifier for emergencies and perhaps for everyday use. One of the best selections is available from Nitro-Pak Preparedness Center (see Resources), where you can find a 16-ounce, two-stage water filtering system that purifies up to one liter every 90 seconds, for under $65. In a 19-ounce device, you can get a three-stage filtering system. Many choices are available, from pocket-size filters to large reverse osmosis and distillation systems that can make sea water potable.

Unless it's labeled otherwise, campground drinking water supplied in the campgrounds of the U.S., Canada and Europe is perfectly safe. Always have a freshly-filled canteen or water bottle with you on the trail or in the car. Unless it's labeled safe, however, all other water from lakes, streams, and waterfalls is suspect. No matter how pure it looks or how high you are above civilization, never drink lake or river water that has not been boiled or treated with a sophisticated filter system. Hazards are many including Giardia Lamblia, which causes travelers' diarrhea. It is spread through feces of mammals that never saw a human being; it has been found in some of the most remote lakes on earth.

Even the highest, purest waterfall can contain dangerous organisms.

Cold Comfort: Hypothermia

I once met an angler who told me how he'd almost died of hypothermia on a warm May day in Tennessee. He'd set off in an open fishing boat, in shirtsleeves. A north wind piped up. He dropped a cotter pin. Waves rose, temperatures plummeted. To make a long story short, he made it back to shore and stumbled to his car, shivering and his teeth chattering. He was only inches away from the warm interior of the car, the starter, the heater. But precious moments passed because he could not remember how to put the key in the car door and unlock it!

That, in a nutshell, is how hypothermia works. First, it numbs your hands, preventing them from grasping the tools that could save you. Then it numbs your brain against the reasoning that could save you. Finally, it reaches vital organs – lungs, kidneys and heart – and death soon follows.

• Dress in layers, discarding outer layers as the day warms up but keeping them with you to go back on as the day cools. A shower or wind shift could pipe up unexpectedly. In many areas that are torrid by day, temperatures plunge dramatically at sundown. Be prepared. When you feel the first shiver, you're experiencing the first sign of mild hypothermia.

• Don't drink alcohol. It makes you feel warmer by dilating blood vessels, sending blood from the body core to fingers and toes, thus robbing vital organs of heat more quickly. In a raw survival situation, it's better to lose fingers and toes than your brain or heart.

• Second only to a coat and good footwear, a hat is essential in preserving body heat. A muffler that can be wound around head, ears and neck, and perhaps pulled over the mouth and nose can be a lifesaver.

* Mittens are warmer than gloves.

Here, from Ruth Wood at BoatUS, the Boat Owners Association of the United States, are additional tips on surviving hypothermia in the water:

• Cold water robs the body of heat 25-30 times faster than air. Within 10-15 minutes, the core body temperature begins to drop. The water doesn't have to be icy. It has only to be colder than you are – that's 98.6 degrees F. – to cause hypothermia. If you suddenly find yourself in the water, don't panic. Flailing around will only cause your body to lose heat more quickly.

Unless you can swim very quickly to the shore or get back aboard the boat, remain as still as possible. Here's where wearing a life jacket comes in. You can tighten up in the HELP position (hug knees to chest) while rescuers reach you. Intense shivering and even pain are natural reflexes. They won't kill you. Heat loss will.

• Don't take off your clothes. Button, buckle and zip up and, if possible cover your head. In cold water, about half your heat loss comes from the head.

• If you're alone, hold your knees to your chest and clasp your arms around your calves to protect your trunk from heat loss. If you're with others, huddle with them.

• Acting quickly before you lose use of your hands, devote all your efforts to getting out of the water. If there is a boat, raft, floating ice chest or anything else that can keep some or all of your body our of the water, use it! Even a capsized boat will support your weight. If you can't climb in, climb on and hoist as much of your body onto it as possible. .

• Dress warmly on cool days. Wind can rob you of heat. Wearing a life jacket adds to survival time in the water by (1) helping to insulate the body, (2) minimizing the motion you must expend to stay afloat and (3) keeping the head out of the water, thus reducing heat loss.

The Cold Truth

Here are your chances of surviving in the water if you're in good health and do not have to exhaust yourself to stay afloat. If you do, these times are cut dramatically. These figures emphasize the importance of getting your body, or as much as possible, out of the water onto some floating object.

Water Temperature	Possible Survival Time
40 Degrees or less	30-90 minutes
40-50 Degrees	1-3 hours
50-60 Degrees	1-6 hours
60-70 Degrees	2-40 hours
70-80 Degrees	3 hours to possibly indefinite

CHAPTER

Getting in Gear

Let There Be Light, Comfort, and Showers

Diogenes started something by setting out with his lantern to search for truth. Having good lights is second only to having adequate shelter on a camping trip. Today's marketplace supplies the most exciting choice of lights since the candle. Costs start at under $20 for a propane lantern and under $10 for battery-operated lanterns, and can go as high as $80 for a top-quality lantern with electric-ignition or remote control.

Here are some things to think about:

• Allow yourself time in a good camping store or mass market such as Kmart or Wal-Mart to research what is available. The choice is mind-boggling. You can even find remote control lanterns that can be switched off and on from up to 50 feet away.

• Battery-operated touch lights, which need only a tap, are inexpensive, quick, and convenient for spots where you need a quick, uncomplicated light for only a few moments. However, touch lights and other lights that turn on with the press or a twist can light so easily that they could get switched on in your duffel bag and be dead by the time you get to camp. Don't put the batteries in until you set up camp.

TOP TIP As much as is practical, stick with one type of fuel for all camping gear. If, for example, your stove uses Coleman fuel, get a heater and lanterns that use the same fuel. Try to use only one or two battery sizes too, rather than an array of lights requiring every size from AAA up. Personal flashlights take AA or AAA batteries, which you probably also need for personal radios and electronic toys. Larger lanterns take Cs, Ds, or lantern batteries. Some lanterns will work on more than one choice of batteries, e.g. two 6-volts or eight D-cells. That's an advantage

Coleman's familiar, single-mantle lantern is a camping standard worldwide. It sells for about $40.

One of the most space-efficient propane lanterns on the market, Coleman's single-mantle Compact slips onto a propane cylinder with a bayonet fitting.

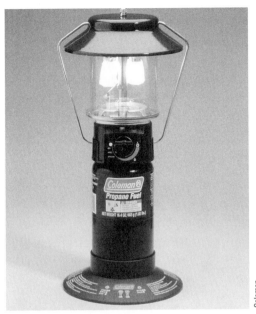

Matchless operation is available for most lanterns. Coleman's two-mantle, electronic ignition lantern operates on High for up to seven hours per cylinder of propane.

One nice feature of one battery model is a night-light that burns for up to 100 continuous hours.

when you're camping overseas or in remote areas where shopping is limited. Don't forget that electronic ignition gas or kerosene lanterns require batteries. Carry spares.

• Consider how the lantern will sit, hang up, or carry in your hand. If it's a hanging type, buy or make a stake with a hanging hook. A hot lantern hung in a tree can weaken or damage bark.

• Note lantern specs about how long a full tank or charge will burn at low light or high. If you camp in

areas with short periods of daylight, you'll go through fuel or batteries faster than you think. Read specs.

• Always have at least one set of extra mantles on hand. They're fragile and, once dropped or even touched, are useless.

• Spiders love the smell of propane. If your lantern burns with a smoky, yellow flame, check the burner and air tube for spider webs. Wrap lanterns in plastic bags for storage and seal with rubber bands to keep spiders out.

Lanterns that will operate on either unleaded gas or Coleman fuel cost more than single-fuel models, but many campers find the versatility well worth the cost. The NorthStar® model has electronic ignition and costs about $80.

You'll pay about $45 for a dual-mantle lantern that can run on two fuels.

A single-mantle propane lantern sells for about $20 and provides up to 15 hours of light on one cylinder of propane.

A lantern that uses the new propane-butane fuel is the compact Xcursion™ that has doors that double as a carrying case. It's refillable from PowerMax™ cartridges.

• Consider adding a No-Bugs Globe (see Resources), especially if you fish at night. It's amber in color, invisible to insects. Sizes are available to fit the most popular camping lanterns.

• If you camp at sites that have electricity, get rechargeable lanterns and plug them in during the day. Lantern batteries can also be charged by day with a solar charger. Also available are solar lights that charge all day and burn for at least part of the night. However, don't count on them as your only lights because their output will vary each day according to how much sunlight was available.

• Note that pressure kerosene lanterns (not wick types) are pre-heated with alcohol. While this requires carrying two fuels, kerosene is a cheap and efficient fuel well worth considering when you're camping in areas where hours of lighting are required.

• Carrying cases are a good investment against damage and rust, and provide safe storage for lanterns, accessories and spare parts. The manufacturer may offer a case made specifically for your lamp.

• Buy a selection of lights for various uses: clip-on lights for reading in bed, stand-alone work lights that can be aimed for hands-free work, chemical light sticks (they're cool and safe, and kids love them), lights that can be hung from a tree or pole, a floating light, and combination emergency units that incorporate a light with a radio, siren, or other features. A hurricane lantern that holds candles makes for romantic dining.

Fluorescent lanterns come in battery and rechargeable models, and cast a very bright light over a wide area. The Trail Lite, available from MPI Outdoors, straps to an arm, belt or bicycle and works as a flashlight or blinking red LED light. The company's Grasshopper is a handy, small flashlight that has its

own stand and its Little Giant provides a floodlight and searchlight in a package the size of half a bread loaf.

TOP TIP

It's a good idea to have one lantern that casts a beam or spotlight, as well as others for general light and task lighting.

• Large flashlights have a way of getting lost in the dark. Place a patch of glow-in-the-dark tape on each flashlight.

• Each camper should have a personal flashlight that clips on a belt or slips in a pocket so he or she is never

Costing about $20, Coleman's two-tube lantern gives up to 28 hours of light and will operate on either D-cells or 6-volt alkaline batteries.

A basic, battery lantern burns up to 16 hours on four alkaline D-cells. Unlike propane and gas lanterns, electric models stay cool to the touch.

Solar aids are increasingly practical and affordable for camping. Choices range from inexpensive combination solar/wind-up radios to solar battery chargers.

without it. Never rely on someone else's light being where you need it, when you need it. A key chain light is handy for getting into the car or a padlocked gear box after dark.

* A hands-free head lamp can be handy for after-dark tasks such as cooking, washing dishes, or changing the baby. Coleman makes one that can be aimed up, down, or 90 degrees in either direction.

• When burning fuels, always be aware of the danger of fire, burns, and oxygen depletion. Have at least some battery lanterns for safety's sake.

• Butane lanterns won't work in extremely cold weather.

• Floating lanterns and flashlights can come in handy for emergencies and for boating or fishing in low-light hours.

Lantern Care

• If a gasoline lantern becomes hard to light or adjust or burns too dimly, replace the generator. It could have been damaged by a bad batch of fuel. A filtering funnel may be available from the manufacturer as an optional accessory. It's a good investment in better fuel and safer filling.

• At least once during the camping season and before storing a gasoline lantern, let it burn out all remaining fuel, cool completely, then rinse out the tank with fresh fuel and put it away clean and dry. Sediment, gum and moisture can build up in the tank and should be flushed away. Take all precautions when working with gasoline.

• Manufacturer directions specify pump maintenance. Yours probably needs oiling once a year or so.

• If a battery-operated or battery-ignition lantern doesn't work, try cleaning the battery terminals with an emery board. They may be corroded, not dead.

Keep Music To Yourself

It's not just bad manners to inflict noise on your campground neighbors, it could get you kicked out without a refund. If you're hooked on entertainment electronics, let each person bring a player with earphones. That way, everyone has his or her own choice of channels, stations, CDs, tapes, games, or MP3 without disturbing anyone else in camp or in the car.

Take a Seat To Go Camping in Comfort

Coleman

Coleman

Folding camp chairs with aluminum frames and replaceable canvas are comfortable seating and light to carry.

Float Your Boat

Chapter 6 covers canoe and kayak camping, but other campers often want boats too for day sailing, fishing, or rowing. In addition to canoes and kayaks, many types of boats can be car-topped as long as you have proper mounting and tiedowns.

AB Inflatables

Deflated, it fits in a bag the size of an armchair, but filled with air it's a magic carpet to fishing and cruising waters.

Inflatable boats stow in a garage, closet or city apartment, yet they swell to seaworthiness with a few whiffs of the air pump. According to Alexandra Heyer of AB Inflatables, you can carry five people or a 1,500-pound payload in an 11-foot boat that weighs only 126 pounds and can take an outboard of up to 25 horsepower. Inflatables are available in models that motor, row, paddle, or sail.

Folding boats are another choice for the camper whose stowage space at home is limited and who prefers a boat small enough to carry on the car top. Folding boats form a long, thin package that carries on a car roof or on the side of a van. An inflatable, by contrast, forms a fat, square-ish package.

The gear also must be considered before you add a boat to your list of camping toys because it also means adding life jackets and other safety gear as required by the U.S. Coast Guard plus oars, an anchor, ropes and so on.

• A boat with an inflatable keel cuts through waves easily and allows the boat to plane with a smaller outboard.

• Floorboards add to the weight and complexity of an inflatable but are important to stability, rider comfort, and structural integrity of the boat.

• Look for a material, such as Hypalon, that is resistant to UV, gasoline and other chemicals. PVC is not as durable.

Binoculars are complex instruments to be chosen and carried with care.

Alpine Outdoors

The Eyes Have It: Binoculars

Binoculars provide the magic in wildlife viewing and, in many kinds of camping, they are also a basic survival tool. In choosing a binocular, you are concerned about compactness, durability, light weight, and optic quality. While many companies make many models in many price ranges, you're basically looking at:

Magnification
Coatings
Aperture
Can the binocs be used without removing your glasses?

Are binocs waterproof, water resistant, or neither?

Do they adjust individually for each eye or do both lenses adjust together?

What is the best choice if you'll be on a boat or other moving object?

Some binocs have a built-compass, which is handy for navigating

Magnification is expressed in a small number, such as 7 X, which tells you that the glasses magnify objects 7 times.

Aperture refers to the opening size, in millimeters. Aperture divided by magnification aperture tells you the exit pupil, which ideally will be 5-7 millimeters, the most that can be handled by the average, healthy eye. Ergo, the popular 7 X 35 binocular will give you an exit pupil, or light available to the eye, of 5 millimeters.

The larger the aperture, the larger and heavier the binocular. Weight is a concern not just to backpackers, who must weigh every ounce, but serious birders, who may tire of holding heavy glasses to their eyes for hours. A higher exit pupil is best for night viewing, in which you want to funnel as much light to the eye as possible.

Coatings affect the quality of the light that gets through, and they also determine the cost because coating is a painstaking, exacting process. The more surfaces that have coatings, and the better the coating material, the greater the price. Spend under about $50, and it's likely the binocs will be coated on the outside, where they'll eventually wear away. The best optics, costing $200 and up, will have coatings throughout.

Construction quality ranges from simple units made with standard quality glass to the best, Bk7 glass prism, which gives a clearer, crisper view. Note too whether the binocs are rated waterproof or by some euphemism such as water resistant, rainproof, or watertight. The best,

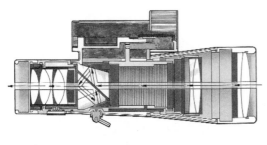

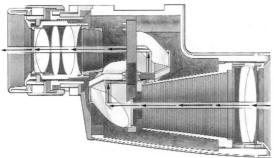

Alpen Outdoors

Diagrams show the inner workings of binoculars.

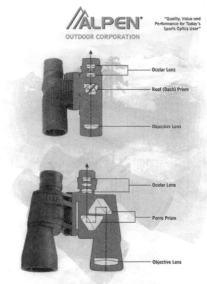

Alpen Outdoors

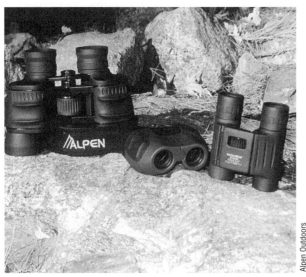

Alpen outdoors offers several types of binoculars.

Ducking the Issue

It's a joke and cliche, but duct tape, also sold commercially as Duck Tape, is still one of the camper's best friends. If you carry no other repair tools, a roll of tape, a tube of Goop* and a can of spray lube (e.g. WD-40) can fix almost anything that can go wrong.

*Although it's sold in several departments at the store under labels for different purposes such as Plumbing Goop or Shoe Goop, this all-purpose adhesive and sealant is pretty much the same. It can glue almost anything to anything.

For car camping, it's easy to throw a roll or two into the tool kit or stuff box. For backpacking and other flyweight camping, an emergency supply of tape can be wound around something else, such as a plastic film canister in which you carry, say, a supply of large safety pins, paper clips, twist ties, and rubber bands. (You're sure to need one or all of them too at some point.) Duct tape is also sold in a flat, wallet-size pack for compact carrying.

According to Theresa Brixius, communications manager for Manco, makers of Duck Tape, the product comes in Industrial, Contractor, Professional, All-Purpose, and Utility grades, but to legally be called "duct" tape (i.e. suitable for use in heating ducts), the tape must meet certain heat resistance standards required by modern heating systems.

Whatever you call it, this miracle product is made up of a layer of polyethylene or vinyl (which gives it its color and makes it waterproof), a layer of cotton cloth (which gives the tape its strength and ability to be torn by hand) and a natural rubber adhesive for strong staying power. The familiar silvery stuff is good enough for most camping repairs and you may also want other colors, such as camouflage or day-glo for special uses.

waterproof binocs are recommended for canoe and kayak use, but to be truly waterproof they probably have individual focus, which is more inconvenient for everyday use. Don't choose the highest magnification for use in a boat underway, because motion, too, is magnified. For spotting markers at night, you need the highest exit pupil that will do the job, with magnification of not more than 7.

Image stabilized binoculars are helpful to canoeists, kayakers, or anyone who has difficulty holding the glasses still. They are offered in a variety of models, some of them waterproof, by major manufacturers including Tasco, Canon, Fujinon, Rigel, and Zeiss. They are new, so try several types for size, weight, and complexity of operation. Some require batteries.

Binoculars: A Test Drive

One way to test binoculars on the sales floor is to try them with and without your eyeglasses on a linear figure such as overhead fluorescent lights. Any waviness you see indicates the degree of distortion. Any glare you observe in the store is a hint of glare you'll experience on the water on a sunny day. Heft the weight for comfort. Adjust the lenses to your own eyes.

Research any company's line of binoculars, and you'll find a confusing array of choices–all of them right for some users in some situations. If you can carry only one pair, find a compromise that is best for size and weight, fit for your eyes with or without eyeglasses, how well they "see" in low light, and ease of focus plus other features you may need such as waterproof integrity or image stabilization.

Any binoculars are better than none. Buy what you can afford, and use and enjoy them.

Duct tape in bright, hunter orange can be placed on gear, not just as protection against stray shots but to make it easier to find.

101 Uses for Sticky Tape

Duct tape can tape up anything that you want to patch, bond, attach, cushion, or bind, at least for a temporary repair. It's the only tape you need except, perhaps, for a small roll of see-through cellophane tape for repairs to maps and books. Here are some things you may not have thought of doing with lowly, homely duct tape:

• Double duct tape over a fraying fabric edge to create a binding.

• In a pinch, use it to hold bandages in place, but watch for a skin reaction. Some people also have an adverse reaction to medical adhesive tape and ready-made bandages.

• Tape up broken knives, blades, or other sharp items before putting them in the campground trash so they can't injure people or animals or tear through trash bags.

• In tick country, wrap pants legs tightly at the ankle and sleeves at the wrist with duct tape.

• Use tape to tack up a sagging hem, patch a tear in a screen or tent, mend a crack in a canoe or kayak, hold together a windbreaker or backpack flap that has a broken zipper, put a new end on a broken shoelace, or re-attach a flapping shoe sole. Tape a wrapped condom to the sleeping pad so you won't have to grope around for it in the dark.

• For the lack of a clamp for a gluing job, wrap the two pieces together with duct tape until the adhesive dries.

• No privacy in the camping cabin? Use duct tape and trash bags to create window curtains.

• Use camouflage-pattern duct tape as a temporary cover-up on gear that is shiny enough to spook wildlife, such as a hunting knife handle or your binoculars.

In tick country use camouflage Duck Tape to close trousers tightly around the ankles.

Duct/Duck Tape Tips

• Like most adhesives, Duck tape works best at room temperature. For the closest, conforming fit, let it warm in the sun.

• It's easier to rip most tape by hand than to cut it with scissors, which can result in a sticky mess.

• Brands differ, but Duck Tape stays removable for up to four weeks - even if exposed to direct sunlight - because it has a UV barrier as an added layer. If any adhesive is left behind when you're ready to remove the tape, keep a supply of Duck brand Adhesive Remover at home. Rubber cement thinner will also work.

Prepare to Repair

In addition to tape(s), it's handy to have a dedicated repair kit, sized and equipped according to your camping style. Buttons, needles, a thimble, and a hank of heavy duty thread or carpet warp, plus scissors if you don't have some in the medical kit, will solve most of your fabric repair problems. Other items that will come in handy for repairs include:

• Heavy duty shoelaces to replace shoelaces or to use anywhere you need a short length of cord. Dental floss, which your hygienist will tell you is a daily essential, also makes a sturdy string, cheese cutter, or butcher twine for trussing a bird.

• A tiny tube of Super Glue.

• A small set of screwdrivers plus an eyeglass repair kit.

• Several lengths of bungee cord with hooks on each end.

• A scrap of sturdy material such as nylon webbing to be used for patching almost anything from britches to the sleeping bag or backpack.

• If you have room to carry spare grommets and a grommet tool, it's nice to be able to put extra grommets into a tarp as necessary to hang it or lash it down as desired.

• A spray-on water dispersing agent such as WD-40 or CRC 6-66.

• Zipper lube according to the types of zippers in your tent and other gear.

Find room for a sewing kit.

It's an added plus if your heater doubles as a cooler.

Heat Pal

Staying Warm, Staying Cool

Fortunately, it doesn't take much to heat or cool the small area of a tent, cabin or camper. If you're staying at a campsite that has an electric outlet, and many tent sites do, throw in an electric blanket, a small electric heater, or an electric fan, and it can make all the difference in sleeping comfort. Many small, wheeled campers including soft-sided pop-ups have roof-top air conditioners. If you have no power at all, a wide choice of battery-operated fans is available in all sizes, and heaters are available in propane, alcohol, and kerosene models.

Points on personal comfort:

• Hand warmers are available in several styles. Some take solid fuel; others take liquid fuel. Some heat with the activation of a chemical, but are good for only one-time use. They're disposable but are handy as a heat pack for unexpected aches and pains.

• Self-adhesive chemical warmers are available in several sizes in camping supply stores. Good for one-time use, they are placed on the body to provide extra heat for sore muscles or cold feet. Read instructions and precautions.

• Think of temperature comforts before choosing a tent site. More sun or shade, wind or shelter, can make a difference of 10-20 degrees. Camped in a low place where cold air pools in the stillness of the night can be much chillier than if you pitch the tent on higher ground. Some land configurations form natural wind tunnels, which could be great on a hot summer night but a disaster in cold or windy weather. Don't hesitate to ask for local advice on where you might find a tent site that is warmer or cooler.

• Get white tent flies for hot weather camping and dark colors for cold weather. Make a wind chute to hang high in a tree to catch breezes and funnel them into the tent. If you want the best breeze all night, pitch the tent so that the entry door or largest windows face the night-time prevailing winds, which may be different from daytime winds.

Necessary Evils: The Potty

If Clean Restrooms are the feature you look for first in the campground guide, or if you have your own bathroom on board, skip this section. Campers don't need to rough it. Plenty of tent sites can be found near bathrooms that are clean and safe. If hot showers, running water, and private stalls are on your list of requirements, insist on them.

However, primitive campers must make their own arrangements at all times, and tent campers may want to have a personal, portable toilet on hand at least some of the time. You might, for example, have a portable biffy to use when you have to get up in the night or a lidded potty that the little ones can use on long car trips.

First, the bad news. Portable potties don't smell like a bed of roses. Chemical cover-ups are used to mask even worse odors, but some people find them as almost as unpleasant as the alternative. This type potty has a reservoir that is filled with water and a chemical. With each flush, everything recirculates until the time comes when it's either full or smells so bad you have to empty it and start anew.

The good news is that portables can be found for $60-$150 in sizes that hold up to a little more than three gallons of "black" water. They are fairly easy to fill, carry, store, and empty, and are comfortable to sit on. The reservoir detaches from the rest of the toilet, so it can be carried to a rest room for emptying and refilling. Chemicals and special, dissolving toilet paper aren't expensive to buy. One brand, Porta-Potti, offers an electric flush model that runs on batteries. It has a lid latch, built-in toilet paper dispenser, battery indicator, and a gauge that tells you the effluent level.

Other, non-flush models use plastic bags, which can get cumbersome and expensive. They also create a disposal problem because it's irresponsible to put sewage-filled bags in the general trash. However, there are situations when such bags can be incinerated, buried, or dropped into a pit toilet to decompose.

You can make your own toilet even if you're not handy with woodworking. Start with a suitable bucket, such as a five- or six-gallon paint bucket, a sturdy waste basket, or a small garbage can. Make sure it's strong enough to hold the weight of the heaviest person who will sit on it. You'll also need plywood and a keyhole saw (for hand cutting) or a power saber saw. Measuring carefully, cut a ring of half-inch plywood that just fits around the top of the can. Cut a hole in the middle of this ring.

Now create a seat that fits atop the can, wide enough for comfortable seating, and cut a hole in the center the same size as the center hole in the ring. Now glue the ring to the bottom of the seat. Buy trash bags in a size that will fill the can with several inches to

spare. Place a bag in the can with the edges extending over the rim. Put the seat down over the can, which will hold the bag in place. After the bag is used, it can be tied off with a twist tie and removed to a large trash bag for future disposal or sealed and left in the can under a new bag. Just be aware that gases build up as the waste breaks down. The hotter the weather, the quicker the buildup and the more quickly you must dispose of the bags before they either leak gas or explode.

You can get a couple of uses out of one bag before sealing, especially if campers visit the can in quick succession and sprinkle the bag liberally with baking soda after use. The can itself stays clean as long as you have an ample supply of bags that are large enough, leakproof, and well sealed after use. Just for peace of mind, give the toilet a good spritz of antibacterial cleaner and a hosing any time you have access to soap and water.

You need only basic woodcutting skills to craft a sturdy camp toilet.

Gordon Groene

TOP TIP For kayaking, children's midnight piddles, and other liquid deposits, you can simply carry a disposable coffee tan, a lidded urinal (sold by some travel catalogs and medical suppliers in both male and female styles), a children's travel potty, or one of the commercial products found in travel catalogs (see Appendix). Several types of leakproof bags are available for male or female use for urine or vomit. Some hold the liquid alone. Others are bulkier to carry but contain a substance that absorbs the urine and turns it into a leakproof gel. In any case, dispose of the results responsibly.

Digging Yourself Into a Hole

In the most primitive camping, you have two choices. One is to leave waste on site, burying it according to safe practices or, in pristine areas where this is not permitted, to pack it out with you.

To dig a hole for one use, use your camp shovel or other suitable camp tool to dig a hole well away from drinking water sources, streams, wetlands, or the high water or tide line. Disturb the soil as little as possible, retaining the ground cover to replace in one piece if possible.

To make a pit for multiple uses, dig a long trench about six inches wide in ground that is stable enough to support your footprints on each side. Pile the dirt you

remove beside the trench. Use the trench starting at one end, filling it in after each use. When it is completely filled, tamp the ground, add more dirt if necessary, and return it to as close as possible to the way you found it.

In any case, use biodegradable toilet paper, and as little of it as possible. As much as you can manage with whatever sticks are at hand, mix dirt into your deposit as you refill the hole, to speed decomposition. Matter that won't break down in the soil, such as sanitary napkins, tampons, and diapers, should be packed out.

In areas where everything must be packed out with you, things get more complicated. You want to stow human waste in as tight a container as possible so you won't have to live with the smell, but a container that doesn't allow for a build-up of the natural gases that occur with decomposition can explode. Don't even think about the result.

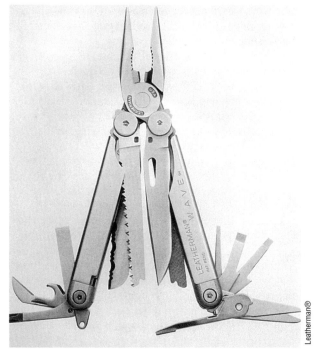

Leatherman®

Leatherman®

A well-made multi-purpose tool is indispensable to camping. Cheap knock-offs are clumsy to work with and often break down or dull. Shop for a respected brand such as Leatherman and look for a model that contains the components you'll use.

Jack(knife) of All Trades

Multi-purpose tools have been an essential part of tenting since the first Neanderthal discovered that a seashell could be used to scrape animals' hides or attached to a stick and used as a hoe. The good news is that the marketplace offers a mind-boggling choice ranging from the family Swiss army knife and Leatherman Pocket Survival Tool to a small ax with built-in bottle opener or a folding shovel that doubles as a hammer. The bad news is that many multi-purpose tools are shoddily made, gimmicky in design, or both.

"Like a lot of outdoor gear, a multi-tool is definitely one of those items where you get what you pay for," says Mark Baker of the Leatherman Tool Group, Inc. "Spend the extra money to get a tool you know you can rely on, because you really don't know how badly you'll need it until the time comes – and you could be anywhere. Size and weight are less important issues for tent camping than for long-distance backpacking, so it's

best to err on the side of increased features and functionality. Look for screwdriver corners that are finely squared to hold a screw, and look for plier jaws that are well-matched and riveted precisely enough to cut paper rather than merely crimping. If the model you are considering also has a file with diagonally-cut teeth, see if the teeth go all the way to the tip of the file. These are among the indicators the manufacturer is taking extra steps to make an excellent product that should provide years of reliable service."

Since the dawn of time, mankind has used tools for four basic functions: to increase grip, to multiply effort, to cut, or to bore. While a multi-purpose knife has a number of blades for cutting and filing, and perhaps a corkscrew or awl for boring, there is nothing that can be used to grip, e.g. a pliers or wrench. Other multi-purpose tools focus on grip, but don't cut. Or they cut but would break if used for prying or hammering. The more functions a tool does well, the better.

Choosing a Water Filter

It's confusing to compare the claims made by all the makers of water filters on today's market. The good news is that the choice of water purifiers is very large, ranging from pocket-size straws to elaborate systems that serve an entire household or campground. Since time began, nature's ways of purifying water have included filtering (through layers of earth and stone) distillation (water is vaporized, drawn up into clouds, then released as rain), and aeration (a waterfall aerates water, which is further purified by sunlight).

First, it's likely that you don't need a water filter at all. Potable water is provided in campgrounds throughout North America. It may taste slightly of iron, sulphur or chlorine, but it's all safe – at least according to government standards. For this reason, campers who are fussy about their coffee sometimes carry a filter to produce water of a consistent taste, regardless of differences in local water supplies. For most of us, however, filters come into the picture only for emergency use or for camping in wilderness areas where waters are of unknown quality. Never drink water from lakes, rivers, pools, springs, or waterfalls unless you have it on reliable local authority that it's safe.

Commercial purification systems still rely on nature's tools: filtering or distillation. Also available are chemical treatments as well as high-tech methods such as reverse osmosis or ultraviolet. As a wilderness camper who is concerned about safe drinking water, your mission is to select a filter that takes out all the biological and mineral contaminants without introducing new ones. And here is where the controversies begin because chlorine, the most common and least expensive water purifier, is considered by some to be a dangerous pollutant. Here are some things to ponder:

• The biggest differences in water filters are initial cost, cost of replacement media, and the time it takes to process a quart of water. The finer and more sophisticated the water treatment, the more time it will take to run water through it and the more you'll pay for replacement filters and/or other supplies.

At one extreme is a rag, which can filter out chunks of sand and rust but is unlikely to produce water that won't kill you. At the other extreme is a stovetop distiller, which will produce water of impeccable pedigree but which takes a great deal of time and fuel to boil the water to make steam, then condense it to water. Somewhere between these two extremes is the right filter for you, one that is workable, affordable, portable, and yet offers protection for your family.

* Some systems involve a chemical additive such as iodine or chlorine that is stirred into the water and given a few minutes to work, followed by filtration to take out particulate matter and some of the chemical as well. The quality of the water in terms of both safety and taste varies according to the quality of the filter.

Jerry Martin Associates

Solar showers are available in a variety of shapes and sizes.

* Solar distillation systems are favored by boaters because they can produce drinking water even from sea water. They're cumbersome and slow, suitable for lifeboat survival but not practical for camping. A solar still can also be created on land by digging a hole and anchoring a sheet of dark plastic over it. Moisture is drawn from the ground, condenses on the underside of the plastic, and drips into a container you put under a low point in the plastic. Again, this is a survival technique that's nice to know about but hardly a part of family camping.

TOP TIP When you're camping along waters that are salt or brackish, you aren't the only ones who are thirsty. Raccoons are too, and they'll chew through a plastic bottle in nanoseconds. Protect your drinking water supply just as carefully as your food supply.

It can be handy to have a home laminator to protect camping maps, recipes, instructions, and checklists. A hand-operated cold laminator costs under $60.

About GPS

Global Positioning Systems take readings from satellites to tell you where you are, usually within a few feet. They're so small, you can carry a receiver in your shirt pocket, so accurate that you can use one to pinpoint where you left your car in the mall parking lot, and so affordable (about $150) that people are using them not just in the wilderness but to find their way around city sidewalks. Take a reading at your hotel in London or New York, set out on foot to sightsee and window shop, and an arrow will always point you back to where you're staying. The same goes for your campsite, the trailhead, or any other point you want to reach or return to. With a laptop computer and a GPS program such as Earthlink, you can find any street address, country road, gas station, or convenience store.

While it's never wise to rely on electronics in place of preparation and common sense, a hand-held GPS plus a cell phone are the two greatest safety aids you can add to your camping gear. It's essential to learn the basics before you leave home, so allot a couple of hours to the new unit before your next campout. GPS receivers come with an instruction book and videos are also available.

Basically, you simply take a reading from a known spot, such as the trailhead or your tent site, and enter it in the unit's memory. Guided by satellites, it will point back to that site (or any other waypoint you supply) and tell you how far you are from it in a direct line. It will also tell you exactly where you are in latitude and longitude, a tremendous help if you're calling for rescue. You'll even use your GPS in games and sports such as orienteering and treasure hunts, and in fishing, where you can pinpoint sea mounts and honey holes.

More and more, maps and other travel information being published with geo-codes (e.g. the latitude and longitude) for important locales, so look for this feature when you're buying new maps. Ships and aircraft have navigated by GPS for years. Divers use it to pinpoint sea gardens that they want to revisit. Archaeologists use it to map sites in an otherwise trackless desert. Some guidebooks use it to report the locations of the nearest McDonald's or Shell station.

For wilderness campers, hikers, kayakers, canoeists and other serious outdoorsmen, GPS has moved from the luxury category into that of basic essential.

PART

2

Let's Go!

Paha Qué

CHAPTER

High-Achiever Checklists Aid Planning

Some campers hate checklists, but lists can be lifesavers – even if you have a memory like an elephant. In fact, the more, the better. One time, we left home without the water jugs – a true disaster because we were headed for a remote site that had no water supply. Water had always been a sort of grey area, not really his job or hers, and we both forgot. As student pilots learn early, there is no substitute for a checklist. If nothing else, it assures that everyone is on the same page and everything gets done.

If you use a computer, start a camping folder with checklists you can print out fresh for each campout. (The computer is also a good place to start a camping recipe file with a shopping list for each menu.) Or, get a loose-leaf notebook just for camping and keep checklists there. They are easily replaced with fresh sheets as needed. Some of our checklists, such as the one for turning off the house, are used so often we laminated them using peel-off, transparent plastic. Found in crafts supply and school supply departments, it's also handy for reinforcing book covers, maps, yearly camping or fishing permits, and other papers that can get dog-eared through use.

Here are some suggested checklists:

☐ See individual chapters for lists of **Gear, Supplies, Provisions,** and **Clothing,** and make up your own checklists for each.

☐ Start with a **Checklist for Leaving the House**, listing such things as:
Stop newspapers and mail.
Set burglar alarms and timers.
Turn off water heater, icemaker, selected electrical circuits. (Make sure you don't turn off power to the freezer and other vital equipment.)
Turn off water supply to the washing machine. (Burst hoses are one of the leading causes of house flooding.)
Add to this list until it's right for your home. You may also need a separate list of phone numbers and emergency instructions to leave with the house sitter, pet sitter, plant sitter, or baby sitter.

☐ Make a **Count-Down Checklist** for pre-departure tasks. Here's just a sample of things you might include:

4-7 Days Before
Make dry mixes (see Chapter 19).
Check supply of stove fuel, batteries, flints (and other specialty supplies that you don't want to pick up at convenience stores along the way).
Gather up and organize maps and guidebooks.
Reserve campsite (if you haven't previously. Some sites have to be reserved months or more in advance).

3 Days Before
Make and freeze casserole to warm up the first night in camp.
Freeze block ice for the ice chest.
Return library books and get new ones for rainy days in camp.

2 Days Before
Have a mechanic check over the car.
Buy the meat and freeze it.
Check over all the cooking gear. (If it has gotten dusty or filmy in storage, there's still time to run it through the dishwasher. Ditto camp clothing and the sleeping bags. If they've gotten musty, there's still time to put them through the washer and dryer.)
Wash and dry ingredients for a tossed salad the first night out. Dry well, seal in a zip-top bag with a few paper towels, and seal shut with plenty of air to protect delicate greens. Refrigerate. In camp, you'll just add dressing, reseal, toss, and serve.

1 Day Before
Assemble everything in one pile (or start packing the car), checking off gear as you do.
Fill the car's fuel tank.
Buy fresh bait.
Pack and refrigerate lunch for the roadside and nibbles for the drive.
Tuck away a bag of "hush money" in the form of games and treats for restless kids.
Get ice chests out of the hot garage or attic.

Night Before

Fill ice chests with sacrificial ice and freeze new ice for tomorrow.

Fill water jugs.

Thaw muffins or sausage biscuits for breakfast, ready to grab for a quick departure.

Check over your **Checklist for Leaving the House** for things that can't be done if you leave very early in the morning, such as taking the dog to the kennel or calling a neighbor to leave the phone number of the campground.

Lay out what everyone is going to wear tomorrow.

Continue packing car, checking off gear list as items go in.

Departure Morning

Check off the rest of the gear as it's loaded, completing checklist.

Drain ice chests and fill with ice and items from the freezer and fridge.

Make sure confirmation number for campsite reservation is on board and handy.

Family members bring their own bed pillows for use in car, camp.

Lastly, go through the **Before Startup** checklist.

Other Checklists

☐ Make a **Before Startup** checklist to use before leaving the house, leaving any spot where you stop in the car, and each time you depart a campsite. It begins with a walk around the car to make sure nothing is falling off, hanging over, flat, bulging, open when it should be closed, closed when it should be open, smoking, hissing, dripping, or otherwise out of place. Double check tie-downs if you use a roof rack, bike rack, or other external storage. Before leaving a campsite, walk completely around it to make sure you haven't left anything behind. The loss of even a small cotter pin or tent stake could be a major inconvenience on your next campout.

First on the Before Startup list and the last thing to do before leaving, especially if you have children, is GO TO THE POTTY.

Once all the kids are on board and seat-belted, yell "Fist," meaning that everyone holds up two fists before you start slamming doors. It's a way to make sure no little fingers will be caught in door latches.

☐ We prefer to have everything loaded on departure morning so we can scoot straight to the campsite and start camping, especially when we're headed for a campground where reservations aren't accepted. If, however, you're a last-minute shopper, create a **Pick Up Along the Way** checklist so you can be quick when you stop at the bait shop, supermarket or convenience store.

☐ Most basic checklists list a first aid kit, period. Go further. Make a **Medical Checklist** that includes the office and emergency numbers for your doctors, dentist, pharmacist, and veterinarian. Know the numbers of your insurance policies, phone numbers for insurance companies, insurance help hotline numbers, and prescription numbers for important medications. (See Chapter 9 for a list of contents for a first aid kid) .

☐ In addition to a checklist of clothing, it's handy if each family member has a **Personal Toiletries Kit** checklist. You'll be visiting campground toilets at different times, so every kit needs soap, toothpaste, floss, tissues, toilet paper, and other items that are in your bathroom at home for everyone to share. In primitive camping, wet wipes or small bottles of waterless hand sanitizer are a plus.

☐ An easy way to provision is to make up a **7-Day Provisioning Checklist** of menus and the foods needed to prepare them, then use it over and over. If you camp only on weekends, it may be years before your family realizes that you always have chili and cole slaw every seventh night in camp. If you camp for a week at a time, make a complete, two-week list of recipes and all the foods needed for them. The family may never figure out that you're serving blueberry pancakes every other Sunday morning and barbecue sandwiches every other Thursday dinner.

☐ Make a **Short-term Lay-up Checklist** for putting camping gear away between weekends. If you camp only in season and put the camping gear away for months at a time, you can also use a **Long-Term Lay-up Checklist** of things that should be done before you put the tent, sleeping bags, and other gear into long-term storage. One of the most common mistakes is to forget about batteries you left in toys, games, flashlights, and the weather radio. Forgotten in the attic or garage for months, they can corrode, and ruin an expensive item.

☐ You might do a checklist of things to do on the **Last Day Out** when you want to, say, make sure the tent is clean and thoroughly dry before packing it up for the last time. This is the day to inventory the kitchen box, discard stale or surplus items that need to be replaced before the next trip, and empty all the water jugs, leaving caps off so they dry completely. Burn off the last of the liquid stove fuel (kerosene, unleaded gas, Coleman fuel), so the stove doesn't gum up during storage. Ditto heaters.

☐ If you're a birder, or think you might be one someday, find a **Checklist of Birds** that are likely to be spotted in the area(s) you camp. Lists are available free from tourism sources, are found in books, or search the Internet. It may take years before you see every bird on the list, but it's very satisfying – and a great family hobby – to check off birds as you identify them.

☐ If you camp with a dog, it's handy to have a separate checklist for the pet and make it the responsibility of one family member. The checklist should list among other needs: food, food dish, treats, a copy of the license and shots records, water dish, leash, collar, stake and chain, crate, vet's phone number, medications, dog's backpack or life jacket if called for, chew toys, and so on. Oh, and don't forget to take the dog! It's also wise to check ahead with the campground if your reservations were made some months ago. Pet policies change; the dog that was welcome last year may be banned this season.

Get a capsule for the dog's collar where you can place your campsite address each time it changes. Check the dog's tags to see if your home phone or other ID are still readable. On an active dog, they wear out before the tag does. If you carry a cell phone, VHF or CB in camping, make sure the dog wears that number in addition to other ID, so you can be reached if the dog gets away from you. See Chapter 17 for more tips on camping with a pet.

In a Pinch

Peg Neely, who has been camping with her husband Bob for 40 years, uses colored spring clothes pins as her checklist, one per item. "They come in at least six colors," Peg says. "We write on each side of the pin with a black marker what is to be checked, then we hang the pins on the gear shift lever so we can't miss them before taking off. Any place is good, as long as they won't be missed."

Clothes pins stow easily in a small stuff bag, and can be clamped on as needed around the house, car or campsite to remind you of, say, Water, Walk Dog, Buy Ice, and so on. They're also bright, inexpensive, and easy-to-use flags for items such as tent stakes or guy ropes that you want to mark with an eye-catching signal. If you use a clothes line in the campsite, always keep a row of bright pins there too. They'll be handy when you want to hang a tea towel or swim suit, and they're a highly visible reminder not to leave the line behind.

 Suggested checklists for a number of camping scenarios are found at www.jackbit.com.

CHAPTER

12

Pack Mule Rules

Getting It All In Your Vehicle

Your camping gear has been purchased, home-made, begged, borrowed, and rounded up from around the house and now it's sitting in a pile, defying you to get it all into the car or van, the canoe, or your backpacks.

Whoa! Simply getting it in is the least of your problems. You also have to find what you want, when you want it. Here's where the real challenge lies. Never has it been more important to be organized, disciplined, and creative.

If yours is a fly-in camping trip, you'll be separating gear into carry-ons and checked baggage, which is another challenge. Or, you may be starting out from home on a motorcycle or bicycle packed with the gear you'll use or replenish along your route. See individual chapters on backpacking and canoe or kayak camping for tips on stowing gear in the boat, backpack, or saddlebag itself.

Among other special situations are those campgrounds that provide a cart at the parking lot so you can transfer everything from the car to a campsite, which can't be reached by car. Or, you're camping the

Pods that are specifically designed to be carried on your vehicle or towed behind it add less drag than makeshift carriers.

Loading in enough gear for a weekend at a campground is easier with a portable equipment carrier.

Virgin Islands, which involves multiple transfers from your car to airplanes, taxis, the ferry boat, a jitney, then a hand cart. You might even transport your gear on the Palm Springs Aerial Tramway, which flies you to an altitude of 13,000 to camp Mount San Jacinto State Park! All these require special packing for special purposes, and that's part of the challenge and fun of camping. You can feel snug and smug, knowing that you have with you just about everything you'll need to create a home for yourself.

It's a Drag

Your vehicle was designed for optimum performance and streamlining, so you always lose fuel efficiency, speed and handling characteristics when you add a boat to the roof, bicycles or skis to a rear rack, or a storage pod to the roof or rear. Still, there is a limit to how many people and how much gear you can carry inside. Compromises must be made.

The marketplace offers a tremendous variety of space stretchers, so there's sure to be something that is the right size and shape for your needs. Some racks or pods ride on the roof. Some are hitch-mounted. Some are open racks, ideal for carrying bulky, odd-shaped objects such as bicycles, snowboards, folding chairs, a folding stroller, and other oddments that can tolerate rain and road slop. Other stowage containers are closed, watertight, and lockable. Here are some considerations when adding exterior storage:

• Keep the load as light as possible. Hanging a stowage pod on the rear hitch and filling it with your heaviest gear will put more weight on the rear axle, unload the front wheels, change your vehicle's center of gravity, affect handling, and aim your headlights too high. Putting a heavy load on the roof will probably weigh equally on each axle but will transfer more weight forward in braking, raise the CG to make cornering more difficult, and will add windage that could make handling difficult on a gusty day or when you're buffeted by a passing truck.

• If you're concerned about a water-tight integrity, look for a pod that is completely sealed and gasketed. On the road, rain and splash will attack the pod from all angles and at stinging speeds, rather like driving through a carwash.

• Consider how you will get at your vehicle's other doors, hatches, and the spare tire once the storage rack is in place.

• Know your vehicle's departure angle when a rear-mounted storage box is in place. If it's mounted too low, it can scrape the pavement.

• The rack itself should provide secure holding to the vehicle and a secure hold on whatever bicycles, boat, or skis it carries, with plenty of chafe protection for everything. Don't underestimate the effects of wear to the vehicle or the load due to road vibration, twisting of the rack or mounts, wind currents, chafe, and shifting of the load.

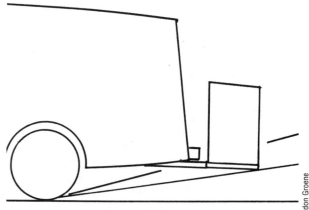

Adding anything to your rear bumper reduces the departure angle. The steeper the hill, the sooner your rear cargo will scrape the ground.

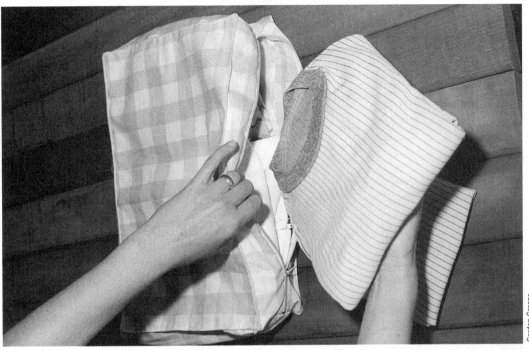

Make or buy small stuff bags to help divide and conquer.

Packing It In

☐ When storing springy sweaters, vests and hats, roll tightly and pull a leg warmer around the bundle to keep it tight. Leg warmers come in handy in a cold snap. Slip them on arms and legs for added warmth under slacks and shirts.

☐ Make or buy stuff bags in different colors for different family members. They're easier to identify in the general jumble that tends to pile up in a tent. It's brighter and more fun too, if you sew up camouflage bags for Junior, frilly pink for Sis, hunter orange for your fledgling bow hunter, Mom's favorite blue and white check, Dad's in his family tartan, and so on.

☐ The new self-sealing, plastic vacuum bags allow you to stow puffy sweaters and down vests in far less space. Two types are available. Some require evacuation with a vacuum cleaner, which is fine for the out-bound trip but not much help when you're packing to go home. Another type is self-evacuating. Put in the garment, zip it closed, and roll tightly. Air is forced out through a one-way valve.

☐ Garments that are folded, then rolled, wrinkle less.

☐ Hats are important protection against any climate, from bright sun to bitter cold. Choose hats that roll for stowage. When crew socks wear out at the heel and toe, cut off the ribbed tops, wash, and save to use as packing bands for springy items such as rolled hats. You'll find other uses for this ribbing in camp too, e.g. surgical stocking to protect a bandage or as a "bootie" around the mayonnaise or other breakable jars.

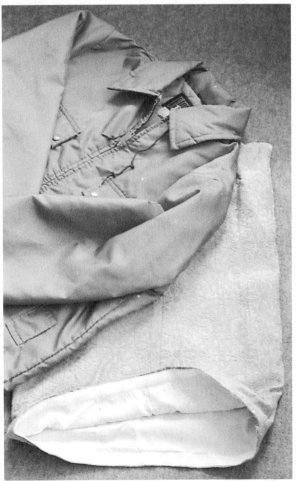

To turn a puffy jacket into a comfortable pillow, button it and fold the arms across the front. Then fold in half with the smooth back facing out. Slip into a pillow case or sham.

A collapsible cart is a great help in loading and unloading. Large wheels can handle rough terrain and beach sand.

Eric Knebel & Associates

Additional Personal Packing Items

☐ Notarized permission for travel and medical care if you're a non-custodial parent or are traveling with a child who is not your own.

☐ An alarm clock on vacation? You'll need it if you have a date with a fishing guide, want to catch the early ferry, or need a reminder to take a pill. If you have laundry in campground machines, either stay with it or set the alarm so you'll be there when the machines finish. An impatient camper who is waiting for the machine might take them out and dump them just anywhere. I once arrived to find that a kindly fellow camper had put my entire wash load in the dryer on High. Her intentions were good but my clothes were fried.

☐ Camera, film, extra batteries for the camera.

☐ A personal toilet kit for each family member. (Make a separate checklist for each). Choose a container large enough for toiletries plus a towel, washcloth or shower puff, and a change of clothes. It's best if the entire kit will hang from one hook, which may be all you have in the shower room or toilet cubicle. Hanging toiletries kits are ideal, providing an entire medicine cabinet that hangs from any nail, hook or rod. However, you also need a larger bag for clothes and the bath towel. One shopping bag-size carrier sewn up from sturdy denim or duck will hold it all.

☐ Personal electronics with earphones and extra batteries.

☐ Individual toy bag for each child to use in the car and in camp.

☐ Personal reading material and reading light.

☐ Your own binoculars.

CHAPTER

Choosing A Campground

Choices Abound, From Rustic To Resort

Tent camping is all about freedom, the open road, and the great outdoors. Nowhere is that freedom more obvious than in the enormous choice of campgrounds available to today's camper. Let's deal first with the bad news. Not all campgrounds welcome tent campers. They're built solely for the use of RV travelers who bring everything with them including the kitchen sink. These travelers want full hookups including cable TV, telephone, sewer, water, and 50-amp power to run their air conditioners, and they're willing to pay for it. If it says in the campground guide that you must be "self-contained," that means there are no public toilets, let alone showers and other facilities that tent campers must have.

The good news is that hundreds of thousands of great campsites are out there just waiting for you. Some are in the same camping resorts used by RVs costing half a million dollars. You may be sleeping in a

Many commercial campgrounds, especially KOAs, offer tent spaces as well as resort facilities, including golf and miniature golf.

With a pack on your back, the world is yours. Hike your way through the fjords of New Zealand or fly to Australia and camp from beaches to mountains.

NZ National Publicity Studios

When you book a campsite, don't forget to ask what tours can be booked at the same time. Add another dimension to your wilderness experience by seeing it from horseback, canoe, or raft.

$50 tent yet you have unlimited access to the campground's golf course, hay rides, square dances, camp store, heated swimming pools, fish pond, spa, club house, ski lift, and tennis courts.

Of course, the tent camper also has the option of getting away from such fancy surroundings and all that goes with them. In some campgrounds, a special section is set aside just for tents. In others, sites are assigned on a first-come basis. Your closest neighbors may be in anything from a motorhome to a pup tent. Less fancy still are designated primitive or backcountry campgrounds where everyone shares one outhouse or water faucet. At the bottom of the luxury ladder, but best of all for those who go tenting to get next to nature, are areas where you're free to pitch a tent anywhere that camping is not expressly forbidden. Such places can still be found. You have to pack everything in and out with you (although a lake or stream might provide water for washing up), but it's a small price to pay for camping off the beaten path.

The range of choices is enormous: government land, commercial campgrounds, condo campsites, membership campgrounds, and private lands (such as those owned by utility companies) where you camp with permission of the owner or manager.

Government parks include:
• U.S. and Canadian National Parks including national seashores, national monuments, and national preserves.
• Canadian Provincial Parks.
• U.S. National Forests.

• U.S. Fish and Wildlife Service lands often provide campsites in wildlife refuges.
• U.S. Army Corps of Engineers lands may have campsites.
• State Parks.
• State Forests.
• State Wildlife Refuges; State Preserves.
• State Fish and Wildlife lands have supervised hunting, fishing and conservation. Many also allow camping.
• County Parks.
• Many city parks allow camping.
• Military bases allow camping by military families (see below).
• State Water Management Districts may have recreational lands.

Non-Profit Campgrounds that may be open to the public or to members only, for free or a fee, include:
• Trails associations, e.g. Appalachian Trail, Rails-to-Trails groups.
• Church campgrounds.
• Elks Club property may allow camping by members.
• Boy Scout, Girl Scout, 4-H, other youth groups' camps.
• Some corporations, such as lumber companies and electric power companies, have large land holdings where camping is allowed with a permit.

Private and commercial campgrounds (not all offer tent sites) include:

• Camper Clubs of America, www.camperclubs.com or (800) 243-2267.

• Coast to Coast Resorts, www.coastresorts.com (303) 790-2267.

• Jellystone Park Camp-Resorts, www.campjelly-stone.com or (800) 558-2954.

• Kampgrounds of America, www.koa.com or (406) 248-7444.

• National Association of RV Parks and Campgrounds, www.gocampingamerica.com or (703) 241-8801.

• Ocean Canyon Resorts, (805) 595-7111.

• Outdoor Resorts of America, www.outdoor-resorts.com or (800) 541-2582.

• Thousand Trails, www.thousandtrails.com or (800) 328-6226.

• Scores of individual campgrounds, most of them owner-operated, are listed in campground guides such as Wheeler's and Woodall's. Woodall's also publishes a campground guide listing only campgrounds available to tenters.

• Many adventure travel operators and outfitters offer campsites in addition to their chief business, which may be whitewater rafting, scuba diving, skydiving, surfing, mountain climbing, auto racing, or presenting concerts.

• Theme parks may have campsites. Among the best known are Cedar Point, Ohio, and Fort Wilderness at Walt Disney World resort in Florida.

Many campgrounds offer bicycle rentals.

Prince Edward Island, Canada, offers plenty of golf courses and campsites galore.

Rating Campgrounds from 1 to 10

Here are some things to consider when you're choosing a campground. Rate them on a scale of 1-10, with 1 being unimportant and 10 being of upmost importance, and have your spouse and older children do the same. Then add up the scores to get an idea of what camping means to each of you.

Activities for children, teens ___
Adults only ___
Adventure, exploring ___
Affordable cost ___
ATVs ___
Bicycling ___
Bird watching ___
Boating ___
Caving ___
Clean restrooms, hot showers ___
Close to home, two hours or less ___
Electric hookup ___
Fishing ___
Handicap access ___
Hiking ___
Horseback riding, horseback camping ___
Hunting nearby ___
Kid-friendly atmosphere ___
Membership, chains, discounts ___
Motorbikes, motorcycles permitted ___
Nature programs, exhibits ___
Pets allowed ___
Privacy, I don't want to see the next campsite ___
Resort atmosphere, planned activities, social life ___
Rock climbing ___
Roughing it versus hot showers, nice bathroom facilities ___
Roller blading ___
Scuba diving ___
Security 24 hours ___
Skiing ___
Swimming___
Water available at campsite ___
Waterskiing ___
Whitewater rafting ___
Other activities that are important to your family (list them, then rate them) _____
Other factors that will affect your choice include:
• Is it open all year or only in season?
• Do I want to go at this time of year? (cold, rain, black flies, mosquitoes, humidity, heat)
• Are reservations accepted or must I take my chances?
• If you don't own a tent and full camping gear, or if you want to fly to a faraway location and rent gear on site, what is available in the way of camping cabins, yurts, rental tents?

Gordon Groene

Choices range from free camping on government lands to campgrounds that have all the facilities of a luxury resort.

Some campsites can be reached only from the water; some drive-in campgrounds offer canoe rentals by the day.

MN Office of Tourism

A Campground Dictionary

Chickee campsites are raised platforms common in tropical areas, often constructed over open water. They're open to let breezes through and have a grass roof, but you'll need a tent or other protection from insects and rain. Campgrounds in other climates may also offer a platform, lean-to or other partial shelter on or in which a tent can be set up.

Grey water is water left over from bathing, cooking, and dishwashing. It's incorrect, and illegal in some places, to pour this on the ground.

Ground sites are raised areas that are cleared for camping in the backcountry of swampy areas such as the Everglades. They're usually high and dry, often on shell mounds.

Hookups, also called umbilicals, provided for RVs, are electricity, water, sewer, and sometimes cable television and/or telephone. Tent sites may have individual power and water, a shared water faucet, or nothing at all. An extra charge is usually made for electrical hookup.

Pack in, pack out. Everything that goes into the outback with you must be brought back out. The only exception may be human waste, which can be buried according to strict rules. Toilet paper and feminine hygiene products must leave with you or be burned in a campfire (where permitted).

Pad. A patch of pavement, gravel, cedar chips, or other surfacing is provided at many campsites to serve as a patio or a tent site.

Potable Water is safe to drink. In some wilderness areas, you may have to bring your own drinking water, but can use local supplies for bathing and dishwashing. Usually water from the hose at a dump station (a sewage disposable station for RVs) is labeled non-potable. Never use water from one of these hoses. Even if the water is potable, the hose is probably contaminated.

Primitive or backcountry camping means few or no facilities at designated sites for which you may need a permit, pay a fee, or both. Sites may be reachable only on foot or by boat.

Self-contained. An RV with its own kitchen and bathroom. The campground may provide no facilities except for hookups to electric, water, and sewer. Tent campers can't be accommodated at campgrounds that specify you must be self-contained.

Picking Your Campsite

Choosing the right campground is half the battle. Finding the right place to make camp is the rest. If you're lucky, you'll be invited to cruise around until you find just the one you want to catch the morning sun, or closest to the swimming pool, or in the most secluded spot. In others, you're assigned to Site 224A and you have to make the best of it.

In developed campgrounds and parks, your site will probably have at least some amenities such as a grill and/or fire ring, water and electric outlets, picnic table and/or a food cache. In wilderness areas where no facilities are provided and no campsites designated, you can make camp anywhere that isn't specified as off limits. (Always check with rangers; some sites may be closed temporarily because of fire danger, high water, or wildlife concerns.)

In both cases, you're looking for a well-drained, level spot for the tent, shelter from harsh winds, and protection from whatever hazards are most common in this terrain. In grizzly country, for example, you want a site that is not near a bear feeding area. In areas that are subject to flash floods, be sure you're well above the highest possible high water mark. Even in flat terrain, be aware of low spots so you don't wake up on an island after an all-night rain. On the shores of tidal waters, always be aware of the state of the tide and its length of travel. In the tropics, it's very little; in Maine, tides devour huge expanses of dry land twice a day.

Always check a week or two ahead to make sure your pet is still welcome. Pet policies are subject to change.

Home, Sweet Campground

We're all brothers and sisters in the camping cause, yet we're all different. Some of us want to camp far from any other humans, and we are willing to paddle or hike all day to get there. At the other end of the scale are gregarious good-timers who want to go where the gang goes. Share a bonfire. Listen to a ranger's campfire talk. Get up a softball game or a potluck. Let your kids play with their kids. Ask an old-timer for advice on a camping problem.

The good news is that there is a campsite for you, no matter how oddball your tastes. If you want a tent site in a campground that welcomes motorcycles and is near a good spelunking cave but not more than half a mile from a pizza restaurant, it's a good bet you can find one. Want a wheelchair-accessible campsite with a fishing pier? A campground that accepts pets? A resort-style campground that has a full activities program, restaurant, golf course, and a masseuse? Yes, there are such places. Here's where it pays to invest in a massive campground guide, such as *Woodall's Campground Directory For North America*. While some of the listings are closed to tent campers, and the guide is weak on information for backcountry campers, it's far more comprehensive than many of the free lists issued by state governments, which may list only state facilities, or state campground associations, which list only commercial campgrounds.

Campground rates start at zero and go as high as $50 and up per night. At a resort campground, you may pay even more plus greens fees, cart rental, tennis lessons, and a tip for the hair dresser. The camping world is a cornucopia. Somewhere are the right campsites for you.

TOP TIP While many free campground lists are available from cities, regions, and states, there is no substitute for a comprehensive guide such as *Woodall's Campground Directory for North America*, published yearly. It lists almost every camping possibility in both for-profit and non-profit campgrounds.

Staking a Claim: Your Campsite

Back in your dad's Boy Scout days, the rule was to find a flat site, rake it clean, pitch the tent, and dig a ditch around the edge, channeling water away from the tent. Today's campers, however, believe in disturbing the site as little as possible. Besides, we now have waterproof, floored tents, that can take most rainstorms. For the lowest possible impact, choose:

• A patch of bare rock, leafy forest floor, pine mulch, or beach sand. Remove obvious lumps such as rocks and pine cones, but don't dig up tree roots or large stones.

• If the site has already had a lot of hard use and erosion, pick a healthy spot that hasn't been overused. Give the abused ground time to recover.

You also want a spot that:

• Won't flood. Look for telltale signs indicating that the area is a dry creek bed, or otherwise a raceway for water in high rains.

• Is sheltered from the coldest winds in cold weather, or open to the best breezes in hot weather.

Paddling down a whitewater stream is a challenge for campers.

Ocoee Rafting

Boot Camp

If you're in the military, active or retired, you're in high cotton, campground-wise. You used to know them as Travel Camps, but the name has been updated to RV Parks. Go to www.pathsacrossamerica.com. Although it's operated by the Army, the campgrounds it lists are open to all members of the military. Click on a state, select where you want to go, click again, and all the military camping parks in that state will be shown plus listings of features, facilities, how to get there, whether reservations are accepted including how to make them and how far in advance they can be made, and who is eligible to use the site. Most are open to all active and retired military members; others are also open to National Guard members, reserves, guests, and/or civilian employees of the Department of Defense.

Listings are extensive for everything from RV sites and furnished cabins to deeply secluded, hike-in tent sites. The parks compete with commercial campgrounds, offering coin laundry, sports areas (baseball, basketball, tennis, volleyball), swimming, fishing, grills, and planned activities. You can also utilize all the privileges of the military base itself, such as health care and shopping. Military campgrounds may also offer free local phone calls and other advantages, and rates are a fraction of those at private campgrounds.

Planning a National Park Campout

Here, thanks to Andrew N. Todd speaking for Amfac Parks and Resorts, are suggestions for planning a national park vacation. While it's always wise to reserve ahead, last-minute reservations are more available than people realize.

• **Educate yourself.** Know something about options before making reservations. Go to www.nps.gov, then to the Web site for the park you plan to visit.

• **Be flexible.** Because of varied occupancy patterns, you may have more luck if you can overnight in a park on a Tuesday or Wednesday this week or on a Thursday or Friday the following week. Travelers with flexible itineraries, especially during the most popular travel months, are more likely to get reservations.

• **Be persistent.** Because some people book far in advance and then have to cancel, availability changes constantly. If you can't get reservations now, try again another day.

• **Be patient and polite.** Reservations agents handle many calls each day. Also, realize that rates are set by the National Park Service, not the concessioners. Rates inside the parks aren't comparable to what you might pay outside the park for a campsite, meal, tour or souvenir. Rates are sometimes not set for several months into the year, so the reservations agent may tell you that rates are subject to change.

• **Don't believe everything you read or hear.** Myths of overcrowding and crumbling facilities abound but improvements are ongoing. Many national parks are in better shape than they have been in years.

• **Book a tour too.** When you reserve a campsite, reserve a tour at the same time. It adds a new dimension to your stay if you take a guided tour by mule, horseback or bus.

CHAPTER

Make Camp, Break Camp

Setting Up Can Be The Start Of Something Big

At one time, it was fairly safe to claim a campsite, drop your gear or set up the tent, then rush off to the day's swimming or fishing. That still works in assigned campsites in well-patrolled campgrounds, but it's almost essential now in some parks that someone stand guard. Horror stories abound about tenters who returned to find that their tent and gear had been stolen, or thrown aside by a claim jumper.

In any case, it's best to set up the tent and organize the gear before doing anything else. You now have shelter and an idea of where to find the grub, sleeping bags, and basic toilet gear.

Come on Baby, Light My Fire

Ever since the first caveman lit the first campfire, there have been two schools of thought on laying a campfire. The Pyromania school of fire building says that a framework the size of a bungalow should be built around a pile of tinder and kindling so that the touch of a match starts the tinder, which starts the kindling, which catches the logs, and suddenly you have a raging inferno. The Milquetoast approach, by contrast, involves lighting a tiny pile of the most tender tinder, then tenderly feeding the fire with additional materials as the flame grows stronger.

In both instances, the idea is to light a suitable fire with only one match.

Building a fire starts with checking the day's fire rules (they may have changed since yesterday) to make sure a campfire is allowed, and it ends with smothering the fire with earth or water until every ember has cooled before you leave the site. If the campsite doesn't already have a fire ring, use your camp shovel to make a clearing so the fire can't spread via twigs and dry leaves. If stones are available to make a fire ring, make one. Keep the fire well inside the perimeter.

Note which way the wind is blowing, so the smoke doesn't blow where you don't want it to. Now, assemble materials to be used as tinder, kindling, and firewood. The campground may sell firewood or you may have brought it with you. It's probably also permissible to gather dead wood. The next requirement is a supply of good matches, preferably waterproof, and a suitable striker. Alternately, you could use a lighter fueled with butane or lighter fluid. A number of types are sold in camping supply stores and catalogs.

Surefire Fire Starters

Theoretically, an experienced camper should be able to prepare a fire with natural tinder, kindling and draft, and light it with one match. In practice, however, most of us end up fuming and sputtering over stubborn fires that refuse to catch. In some terrain, good tinder is impossible to find. Any time it's damp or raining, nature needs a helping hand. The type and number of fire starters you'll need depends on the fuel and the kind of fire you need and, if you're kayak camping or backpacking, you're also limited by what you can carry. Here are some ideas:

* Scout the surrounding wilderness for likely tinder such as dried weeds, an old bird's nest, and the tiniest twigs.

* Use a solid fuel cube sold for use in pocket stoves. Tea lights are small circles of wax with a wick, each in their own foil container. They don't burn as hot or as long as solid fuel cubes, but cost only about a dime each

* The price is high ($4-$5 each), but a fire starter from Skyblazer, the company that makes signal

Skyblazer Signal Products

HotShot is an expensive, but surefire way to get a blaze going even on a wet day when you have little or no tinder. Sold in camping supply stores, the igniters burn at more than 1,200 degrees F. for up to two minutes.

devices, burns for up to two minutes at 1,200 degrees F. to start the most stubborn fire. It ignites with a scratch, so no match is needed. Ask for HotShot in camping supply stores.

* Whittle wood shavings and chips. They'll usually light even when wet.

* Save dryer lint in generous gobs, and wrap each in a twist of waxed paper to take on your next campout.

* Cut strips of corrugated cardboard as wide as a small tin can is high. Tuna cans are ideal. Coil the cardboard as tightly as you can around a candle stub, which will serve as a wick, to fit as much cardboard in the can as possible. Melt wax (take care! It can flare up)

and pour it into the cardboard until it's saturated. If you save candle stubs, old jelly wax, and broken crayons, you'll always have plenty of scrap wax on hand. Melt it in a large tin can and let debris settle to the bottom. Then pour.

To proceed, build a pyramid of charcoal or kindling around the can, leaving plenty of air circulation, and light the wick. By the time the waxed cardboard burns away, the fire will be able to support larger sticks and logs. Properly dispose of the can, which will remain after the fire is cold.

• Fireplace "logs" are sold in home stores and supermarkets. They light with a match and burn long enough to ignite kindling, which in turn can light hardwood logs. Their disadvantage is that they are bulky to carry and expensive to buy.

• Roll old newspapers very tightly into log-size coils and secure with a string. Soak the bundles in leftover wash water. Drain well, stack on a rack, and dry thoroughly. Puncture with an ice pick or an electric drill to make air passages, and use these "logs" as kindling.

• Tear off and discard the glossy covers of any old, pulp, paperback book and put the book in a plastic bag with a dollop of lamp oil, kerosene or diesel oil. It takes no more than a tablespoon or two, so don't overdo it. Store in a closed tin box for several days until the oil permeates the entire book. It will light with a match and burn hot and long enough to start wet kindling or a dry, hardwood log.

Fire Styles

Thanks to Patrick McHugh of MPI Outdoors, here are three ways to shape a campfire. "Don't forget," he says, "that you need three things: heat, fuel, and air."

The Teepee is the traditional campfire, in which you form a teepee-shaped cone of kindling around tinder stacked in the center. "This normally works well with damp wood," McHugh explains.

The Lean-To is a good style to use in windy or damp conditions. Place a green stick in the ground at an angle of about 30 degrees, pointing at the direction of the wind. Place the tinder at the end where the stick enters the ground and lean kindling against the stick for its entire length. As the kindling catches, add larger kindling.

The Cross Stitch starts with scratching a cross into the ground about 12 inches square and 3-4 inches deep. Place the tinder in the center and build a pyramid of kindling over it. The cross cut in the ground provides good draft to start the fire, no matter which way the wind blows.

TOP TIP Don't use charcoal lighter or any other fuel on a fire, even a fire that appears to be lifeless. If you must use flammable chemicals, use them only before lighting the first match on freshly-laid tinder and kindling.

Sparkers and Lighters

For backpacking and other lightweight camping, waterproof matches are the lightest choice. If you have more space, however, other fire lighters are more reliable and longer, so there's less chance you'll burn your fingers. Shop a camp supply store for both a stove sparker and a flame stick. The sparker is best for lighting any gas stove, lantern or heater that does not have a built-in igniter. However, it produces only brief sparks. The flame stick lights a flame that can be used to light a campfire or candle.

Sparkers come in models that use a flint, which wears out and must be replaced, batteries, which die, or in piezo-electric styles that cost more but last forever. The best and most common flame sticks take a cigarette lighter cartridge, which follows Murphy's Law and runs out at the worst possible time. Whatever lighters you carry, stow and carry them safely, keep them away from children, and always have a spare flint, batteries, or fuel cartridge on hand.

Parting is Such Sweet Sorrow

It's time to break camp, which means getting your gear home safely and complete, and leaving the campsite in better shape than you found it. Get into a routine that becomes habit, one that will help you work as a family or team to pack the car, backpack, boat, or horse properly for the return trip. Then take one last stroll around the campsite including any public toilets, the laundry, and any other common areas. Make sure nothing was left behind. Walk completely around the car to see that everything is lashed down, no tires are flat, and no straps are hanging out of the trunk. Here are additional tips on breaking camp:

• Make sure the fire is out. Clean out the grate or fire ring. Dispose of all trash including any unburned items in the fire.

• Sweep out the tent. Shake sleeping bags and ground cloths. Dry and air the tent and sleeping bags if possible. If not, do this as soon as you get home. Soil you bring back from the campground has a way of multiplying like a giant amoeba. The longer you wait to dry and clean your gear, the grottier and stinkier it becomes.

• Don't bury the food box and cooler under all the gear in the car. Keep some food and drink where you can get at it while breaking camp and during the drive home.

• Give the children age-appropriate jobs. If they get bored while adults are still struggling with stowing the tent and other difficult tasks, send them on a Trash-ure Hunt. The simplest way is just to give each of them a trash bag and give a prize for the most weight, or most volume at the end of, say, 45 minutes. Set boundaries so they don't wander too far afield. The idea is to leave your campsite clean and green.

• Check out if necessary with the campground front office. Close any float plans.

• Last stop is the potty for people and walkies for the dog.

Don't forget that you need three things: heat, fuel and air.

CHAPTER

Four Season Camping

Cooler Weather Doesn't Mean The Season Is Over

Campers who are willing to put up with a little sass from the Weather Channel can camp not just in summer, but around the calendar. The weather may be a little more unpredictable in low seasons, but so is everything else – nature's symphonies, the people you meet on the trail, and souvenir shops that are now having year-end close outs. You'll find year-round tent sites available in a surprising number and variety of campgrounds in all parts of the country, from the hottest desert days to the wind-whipped snowstorms of winter in the Rockies. Where tenting areas are closed, the same parks may offer snug shelters and cabins that are just as campy and are a nice change from tenting.

It's always wise to seek expert local advice and it's essential in off seasons. Ask rangers what hazards are likely to be encountered during this special season and heed their warnings. Do homework ahead of time to see what kinds of temperatures and rains can be expected. Tourist crowds are often driven by school holidays rather than weather. The "off" season may be best of all.

Learn what natural phenomena are expected in this area during this time. It could be anything from the spectacle of aurora borealis to the irksome attack of sandflies. For better or worse, forewarned is forearmed. Also see individual chapters for more on camping and coping in extreme heat or cold.

Dress and Undress

Except for camping equatorial jungles where it's always broiling hot, it's always essential to dress in layers. Hiking El Junque, Puerto Rico's steamy rain forest, I thought I'd melt as I hit the trail, but was shivering by the time I reached the misty hills. Temperatures drop as altitude rises, so it can be cold even at the Equator if you're high enough. Nor can you count on southern latitudes to be as warm as you expect. Winter cold fronts blast through Florida as far south as the Everglades, and the strongest ones may make it all the way to the campgrounds of St. John in the U.S. Virgin Islands.

In short, be prepared.

When packing for tropic heat, take at least one outfit that has long sleeves and long trousers for sun and insect protection, plus a wide-brim hat, a windbreaker if you'll venture higher than 1,000 feet and, for anything other than sashaying around the swimming pool, sturdy shoes with good socks. Some tropical thorns can go right through sneakers or flipflops. Water shoes are also welcome for beachcombing rocky shores or swimming off pebbly beaches.

See Chapter 7 for more about clothes for camping.

TOP TIP Catalytic propane heaters should be used only in well-ventilated areas. Heaters with Oxygen Depletion Systems (ODS) have a sensor that shuts off the heater if oxygen supplies fall below acceptable levels. Both should, of course, be used with extreme caution in regards to fire safety, carbon monoxide, and awareness of oxygen depletion.

Essentials for Off-Season Camping

• Carry at least two extra pairs of socks, and unless you're flyweight camping, at least one extra pair of shoes. During World War I, more soldiers were felled by foot ailments than by enemy bullets. It's essential to keep feet dry in all seasons.

• The body loses at least 10 percent of its heat through the head. In cold weather, keeping the head and neck warm is crucial. In summer, a ventilated hat that shades the head allows the head to behave as the efficient radiator it is.

• Always call ahead to make sure a campsite, and whatever facilities you will rely on, are available. Many campgrounds close seasonally, and not always on the same dates each year. Some campgrounds may close during the week in colder seasons but open on weekends. Some campgrounds may be open but shower houses are closed or water lines turned off.

Other Natural Wiles and Wonders

Be aware too that hours of daylight vary by latitude and month by month. The hours from sunrise to sunset are as long as about 12 hours at the Equator for every day of the year and 24 hours of daylight at the poles during their summers, to as short as zero hours of daylight at the poles during their winter months. Rather than wrestle with the entire chart here, however, it's better just to remember that it's something to look into before you fly into, say, southern Australia or northern Canada, and plan to hike X miles before dark each day.

Tides, too, can play a huge rule in beach camping or island hiking. The closer to the Equator, the smaller the tidal range. Huge tides in northern areas can strand an unwary hiker, sink a naive tenter, and confound canoe or kayak campers who find themselves paddling furiously and still being swept backwards in a current that, just minutes before, was flowing the other way. Even in the Caribbean where tidal ranges are only a foot or two, a coastal path could disappear between low tide and high. If you are boating in tidal areas, invest in a tide chart. Otherwise, learn the local tide clock. Depending on the location, it could be anything from a mere curiosity to a matter of life and death.

"Spring" tides don't have to do with springtime but with the full moon, when tides are extra high or extra low. In most instances, they won't have much to do with camping life.

TOP TIP

Know where to find the weather channel on your radios or, better still, invest in a NOAA weather radio that sounds an alert if threatening weather is in the area.

Do homework ahead of time to see what kinds of temperatures and rains can be expected.

How Cold Was It?

Except for the United States, the entire world uses the metric system for everything including temperatures. Listening to weather reports when camping elsewhere, it's useful to know at least the basics of the Centigrade scale. To convert Centigrade to Fahrenheit for temperatures that are above freezing, multiply by 1.8, then add 32 degrees. To do it in your head, multiply by 2 and you'll be close enough for most planning purposes. Ergo, 10 degrees C times 2=20+32= about 52 degrees F.

It's also helpful to remember that 100 degrees C is boiling, 0 degrees C is freezing. Any day hotter than about 28 degrees Centigrade is too darned hot. And, just for the record in case you're camping in Antarctica, minus 40 degrees C is also minus 40 degrees F.

To convert Fahrenheit to Centigrade in round numbers, subtract 30 and divide by two. Don't try it on a math test, but it works well enough in camping that you can listen to the weather forecast and decide whether to wear your parka or a sleeveless tee shirt. Note that an inch of rain is 25 millimeters.

As a rule of thumb, temperatures usually drop about 3 degrees F. for each 1,000 feet you climb.

 Wind Chill Chart

		Temperature (°F)																
		40	35	30	25	20	15	10	5	0	-5	-10	-15	-20	-25	-30	-35	-40	-45
Wind (mph)	5	36	31	25	19	13	7	1	-5	-11	-16	-22	-28	-34	-40	-46	-52	-57	-63
	10	34	27	21	15	9	3	-4	-10	-16	-22	-28	-35	-41	-47	-53	-59	-66	-72
	15	32	25	19	13	6	0	-7	-13	-19	-26	-32	-39	-45	-51	-58	-64	-71	-77
	20	30	24	17	11	4	-2	-9	-15	-22	-29	-35	-42	-48	-55	-61	-68	-74	-81
	25	29	23	16	9	3	-4	-11	-17	-24	-31	-37	-44	-51	-58	-64	-71	-78	-84
	30	28	22	15	8	1	-5	-12	-19	-26	-33	-39	-46	-53	-60	-67	-73	-80	-87
	35	28	21	14	7	0	-7	-14	-21	-27	-34	-41	-48	-55	-62	-69	-76	-82	-89
	40	27	20	13	6	-1	-8	-15	-22	-29	-36	-43	-50	-57	-64	-71	-78	-84	-91
	45	26	29	12	5	-2	-9	-16	-23	-30	-37	-44	-51	-58	-65	-72	-79	-86	-93
	50	26	19	12	4	-3	-10	-17	-24	-31	-38	-45	-52	-60	-67	-74	-81	-88	-95
	55	25	18	11	4	-3	-11	-18	-25	-32	-39	-46	-54	-61	-68	-75	-82	-89	-97
	60	25	17	10	3	-4	-11	-19	-26	-33	-40	-48	-55	-62	-69	-76	-84	-91	-98

Frostbite Times □ 30 minutes □ 10 minutes □ 5 minutes

Wind Chill (°F) = $35.74 + 0.6215T - 35.75(V^{0.16}) + 0.4275T(V^{0.16})$
Where, T= Air Temperature (°F)   V= Wind Speed (mph)   *Effective 11/01/01*

National Weather Service

Chart for the wind chill factor.

Lightning

Lightning is a powerful force and a formidable killer that may strike without warning out of a clear sky. Usually, however, it gives ample warning. The time to put your safety plan in place is when you first hear thunder. Don't wait for the rain to drive you indoors. Lightning usually comes first. The most obvious shelter and one of the safest is your car. Or, take shelter in a campground building such as a clubhouse. If the only building available is the shower house, stay well away from plumbing fixtures.

Caught in the open, stay away from water, high ground, open spaces, and metal objects including fences. Trees, tents, and open picnic shelters aren't good places to hide. In fact, when lightning hits a tree the charge can spread out along the root system for many feet around. Pick a low spot and assume the "lightning crouch." With feet together, crouch down to make yourself as small as possible and cover your ears with your hands to avoid hearing damage from a loud thunderclap. Don't cluster with other people in the open, forming a more attractive lightning rod. Try to maintain about 15 feet between yourselves. Wait about half an hour after the last lightning strike or thunderclap before resuming normal activities.

It's safe to touch a lightning victim; no charge remains. Give whatever first aid you can while summoning professional help as quickly as possible.

Flash Floods

Even experienced campers are sometimes caught by flash floods, not realizing that they aren't always preceded by heavy rain. Rising water could be sudden and unexpected due to snow melt, a dam burst, or even a controlled release that goes awry. The steeper the hills, the more chance that low places can turn into raging torrents. Local knowledge is an excellent guide. So is your own, keen sense of observation. Note high-water marks, the lay of the land, sources for any water than might come your way, and likely places for water to collect.

In hurricanes, flooding caused by the storm surge in the sea kills more people than are killed by winds. Seek shelter on high ground.

Hurricanes

Hurricanes and typhoons are annual threats in many tropical locales and, while they deserve respect if not outright terror, they are so random that most travelers no longer avoid the hurricane belt during storm season. To do so would mean skipping entire continents for six months of the year. In the Caribbean, for example, hurricanes might be seen in any month (except, perhaps, April) and are most common June through October. These are also months that offer great diving, snorkeling, sightseeing and camping, often at off-season discounts.

The good news is that hurricanes give plenty of warning. In Florida and the entire eastern seaboard, around the Gulf coast, and throughout the Caribbean, weather forecasts are good and authorities well organized. While a vacation may be disrupted by a hurricane, deaths are rare among people who evacuate or take shelter when advised to.

Those people who haven't experienced a high-level hurricane don't understand the furies that are produced.

A man who survived a disastrous hurricane on the little island of Cayman Brac in the 1930s told me his story. The family knew a severe storm was coming and took shelter in caves in the island's only high ground. They didn't know that a second, more vicious storm always passes over after the calm that is the eye of the hurricane. Many people left the shelter and were killed. Those who survived were met with another world when they emerged from the caves. "There wasn't a fence, a house, a tree–nothing that would help us identify our own property or tell us where our homes had been," he remembered.

While volumes can be written on hurricane preparedness, it boils down to: have a radio and heed warnings; evacuate when authorities advise it (evacuation routes can become clogged later); and follow the instructions of emergency crews. The time comes when they can no longer answer Maydays from people who waited too long.

Tornadoes

Awesome forces are contained in these whirling winds. If you have a weather radio, a tornado watch means that weather conditions are right for a tornado to form. A tornado warning means that one has been spotted. The wind alone is enough to blow you away, tent and all. It may be filled with junk up to and including huge chunks of metal that can batter you and it can easily blow down buildings or trees to crush you. Seek shelter in a sturdy building or, if none is available, in a ditch and cover yourself with your sleeping bag and anything else that can cushion you from flying debris. Eerie darkness and/or continuous thunder and lightning usually accompany a tornado. Its approach is described as the sound of a freight train.

Driving Ambitions

Even if you are an experienced winter driver, it's a plus to take an ice driving course so you'll be a better, safer driver on your way to the trailhead. Many areas are sure to have at least some ice from autumn through spring, and others have snow all year. Conditions change when you leave the city and head for the outback, and "black" ice may be encountered on bridges even when the rest of the highway is clear and above freezing. Courses at the Bridgestone Winter Driving School in Crested Butte, Colo., last a half day, full day, or several days. They are fun, fast-paced, and challenging for people from all climates and terrains. The local KOA is open all year. Call 800-WHY SKID or (303) 879-6104, www.winterdrive.com.

It's always wise to check ahead on road conditions. Some of these numbers apply for all conditions, including construction, all year. Some operate only in winter to report on snow conditions. Also see state tourism office listings in Resources, and contact individual states. Many have special hotlines to report on fall color during leaf peeping season or road conditions for skiers, and others create special numbers during floods, forest fires or other natural occurrences that affect highways.

Alabama (334) 242-4378

Arizona (602) 651-2400, ext. 7623; construction information (602) 255-6588

Arkansas (501) 569-2374

California (916) 445-7623 or 445-1534

Colorado (303) 639-1111

Connecticut (860) 865-2650

Florida (800) 475-0044

Georgia (404) 635-6800

Idaho (208) 336-6600

Illinois (312) 368-4636, winter conditions (217) 782-5730; construction, (800) 452-4368.

Indiana (317) 232-8298, construction (317) 232-5533

Iowa (515) 281-5824

Kansas (785) 291-3000 or (800) 585-7623

Kentucky (800) 459-7623

Louisiana (225) 379-1541

Maine (207) 287-3427

Maryland (800) 327-3125

Massachusetts (617) 374-1234

Michigan (800) 337-1334

Minnesota (800) 542-0220

Mississippi (601) 987-1212

Missouri (800) 222-6400

Montana (406) 444-6339 or (800) 332-6171

Nebraska (402) 479-4545, winter (402) 471-4533

Nevada has three regions, south, (702) 486-3116; northwest, (775) 793-1313; northeast, (775) 738-8888.

New Hampshire (603) 271-6900

New Jersey (732) 247-0900 Turnpike; (732) 727-5929, Garden State Parkway

New Mexico (505) 827-5154 or (800) 432-4269

New York (800) 847-8929 (Thruway only)

North Carolina (919) 549-5100, ext. 7623

North Dakota (701) 328-7623; construction (701) 328-2565

Ohio (888) 876-7453 Turnpike; (614) 466-7170 elsewhere

Oklahoma (405) 425-2385

Oregon (503) 588-2941; winter, (800) 977-6368

Pennsylvania (800) 331-3414 or (888) 783-6783

Rhode Island (401) 222-2468

South Carolina (803) 896-9621

South Dakota (605) 367-5707

Tennessee (800) 858-6349

Texas (800) 452-9292

Utah (801) 964-6000

Vermont (802) 828-2648

Virginia (800) 367-7623

Washington (800) 695-ROAD; construction (360) 705-7075; mountain passes in winter, (888) 766-4636

West Virginia (304) 558-2889

Wisconsin (800) 762-3947

Wyoming (888) 996-7623 or (307) 772-0824; construction, (307) 777-4437

CHAPTER

Camping Clubs

The More, the Merrier Is Their Motto

To some campers, "joining" is the antithesis of the total escape that camping can provide. Most of us, however, want to get involved for some reason. It may be social, especially for campers who have families and want to camp in places that have activities for children or teenagers. There are also special interest groups among campers who are, say, handicapped anglers or barbershop musicians or square dancers, or people who band together for volunteer projects such as cleaning up a park or re-roofing a church.

Or, you could join a club for purely economic reasons. Good Sam and KOA are among groups whose members get discounts at campgrounds. Other groups are formed by people who have the same brand of RV. They get together periodically for shop-talk about their rigs' problems and quirks. Still others are political, organized for general conservation support or for a particular interest such as saving some endangered species. One or more of the following clubs may be right for you.

National Camping Clubs

Escapees RV Club
100 Rainbow Drive
Livingston, TX 77399
(936) 327-8873 or (888) 757-2582
www.escapees.com
Members are mostly full-timers, who live in their RVs as a lifestyle. The group owns its own campgrounds and provides many social and financial benefits.

Family Campers and RVers
4804 Transit Road, Bldg. 2
Depew, NY 14043
(716) 688-6242
www.fcrv.org

Family Motor Coach Association
(Motorhome owners only)
8291 Clough Pike
Cincinnati, OH 45244
(513) 474-3622
www.fmca.com
Membership is open only to those who own motorhomes. Hundreds of chapters serve members according to special interests, RV brand, and/or geographic location. Benefits are many including a color magazine, towing service, insurance, and much more.

Family Travel Trailer Association
P.O. Box 5867 - CM16
Titusville, FL 32783
(800) 603-1101

The Good Sam Club
2575 Vista Del Mar Drive
Ventura, CA 93001-3920
(805) 667-4100
www.goodsamclub.com
One of the oldest camping clubs, Good Sam offers campground discounts, a monthly magazine, get-togethers, volunteerism, and much more.

The International Family Recreation Association
P.O. Box 520
Gonzalez, FL 32560-0520
(800) 477-7992
www.rvsite.com

KOA Value Kard
Buy it at any KOA campground or see www.koa.com.
For a small, yearly fee this card is good for a 10 percent discount at all 500 KOA campgrounds plus other benefits and access to special promotions.

Loners on Wheels
P.O. Box 1355
Poplar Bluff, MO 63902
Fax: (573) 686-9342
www.lonersonwheels.com
Singles of all ages travel in campers of all types.

National African-American RVers Association
P.O. Box 341
Somerdale, NJ 08083
(856) 784-6897
www.naarva.com

RV Elderhostel
75 Federal St.
Boston, MA 02110-1941
(617) 426-7788
www.elderhostel.com
This group organizes Elderhostels for RVers who travel and study while overnighting in their own campers.

Rainbow RV Club International
627-340 Island Hwy.
Victoria, BC
V9B 1H2
(250) 708-0040
www.rainbowrv.com

RVing WOMEN
P. O. Box 1960
Surprise, AZ 85378-1960
(623) 975-2250 or (888) 55-RVing
www.rvingwomen.com

S*M*A*R*T
Special Military Active Retired Travel Club Inc.
600 University Office Blvd., Suite 1A
Pensacola, FL 32504
(850) 478-1986
www.smartrvclub.bizland.com

RV Brand Name Clubs

Whatever other memberships you have, it's always a plus to join a brand-name group that has factory support, newsletters, discounts, product updates, and "insider" news about your equipment.

Alpenlite Travel Club
P.O. Box 1726
Clackamas, WA 97015
(503) 698-4461

American Clipper Owners Club
322 Cavanaugh Street
San Mateo, CA 94401
(650) 344-3750

Avion Travelcade Club
101 E. Sioux Road, #1078
Pharr, TX 78577-1719
(210) 787-0445

Beaver Ambassador Club
P.O. Box 6089
Bend, OR 97708-6089
(541) 389-1144

Bounders United Inc.
3298 Anniston Drive
Cincinnati, OH 45248
(513) 922-3131

Carriage Travel Club, Inc.
P.O. Box 246
Millersburg, IN 46543-0246
(219) 642-3622 Ext. 252

Country Coach International
P.O. Box 207
Junction City, OR 97448
(503) 998-3712

Fireball Caravaners, Inc.
16339 Septo Street
North Hills, CA 91343
(818) 892-0861

Foretravel Motorcade Club
1221 N.W. Stallings Drive
Nacogdoches, TX 75964
(409) 564-8367

Georgie Boy Owners Club
8650 S.E. 66 Circle
Trenton, FL 32693
(219) 258-0591

Gulf Streamers International RV Club
P.O. Box 1005
Nappanee, IN 46550-0905
(219) 773-7761 Ext. 3521

Hitch Hiker of America International (NuWa)
325 W. Main St.
Melrose, MN 56352-1065
(320) 256-4933

Holiday Rambler RV Club
600 E. Wabash St.
Wakarusa, IN 46573
(219) 862-7333

International Allegro Family Motorcoach Club
P.O. Box 1457
Red Bay, AL 35582
(256) 356-0210

International Coachmen Caravan Club
P.O. Box 30, Hwy. 13 N.
Middlebury, IN 46540
(219) 825-8245

International Skamper Camper Club
220 Church St.
St. Marys, PA 15857
(219) 875-3246

Jayco Jafari International Travel Club
1660 Nash
White Cloud, MI 49349
(616) 689-6370

Lazy Daze Caravan Club
4303 Mission Blvd.
Montclair, CA 91763
(909) 627-1219

National Collins RV Club
2206 Kimberly Drive
Klamath Falls, OR 97603
(541) 884-2749

Newmar Kountry Klub
P.O. Box 30
Nappanee, IN 46550-0030
(877) 639-5582

Shasta Wings RV Club
P.O. Box 171
Osceola, IN 46561-6171
(219) 258-0571 or (800) 262-5178

SOI Club
3550 Foothill Boulevard
Glendale, CA 91214
(818) 249-4175

Starcraft Camper Club
4921 Rosecroft St.
Virginia Beach, VA 23464
(757) 495-1607

Sunnybrook Travelers
173 Morningstar Road
Venice, FL 34292
(941) 488-8399

Supreme Travel Club
2703 Belknap Lane
Mishawaka, IN 46544
(219) 258-0591

Wally Byam Caravan Club
International (Airstream)
803 E. Pike St.
Jackson Center, OH 45334
(937) 596-5211

Winnebago Itasca-Travelers
P.O. Box 268
Forest City, IA 50436
(515) 582-6874

CHAPTER

Take Me Along

Kids and Pets Enjoy Camping, Too

Kids and camping go great together. In today's campgrounds, you'll see children from newborns to teen-agers participating in family camping. For an increasing number of single parents, especially single mothers, camping is one of the few affordable ways to vacation with children. You can sleep and feed them for a week in a campground for the cost of one or two days in hotels and restaurants. As for fun, a $15 state park beats out a $50 theme park any day!

Parenting kids in camp is much the same as parenting at home. Job One is to keep the kids safe, well fed and hydrated, and clean enough to be healthy. Camping takes care of all the rest, from entertainment to educational opportunities.

Camping With Kids by Don and Pam Wright is out of print now but is available from used book sources including amazon.com (where you'll find an impressive selection of books on camping with children, outdoors life with children, and related topics. Search for key words camping+children). While the Wrights are more into RVing than tenting, their book focuses on participation, responsibility, making children full members of the camping family and, most important, having *fun*. The Wrights' children had camping chores to do from an early age. The family found, as so many campers do, that chores such as dish washing or sweeping up somehow aren't the drudgery in camp that they are at home, usually because everyone pitches in at once.

Birdwatching provides hours of learning and adventure.

Alpin Outdoors

Specialty Gear

Today's parents are active and even adventurous campers. As a result of this trend, most outdoor catalogs offer a good selection of rugged gear that enables you to take infants and children into the great outdoors with you – not as couch potatoes but as budding anglers, hikers, rock hounds, and paddlers.

L.L. Bean, for example (see Resources), offers strollers with large wheels that can be used on rougher terrain than can be managed with conventional strollers. Mom and Dad don't have to miss their morning jog because junior goes along. Also available are backpack-style baby carriers with a sturdy frame suitable for long hikes with a child up to 45 pounds. Bean's infant carrier, structured of ripstop nylon for serious, outdoor use, allows you to carry the child facing outwards or towards your body.

For bikers, L.L. Bean and other outfitters sell helmets for adults and children, child seats, and a Papoose Caboose that tows behind a bicycle. If you do a lot of bicycling in the campground, look into a kids' tandem. It's a half bicycle that attaches behind an adult bike and allows a child to pedal or coast. It's good for kids up to 80 pounds. We once did a three-day bicycle/camping trip, covering up to 30 miles a day, in which children as young as 8 and 10 rode their own bikes. We were amazed at how well they kept up, even on one-speed bicycles. What they lacked in fancy gearing and lightweight frames, they made up in boundless energy.

If you camp on or near the water, it's essential that children have Personal Flotation Devices (PFDs). See Chapter 6 for the full story. This is an extreme example, but a couple who camp often at a canal-side campsite keep their toddlers in PDFs every waking moment. At their age, the kids never knew camping any other way and they take the vests for granted. The moment they get out of the car, the life vests go on. Except for bedtime and baths, the PFDs don't come off again until everyone is back in the car.

Some parents also keep small children in a harness or leash while on the trail. Almost every year we hear stories of children who wandered off from the group and got lost, sometimes with tragic endings. Use a leash, a strict buddy system, or both. Usually trouble starts when there is no clear understanding of who is looking after whom. A child wanders off after a butterfly and Aunt Maude thinks he's with Mary, who thought he was with Ken.......

A child who is old enough to walk with the group can carry a pack too, even if it holds nothing more than the child's own drinking water, whistle, and extra sweater. Invest in a real pack, one designed for comfort and sound, orthopedic support. Book bags aren't suitable for serious hiking and, heavily loaded, could be bad for a child's skeletal health.

With the right carrier, parents can hike all day with comfort and safety for themselves and the child.

Tough Traveler offers carriers for infants, children, books and pets, all in top quality materials and designed for the wearer's safety and comfort.

Play Along

It's a common complaint from bored children that they have nothing to do. Here's how to keep them busy during those odd moments in camp when the chores are done and they still have energy to burn off. Turn off the personal electronics and get them moving!

* Don't overlook chores as a way to entertain, involve and educate children. The jobs you can't get them to do at home become funky and fun in camp.

* Have a litter-getter contest as a way of cleaning up the campsite or even the entire campground. First, have a parent-child talk about privacy rights in regard to other campsites, then give each child a plastic bag and a list of litter to find: a diet drink can, something red, something sparkly, something plastic, a gum wrapper, and so on. Announce you are also looking for a "secret item" so the kids will pick up all the junk they find. When they get back to camp, there are prizes for those who find the most things on the list and for those who find the "secret" item.

* Make up a kitchen band: beans in a coffee can make a tambourine, waxed paper over a comb makes a kazoo, an empty oatmeal box (cardboard box, plastic lid) makes a tom tom, whistles, bells, seed pods known as "shak-shaks," castanets made from nutshells. See how many different instruments you can devise with what's on hand.

* To play Drop the Bean, use a can punch to make three holes in the bottoms of several clean tin cans. Make sure the hole is just a little larger than beans. In each, place a cup of dry beans. At the signal, each player stands over a cardboard box and begins shaking the can. The first person to empty his can wins.

• Involve children in creative projects. You might, for example, bring an inexpensive plain paper tablecloth and let the children color it to make an elegant tablecloth for dinner. Build a birdhouse out of a discarded plastic bleach bottle. Weave dry grasses into

Bring crafts supplies for creative projects.

place mats or baskets. Make a scrapbook for the prettiest fall leaves or to hold picture postcards bought in your travels. Write a letter to Grandma. For more ideas, get books from the library and visit www.verybestkids.com.

• It's hard to keep teen-agers interested in camping with family. Join a camping club with other families that include teens, or seek out campgrounds that have activities programs for all age groups.

Kids Can Help

Here are just a few of the jobs that children can be assigned:

Ages 4-6

* Pick up loose gear and toys around the campsite and put in a bucket or milk crate.

* Clean up litter around the campsite and place in trash bag.

* Roll up their own sleeping bags.

* Count tent stakes, poles, silverware, etc. to make sure nothing is left behind.

* Help set the table.

* Learn to tie knots needed in camp.

Ages 6-12

* Gather tinder and kindling.

* Scrub potatoes for campfire baking and wrap individually in foil.

* Sweep out the tent with a whisk broom and dust pan.

* Serve as camp secretary, diarist or scrapbook keeper.

* Take full responsibility of the family pet and its gear, including clean-up.

Ages 12 and up

* Teach camping skills, e.g. knot tying or laying a campfire, to younger siblings.

* Plan some menus and shopping lists.

* Take responsibility for some checklists.

* Haul water.

* Take trash to dumpster.

* Take charge of weather report, maps or nature guidebooks.

* Use the Internet to do research on nature, campgrounds, routes.

Pets in the Campground

Blake Hawley, veterinarian for Hill's Pet Nutrition, says, "If pet owners plan to travel with their cat or dog, it's important to ensure the pet's health and comfort during the trip." He recommends making a checklist of things to pack for pets including medications, the food that the pet is accustomed to eating, and a leash or carrier. More tips are available at www.hillspet.com.

Dr. Hawley also suggests:

• Feed pets several hours before departure to reduce the likelihood of motion sickness.

• Help pets adjust to the car ride by taking them on practice drives.

• Bring toys, food, and water from home so pets feel more secure.

• If a pet gets nervous and starts to howl, soothe it by talking to it or playing relaxing music.

• Never leave pets unattended in hot vehicles and never leave the vehicle without having your pet on a leash or in a carrier.

• Make sure pets wear proper identification in case they get lost.

• Check pets for ticks daily, recommends Dr. Hawley. "While on vacation, keep your pet from roaming through tall grasses and woods. Consult a veterinarian for one of the many highly effective topical and oral products now available to control flea and tick problems," he says.

• Mosquitoes thrive in lakes and parks and frequently spread heartworm to untreated pets. Often fatal, heartworm is preventable. A veterinarian can offer a heartworm preventative and appropriate testing for pets.

"It is important for pet owners to realize that health problems can develop both inside and outside the house. This is especially true with allergies," Hawley finds.

"The same pollens and house dust that cause allergic reactions in people could cause allergic dermatitis in dogs and cats." If a pet shows signs of hair loss or licks and scratches excessively, it may have allergic dermatitis. Your vet can recommend a solution, which could include nutritional management, injections, oral medications, topical shampoos, dips, ointments and environmental treatments.

Martin Coffman of Iams, makers of specialty pet foods, also suggests:

• Before traveling to remote areas, stop by your local veterinarian's office for a list of veterinary clinics in the area of your destination. That way, you don't spend valuable time finding phone numbers in an emergency.

• Make sure your dog has plenty of identification on its collar to insure its return should it get lost. If your dog does get lost, leave an article of clothing, such as an old jacket, near the area. Often, the dog will be discovered curled up on the jacket the next morning.

• In case of snakebite, don't waste valuable time

Gordon Groene

In addition to a leash, which is required in any campground where pets are permitted, it's a wise precaution to have a PFD for your pet too. If a dog falls off the edge of a canal or swimming pool, it can't get out without help. A good PFD keeps it afloat and also provides a handle for rescuers.

with first aid in the field. Rush the pet to a veterinary clinic. Ask your veterinarian in advance what to do if you are truly isolated and a snakebite occurs.

In the Wink of an Eye

Kids and dogs can slip away into the night and be gone in seconds. It could be useful to buy a battery-operated flasher from a bicycle shop, and fasten it to a child's clothing or a dog's collar. The Red Alert (MPI Outdoors) runs for more than 200 hours on two AA alkaline batteries and flashes in red or amber. It's also popular for after-dark roller blading or jogging. Children who are old enough to understand can also be equipped with a rescue whistle, with the instruction, of course, that it's to be used only for emergencies.

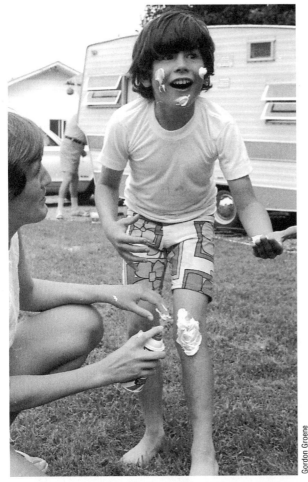

Gordon Groene

Gordon Groene

An inflatable, child-size swimming pool carries in little space, inflates by mouth if you don't have a compressor, and comes in handy for toddlers' bath time and playtime.

TOP TIP Carry an inflatable, child-size swimming pool to use for bathing toddlers.

Job one is to keep the kids safe, well fed and hydrated and clean enough to be healthy.

TOP TIP Carry a couple of instant stain wipes (such as Shout Wipes) on every camping trip so you can treat accidents to expensive jackets, stuff bags, or sleeping bags. Treated early, the stain is much more likely to come out completely when you launder or dry clean it at home.

Gordon Groene

An easy way to get kids clean in campground showers is to "paint" them, Indian style, with shaving cream, then let them rinse clean.

Buy a garden sprayer to be used as a portable shower. Add stove-heated water, pump up pressure, and you'll get a generous shower from a couple of quarts of water.

Improvise a solar shower by heating a gallon or two of water in a dark plastic bag in the sun. Hang it high enough to stand underneath, then quickly stab it with an ice pick to create a shower. Leave a little reserve at the bottom of the bag for a second rinse. The bag can still be used as a garbage bag

TOP TIP

If your family keeps losing or forgetting soap and washcloths in campground showers, squirt a little shampoo into a sandwich-size plastic bag for each person. Step into the shower to get wet. Then turn the bag inside out, and use it as a shower mitt. Dispose of it responsibly. An ounce of shampoo concentrate is enough to lather all over. No more wet, smelly washcloths in your toilet kit!

CHAPTER

Fun and Games

Orienteering, Hashing Are Among Popular Activities

Camping is a sport in itself, one of the best. It's about nature, cooking, outdoor skills, and embracing the great outdoors. It's also a way to travel on the cheap while pursuing other sports. You'll find tent campers at the annual EAA fly-in at Oshkosh, Wis., at the airport in DeLand, Fla., during international parachute meets, in the infield during the Daytona 500, and in campgrounds anywhere famous for surfing, BMX, skateboard ramp, spelunking, bass tournaments, mountain biking, whitewater rafting, rock climbing, mountaineering, and every other outdoor sport you can imagine plus legions of indoor sports too. Many campers are hunters, fishermen, hikers or bikers first and campers second.

In addition to those outdoor sports that are already part of your life, here are some that go especially well with camping:

Orienteering

Using a compass and map, you'll learn valuable navigation skills while scrambling over hill and dale. Orienteering is a delightful family sport, with events for even the smallest learners.

Anyone can start out simply, then add a fancier compass and tackle tougher courses as your skills increase. Groups are available at the local, regional, state, national, and international levels. Contact the U.S. Orienteering Federation, P.O. Box 1444, Forest Park GA 30051 or www.orienteering.org.

Hashing

Groups that call themselves Hash House Harriers start with a wild game of running and end with convivial cascades of liquid refreshment. It all began in Malaysia in the 1930s when some resident Brits decided to create a hare-and-hounds hunt with humans. The sport died out during World War II but has reappeared and gained popularity in many countries worldwide. Do

Gordon Groene

Treasure hunting is an addictive game for the whole family. Hunt responsibly, however. Metal detectors aren't permitted in many public parks.

an Internet search for the key word *hashing* to find an organization near you, or instructions on how to create your own using official lingo and rules.

A day or two before the run, one or two hashers, or "hares" lay a trail of about four to six miles and mark it with chalk, shredded paper, flour, or pieces of toilet paper hanging in the bushes, depending on local practice, tradition, or terrain. Another method is to start the hare only 15 minutes ahead, as "live hares," marking the trail while trying to stay ahead of the pack. At a signal, the pack (also know as harriers, harriettes or hounds) give chase. The idea is to mislead the hounds by sending them up false trails, dead ends, and on time-consuming loops.

At the end of the trail, everyone is hot, exhausted and ready for gallons of cold comfort. Traditionally, great quantities of beer are consumed but any cold drinks will do. The important thing is the camaraderie, a rowdy party, and all the ritual and lingo that one learns in hashing.

Volksmarching

Picture a group of happy wanderers, strung out along a trail at their own pace, yet proceeding in happy companionship. The trail has been chosen ahead of time, well marked, and checked over for hazards. The game is simply to enjoy the walk, not to win a race or get your competitors lost, so don't look for hidden agendas. Along the path you'll encounter people to stamp your passport, give you an cold drink, or offer a bandage for your blisters.

Volksmarches (Peoples' Walks) are well organized, are designed to include as many ages and interests as possible, and are among the most pleasant ways to enjoy the outdoors in the company of nice people. Do an Internet search using the key word Volksmarch to find a group in your area. Many city, state, and regional groups exist. The American Volkssport Association publishes *The American Wanderer* for avid folk-walkers. See www.ava.org for information on U.S. and Canadian volkssport groups.

Play Ball!

Many campgrounds have large playing fields where campers are welcome to get up a game of touch football, soccer, or baseball. There may also be volleyball, tennis, and basketball courts. Take the necessary equipment. The campground's outdoor sports equipment, if they have it at all, is probably in sorry shape.

CHAPTER

Meals Afield
Good Planning Is The Key To Success

Cooking in camp is different for every camper in every camp, and that's part of the fun. One day you're cooking on your knees in the wilderness. The next, you may have a real campsite with water, grill, a sturdy picnic table to work and eat on, and perhaps even electricity. Back in chapter 8, you assembled a good selection of gear. Now it's time for the grub.

It takes a math whiz to figure how much food is needed for two adults and two kids for a long weekend, a couple for a week, or for one person on a three-day backpack trip. You don't know how hungry you'll be or what supplies you will be able to buy or forage along the way. There's a lot of guesswork, but they can be educated guesses and they'll get closer to the mark as your camping skills grow.

We once stumbled on a mountain of wild blackberries while camping our way through England, acres of rose hips while camping Martha's Vineyard, and seas of blueberries and raspberries in Nova Scotia. We ate ourselves silly on the fresh food and made fruit leather to take home. While it's no longer possible to live off the land, especially in public lands where you can't pick so much as a sorrel leaf, there are fish to be landed, roadside stands to be browsed, wild berries and nuts to be harvested where allowed, and local bakeries to be sampled.

Provisioning

• Basically, you need at least a half cup of flour, one egg, and one cup of milk per person per day for eating and/or cooking. You'll use less, of course, if all cooking is done from mixes.

• As a rule of thumb, consider 4-6 ounces of well-trimmed, boneless meat or 8-10 ounces of cleaned, bone-in fish as one adult portion. Therefore, a pound of ground beef will feed four, more or less. It can be stretched to feed 14 if you make chili with beans and other fillers, but it will feed only two if your crew insists on half-pound burgers. If you're serving whole birds, plan on a pound per person. There's a lot of waste.

Even if you never use them at home, canned and packaged foods can play an important role in camping.

Gordon Groene

Peanut butter can be stirred into a hot cereal, used as an ingredient, or spread on bread or crackers.

Skippy ®

• Plan at least a quart of drinking water per person per day and more in hot weather, not counting water for dishwashing, cooking, and bathing.

• Carry a supply of "just-in-case" foods to fill gaps in menus, to expand meals that prove too skimpy for appetites that swell greatly in the outdoors, or to fall back on in an emergency. If you can't cook in the rain or if you lose some supplies to an animal or bugs, you'll bless the day you slipped a six-pack of Slim Fast into the trunk of the car.

Lifesaving backups to have in your food cache include popcorn, regular or brown rice, peanut butter, canned date and nut bread, well-wrapped hardtack-type rye crackers, your own or purchased trail mix, dried fruits, unsalted nuts, hard cheeses, and pemmican or jerky.

Campfire Cookery

After environmental safety concerns, the first rule of campfire cooking is to keep it small and manageable. You don't want a bonfire big enough for a pep rally. Aside from being a menace, a fire that's too large is so hot you can't get near it to arrange and stir pots. You want a supply of well-started coals that you can stay near to monitor temperatures, stir in ingredients, reposition pots as needed, and test for doneness. Without pushbutton controls, a cook has to be exceptionally alert to the look, sound and smell of foods to keep things at the simmer or at the boil and to bring them to perfection without burning or undercooking.

Start a small fire and have enough logs or charcoal briquets in reserve to feed it as needed to keep it at the right cooking temperature. Often this is done with two

The secret to deep frying is to keep the fat hot enough, which requires expert fire management.

Gordon Groene

fires, the cooking fire and the "feeding" fire that produces pre-started coals for the cooking fire.

One of the finest campfire meals I ever ate was a shore dinner in the Thousand Islands of the St. Lawrence in upstate New York. The guide built a crackling wood fire, filled a big, iron skillet with a couple of pounds of lard, and kept it at a rolling boil as he quick-fried a mess of perch. For dessert, he brought the lard to a hard boil again, and deep-fried French toast. If he'd let the lard get too cool even for an instant, the food would have absorbed it and tasted lardy and fat. Learning to manage campfire temperatures is an art in itself, crucial to everything from deep-frying fritters or searing a steak to frying flapjacks and the long, slow braising of a lamb stew. Half the battle is to have enough charcoal or wood in reserve.

Many methods are used to hold a pot over a fire. Some campsites come equipped with a grill or grate so, depending on where you camp, you may never need more than that. Or, you might bring a grate, improvise one by positioning large logs to hold the pot, or bring a steel tripod made for hanging a pot over an open fire.

Forget the pictures you've seen in old scout manuals, showing a pot hanging from a green stick suspended between two forked sticks stuck in the ground. It isn't good scouting to cut live trees and, even if you can find dead trees in the right shape, it's hard to keep the pot suspended over the fire and at the right height.

Rocks can also be arranged to hold a rack that will be your "stove." Form them into a fire ring with a corridor off one side, shaped like a big keyhole. The whole thing can be as small as a ring not more than 1 1/2 feet in diameter plus an ell of, say, 12 X 15 inches, edged with rocks that will hold your grate.

Build the main fire in the round part, then rake enough hot coals into the ell to begin your cooking. Place a grate over the rocks that form the rectangular ell, and your "stove" is ready to go. Rake additional live coals under the grate from the main fire as needed. Folding grills are sold at camp suppliers in many styles. They're light to carry, but can be tippy, so use one with care and don't overload it. It's worth the extra weight to carry a sturdy, iron grate or rack. Two cautions. First, some rocks can explode when layers of moisture inside them expand from heat. In each area where you camp, ask local advice on what kinds of rocks are recommended for a fire ring. Second, don't grill or smoke foods directly on an old refrigerator rack. Food could be contaminated from the metal plating.

For slow, all-day cooking in a Dutch oven, dig a hole a foot or two from where you'll build the main fire, with a shallow ditch connecting the two. Fill the Dutch oven (preferably a cast iron one with a flat lid) with ingredients, cover, and set it near the main fire so it begins to heat through. (Or quick-start it over the camp stove.) Rake a good bed of hot coals into the hole, add the Dutch oven, then shovel coals around the edge and over the top. Loosely shovel a little dirt over the top to keep the heat in but not so much that the coals are smothered. They continue to need oxygen to burn. If the hole is deep enough and the coals sufficient for the size of the pot and what's in it, you should be able to retrieve a perfectly cooked meal by sundown.

You can now keep the main fire going if you need it, or let it go out. A Dutch oven that has been preheated and well buried in coals should need no further tending for the day.

TOP TIP

Cooking in a fire hole can be dangerous for careless adults or heedless kids, and it isn't recommended if you have toddlers who could step into the fire. Note too that charcoal, which is white when it's at cooking temperature, may look cool to youngsters. It stays hot for hours, and could be missed in the dark. You can't be too careful with a any fire; a ground fire requires double vigilance.

Fearless and Fireless

Fireless cookers have been around since the covered wagon. Pioneers soaked their dried beans all night, then brought the pot to a full boil over the breakfast fire. The hot pot was then put in a box of straw. By the time they made camp that night, the beans were hot, tender, and ready to eat.

The same technique works today, rather like having a non-electric crock cooker. You'll need an ice chest or other heavily insulated container, a pot, and enough insulation to fill the cooler completely except for the space taken up by the pot. Insulation can be white "peanuts," newspaper, Styrofoam, feathers, straw, bricks, or anything that holds the heat. Make sure that the hot pot does not touch any part of the ice chest. The plastic liner will melt.

The thicker and more dense the insulation, the longer it will hold the pot at cooking temperature. The more air space, the quicker it will cool. If you can cut and carve foam to the exact shape of the pot so insula-

While fireless cookers are occasionally found on the market, you can make your own using a box and Styrofoam, straw, hot bricks, pellets, or other insulation. The secrets are to (1) use a large amount of insulation completely surrounding the pot and (2) bring the pot to a full boil before burying it in the cooker.

Gordon Groene

tion is at least 4-6 inches thick around, above, and below the pot, it will cook a beef stew and serve it hot in eight hours. You might also make a fireless cooker by using fat pillows to line the cooler, providing a thick, insulated nest for a pot. Sew up your own using denim or another sturdy fabric. Fill them with "bean bag" pellets, and leave enough space in the ticking so they mold closely around the cook pot.

Bring the covered pot to a boil over your morning fire, place it in the fireless cooker, make sure it's com-

pletely surrounded with insulation, and close the lid of the cooler. Place the cooler in a warm spot, sheltered from the wind, and don't peek all day. You can even put it in the trunk of the car, and have hot stew when you arrive in camp. Until you get the hang of fireless cooking, be prepared to warm up the pot over the camp stove in case it has cooled too much. It takes practice because everything depends on the size of the cooking pot, the amount and type of food, and the quality and quantity of the insulation you provide.

Provisioning the Camp Pantry

According to a survey by Kraft Foods, these are the items most commonly found in American larders. No camper is going to carry all 100 items, and there is some repetition, but keep the list handy as a mind-jogger when you're putting together your own provisioning list.

1. Eggs
2. Granulated sugar
3. Flour
4. Peanut butter
5. Ground black pepper
6. Ketchup
7. Baking soda
8. Yellow mustard
9. Vanilla extract
10. Baking powder
11. Ground cinnamon
12. Spaghetti or vermicelli
13. Brown sugar
14. Barbecue sauce
15. Yellow onions
16. Spaghetti sauce
17. Canned tomato sauce
18. Margarine
19. Idaho baking potatoes, fresh
20. Oregano
21. Corn
22. Beef, hamburger
23. Vegetable oil
24. Saltines
25. Salad dressing (bottled)
26. Carrots
27. Paprika
28. Apples
29. Bananas
30. Chili powder
31. Nonstick cooking spray
32. Nutmeg
33. Canned tuna
34. Canned tomato paste
35. Confectioner's/powdered sugar
36. Green beans
37. Garlic powder
38. Worcestershire sauce
39. Lemon juice
40. Flavored gelatin (JELL-O)
41. Cornstarch
42. Parmesan/Romano cheese, dry, grated
43. Grape jelly
44. Lettuce - Iceberg
45. Dried parsley flakes
46. Milk (any white)
47. Elbow macaroni
48. Mayonnaise
49. Macaroni and cheese
50. Peas (any)
51. Microwave popcorn
52. Honey
53. Soy sauce
54. Applesauce
55. Dill pickles
56. Sliced white bread
57. Regular tomatoes
58. Potato chips
59. Seasoning salt
60. Garlic salt
61. Cola
62. Hot cocoa mix
63. American cheese slices
64. Cloves (any)
65. White rice (any)
66. Tomato sauce - plain
67. Orange juice
68. Ground coffee
69. Bouillon cubes
70. Peas - green
71. Baking mix
72. Prepared pasta
73. Onion powder
74. Bay leaves
75. Salad dressing - Ranch
76. Cider vinegar
77. Garlic - fresh
78. Dried basil
79. Egg noodles
80. Butter
81. Pickle relish
82. Solid shortening - can
83. Salad dressing - Italian
84. Canned chopped tomatoes
85. Pudding mix (instant)
86. Chicken broth
87. Ground cloves
88. Strawberry jelly
89. White rice - regular
90. Ground ginger
91. Italian seasoning
92. Boneless/skinless chicken breasts
93. Sage
94. Oranges
95. Chicken bouillon cubes
96. Mayonnaise - regular
97. Pancake/waffle (baking mixes)
98. Bacon
99. Green peppers
100. Celery

Making a List and Checking it Twice

Start with a list of the meals you'll be making in camp, keeping in mind that routines, tastes and appetites may be different in camp than at home. By the time everyone gets organized in the morning, breakfast is welcomed even by those who never eat breakfast at home. To your family, lunch may mean a nosebag of trail mix or a bag of sandwiches to take out in the fishing boat, or you may make the noonday meal the big dinner of your day. At home, you may have dinner quite late, but in camp it's more practical to eat and clean up in daylight, then have popcorn or s'mores around the campfire before turning in.

The main difference, though, is that your gang will eat as they never ate before. Kids will scarf down foods they won't touch at home. Light eaters become hungry eaters and heavy eaters turn into shop vacs. Be prepared.

You might fill it in like this:

To make Big Lie Homemade cookies, start with a can of frosting and a tin of Danish butter cookies. Frost the cookies, use any sprinkles and trims you have, and voila! They're homemade!

Friday Lunch
Stop at Wendy's on the way out of town

Friday Supper
Cranberry juice cocktail, Triscuits, cheese
Chicken Chili

Italian bread
Raw veggies with dip
Canned pineapple rings, Big Lie Homemade Cookies
Coffee

Start by listing all the meals you'll need while you're gone, including those you plan to have at restaurants. Your menu list might look like this:

Friday Lunch _____

_____

Friday Supper _____

_____

Friday Late Snack _____

_____

Saturday Breakfast _____

_____

Saturday Lunch _____

_____

Saturday Supper _____

_____

Saturday Late Snack _____

_____

Sunday Brunch _____

_____

Sunday Supper _____

_____

Late Snack

Apple juice, soft pretzels

Saturday Breakfast

Canned ruby red grapefruit sections

Biscuits with sausage gravy

Coffee

Saturday Lunch

Tuna salad sandwiches

Pringles

Tangerines

Milk

Saturday Supper

Pre-dinner: V-8 cocktail, peanut butter-stuffed celery, crackers

Ham and beans

Cornbread with honey butter

Tossed salad

Canned peach halves with whipped cream from a squirt can

Beverage

Saturday Late Snack

Cheese-veggie wraps, hot cocoa

Sunday Brunch

Orange juice

Blueberry pancakes

Sausage patties

Coffee

Plenty of nibbles for the drive home

Sunday Supper

Apples and popcorn at home

This is the simplest of menus, but look what happens when you take it to the supermarket and start thinking it through. Your shopping list would look like this:

Salt, pepper for the table

1 can nonstick spray

1 bottle cranberry juice cocktail

1 box Triscuits

Small round of brie

If you'll make the chili in camp instead of bringing it from the freezer at home, list the ingredients on your shopping list, e.g. 1 pound boneless, skinless chicken breast, 1 packet chili seasoning, large onion, 1 green pepper, 1 can diced tomatoes, 1 can pinto beans

1 loaf Italian bread

1 tub margarine

1 package cut-up raw vegetables

Small tub onion dip

1 can pineapple rings

Frosting, cookies

Coffee (also tea, cocoa mix, cream, sugar)

Milk

1 bottle or can apple juice

1 package soft pretzels

1 can ruby red grapefruit sections

1 package biscuits (or ingredients for making your own)

1 pound sausage

1 packet country gravy mix

1 loaf sandwich bread

1 pound tuna salad from deli

1 tube Pringles

1 tangerine per person

1 bottle vegetable juice cocktail

1 jar peanut butter

Box round crackers

Bunch celery

Canned ham

2-3 cans baked beans

Brown sugar

1 onion

1 box cornbread mix

Eggs (for the cornbread mix and pancakes)

Oil (for the cornbread mix and the pancakes)

1 carton honey butter

1 package torn salad greens

Tomato for salad

1 bottle salad dressing

1 can peach halves

1 aerosol can whipped cream

1 package flour tortillas

1 package shredded carrots

3-ounces cream cheese

Scallions (make veggie wraps with tortillas, cream cheese, carrots and sliced scallions)

Hot cocoa mix

Orange juice concentrate

1 box pancake mix

1 can blueberries

1 package sausage patties

Baby carrots, whole wheat crackers, juice etc. for the drive home

Apples plus microwave popcorn for when we arrive home

Two types of canned ham are available, refrigerated and non-refrigerated. If you buy the refrigerated type, don't forget to keep it refrigerated.

National Pork Board

In addition to all the ingredients needed for your menu, and any staples you'll need for things you'll make from scratch, your shopping list must also include non-food items.

A Non-Food Shopping List

Make up your own list. Here are some thought starters:

Aluminum foil (roll, cooking bags, wraps)
Charcoal lighter
Dishwashing detergent, scrubber-sponge
Facial tissues
Food wrap, bags in various sizes
Garbage bags
General clean-up spray
Matches
Paper towels (get plenty and use them as napkins too)
Toilet paper

Pantry Raids

At home, you have to maintain some control over the refrigerator and pantry. In camp, it's essential because you have limited supplies, a carefully planned menu, and an ice supply that won't last if everyone is in and out of the ice chest all day long. Food safety could be threatened. Have a family powwow to set rules about snacking. One solution is to set aside one box or bag of healthful snacks that are up for grabs any time, plus an ice chest that you fill anew each morning with that day's limit of ice and cold drinks. When they're gone, there is always tap water. All other supplies are off limits to anyone but the cook. It all works surprisingly well as long as everyone helps make the rules and understands them.

Shortcuts

The most versatile convenience food you can carry doesn't cost any more than ordinary flour. It is self-rising flour, which contains flour, baking powder, and salt. Add eggs, oil, and milk (plus sugar and other ingredients as needed) to make muffins, pancakes, or coffee cake. Or, just add milk and oil to make biscuits. A little wheat germ, cornmeal, and/or uncooked oatmeal add texture and nutrition if you like a grainier product. Self-rising flour is made with soft winter wheat flour, which is the best choice for fluffy biscuits. That's why it's so popular in the South, where biscuits rather than toast are the breakfast staple. It may give slightly different results with other recipes than you would expect with all-purpose flour, but do give it a try.

TOP TIP Remember to use self-rising flour only in place of a flour-baking powder-salt combination, never in place of regular flour in pie crusts, yeast bread, or other applications.

Convenience foods make camp cuisine more carefree, and they simplify planning too. However, they create extra bulk and trash, they often contain chemicals and other undesirable ingredients, and they're sometimes outrageously overpriced. Here are some other convenience foods that sell at ordinary prices:

Combination seasonings such as seasoned salt, lemon pepper, Italian seasoning
Peanut butter and jelly in one jar
Flavored nonstick pan sprays (butter, garlic, olive oil)
Condensed soups (not semi-condensed or ready-to-serve)
Bouillon (use as ingredient, flavoring, beverage or broth)
Flavored bread crumbs with herbs
Instant puddings cost the same as cook-and-serve
Powdered drink mixes cost less than ready-to-drink liquids, and carry in less space
Bottled lemon juice costs less than fresh squeezed

Hello, Jell-O

Boxes of flavored gelatin dessert are inexpensive little lifesavers even if you never make them into the jiggly dessert. Use the powder sparingly or to taste because it's highly concentrated. Buy regular or sugar-free gels in a variety of flavors and use to:

• Dissolve a little of the dry gel powder in boiling water to make a tart, colorful, bracing hot drink.

• Buy a frozen pound cake in an aluminum pan and, without removing it from the pan, poke 12-20 holes in it with the round handle of a wooden spoon. Dissolve a packet of fruit-flavored gel in a half cup of boiling water and slowly drizzle it over the cake. Return it to the cooler. When you slice or spoon it, it will have streaks of color and flavor throughout.

• Sprinkle freshly made popcorn with dry gelatin and mix well for a sweet, fruit dessert. You'll need about four quarts popped corn for each four-serving packet of gel.

• Fold a package of fruit gelatin and a can or two of well-drained fruit into a large carton of thawed, whipped topping for a heavenly dessert.

• Mix together a package of fruit-flavored gel and a half cup of sugar in a brown paper bag. Shake freshly baked donuts or biscuits in it to coat, and serve hot.

• Sprinkle dry orange gelatin atop servings of instant vanilla pudding for a flavor similar to Orange Julius.

• Make up an eight-serving batch of biscuit mix according to package directions. Knead on wax paper or paper toweling sprinkled with flour or dry biscuit mix, then pat into a rectangle. Sprinkle lightly with cherry or strawberry gelatin powder, roll up, slice, and bake as for biscuits. You'll have flavorful pinwheels.

• Make a gourmet tea by brewing two tea bags, 1 to 1 1/2 quarts of boiling water, and a packet of any flavor gelatin. Let steep five minutes, then drink hot.

All Mixed Up

When you make your own mixes at home, you save money, save time in camp, save having to carry tons of extra supplies, and, best of all, you can tailor the recipes to exactly the ingredients you want and the quantity that is right for your family. Cutting down on salt and sugar? Prefer brown rice to white? Rather serve whole wheat flour than white? Want to make only eight pancakes or two biscuits? Homemade mixes are just the ticket.

Make them up in big quantities, then package them according to what constitutes one batch for your crew. Then add a note of ingredients and instructions for completing the recipe. For example, say your home-made pancake mix contains flour, leavening, salt, and powdered milk. For each two cups of the mix, you would add 1-2 eggs, 1/3 cup oil, and 1 1/2-2 cups water to make your batter (depending on how thick you like your pancakes to be).

Or, package up a cup of raw rice plus the ingredients to make your favorite rice pilaf. To complete the recipe, you'd bring two cups of water to a boil, stir in a cup of the rice mix, and simmer over a very low flame until the rice is tender. In a snack-size bag, zip all the dried herbs and spices you use in one batch of your famous, homemade spaghetti sauce. In camp, you'll simply dump it into whatever else you do to make the sauce. Instead of carrying along half a dozen spice jars, you need only one bag of pre-measured herbs.

Get the picture? Let's mix it up!

Biscuit Mix

8 cups flour, can be up to 25 percent whole wheat
4 tablespoons plus 1 teaspoon baking powder
1 tablespoon salt

1 1/2 cups nonfat dry milk
1 teaspoon baking soda
2 cups shortening

Mix the dry ingredients well in a large bowl and cut in the shortening with a pastry blender or two knives until the mixture is fine and mealy. Measure into zip-top bags in the amounts you need, planning a half cup per person per serving.

• To make pancakes: add milk and an egg to make a medium batter
• To make muffins: add milk, eggs and sugar, plus dried fruit, nuts, or other flavors, to make a thick batter.
• To make "impossible" pie, whisk together a half cup of biscuit mix, 2 eggs and a cup of milk. . Arrange (precooked) ingredients for a fruit, vegetable, or meat pie in a buttered pie tin and pour the batter atop the filling. As it cooks, the crust will rise to the top. Bake at 400 degrees until the top is golden.
• To make biscuits: add milk to make a very thick dough, knead briefly on a floured paper towel, cut and bake.
• To make shortcake, add sugar to the mix, then add milk and bake as for biscuits. Split the sweet biscuits and top with fresh or canned fruit.
• To make cobbler: place canned or fresh fruit in a baking pan. Make sweet biscuit dough, drop by teaspoons atop the fruit, and bake until the top is golden and crusty.
• To make coffee cake: add a little sugar and whisk biscuit mix with an egg and enough milk to make a thick batter. Place in a buttered baking pan. Make a streusel topping by cutting butter into a mixture of dry biscuit mix, cinnamon, and brown sugar. Bake.
• To make cornbread, add a cup of self-rising cornmeal per cup of biscuit mix. Add sugar, milk and an egg or two to make a medium batter. Bake in a buttered pan.

Through Thick and Thin: A Definition

* Thin batter: think buttermilk. For making thin pancakes or crepes.
* Medium batter: it pours, but puddles up quickly on the griddle, as for thicker pancakes.

* Thick batter: has to be spooned out of the bowl and into pan, as for cornbread or muffins.
* Dough: has to be scraped out of the bowl, as for bread or biscuits.

Master Meat Mix

If you freeze batches of this mixture, you'll eliminate the messy, tiresome step of browning and draining meat and vegetables. Package it in lots of 1-1 1/2 cups for each two servings. This recipe is easily doubled or tripled, but it gets harder to manage unless you have a very large pot. You must be able to stir and break up the meat as it cooks. If you have trouble getting vegetables into your family, add finely diced carrots, grated cabbage and celery to this mix and they'll go unnoticed.

3 pounds lean, ground beef or a mixture of ground beef and turkey
2 medium onions, diced
3-4 cloves garlic, diced
Medium green bell pepper, diced
Salt, pepper

Optional:
2-4 carrots, finely diced
2-4 ribs celery, diced
Half a small cabbage, grated
16-ounce can pumpkin

Brown the meat in a large pot over high heat, breaking it up until it's crumbly. Drain off any excess fat. Continuing over high heat, add the vegetables and stir-fry until they are well mixed. Cover, reduce heat, and cook until the vegetables are tender. Stir in the pumpkin, cool, package, and freeze.

• To make chili, add canned beans, canned tomatoes, and chili powder to taste. Pass the hot sauce.
• To make hamburger soup, cook the mixture with canned chicken broth, diced potatoes and diced, mixed vegetables. Add a can of diced tomatoes if you like.
• To make hamburger stew, cook a pot of diced potatoes, sliced carrots, and quartered onions until tender. Drain almost all the water. Stir in the meat mixture and season to taste. To make a thicker gravy, stir a little cornstarch or instant-blending flour into cold water and stir into the simmering stew until it clears and thickens.
• To make Sloppy Joe, stir canned tomato sauce into the meat mixture, heat, and spoon into buns.

Cowboy Campfire Coffee

1 cup perc-grind coffee

2 quarts water

This is traditionally made in an old-fashioned, enameled steel coffee pot, but any tall, thin pot will do. Put the coffee in a pot with all but one cup of the water. Bring it to a hard boil, then turn down the flame and simmer 2 minutes. Remove from the heat and slowly add the last cup of water, which will settle the grounds. Let it stand 3 minutes, then pour into cups, taking care not to disturb the grounds in the bottom.

Stirrup Biscuits

You'll find heavy cream, or whipping cream, in the refrigerated dairy shelf. Kept cold, it can keep for several weeks. Note use-by dates.

2 1/2 cups self-rising flour or
2 1/2 cups flour plus 1 tablespoon baking powder and 1 teaspoon salt

1 tablespoon sugar (more or less to taste)
2 cups (1 pint) cold, heavy cream

Stir together the dry ingredients and stir in the cream.
If you have an oven: Preheat the oven to 400 degrees, grease a pan that will fit the oven, and drop the biscuits by the scoop (about 1/4 cup each) onto the pan. Allow about an inch between them to allow for spreading. Bake 18-20 minutes or until golden brown.
If you have no oven: Grease a cold, cast aluminum skillet. Drop the biscuits by scoops onto the cold pan, then cover, place over a medium flame, and bake 6-10 minutes or until one side is browned. Turn the biscuits and press gently to flatten only slightly (biscuits will be heavy if you force out all the air), cover, and bake another 3-4 minutes. Turn again, cover, and bake another 2-3 minutes. Biscuits should be golden brown on both sides, and done in the middle. Break one to be sure. Serve hot.

Potato Pan Dandy

This meatless main dish can be served for breakfast or supper. Use a non-stick skillet and you'll have no pan to wash. Just wipe it clean with a paper towel.

3 tablespoons olive oil
Medium onion, diced
3 cloves garlic, mashed
16-ounce can whole potatoes, drained and quartered

8 eggs, shaken to mix*
Salt, pepper
1 pint cherry tomatoes, cut in half
1/2 cup grated Parmesan cheese

Sizzle the onion, garlic, and potatoes in the hot olive oil over medium heat until the onion and garlic are tender. Reduce the flame. Pour in the eggs, shower with salt and pepper, scatter with the tomatoes and sprinkle with the cheese. Cover and cook over low flame until the eggs are set. Using a coated utensil that won't damage the non-stick skillet, cut into wedges and serve. Serves 4.

Variations: Add 2-3 tablespoons real bacon bits when you add the tomatoes
• Spice it up by adding a teaspoon of dried Italian seasonings with the salt and pepper
• Use grated Cheddar cheese or jalapeno pepper-jack cheese instead of Parmesan

• You can whisk the eggs in a bowl, but you will have less dishwashing if you use a jar with a tight-fitting lid, preferably a jar that was able to go into the recycle bin anyway.

Soups and Stews

Corn Chowder Et Cetera

Make it meatless, or add canned tuna or chunk chicken. The "et cetera" part is the way you can make this a little different each time.

4-6 slices bacon or 2 tablespoons olive oil
Large onion, diced
2 medium potatoes, scrubbed and diced or
16-ounce can whole potatoes, drained and quartered
Pinch dried thyme (optional)
Water
2 tablespoons cornstarch
1/3 cup nonfat dry milk
1 cup water

16- or 17-ounce can cream-style corn
1 can evaporated milk
Salt, pepper
Optional additions:
12-ounce pouch tuna in water or
10-ounce can chunk chicken or
16-ounce can salmon, drained and picked over
8-ounce can peas and carrots, drained
Butter

Fry out the bacon and pour off all but a tablespoon or two of the fat. Set bacon aside on paper towels to drain, then cut into small bits. Or, start with the olive oil. Stir-fry the potatoes and onions in the hot fat, add thyme, and add enough water just to cover. Cover and simmer over low flame until the vegetables are tender. Mix the cornstarch and dry milk, then gradually add water to make a paste. Stir into the chowder with the bacon, corn, evaporated milk, and other ingredients you choose to and stir constantly over low flame until it bubbles and thickens. (Watch for burning. Milk scorches easily.) Thin with milk or water if it's too thick for your taste.   Place a pat of butter, if desired, into each soup plate and add chowder. This makes 4-6 servings. Complete the menu with pilot crackers and apple butter, canned bean salad served in bathroom-size plastic or paper cups, and a dessert of golden Delicious apples and a pocketful of chocolate kisses to eat on a sunset hike.

Expandable Brunswick Stew

Ever since pioneer days, Brunswick Stew has been a kettle classic. To make it from scratch, you need three meats including at least one game meat such as squirrel or rabbit, plus lima beans and cream-style corn. They're what make it Brunswick Stew.

This is a recipe for the 21st century, one you can expand to feed a crew or a crowd. For larger batches, introduce a third meat such as canned pork or beef in gravy and chunk turkey in addition to the chicken and ham. Canned corned beef can also be used sparingly, no more than one can per triple batch. It's salty, so be skimpy with seasonings. This recipe serves four but is easily multiplied. If you do the math, large, economy-size cans can be used.

15- or 16-ounce can lima beans, divided
1 quart water
10-ounce can chunk chicken
6-ounce can chunk ham
15- or 16-ounce can diced tomatoes
Medium potato, scrubbed and diced

Small onion, peeled and diced
15-ounce can cream style corn
Salt, pepper, and a tiny pinch of sugar
Butter (optional)
Hot sauce

Place half the limas and their juice in a kettle with the water and mash the limas. Break up the chicken and ham with a fork and add them, with the juice. Add the tomatoes, potato and onion. Bring to a boil over medium flame, cover, reduce heat, and simmer until the potato and onion are tender. Stir in the corn, remaining limas, sugar, and salt and pepper to taste and heat gently until it's thoroughly hot. (Watch it! It can burn easily after the corn is added.) Place a pat of butter in each soup bowl and ladle in the soupy stew. Pass the hot sauce.

Ham 'n Tatters

Start out with the frozen potatoes in the ice chest, keep them cold, and use within two days after they thaw. If you buy mayonnaise in small jars and use the entire jar at once, you don't have to worry about measuring or spoilage.

1-pound canned ham, cut into bite-size chunks
28-ounce package frozen hashed brown potatoes, thawed
10 3/4-ounce can condensed cream soup (mushroom, chicken, celery, broccoli)

8-ounce jar mayonnaise, regular or diet
1/2 cup milk
4-ounce package shredded Cheddar or jack cheese

In a heavy, cold, sprayed skillet, spread the ham and potatoes. In a bowl, whisk together the soup, mayonnaise, and milk and spread over the ham mixture. Place over low-medium flame with a flame tamer and bake, tightly covered, about 30 minutes or until everything is bubbly. Sprinkle with the cheese, turn off the fire, cover, wait 5 minutes then spoon onto serving plates.

Complete the meal with crunchy baby carrots, celery sticks, cherry tomatoes, pickle spears, and crusty chunks of Cuban bread.

Corn on the cob steams carefree on the grate in a foil packet, the perfect side dish.

Jambalaya

Take a simple meal of chicken and rice and add sausage for spicy flavor, and you have a meaty, one-dish feast for 6-8 campers.

2 cans, 10 ounces each, chunk chicken, undrained
1 tablespoon oil
Medium onion, diced
3 ribs celery, diced
Medium green bell pepper, diced
16-ounce packaged fully cooked smoked sausage, cut into bite size pieces
2 cups raw rice
2 cans, 10 1/2 ounces each, chicken broth or
1 can chicken broth and 1 can diced tomatoes with their juice
Salt, pepper to taste

Drain the chicken into a 4-cup measure. In a large pot, heat the oil and sizzle the onion, celery and pepper. Stir in the sausage, canned chicken and rice. Add the chicken broth and tomatoes to the measure and add water until it's full to the 4-cup mark (one quart). Stir the liquid into the meat mixture, reduce flame, cover tightly, and simmer 20-30 minutes or until the rice is tender. Spoon onto serving plates and complete the menu with crisp bread sticks, cut-up raw vegetables with a creamy dip, and Pineapple Fried Eggs for dessert.

Big Chief Make-Ahead Ham and Macaroni

Double or quadruple this recipe at home, then freeze it in batches, using boilable bags. It's a great way to use leftovers from a big ham. It keeps up to four days in the ice chest. To heat, just vent the bag and lower it into a pot of boiling water. At the same time, heat your favorite boil-in-the-bag vegetable(s). No pots to wash!

8-ounce package pasta twists
8 ounces cooked ham, diced
4 ounces grated Cheddar cheese
1 cup frozen peas
1 can cream of celery soup
Take along: Small can French's Taste Toppers™ French-fried onions

Cook the pasta according to package directions. Drain and fold in the remaining ingredients except the onions. Divide into boilable bags (e.g. Reynolds roasting bags, Seal-a-Meal bags) and freeze. Heat, spoon onto serving plates, then sprinkle with crisp onion topping. To make this dish in camp, cook the pasta, drain off excess water, fold in the ham, cheese, peas and soup, and cover. Cook a few minutes over very low flame until everything is heated through. Spoon onto plates and sprinkle each portion with crispy onions.

French's

A variation on an old favorite, macaroni and cheese with ham, is to add a vegetable and a crisp topping.

Pineapple Fried Eggs with Spicy Salsa

Fool the eye with these sunny-side up desserts. The donut hole becomes the "yolk" and the redhots and syrup are your spicy salsa.

Large can sliced pineapple in its own juice
Squeeze bottle of strawberry syrup

1 package donut holes
Small package redhot candies

Drain the pineapple, saving the juice for another purpose. Put a thin layer of strawberry syrup in a large, nonstick skillet. Add the pineapple slices in a single layer (or stack two slices for a larger dessert). Place a donut hole in the center of each. Cover and heat gently just until it's warmed through. Remove each pineapple "egg" to a serving plate, sprinkle with a few redhots, then drizzle with more strawberry syrup.

Creamy Rice Pudding

If you have a pressure cooker, this can be ready in minutes, and it cooks off the burner. It's delicious for breakfast, or bring the cooker to full pressure just before you sit down to dinner, and the pudding will be ready for a hot dessert. You don't add sugar. The dried fruit and condensed milk add all the sweetness needed.

1 cup raw rice
2 tablespoons butter
1 1/2 cups water
14-ounce can evaporated milk
1/2 teaspoon cinnamon

1/4 teaspoon nutmeg
1/2 cup dried cranberries, cherries, or raisins
1 can sweetened condensed milk
1 teaspoon vanilla

In a pressure cooker, melt the butter over medium heat. Stir in the rice to coat the grains. Stir in the water, evaporated milk, cinnamon and nutmeg. Lock on the lid and bring the cooker to full pressure, then turn off the fire. Let pressure return to normal of its own accord, then remove the lid. Stir in the dried fruit, condensed milk and vanilla. Cover again (do not lock) and let stand 5 minutes. Stir and spoon into dishes. Serves 4-6.

Note: This is tricky to make without a pressure cooker because milk burns easily. Proceed as above, using a flame tamer or a double boiler to cook the rice 20 minutes or until it's tender. Then stir in the other ingredients.

Gordon Groene

Complete menus can be made entirely from foods you can carry without refrigeration. This meal consists of cold asparagus vinaigrette, mashed potatoes, salmon patties, green beans with almonds, and tapioca pudding garnished with coconut and pineapple wedges.

When You Need a Stretcher

Here are some ways to stretch a skimpy meal when rations run low.

• **Cream it.** Make a basic white sauce with two tablespoons instant blend flour, a cup of milk, and salt and pepper to taste. Cream cooked or canned vegetables, canned or leftover cooked meats, hard-boiled eggs, dried beef, or smoked or canned fish, and serve over toast or biscuits.

• If the steaks or chops are too small for tonight's appetites, or if the burgers look too thin, top each portion with a slice of **cheese** or a sizzling-hot **fried egg**.

• **To stretch a small catch,** have on hand a selection of canned oysters, shrimp, crab, tuna, salmon, and lobster. Use as much as necessary with whatever bits of fish you have to make a sensational chowder. The more varieties of seafood it contains, the better it tastes.

• **Make a salad side dish from your pantry shelf.** Canned vegetables that make good cold salads when tossed with a simple vinaigrette include drained green beans, Mexi-corn, drained baby carrots, or green beans with potatoes. Put together well-drained green beans, black beans, and kidney beans for a calico salad. Canned, stewed tomatoes can be doctored up with grated cheese, croutons, or minced sweet onion.

• **Powdered milk** doesn't win popularity contests as a beverage, but it can be used for cooking or made into cocoa. Add chocolate or fruit-flavored syrup to make a shake. Use it to make instant puddings. To stretch supplies of fresh milk, add up to 50 percent reconstituted dry milk. Chill thoroughly.

• **Make soup.** Many dishes can be turned into soup by adding a can of this and that. Make chili into a hearty soup by adding tomato juice and another can of beans. Make chicken chowder by adding chicken broth and a can of chunk chicken to scalloped potatoes. Make minestrone by combining canned tomatoes, kidney beans, spaghetti sauce and broken spaghetti. Keep bottled clam broth on hand and add canned seafood and condensed potato soup to make chowder.

If any soup is too thick, thin it with juice, bouillon, or broth. If it's too thin, thicken with instant blending flour, potato flakes, or cornstarch, made into a paste first with a little water before adding to the hot liquid.

• **Smother it with cheese.** Meat or eggs loom larger when you make cheese sauce, or simply lay a square of process cheese on top and let it melt. Make a cheese sauce for toast and you have a rarebit.

• **Nuts to you!** Use walnuts to stretch chicken salad, peanuts to add crunch and bulk to cole slaw, slivered almonds to green beans, or pecan meal to stretch ground chicken or turkey to make burgers or meatloaf.

• **Wrap it in dough.** Keep extra crescent roll in your cooler to make strombolis, pasties, pigs-in-a-blanket, meat pies, or tarts. You can also seal small bits of meat or vegetables in egg roll wrappers, which keep well in a cooler. Steam, drop into boiling broth, or deep fry. Wheat tortillas also keep well in the freezer, and can be used to wrap meat, cheese or vegetables.

Reynolds

Reynolds

Line camp pots in foil for baking or warming leftovers so the pan doesn't get dirty

Camp Stove Smarts

☐ Check out the stove and other equipment before you leave home, not just to confirm that everything is in working order but to re-familiarize yourself with knobs and buttons. In camp, you will be working under more difficult conditions. Don't light the campstove or stoke up the campfire until you've checked fuel, filled the fuel tank or stacked up firewood, and are ready to give the fire your undivided attention. Once the flame is burning, it's important to make full use of it to save fuel, get the meal together seamlessly so everything comes hot to the table at once, and prevent accidents to the food, people, or nearby gear.

☐ Before lighting up, line up the pots you want to use, and grease or oil them if necessary. Chop and dice. Open cans and bottles. Measure ingredients so they are ready to dash into the pot. (Bathroom-size paper cups are ideal containers for small amounts of herbs and other ingredients.)

☐ Take a cue from television cooks, who have everything ready when the camera rolls. Find pot holders, and have hot pads or trivets ready for any hot pots you need to remove from the stove. (Pot shuffling, when you have a two-burner stove, is an art.) Have serving dishes handy, and the table set with everything but the plates of hot food. Then, let 'er rip!

☐ A watched pot does boil eventually, but it will come to a boil faster if you leave the lid on. You'll use less fuel too.

☐ It's always wise to have a bucket of water or sand, a fire extinguisher, and/or a box of baking soda handy to the cooking area. Never throw water on a gas or electric stove.

TOP TIP According to the Bertolli people, light olive oil can be substituted for butter. When a recipe calls for 1/4 cup butter, use 3 tablespoons olive oil or substitute 3/4 cup olive oil for a cup of butter. It makes for delicious muffins and cakes, and it can be mixed with a whisk instead of having to cream butter and sugar using elbow power.

A Natural High

Cooking at high altitudes is different from cooking at sea level. The water that boils at 212 degrees F. at sea level, bubbles at 208 degrees at 2,000 feet, 203 degrees at 5,000 feet, 198 degrees at 7,500 feet, and 194 degrees at 10,000 feet. If you're just heating water for coffee or to rehydrate freeze-dried foods, it is merely a difference in temperature, but leavened foods such as pancakes or muffins will need less baking powder or baking soda. Up to about 3,000 feet, you probably won't notice much difference. Just don't whip too much air into the batter. However, above 3,000 feet it's time to start reducing the amount of leavening. Above 7,000 feet, meat will probably need a longer cooking time. Pressure cooking also requires adjustments.

First, read labels. Most commercial mixes have high altitude instructions on the package, and your pressure cooker cookbook explains high altitude cooking. (You may need a special pressure regulator gauge, which can be ordered from the manufacturer.) If you'll be doing a lot of camping at high altitude, get a specialty cookbook, or contact a county extension home economist in the area for special instructions.

No Pot to Hiss In

It takes courage to try it the first time, but you can cook many foods directly on the embers of a wood fire. Foil-wrapped baking potatoes, tossed into a fire, come out perfectly roasted in about 45 minutes. Choose large potatoes, scrub, prick, and wrap well. After 35 minutes, test one. If you don't eat the skins anyway, you don't even need the foil. Steaks, plain or dipped first into a pan with a thick layer of salt, can also be placed directly atop an even bed of glowing embers of a wood fire. (This isn't recommended for charcoal). Ashes and salt brush away, leaving a juicy, tasty steak. Use tongs for handling steaks. Whole, gutted fish can also be roasted on wood coals, but it's best to use a grill basket for easier handling.

Better Safe Than Sorry

Food safety experts say, "When in doubt, throw it out," but my brother's scout troop put it more colorfully, "Better to throw it out than throw it up." Food safety concerns have mushroomed in recent years because organisms have gotten smarter, faster, and more resistant to antibiotics. Where a temperature range of 40-45 degrees F. used to be considered safe, authorities now say that 40 degrees is a minimum, and some chefs never let their refrigerators fall below 38 degrees. Tyson Foods recommends keeping raw chicken at a maximum of 40 degrees, preferably colder.

Here's how to keep your family safe:

• Keep a thermometer in the ice chest. Don't expect it to keep fresh meat, salads made with mayonnaise, or leftovers the way they'd keep at home. Strive to keep fresh foods close to 40 degrees.

• Rely on canned meats, fully cooked vac-pac meats and sausages, and meats that you freeze at home to be cooked as soon as they thaw. Better still, cook and freeze meats at home both for safety and convenience. If you carry raw meat, think of its juices as a poison that could contaminate other foods. Don't store meat where juices can drip onto fruits and vegetables. Don't put cooked meat on the same platter that held the meat when raw. Marinades should be cooked or discarded after contact with raw meat.

• Defrost in the ice chest, never at "room" temperature.

• Wash your hands before and after working with raw meat and any time during meal preparation after

Why wash pots when grilled vegetables taste so good?

Gordon Groene

you blow your nose, change the baby, or otherwise introduce harmful organisms.

• Clean the cutting board with soapy water and/or bleach and a thorough rinse. Use one side for fruits and vegetables that will be eaten raw, the other side for raw meat. Don't use a sponge or dishcloth for cleaning after it has touched a place where raw meat has been.

• Buy an instant-reading meat thermometer to use as you cook. Here are what readings you should get, according to the American Dietetic Association. Take the reading in the thickest part of the meat or casserole, away from bone, fat, and gristle.

Type of Meat	Degrees F.
Beef, Veal, Lamb	
Ground	160
Whole roast, steak, medium rare	145
Medium	160
Well done	170
Poultry	
Ground	170
Whole	180
Boneless roasts	170
Dark Meat including whole duck	180
Stuffing, alone or in bird	165
Pork	160-170
Fully cooked ham	140
Egg dishes	160
Leftovers	165

Cut Down on Dishwashing and Mess

While responsible camping calls for fewer disposables, there are times when water itself is far more precious than the small amounts of paper, foil or plastic you could use to avoid cleanup. My own camping has occurred in areas where:

• Unlimited water is available for drinking and cleanup.

• Drinking water is limited, but unlimited water is available for dishwashing. If it's lake or river water, it may need filtering, boiling or the addition of chlorine to make it clean enough for sanitizing dishes. In some cases, it's sea water. Clean ocean water is fine for washing dishes but a freshwater rinse is recommended because salt leaves behind a sticky residue. It also rusts steel and can even leave rust stains on some grades of so-called stainless steel.

• All water has to be brought along.

Each situation calls for different planning and different economies of water usage, but here are some ways to cheat on dishwashing and allow more time for camping fun.

• Buy nonstick pots and take care of them well. Most will clean up with paper towels.

A pot with a strainer insert is handy for boiling or deep-frying.

Gordon Groene

Have a Great Lakes Fish Boil

It's a delicious meal in one pot. Bring heavily salted water to a hard boil, add scrubbed potatoes and bring to a hard boil again. When the potatoes are almost tender, drop in corn. As soon as the water is boiling hard again, drop in fillets of fish just until they turn white and firm. It's essential to have water at a rolling boil to sear and seal the fish.

Foil baking bags make it easy to bag complete meals for the grill.

Create a Stir!

Stir-fry dishes are a boon for camp cooks because all the cutting can be done ahead of time, in home or in camp. Once you start the stove, everything cooks in a few minutes. Cook rice on the second burner and you have a full meal. This recipe is deliberately vague so you can make it every day and still have a different dish. If you start with raw meat, it's easiest to cut it into very small slices while it's half frozen. Or, use cooked beef, pork, or chicken or your own, fresh-caught fish. For vegetables, choose the most colorful variety. Cut slow-cooking vegetables, such as carrots, into paper-thin slices. Everything should be crisp-tender.

2 tablespoons cooking oil, preferably peanut oil
2-3 cloves garlic
1 pound meat, poultry or fish, cut into small pieces
4 cups vegetables in bite-size pieces (squash, onions, red and green sweet pepper, scallions, fresh bean sprouts, eggplant, shredded cabbage, etc.)

1 cup water
2 tablespoons cornstarch
Optional items:
A little grated, fresh ginger or
1 teaspoon toasted sesame oil or
Chili paste to taste
Soy Sauce

Heat the oil with the garlic in a wok until the garlic is fragrant. Keeping the burner at its hottest, stir in the meat or fish, stirring constantly, then stir in the vegetables. Don't add foods too quickly. Keep the pan fiery-hot. Stir the cornstarch into the water.

When the meat is done and vegetables crisp-tender, stir in the cornstarch mixture until it boils and clears. Add any optional items. Serve over hot rice and pass the soy sauce.

Learn to wrap heavy duty foil to make leak-proof packets to place in the ashes or on the grate.

A bushel of oysters and a campfire add up to an oyster roast. Oysters pop open and are eaten right from the shell.

Many dishes can be cooked in a wok, which is a good pan to use on a camp stove because it is very thin and has a small bottom for good contact with the heat.

A new, nonstick foil is ideal for cooking or covering some-mores, spaghetti, and other sticky foods.

It isn't necessary to refrigerate regular (not soft or liquid) margarine. Buy margarine in sticks, let it come to room temperature, press into clean containers, and keep it in the coolest place available.

Don't rely on freeze-dried foods you haven't rehearsed at home first. Some reconstitute ready to eat; others are rehydrated and then cooked. Manufacturers' definition of a "serving" may be your idea of starvation rations.

Life Without Refrigeration

During the 10 years when my husband and I lived full-time on the go, spending months at a time on remote, tropical islands, we soon learned that it was easier to manage without ice or refrigeration than to spend all the time and money necessary to keep ourselves supplied with ice or energy to run a refrigerator. It's less of a problem for campers who can simply buy fresh ice at the camp store every day, or who camp in areas where nature supplies refrigeration, but here are tips for those who want to live with less ice or no ice at all:

• Long before refrigeration was invented, people ate cheese, yogurt, pickles, jams, sausages, jerky, pemmican, and other foods that were preserved by natural means.

• Pay special attention to cleanliness when you have little or no cooling. Use a clean spoon to dip into jelly, a clean knife to dip into peanut butter. Don't lick utensils and put them back into a jar.

• Buy small sizes of ketchup, relish, pickles, mustard, preserves and other condiments and use them up.

• Eggs keep up to several months without refrigeration, depending on how old they were at purchase. For longer keeping, rub uncooked eggs with margarine or oil. This seals the shells, which are porous, and keeps eggs fresh longer.

• Take a clue from the supermarket, where you'll find some sausages and cheeses on the shelf. If the market didn't refrigerate it, you don't have to either.

• Strictly observe labels, use-by dates, and any instructions to "refrigerate after opening."

• Discover new ways of doing things. Make vinegar-and-oil salad dressing as needed. Try freeze-dried eggs and cottage cheese, unusual canned foods you don't use at home (e.g. bean salad, Boston brown bread, tortillas all come in cans), and shop the supermarket with fresh eyes. You'll find things there you've overlooked before, and at everyday prices.

• Plan more carefully. Eliminate leftovers.

CHAPTER

Housekeeping Under the Sky

Chores that are drudgery at home don't seem nearly as burdensome when you do them in camp. Everyone pitches in with a pioneer spirit, hauling and heating water, tidying up, tending the fire, stowing and spiffing things up. Let's talk about cleaning and coping in the campsite.

Talking Trash

In camp, cleanliness is more than neatness. Bits of food, packaging, and other trash attract animals and bugs. A bear can smell the greasy film on your campstove from miles away; raccoons will figure out a way to get at your carrot peelings if it takes all night. Cleanliness is a survival tool.

In fly-weight camping, in which everything is packed in and packed out, seal garbage in plastic bags and hang it between two trees or secure it in the food cache if one is provided at the campsite. If the burying of biodegradable trash is permitted, dig a hole well removed from your tent site, high above any tide or high water line, and cover it well with soil. Then replace the ground cover as close as possible to the way it looked before. Some campsites, even in the most primitive settings, provide containers for trash that is collected regularly by park personnel. Make sure you replace and secure the lid properly.

Don't leave anything out overnight, not even in your screen room. A hungry, determined, wild animal can get into almost any camping containers including locked ice chests and plastic boxes with simple, lock-on lids. At best, it can make a mess. At worst, screens could be ripped and ice chests battered.

Coming Clean

Here are some clean-up tips for the campsite:
• Carry a turf-type doormat to place in front of the tent door. It will scrape off a lot of dirt, wet or dry. Carpet samples also make good doormats and are cheap enough to be discarded after a campout or two. If yours is a truck or pop-up camper, one that requires a step up to enter, use an overturned milk crate as the step. Debris from your shoes falls through to the ground.
• An old-fashioned whisk broom takes little space, yet effectively sweeps out a tent, brushes crumbs off the picnic table, and whisks loose, dry dirt off boots. If you carry a small, rechargeable, fully charged vacuum cleaner, it will clean the tent for up to a week on one charge.
• If you can rig a clothes line that is sturdy enough, throw the tent over it after taking it down, and beat off loose dirt. Ditto with the ground cloth.
• Inexpensive bamboo beach mats can be placed on the tent floor as throw rugs. They are light to carry, smell fragrantly of sea grass, and are easily rolled up for storage and shaken to clean. They're cheap enough to discard when they get worn or stained. Buy a good supply at the end of summer at sell-out prices.
• Don't wear trousers or shorts with cuffs. They pick up chaff, sticklers and debris, which ends up in your tent or sleeping bag.
• Buy inexpensive, flannel-back, vinyl tablecloths on sale for use on the campsite's picnic table. The plastic wipes clean, can be spread over gear if it rains, and can be machine-washed when you get home.

Rub-a-Dub-Dub: The Laundry

Everything you packed so carefully into your camp kit and arranged so neatly in tent and campsite is thrown into a frenzy after the first night, when you peel off the first pair of dirty socks and realize you need a place to keep laundry. If you stay out long enough, you'll also need to *do* laundry.

Start out with an empty bag, preferably two, for dirty clothes – one for whites, one for colors. Large, canvas "ice" bags sold by boating and camping suppliers are sturdiest and best, with hefty handles so you can hang them up. Or, sew up your own using a sturdy fabric such as denim or duck. You don't have to be a tailor. Just zip up a couple of big sacks, hem them, and sew on some handles. When the bags are full and you're in a campground with a coin laundry, simply throw a compressed detergent "pill" into each bag, empty the whole thing into the machines, feed in your quarters, and sit back with a good book while your clothes clean themselves.

If you wash by hand, a bucket will do for small loads or, if you are in the boondocks for a lengthy period and must do large loads including towels, sleeping bag liners or sheets, carry an inflatable, child-size swimming pool and a toilet plunger. Fill the pool with water, soap and clothes, let them soak 20 minutes, then plunge away to remove stubborn dirt. Wring, rinse, wring, rinse again, and wring one last time.

Another way to wash effortlessly is to place clothes, water, and soap in a lidded trash container that has a

Shurhold Industries

Soap and water are part of camping life, but don't wash a vehicle in the campground without permission. Run-off of road salts and chemicals can harm park plants.

lock-on lid, and drive for a couple of hours. Give them a rinse or two and they're ready to dry.

• Observe campground rules. Clotheslines may not be permitted.

• Carry a good supply of sturdy clothes pins, preferably spring-loaded wooden pins, for the best grip. Even if you don't do laundry, you'll probably be drying wet towels and swim suits.

• Don't trust an expensive sleeping bag or other garment to a coin washer or dryer you haven't tried before. A dryer could have little burrs or could have just been used by someone whose kids left crayons in their pockets. The washer could be hooked up to water that stains or is too cold or hot.

• Keep a good supply of coins on hand just in case you find a coin laundry. You may need just the dryers if your tent leaks and wets the sleeping bags. A film canister is the perfect size to hold a stack of quarters.

• Keep a stain stick handy to treat stains as you remove garments to the laundry bag.

• Detergent tablets are lighter and less messy to take along than liquids. Fill a snack-size plastic bag with scented fabric softener sheets to take, too. A couple of these sheets and a run-through in the dryer on low heat will perk up a musty sleeping bag.

• Clean sea water can be used to do laundry. Powdered detergents don't make suds, but liquids do. So does Vel bar soap. Rinse several times with salt water, then do at least one fresh-water rinse so no salt remains. If you don't, the salt draws moisture back out of the night air and garments will feel clammy.

• There is another solution to the laundry problem and that is simply to discard garments and towels as you go. As you fold the laundry at home, set aside underwear, tea towels, socks and other items that are good for one more use and take them camping. When they are soiled, put them in the trash. You'll go home with a lighter load.

• Don't laugh at the suggestion that tea towels for camping be starched and ironed. They'll stay fresh twice as long as towels that you just wash, dry, and fold. Try it on your next campout.

• Sleeping bags will stay fresh longer if you use inner liners. Some bags have inner sheets, attached by Velcro. If yours doesn't, sew up a percale envelope that will slip inside the bag. Travel specialty catalogs such as Magellan's also carry silk sleeping bag liners. Silk takes up almost no room. It washes like a handkerchief and dries swiftly.

• Even if you're able to keep ice chests cold by adding new ice, empty them at least once a week and clean with a chlorine solution. Bits of food, paper labels, and other contaminants take on a life of their own.

TOP TIP

Improper cleaning can shorten your tent's life, ruin its looks, compromise its water repellency, and/or destroy the fire retardant. Follow manufacturer's directions for tent care.

C H A P T E R

How Green Was My Valley: Responsible Camping

Most of us think we're pretty good citizens when it comes to the outdoors, but there is more to "green" camping than simply picking up after yourself at the campsite. Here is a checklist of ideas to make your campout less intrusive on the environment.

__ First, don't lay a guilt trip on yourself. Whether you're camping in a pup tent or a Class A motorhome, you are using less energy that if you were at home using heat, air conditioning, and an arsenal of appliances.

__ When checking in at a campground or wilderness area, ask to use an area that can best tolerate human impact under today's conditions. Impact takes a different toll at different times depending on rainfall, the state of any seasonal growth, wildlife migrations/nesting, or fire danger.

__ Try to avoid camping during high-use times such as weekends and holidays.

__ Pre-cook, pre-plan, and pre-package foods to minimize cooking and trash.

__ Choose equipment (except for safety gear) in colors that will blend with the natural environment.

__ Report illegal dumpers, poachers, and polluters to the toll-free hot lines that are available in most wilderness areas. They are stealing your children's legacy.

__ Mix your own drinks using powders or concentrates, rather than using canned sodas. Carry fresh fruits and vegetables. Buy wood and fabric camp chairs, and paint and re-seat them as necessary. Protect camping equipment from rust, corrosion, sun fade, mildew and other destroyers. Make things last.

__ Observe the laws of aerodynamics. The more luggage, storage pods, boats, bikes, and other junk you hang on the roof of your car or the back of the van, the less fuel efficient it becomes. Travel light.

__ Never forget that you and your pets are the outsiders here. Nature and its creatures come first. __ Recycle just as religiously as you do at home, but observe campground rules. Each area separates recyclables differently.

__ Don't hang lanterns on trees. High heat can blister the bark, creating breaks where disease or insects can enter. Bring lantern posts that stick in the ground.

Gordon Groene

The heat of a lantern can damage tree bark, inviting borers or disease.

Paths, steps, boardwalks and other trail features have been placed where they are to protect the terrain. Stay with the trail.

Gordon Groene

__If you have room to carry a screen room for daytime living, in addition to the snug tent for the night, you won't have to use bug sprays. Fly paper can still be bought in familiar coils. If flies are a problem, try hanging it around the perimeter of the campsite.

__Don't carry a boom box or anything else that will disturb nature's sound track. An exception, of course, is noisemakers that may be required for search and rescue. Talk and walk quietly. The quieter you are, the more you'll be rewarded with wildlife sightings and sounds. An exception is bear country, where you may be advised by rangers to wear bells and make a racket.

__ Keep a safe distance between yourself and other hikers, so branches released by one don't snap back and injure the next person in line. Walk single file in the center of the trail. Keep groups small, six or less, and don't disturb plants, rocks, or other trail surfaces any more than necessary.

__Buy nonstick cookware that wipes clean in most instances without dishwashing.

__ Carry a good supply of freshly laundered rags to use in camp as dish towels and cleaning cloths instead of paper towels. Favor natural fabrics (linen, cotton), which are the best rags and will also decompose in landfills.

__ Carry foods in natural packaging: garlic by the braid, nuts in the shell, sausages in natural casings, cheese in wax coatings, eggs in their shells.

__ Don't use steel wool, sink cleanser or other cleaners that could leave residue on dishes or pots, especially if you're scrimping on rinse water. Baking soda is a food-quality abrasive. So is a cut lemon dipped in salt.

__ Don't flush chemicals that could kill helpful bacteria in the campground's septic system. The most common culprits are formaldehyde toilet deodorants, but even leftover medications, especially antibiotics, could interfere with the natural decomposition.

__ Even if you think you know a better or easier way, stay with the main trail. Rangers have probably designed it this way for a reason. Where switchbacks, boardwalks, steps, paving, and other design features have been added, don't shortcut them.

__ Try solar cooking and a solar sun shower.

__ Use tinder and kindling rather than chemicals, and dead wood from the forest rather than charcoal. Propane cooking is the most energy efficient, odor-free fuel.

__ Don't put anything in the campfire that won't burn away to clean ash.

__ In choosing a primitive campsite, stay out of sight of the trail and other campers, and a good distance away from springs and other water sources that are used by wildlife. If a campsite appears over-used, pass it by. One day's damage may take decades to heal.

__ Don't foul a natural water supply. Even "clean" rinse water should be dumped well away from drinking water sources. Use biodegradable cleaning agents. Don't dump cooking water on plants, even after it cools. It contains salts, herbs, and other things that may harm plants.

__ Don't cut or collect plants. Use only dead trees for firewood (where allowed). Don't discard anything in the wilderness, even a small piece of paper that you think will dissolve in the next rain storm.

__ Buy food, cleaners, and personal products in bulk and repackage them in reusable containers for camping. Remember, though, that not all plastics are food safe. Don't repackage edibles in soap dispensers or garbage bags.

__ In winter camping, don't wash a salty car where water runoff will damage nearby metals or plants.

__ Buy a different mug for each member of the family to cut down on dishwashing without using paper cups.

__ Buy as many things as possible in powdered, dehydrated, concentrated, dried, boneless, or compressed form so you don't spend fuel dollars hauling around packaging, bone, skin, and trash that will burden the campground environment.

__ Check local campfire laws daily. They can change from day to day according to weather conditions.

__Don't drive on fragile lands or walk on dunes or other threatened land. Once erosion begins, it may not be stoppable.

__ In the campground laundry, use cold water. Clean the washer and dryer filters before each use, and measure detergents and rinses, using no more than the manufacturers recommend.

__ Dispose of all chemicals, dead batteries, and other hazardous waste, worn out tires and tubes according to state or local law.

__ A pressure cooker saves time and fuel and in many instances is faster than a microwave.

__ Invest in a portable water filtration unit so you can have potable water without carrying heavy bottled water.

__ Don't drive nails into trees to hang clotheslines or hammocks.

__ Bring your own screw-type stake and put the dog's lead through that, rather than around a tree or shrub. Even the small abrasion caused by tying a pet or a clothesline to a tree could allow pests to get a foothold in tender bark.

__ Buy or repackage peanut butter, margarine, mustard, ketchup, mayonnaise, and jelly and other sandwich makings in squeeze containers or tubes. It's more sanitary to squeeze them onto the bread, and you won't have to wash extra spreaders and spoons.

__ Use rechargeable batteries; consider investing in a solar or hand-operated charger.

__ Buy refills for pump and spray type soaps and cleaners.

__ Buy eggs in bulk and carry them in reusable plastic egg carriers sold in camp supply stores.

__Redouble your water conservation efforts. Hot water drained from pasta can be saved for dishwashing. Water used to rinse dishes is slightly soapy, but can be used to do hand laundry.

__Remember your folks telling you time and again, "Look, don't touch"? It's still a good wilderness rule.

CHAPTER

Home, Sweet Homecoming

You've checked out of the campsite, notified rangers and everyone else who should be told that you're no longer Out There, and now you're safe at home.

Your camping trip isn't really over until all the gear has been cleaned, repaired, replaced, and stowed in readiness for the next campout. It's human nature to collapse in a heap at the end of a trip, wrapped in wonderful memories of the campout. Yet it can also be fun to keep one oar in the camping waters at all times, making camping an ongoing family project. Between trips you can plan new campouts, take courses in new outdoor skills, renew gear. Plan menus. Freeze dishes for future campouts. Watch for sales on gear you want to add or replace.

Sometime between now and your next camping trip, the sooner the better, here are steps to take:

• Immediately empty ice chests, clean with a bleach solution, dry thoroughly, and put away with the lids ajar and any removable plugs removed, so air can circulate.

Even the cleanest ice chest can get musty if it's stowed closed. If odors persist, fill the interior with loosely crumpled newspaper, a scattering of baking soda, or a few cups of kitty litter.

Periodically de-rust the stove with a wire brush to keep air passages open.

Gordon Groene

Your camping trip isn't really over until all the gear has been cleaned, repaired, replaced and stowed.

• Degrease the stove. The buildup will get more stubborn as time goes by, so attack it soon after you get home. Too, grease could seal in moisture and hasten rust. If yours is a liquid fuel stove, the best way to keep the carburetor from gumming is to burn off all the fuel on the last day of the campout. Store it with the tank empty.

• Even if you swept the tent and packed it dry at the campsite, it's good practice to get it out again once or twice a season. Set it up enough to vacuum the interior thoroughly, using a crevice tool to get into all corners and pockets and an upholstery brush attachment on the fabric, flies, and screens. Dirt takes a toll on fabric, abrading, and staining. Moisture is even worse. If mildew gets a start, it can eat, destroy, and leave odors that make the tent smell musty forever.

• Sleeping bags should be stowed clean and dry. If yours are washable or have removable sheets for easy laundering, get them into the first available wash load. Don't stow them again until they are bone dry.

• Inventory the medical kit. Replace supplies you used and get fresh medications for those that are past their use-by date.

• Sort through personal toiletries kits, remove anything that is damp, and refill with fresh soap, shampoo, wash cloth, and so on before the next campout.

• Be especially alert for any strange rashes or illnesses that pop up in your family or pets soon after your return, and tell the doctor or vet when and where you camped. One of my friends came down with an often-fatal tropical disease, one almost never seen in Canada, after returning home to Toronto from a camp-ing trip deep in the Amazon jungle. Fortunately, a family member remembered to tell her doctors where she had been. Quick diagnosis and treatment followed, and she survived. It could be very helpful to doctors to know that you just returned from a place where you could have been bitten by a tick that carries Lyme disease or a mosquito that carries malaria.

• Send for brochures. Make campground reservations weeks and even months ahead. The more homework you do on travel, history, flora and fauna, the richer your next camping trip will be.

• Start tucking away special treats for the next campout: little toys for the children, special recipes, or a book you want to read by lantern light.

• At our house, all garments get a thorough shake-out, then go into the washing machine. Ticks, redbugs, or other pests could be lurking even in clothing that was never worn.

• Put all galley gear through the dishwasher to remove grime that was missed in campground dishwashing. The harsh detergent and scalding water of a dishwasher also remove stains and discoloration that hand dishwashing cannot.

• Take all opened packages and bottles out of the pantry box and use leftovers in the kitchen as soon as possible. Even long-life foods were exposed to added heat, cold or moisture in the outdoors and will get stale faster.

• Plunge shower clogs into a bucket with a mild bleach solution. Soak, rinse, and dry. Nasty things may have been brought home from public showers.

• Wash and rinse swim suits in clean water to remove salt, chemicals, and other contaminants that could damage the fabric.

• Remove batteries from anything you're stowing for more than a week or two.

• Keep a running checklist of gear that has to be repaired or lost items that must be replaced.

PART

Camping on wheels

Saga

Chapter 23: Choosing A Wheeled Camper

Appendix 1: Great Places To Camp

Appendix 2: Useful Addresses and Recommended Reading

Bayside

CHAPTER

Choosing a Wheeled Camper

It happens to most of us sooner or later. The kids come along, or your bones long for a softer bunk, or maybe you just want to spend more time sightseeing or fishing and less time setting up a tent and cooking over a campfire. The transition to camping on wheels is a snap except for one thing. Now you must choose campsites that are accessible to a vehicle. That rules out all the secluded hideaways you camped when you walked or paddled in, but it also means you can hop into the car or camper when you want to go into town for provisions, drive a sightseeing loop of the area's best Civil War battlefields or treat yourself to a night out at summer theater or a square dance.

Basic Decisions

Your first decision is whether you'll drive the wheeled camper or tow it. Towables cost less because you're not buying an engine and transmission. In the off-season, store your travel trailer and forget it. When you reach a campsite, unhitch the camper and you now have a car for errands and sightseeing. **Towables** come in an enormous range of sizes, layouts, and prices from featherweight pop-ups that can be towed by an economy car to leviathans that need a powerful tow car or truck.

The disadvantage to any of them is the hassle of towing, backing, and parking. On the highway, you

With an SUV conversion, you can have the comforts of home off-road and on.

Sportsmobile

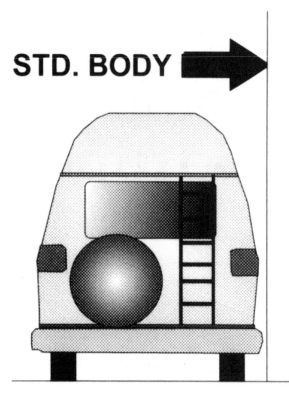

STD. BODY ➡

WIDE BODY ⬅ ➘

Great Western Van

Van conversions are available in wide-body models that drive like a car but sleep like a small motorhome. Fully equipped with sleepers, galley and a bath or partial bath, they sell for $50-$60,000.

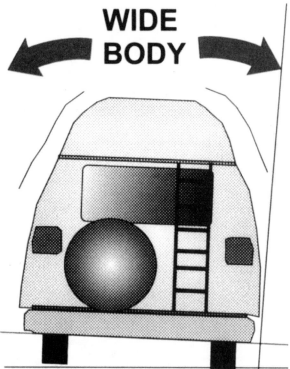

must drive slower, with more planning and care about changing lanes and maneuvering. Towing also means extra hazards on the highway, extra tires, extra tolls. When you stop for lunch, you have to get out in the rain to get into the trailer and, if it's a folding type, you won't have shelter until you get to the campground and set up. You can't park just anywhere. In fact, your homeowner association's rules may prohibit your parking your travel trailer in your own yard.

A driveable camper (van, pickup, station wagon, SUV) costs more to buy and maintain, but it can also be used year-round as your family van, personal car, or the pickup truck you use in your work. Some vans are fitted out as permanent campers; others have removable seats that allow a passenger van to be converted to a camper. A van camper, also called a Class B motorhome or van conversion, has all the comforts of home and it can also tow a small boat or a trailer for your PWCs or motorcycles. Another plus is that it's one unit. Pull over and make lunch, take a nap, or use the bathroom without having to leave the vehicle.

The disadvantage, in addition to cost, is that everything goes everywhere with you. When one family member wants to go into town, your entire household goes into town.

There are, of course, endless combinations: a pickup truck with a camper bed and towing a travel trailer; a van fitted out with a galley, towing a boat that has bunks; a 4WD that tows a pop-up tent trailer; a pop-up tent trailer that can be towed by Mom's car or Dad's.

Only you can decide what wheels are right for you.

Aliner

This little A-frame Sportliner is only 12 feet long with a hitch weight of 130 pounds yet it provides hard-side camping and indoor-outdoor living for up to four people. It's priced at under $7,000.

The 18-foot Cabin Cruiser is 18 feet long, has a hitch weight of 150 pounds, and can be furnished with an optional flush toilet, pressure water, air conditioning, outside shower, and other luxuries. Prices start at under $10,000.

Low-profile on the road and weighing only 450 pounds, the Aliner Truck Cabin fits the bed of a pickup truck. It's priced at under $4,000.

A Glossary of Wheeled Campers

Fifth Wheel is a trailer designed to be towed by a pickup truck fitted with a special connection. It's easier to tow than a travel trailer. Very luxurious models with slideouts are available.

Mobile Home is a term that causes a lot of confusion because it applies to what we now call manufactured housing. Wheeled campers are mobile and they can be homes, but they are not mobile homes.

Motorhome, a single unit that drives like a bus and lives like a fully-equipped house. A **Class A** motorhome, sometimes called a motor coach, may have a diesel or gasoline engine and is usually 21-40 feet long. A **Class C** motorhome, also called a mini-motorhome, is built on a truck chassis but could be as large or larger than some Class A's. You can walk from the cockpit to the living area. A **Class B** motorhome, also called a van conversion or camper van, is a van with living facilities that may include at least a partial bathroom, a raised roof for standing headroom, a slide-out or two, and a basic kitchen.

Pop-up, Fold-Down, or Folding Camper is a travel trailer that folds to form a very low profile for the road. Many models are small enough to be towed by a small car, yet they set up to make very spacious quarters. Most have at least some cooking facilities and some have a bath with shower.

Truck campers are priced from under $15,000, are available with layouts ranging from basic bunks to full living facilities, and can turn your everyday pickup truck into a camper.

Folding travel trailers tow easily and stow off season in a small space, yet they pop open to sleep four or more. Prices start at under $10,000.

Self-contained is an important word because it means full living facilities including a bathroom and holding tanks for sewage (black water) and sink and shower drainage (grey water). Many campgrounds don't have public toilets and showers, so tent campers and RVs that are not self-contained can't be accommodated.

Slide-outs are found on RVs of every size. They're sections that can be slid out like a dresser drawer, to increase interior space after the RV is set up in the camp-site. The slide-out could be in the kitchen, bedroom or living room or could be just a bay window. It isn't uncommon for an RV to have two or three slide-outs.

Travel Trailer is a towed trailer that could be anything from a soft-sided trailer that folds up for the road to a rolling home 40 feet long.

Truck Camper is put on the bed of a pickup truck. Most have bunks and at least some cooking facilities; some have a partial bathroom.

Jayco

Before You Buy

Before adding another set of wheels to your family stable, first get the towing-versus-driving decision settled, then consider:

• How many will it accommodate? How many will it sleep and how are bunks arranged?

• Is there a seat belt for everyone on board?

• Where will you park the camper when you aren't using it. If zoning doesn't permit parking it at your home, check out the cost of storage lots.

• Look beyond initial cost. There's also insurance, extra fuel and tolls, licenses, storage, equipment, and maintenance.

Jayco

Many tent campers make the transition into wheeled camping by buying a compact trailer that pops up and open to create a spacious camper that has a kitchen, perhaps a partial bath, and bunks for the family. Many models can be towed by economy cars.

APPENDIX

Camping Resources
Useful Information For Travelers

Travel Information By State and Province

Note: Some of the following telephone numbers answer only during business hours; some are automated and are able only to take your name and address for sending literature. Start with these contacts, then fine-tune your search to learn more about the regions you plan to visit and your special interests such as birding, mountain bicycling, or whitewater rafting as well as the right campsite. The trail can be a long one leading to departments that issue hunting and fishing permits, regional tourism agencies such as Pennsylvania Dutch Country or California Wine Country, and individual departments that handle state forests, state parks, and so on. Note that the state park guide issued by many states is not a complete guide to campgrounds; commercial campgrounds publish their own directory and each state also has many regional, county and city parks that offer camping.

Alabama Bureau of Tourism & Travel
P.O. Box 4927
Montgomery, AL 36103
800-ALABAMA, www.touralabama.org.

Alaska Division of Tourism
P.O. Box 110801
Juneau, AK 99811
(907) 465-2010, www.dced.state.ak.us/tourism/

Arizona Office of Tourism
2702 North 3rd St., Suite 4015
Phoenix, AZ 85004
(602) 230-7733, www.arizonaguide.com

Arkansas Department of Parks & Tourism
One Capitol Mall
Little Rock, AR 72291
800-NATURAL, www.arkansas.com
California Division of Tourism
P.O. Box 1499
Sacramento, CA 95812
(800) 862-2543, www.visitcalifornia.com
For state park campsite reservations only,
(800) 444-7275

Colorado Tourism Office
1625 Broadway, Suite 1700
Denver CO 80202
800-COLORADO or (303) 892-3885,
www.colorado.com

Connecticut Office of Tourism
505 Hudson St.
Hartford, CT 06106
800-CT-BOUND or (860) 270-8080

Delaware Tourism Office
99 Kings Highway
Dover, DE 19901
866-2-VISIT-DE or (302) 739-4272,
www.visitdelaware.com.

District of Columbia Convention & Tourism Corporation
1212 New York Ave. SW #600
Washington, DC 20005
(202) 789-7000, www.washington.org
(For information on camping, contact state tourism offices for Maryland, Pennsylvania, and Virginia. There are no campgrounds in the District itself, but many campgrounds in surrounding states offer tours or transportation into the capital.)

Florida Department of Environmental Protection, Parks Information
Mail Station 535, 3900 Commonwealth Blvd.
Tallahassee, FL 32399
(850) 488-9872, www.dep.state.fl.us/parks or
www.myflorida.com
Campground and cabin reservations in state parks,
(800) 326-3521
General tourism information, 800-7FLA-USA,
www.flausa.com

Also
Florida RV Trade Association
401 N. Parsons Ave., Suite 107
Brandon, FL 33510
Request the free campground guide, which lists only commercial campgrounds that are members of the Association.

Georgia Department of Tourism
285 Peachtree Center Ave. NE
Marquis Tower Two, Suite 1000
Atlanta, GA 30303
800-VISITGA or (404) 656-3590, www.georgia.org, also www.gastateparks.org

Hawaii Visitors & Convention Bureau
2270 Kalakaua Ave.
Honolulu, HI 96815
(808) 924-0260, www.GoHawaii.com

Idaho Travel Council
P.O. Box 83720
Boise, ID 83720
800-VISIT-ID, www.visitid.com

Illinois Department of Natural Resources
524 South Second St.
Springfield, IL 62701
(217) 782-2965
Also
Illinois Bureau of Tourism
100 West Randolph St.
Chicago, IL 60602
800-2-CONNECT, www.enjoyillinois.com

Indiana Tourism Division
1 North Capitol St., Suite 700
Indianapolis, IN 46204
877-ENJOY-IN, www.enjoy.indiana.com

Iowa Division of Tourism
200 East Grand Ave.
Des Moines, IA 50309
800-345-IOWA or (515) 242-4718, www.traveliowa.com

Kansas Department of Tourism
1000 SW Jackson, Suite 100
Topeka, KS 66612
800-2-KANSAS or (785) 296-2009, www.travelKS.com

Kentucky Department of Travel
P.O. Box 2011
Frankfurt, KY 40602
(800) 225-TRIP, extension 67, www.kentuckytourism.com

Maine Campground Owners Association (MECOA)
655 Main St.
Lewiston, ME 04240
(207) 782 5874; www.campmaine.com
Also
Maine Office of Tourism
33 Stone St., 59 State House Station
Augusta, ME 04333
888-MAINE45, www.visitmaine.com

Maryland Office of Tourism
217 East Redwood St.
Baltimore, MD 21202
(800) 543-1036 or (410) 767-3400, www.mdisfun.org

Massachusetts Office of Travel & Tourism
State Transportation Building
10 Park Plaza, Suite 4510
Boston, MA 02116
800-277-MASS, www.massvacation.com

Travel Michigan
4225 Miller Road, Suite 4
Flint, MI 48507
888-78-GREAT, www.michigan.org

Minnesota Office of Tourism
100 Metro Square
121 Seventh Place East
St. Paul, MN 55101
(800) 657-3700 or (651) 296-5029, www.exploreminnesota.com.

Mississippi Division of Tourism
P.O. Box 1705
Ocean Springs, MS 39566
800-WARMEST, www.visitmississippi.org.

Missouri Division of Tourism
P.O. Box 1055
Jefferson City, MO 65102
(573) 751-4133, www.visitmo.com

Travel Montana
P.O. Box 200533 or 1424 9th Ave.
Helena, MT 59620
800-VISIT-MT or (406) 444-2654, www.visitmt.com

New Hampshire Office of Travel & Tourism
Box 1856
Concord, NH 03302
(603) 271-2665 or 800-FUN-IN-NH, www.visitnh.gov

New Jersey Office of Tourism
P.O. Box 820 or 20 West State St.
Trenton, NJ 08625
800-VISIT-NJ or (609) 292-2470, www.visitnj.org

New Mexico Department of Tourism
491 Old Santa Fe Trail
Santa Fe, NM 87503
800-SEE-NEW-MEX, www.newmexico.org

New York Division of Tourism
P.O. Box 2603
Albany, NY 12222
800-CALL-NYS or (518) 474-4116,
www.iloveny.com

Nevada Commission on Tourism
401 North Carson St.
Carson City, NV 87901
800-NEVADA-8 or (775) 687-4322,
www.travelnevada.com

North Carolina Tourism Division
301 North Washington St.
Raleigh, NC 27601
800-VISIT-NC or (919) 733-4171, www.visitnc.com

North Dakota Tourism
604 East Blvd.
Bismark, ND 58505
(800) 435-5663 or (701) 328-2525,
www.ndtourism.com

Ohio Division of Travel & Tourism
P.O. Box 1001
Columbus, OH 43266
800-BUCKEYE, www.ohiotourism.com

Oklahoma Tourism
P.O. Box 60789
Oklahoma City, OK 73146
(800) 652-6552 or (405) 521-2409,
www.travelOK.com

Oregon Parks & Recreation Department
1115 Commercial St. NE, Suite 1
Salem, OR 97301
(503) 378-6305 or (800) 551-6949

Pennsylvania Office of Tourism
Commonwealth Keystone Building, 400 North St.,
4th Floor
Harrisburg, PA 17120
800-VISIT-PA or (717) 787-5453,
www.experiencepa.com

Rhode Island Tourism
One West Exchange St.
Providence, RI 02903
(800) 556-2484 or (401) 222-2601,
www.VisitRhodeIsland.com

South Dakota Department of Tourism
711 East Wells Ave.
Pierre, SD 57501
(800) 732-5682 or (605) 773-3301,
www.travelSD.com

Tennessee Tourism Development
320 Sixth Ave. North, 5th Floor, Rachel Jackson
Building
Nashville, TN 37243
800-GO-2-TENN

Texas Tourism
P.O. Box 12728
Austin, TX 78711
(800) 888-8839, www.TravelTex.com

Utah Travel Council
Council Hall
Salt Lake City, UT 84114
(800) 200-1160 or (801) 538-1030, www.utah.com

Vermont Department of Tourism and Marketing
6 Baldwin St., Drawer 33
Montpelier, VT 05633-1301
800-VERMONT, www.1-800-VERMONT.com
email: vttravel@dca.state.vt.us

Virginia Tourism Corp.
901 East Byrd St.
Richmond, VA 23219
(800) 932-5827, www.VIRGINIA.org

Washington Tourism Office
P.O. Box 42500
Olympia, WA 98504
(800) 544-1800 or (360) 725-5050,
www.experienceWashington.com

West Virginia Division of Tourism
201 E. Washington St.
Charleston, WV 25305
800-CALL-WVA, www.callwva.com

Wisconsin Department of Tourism
201 W. Washington Ave.
Madison, WI 53707
800-432-TRIP, www.travelwisconsin.com
Also (800) 373-2737 for travel information on
Wisconsin and neighboring states

Wyoming Division of Tourism
I-25 at College Street
Cheyenne, WY 82002
(800) 225-5996 or (307) 777-7777,
www.wyomingtourism.org

U.S. Virgin Islands Department of Tourism
c/o Martin Public Relations
One Shockoe Plaza,
Richmond, VA 23219

**Yellowstone Association for Natural Science,
History & Education**
P.O. Box 117
Yellowstone National Park, WY 82190

(307) 344-2293, www.YellowstoneAssociation.org The institute offers a selection backcountry courses for backpackers, horsepacking courses, and courses in sea kayaking.

U.S. Bureau of Land Management oversees many federal lands where camping is permitted. Call (202) 452-0300 or go to www.blm.gov.

U.S. National Park Service, 800-365 CAMP (reservations only) or www.nps.gov. If you are age 62 or better, get a lifetime Golden Age pass that allows free admission (not camping fees) to all national parks. It's available at any national park. Admission to some national parks including Gulf Coast, Big Cypress, Biscayne, and Dry Tortugas is free. For an additional fee, get an upgrade to the Golden Eagle pass good for public recreation areas managed by other federal agencies including the U.S. Corps of Engineers and U.S. Forest Service.

U.S. Department of the Interior, 1849 C Street NW, Washington, DC 20240, www.doi.gov for agencies including the Bureau of Land Management, National Park Service, and Fish & Wildlife Service. For a directory of national wildlife refuges, go to refuges.fws.gov.
.

U.S. National Fish & Wildlife Service
849 C Street NW
Washington, DC 20240
(202) 208-4131, www.refuges.fws.gov

U.S.D.A. Forest Service
201 14th Street SW, Washington, DC 20001 or P.O. Box 96090, Washington, DC 20090 (202) 205-1248; for camping reservations in national forests, call (877) 444-6777.
Web site: www.fs.fed.us

U.S. Army Corps of Engineers
1000 Independence Ave. SW
Washington, DC 20003
(202) 761-0660, www.usace.army.mil
Some Corps lands are open to camping, sometimes in developed campgrounds.

Canada

Travel Alberta
Box 2500
Edmonton AB T5J 2Z4
(800) 661-8888, www.travelalberta.com

Canadian Heritage, Pacific & Yukon Region Office
Room 300, 300 West Georgia St., Vancouver, British Columbia, Canada, V6B 6C6. Tel: 604-666-0176
Contact this office for information on parks in British Columbia and the Yukon.

Travel Manitoba
7th Floor, 155 Carlton St.
Winnipeg, MB R3C 3H8
(800) 665-0040, www.travelmanitoba.com

New Brunswick Tourism
P.O. Box 12345
Woodstock, NB EOJ 2BO
(800) 561-0123 or (204) 945-3777,
www.tourismnbcanada.com

Newfoundland and Labrador Tourism
P.O. Box 8730
St. John's, NF AIB 4K2
(800) 563-6353 or (709) 729-2830,
www.gov.nf.ca/tourism

Nova Scotia Tourism
World Trade & Convention Center
1800 Argyle St.
Halifax, NS B3J 2R7
(800) 565-0000 or (902) 424-5000,
http://explore.gov.ca/virtualns

Ontario Ministry of Tourism
Queen's Park
Toronto, ON M7A 1C6
800-ONTARIO, www.tourism-toronto.com,
www.rainbowcountry.com,
www.ontarionearnorth.com or
www.ontarioeast.com

Prince Edward Island Tourism
129 Queen St.
Charlottetown, PEI C1A 4B3
877-MEET-PEI or (902) 368-3688,
www.meetingspei.com

Tourism Saskatchewan
1922 Park St.
Regina, Saskatchewan S4P 3V7
(306) 787-2300 or 877-2ESCAPE,
www.sasktourism.com

Tourism Quebec
P.O. Box 979
Montreal, QE H3C 2W3
(514) 864-3838, www.bonjour-quebec.com

Mexico

Mexican Consulate
610 A Street
San Diego CA 92101
(619) 231-8414
Mexican Tourism, 800-44-MEXICO
Also contact the Discover Baja Travel Club, 800-727-BAJA or the Vagabundos Del Mar Travel Club, 800-474-BAJA. Read Travelers Guide to Mexican Camping (Moore) and Foghorn Outdoors: Baja Camping (Jones). Special planning is needed for driving to Mexico, where every traveler must have insurance issued by a Mexican company. A good listing of campgrounds in Baja and mainland Mexico is found in Woodall's Campground Directory for North America.

Among nations that are camper-friendly are:

Australia: Destination Queensland
c/o Fontayne Group
430 Colorado Ave.
Santa Monica, CA 90401

Belgian Tourist Office
780 Third Ave. #1501
New York, NY 10017
www.visitbelgium.com

British Tourist Authority
515 Fifth Ave. #701
New York, NY 10176, www.travelbritain.org

Caribbean Travel Organization
c/o Kahn Travel Communications
77 North Centre Ave. #215
Rockville Centre, NY 11570

Danish Tourism Board
655 Third Ave., 18th Floor
New York, NY 10017
www.visitdenmark.com

Finnish Tourism Board
655 Third Ave.
New York, NY 10017

French Government Tourist Office
444 Madison Ave., 16th Floor
New York, NY 10022
www.francetourism.com

German National Tourism Office
122 West 42nd St., 52nd Floor
New York, NY 10168
www.germany-tourism.de

Israel Ministry of Tourism
800 Second Av.
New York, NY 10017

Japan National Tourism Organization
One Rockefeller Plaza #1250
New York, NY 10020
www.jntonyc.org

Netherlands Board of Tourism
355 Lexington Ave., 19th Floor
New York, NY 10017
888-GO-HOLLAND, www.goholland.com

New Zealand Tourism Board
501 Santa Monica Blvd., Suite 300
Santa Monica, CA 90401
866-NEW ZEALAND, www.tourisminfo.govt.nz

Norwegian Tourist Board
655 Third Ave., Suite 1810
New York, NY 10017
www.norway.org, www.tourist.no, or 212-885-9757.

Portuguese Travel & Tourism Commission
60 Bloor St. West #1005
Toronto, ON M4W 3B8
(416) 921-7376

South African Tourism
500 Fifth Ave.
New York, NY 10110-0002
www.southafrica.net

Tourist Office of Spain
666 Fifth Ave., 35th Floor
New York, NY 10103
www.okspain.org

Switzerland Tourism
608 Fifth Ave.
New York, NY 10019
www.switzerlandtourism.com

Gear and Services

Adventures Medical Kits, Box 43309, Oakland, CA 94624, (800) 324-3517, www.adventuremedicalkits.com offers specialized first aid kits.

Atsko/Sno-Seal, Inc. 2664 Russell Street, Orangeburg, SC, (800) 845-2728, www.atsko.com makes essential, high-quality products including odor-free soaps and shampoo, waterproofers for clothing and footwear, spray-on UV protection for skin or clothing, and Sport-Wash, a residue-free laundry detergent that won't compromise the qualities of high-tech fabrics.

Boat/US, 880 South Pickett St., Alexandria, VA 22304, (800) 937-2628, www.boatus.com is a multi-service organization that provides indispensable help to boat owners, but membership is so inexpensive, under $10 a year, that tent campers can benefit from membership even if they are not boaters. The Boat/US catalog, free with membership, is one of the best sources of boating, fishing, and outdoor gear available. The group also has retail centers in 20 states.

Camping World, P.O. Box 90017, Bowling Green, KY 42102 is the nation's largest chain of camping supply stores. While it's highly RV-oriented, there's plenty here for the tent camper. Request the address of the store nearest you, or shop by catalog, (800) 626-5944, www.campingworld.com. Ask about joining the President's Club. Members get a discount on goods and shipping, a magazine, and other perks for less than $20 a year.

Camper's Choice, 502 4th St. NW, Red Bay, AL 35582 is located on the Mississippi border west of Russellville, AL, a retail location with a big choice of camping gear and a welcoming cup of coffee. If you can't shop in person, shop www.camperschoice.com,

Canvas Replacements, W2299 Highway 98, Loyal, WI 54446, (800) 232-2079, www.canvasreplacements.com specializes in tent repairs and in new canvas for pop-top travel trailers.

Current Designs kayaks and accessories, P.O. Box 247, Winona, MN 55987, (507) 454-5430, www.cdkayak.com, e-mail wenonah@luminet.net.

Eddie Bauer has a catalog, Web site, and stores selling high quality outdoor garments and gear, (800) 426-8020, www.eddiebauer.com.

C.C. Filson Company, P.O. Box 34020, Seattle, WA 98124, (800) 624-0201, www.filson.com. A maker of high-end outdoor wear in fine cotton and wools, the company offers a large selection of garments as well as custom sizes such as extra long or short, longer rise, one arm or leg longer, footwear in extra lengths or widths, right or left-hand shooting patch, snaps instead of buttons, and much more. The company has been in business since 1897, and can reproduce some of its discontinued garments to special order.

Get Organized, 600 Cedar Hollow Road, Paoli, PA 19301, (800) 803-9400, www.getorginc.com is a source of storage and carrying containers, and unusual household accessories that are useful for camping. Their Aero Bed has a built-in pump and comes in child's, twin, full and queen sizes. Mattress covers and folding frames are available.

The Baker's Catalog, P.O. Box 876, Norwich, VT 05055, (800) 827-6836, www.KingArthurFlour.com is a good source for offbeat cooking gear and ingredients. Their ClickClack airtight containers keep dry foods fresh far longer than conventional containers. They come in sizes from 8 ounces to 5 pounds.

Lands' End, 1 Lands' End Lane, Dodgeville, WI 53595 sells casual clothing in high-tech fabrics as well as shoes for the outdoor life. Call (800) 356-4444 in the U.S. and Canada, www.landsend.com.

Leatherman Tool Group, Inc. P.O. Box 20595, Portland, OR 97294, (800) 762-3611, www.leatherman.com manufactures a full line of high quality, stainless steel, multi-purpose tools including the original Pocket Survival Tool.

Lehman's Hardware, P.O. Box 41, Kidron, OH 44636, (330) 857-5757, www.lehmans.com is a major supplier of non-electric items to the Amish community. Stop in, or call and order a catalog (about $5). It's a source for wind-up lights, old-fashioned lanterns, solar cookers, enamel speckleware, and hundreds of other items suitable for camping.

Let'sGoAERO, 6950 South Tucson Way, Suite C, Englewood, CO 80112, LetsGoAero.com, (303) 660-6113 makes open and enclosed cargo carriers for cars, minivans, pickup trucks, SUVs and RVs. Clamshell designs are space-efficient, aerodynamic, and leakproof.

MPI Outdoors, 10 Industrial Drive, Windham, NH 03087, (800) 343-5827 or outdoor1@ix.netcom.com. The company doesn't sell direct but can steer you to a dealer. For a complete description of their camping gear, see www.mpioutdoors.com. Products include Space® blankets, specialty flashlights, pocket stoves and fuel, a xenon strobe and other survival and safety gears.

Manco, Inc., 32150 Just Imagine Drive, Avon, OH 44011, (800) 321-1733 www.manco.com makes Duck Tape and the ezLaminator, which needs no electricity to laminate checklists, recipes, maps, and other important papers used in camping.

Modern Farm, as the name indicates, is primarily a supply house for ranchers but the catalog lists many offbeat items that can be a boon to camping. Among them are specialty and multi-purpose axes, unusual outerwear, lanterns including a solar lantern, portable stoves not found elsewhere. Contact (800) 443-4934, www.modfarm.com.

Mountainsmith, 18301 West Colfax Ave., Building P., Golden, CO 80401, (800) 551-5889 or (303) 279-5930, www.mountainsmith.com makes a full line of backpacks and accessories that carry a lifetime warranty.

Nitro-Pak are specialists in survival equipment including water filters, freeze-dried food, staples canned in long-life tins, and other supplies that campers can't find anywhere else.

No-Bugs Globe is an amber shade that fits the most popular camping lanterns. See www.nobugsglobe.com or call (877) 662-8477.

Passport America, (877) 990-2267, www.passportamerica.com is a membership organization whose members get a 50 percent discount at 800 member campgrounds nationwide. Dues are $44 per year. For those who prefer resort campgrounds, it's a plus; discounts don't apply to primitive camping or government parks.

Plow and Hearth, P.O. Box 6000, Madison, VA 22727, (800) 627-1712, www.plowhearth.com offers a wide array of accessories for country living. Of special interest to campers are such items as Polartec-lined jeans, waterproof outdoor clogs, silk undergarments, boots, and other specialty clothing for the outdoors.

Professional Cutlery Direct, 242 Branford Road, North Branford, CT 06471, (800) 859-6994, www.cutlery.com offers a free catalog of upscale, unusual, gourmet cookware, and the finest knives from all over the world. Campers will be interested in the nonstick griddle, individual stainless steel pans that you can cook in and eat from, a high-heat spatula, a universal lid that fits most pots, and other gear found nowhere else.

R.E.I. sells clothing and gear for the camper, climber, paddler, and hiker through its stores, Web site and catalogs. (800) 426-4840, www.REI.com. The company also books organized adventure travel trips worldwide. Hike, ski, backpack, kayak, climb or cruise with a group led by experts.

Skyblazer, 4275 North Palm St., Fullerton, CA 92835, (714) 447-5409, www.skyblazer.com makes signal devices for rescue on land the sea and the HotShot fire starter.

Sun Ovens International, Inc., 39W835 Midan Drive, Elburn, IL 60119, (800) 408-7919, e-mail sunovens@execpc.com. Offers solar cookers retail or wholesale.

Tough Traveler, 1012 State St., Schenectady, NY 12307, (800) GO-TOUGH or (518) 393-0168, www.toughtraveler.com.

Travelsmith, 60 Leveroni Court, Novato, CA 94949, (800) 950-1600, www.travelsmith.com, specializes in top quality, hard-to-find aids for the international traveler. Shop the catalog for high-tech clothing, compact travel accessories, and useful oddments not found elsewhere.

Travillo, 4376 South 700 East #200, Salt Lake City, UT 84107, (801) 904-1142, www.travillo.com makes a fleece pillow that contains a small, fleece blanket.

Vermont Country Store, P.O. Box 6999, Rutland, VT 05702, (802) 362-8440, www.vermontcountrystore.com specializes in old-fashioned necessities and whimsies that can't be found in stores any more. While only about 10 percent of the merchandise is of interest to tent campers, it's worth a look because of the practical clothing and gear found here and nowhere else.

Walnut Acres, Penns Creek, PA 17862, (800) 433-3998, www.walnutacres.com is an organic farm offering granolas, nuts, dried fruits, fruit leather, popcorn, trail boxes, canned meats and vegetables, and many other health foods for concerned campers.

We-non-nah Canoes, P.O. Box 247, Winona, MN 55987, (507) 454-5430, www.wenonah.com, email wenonah@luminet.net. See the Web site, or ask for a catalog.

Wintergreen North Woods Apparel, 205 East Sheridan, Ely, MN 55731, (800) 584-9425, www.wintergreendesigns.com offers wind wear, canoe shorts and other handmade outdoor wear

Recommended Reading

ABCs of Boat Camping (Sheridan House) by Gordon and Janet Groene covers camping with small boats including sailers, canoes, rowboats and power boats.

The American Mustang Guidebook (Willow Creek Press) by Lisa Dines tells the history and behavior of wild horses, where to find them state by state, and how to adopt one.

Be Alert Be Aware Have a Plan (The Lyons Press) by security expert Neal Rawls has a suggestion for almost every emergency from hurricanes and road rage to biological warfare. It's interesting armchair reading that heightens awareness.

Birds of North America (Smithsonian Books) is issued in Eastern and Western editions. Sturdily bound and color illustrated, these books are indispensable for serious birders.

Camping Your Way Through Europe (Affordable Travel Press) by Carol Mickelsen gives instructions on how to organize a dream trip abroad.

The Cast Iron Way to Cook (Simon & Schuster) by Sue Cutts is available at places where LeCreuset porcelainized cast iron ware is sold. It's for cast iron cooks who prefer a gourmet approach.

Cooking Aboard Your RV (Ragged Mountain Press) by Janet Groene is a book of simplified recipes, suggested gear, and tips for the camp cook. Groene's Cooking on the Go (Hearst) is available from stores that carry out-of-print books. It's for campers who have no oven nor refrigeration.

Complete Idiot's Guide to RVing by Brent Peterson (Alpha Publishing) is for the reader who camps on wheels but tent campers will also learn from it.

Cougar Attacks, Encounters of the Worst Kind by Kathy Etling (The Lyons Press). Etling's knowledge of these big cats and their ways is extensive, and reassuring. She recounts many case histories, some of them fatal but others recounted by survivors who sustained injuries. The book is exciting armchair reading as well as a valuable guide for anyone who ventures into cougar country.

Dangerous Wildlife in the .... is a series of books from Menasha Ridge Press. Volumes are available for each part of the country, providing invaluable insight on what to avoid, how to avoid it, and what to do if you're a victim. They are exhaustively complete and highly recommended. Be sure to get the volume for the area you camp, e.g. Dangerous Wildlife in the Southeast.

Knowing the Ropes (International Marine) by Roger Taylor teaches everything you'll ever need to know about knots, lines, painters, and sheets for boating and camping.

A Paddler's Guide to Everglades National Park by J. Malloy.

Peterson Field Guides (Houghton Mifflin) are available to a wide variety of outdoor interests from birding to geology. They are well organized for reference, comprehensive, and sturdily bound for outdoor use.

Florida Camping, a Foghorn Outdoors book (Avalon Travel) is a comprehensive guide to camping the Sunshine State's private and public campgrounds. The series also has books titled Baja Camping, California Camping, Colorado Camping, Easy Camping in Northern California, Easy Camping in Southern California, New England Camping, Pacific Northwest Camping, and Utah Camping.

Florida State Parks, a Complete Recreation Guide by Michal Strutin (Mountaineer Books) educates the reader about Florida's nature and terrain, as well as where to camp.

How to Shit in the Woods by Kathleen Meyer (Ten Speed Press) is the bravest and best book about piddling and pooping in the outback. It's a must for primitive campers. Also available are two books, *Sh##ing Pretty* and *Going Abroad* by Dr. Jane Wilson-Howorth (Travelers' Tales). Both books deal with bathroom and hygiene concerns, especially for the overseas traveler. Restroom facilities in campgrounds abroad may be below, equal to, or superior to North American standards.

Mexico by RV (Sunseeker Publications) by Kathy Olivas is a comprehensive guide to highway travel and camping south of the border.

Ohio State Parks by Art Seber (Glovebox Guidebooks) covers all the Buckeye State's parks in alphabetical order, with everything you need to know about camping there.

Survival Tips, 150 Ways to Survive Emergency Situations (Globe Pequot) is a pocket-size book packed with ideas for surviving in the outdoors. It's a sensible guide as well as fascinating armchair reading.

The Tenting Directory (Woodall Publications) is a where-to guide listing hundreds of campgrounds that are tent-friendly. It's a slimmer, less expensive volume than those guidebooks that list all campgrounds including those that have no tent sites.

Where the Birds Are is a National Wildlife Federation Book (Grand Central Press imprint of DK Books). Subtitled, *The 100 Best Birdwatching Spots in North America,* it is the finest guide available to bird lovers who want to plan camping trips around birdwatching. Sites and their bird life are covered extensively, and some campground information is provided. Also published by DK are Smithsonian guides to *Birds of North America,* in regional editions.

Woodall's Campsite Cookbook (Woodall Publications) will give you plenty of ideas for new dishes and instructions on how to cook old favorites. Also included are tips on Dutch ovens, fire building, and cooking in foil. *Woodall's Go and Rent...Rent and Go* is an annual magazine-style guide to over-the-road RV rentals and campgrounds that have on-site rentals on cabins, rents, RVs or other static accommodations.

Woodall's Campground Directory, published annually, lists campgrounds state by state. To save weight and money, you can also buy just the Eastern version, the Western version or regional versions or just the *Tenting Directory.* A free KOA campground directory is available at any KOA campground.

Wheeled Camper Manufacturers

For a complete list of RV manufacturers in all types and sizes, contact the Recreation Vehicle Manufacturers Association, P.O. Box 2999, Reston, VA 20195 or www.rvia.org. Also see www.gocampingamerica.com. All manufacturers of towables and motorhomes are also listed in a recommended guide to all phases of RV travel and life, *Living Aboard Your RV,* available from online book services of (800) 262-4729.

Manufacturers mentioned in this book include:

Aliner, Columbia Northwest, Inc., One Main St., Kecksburk, Mammoth, PA 15644, (724) 423-7440, www.aliner.com.

Coleman Folding Trailers, are manufactured under license by Fleetwood Enterprises, 3125 Myers St., Riverside, CA 92503. Contact local dealers or www.colemancaravan.com.

Great Western Van, 329 Parkdale Road, St. Andrews, Manitoba, Canada R1A 3N9, (204) 338-9303 or (888) 498-8267, www.greatwestvans.com.

Lance Camper Manufacturer Corp., 43120 Venture St., Lancaster, CA 93535, (661) 949-3322, www.lancecamper.com.

Sportmobile West, Inc. 3631 South Bagley Ave., Fresno, CA 93725, (800) 827-3071, www.sportmobile.com.

Working the Web

Here are some Web sites where you'll find information, instructions, resources and gear that may not be available elsewhere.

Adventure travel gear is offered by Brigade Quartermasters, www.actiongear.com

Arctic camping gear that is guaranteed for life is from www.wiggys.com/index.hml

Bargains in closeouts, seconds and discontinued outdoor gear, see www.sierratradingpost.com

Chlorine water treatment for safe drinking water is from www.readychlor.com

Clothing suppliers include www.railriders.com

Discover The Outdoors is an encyclopedia of information and instruction on camping and all phases of outdoor sports. Go to www.dto.com.

Earth Chair is a denim, beanbag-type that is sold without filling. Take it camping with you and stuff it with whatever you can find. It costs about $50 from www.earthchair.com.

Emergency and survival gear of all sorts is from www.escape-co.com, www.beprepared.com, www.life-link.com, www.ewalker.com, and www.surplusnavy.com. At www.equipped.org see unbiased reviews of survival and outdoor gear. A belt-pouch survival kit is from www.sharplink.com/jkits

Family Camping, try www.thefamilytravelfiles.com. It's an ezine that covers all kinds of family travel worldwide, so dig for camping sites.

Fire starters are from www.meteorlites.com, www.light-my-fire.se, and www.supercedar.com.

Frontier Soups offers American classic recipes in package form. While pricey, they are complete, easy to cook, and deliciously complex in taste and nutrition. Products include California Gold Rush White Bean Chili, Kansas Farmhouse Split Pea Soup, Wisconsin Lake Shore Wild Rice Soup, and much more. Go to www.frontiersoups.com.

GORP.com is a Web site packed with information on all aspects of camping and the outdoors.

Go RVing at www.GoRving.com or 888-GoRving will send you a free video. While it's heavily weighted towards wheeled camping, the organization will provide a list of dealers, most of whom carry pop-ups and other small RVs, and commercial campgrounds, many of which have tent sites.

Knives and multi-purpose tools are offered by www.knifecenter.com, www.coldsteel.com, www.uniqueknives.com, www.knife-dealer.com, www.multitoolsource.com, www. swiss-knife.com, and www.cutleryshoppe.com

Lanterns, the old-fashioned oil and kerosene kind, are at www.y2klanterns.com

Medical supplies for the outdoors are shown at www.chinookmed.com; a first aid checklist can be found at http://nene.essortment.com

MRE's, military-style Meals Ready to Eat are sold by www.marrich.com, also www.survivalinc.com . A full line of dehydrated and freeze-dried foods is from www. longlifefood.com, www.ginestead.ebz.com

Optics including binoculars and spotting scopes are at www.skyoptics.com

Outdoor products can be ordered from www.beoutdoors.com. Also www.back-countryequipment.com, www.akgear.com

Outdoor clothing is seen at www.earlywinters.com

Shelter systems including tents, yurts, tarps, and emergency shelters are seen at www.shelter-systems.com

Steri-Pen is an electronic device that emits ultraviolet light that kills microbes in a glass of water. It's battery operated, carries in a space the size of a stapler, and weighs less than 8 ounces. Once put into a pint of water, it calculates how much treatment is needed and it operates automatically for 38-48 seconds. Learn more at www.hydro-photon.com. Keep in mind that it kills microorganisms only; water could still be harmful because of silt, salts, heavy metals, petroleum products, and other pollutants. It's ideal for backpackers who have access to good lake and river water that, even in remotest wildernesses, can contain bacteria, protozoa and other life-threatening organisms.

Surplus is a natural for Web storefronts. They include www.sportsmansurplus.com, www.hahnsurplus.com, www.vtarmynavy.com, and www.majorsurplusnsurvival.com

Survival supplies and military surplus are available from saf-t-pak.com, cumbria.com/survival, www.tacticalplus.com and www.greatlakestd.com. All Alive is a complete survival kit in a waterproof shoulder bag, www.all-alive.com

Water purification systems are manufactured by www. aqua-sun-intl.com .

Great Places to Camp

From Alaska To Florida, Good Campsites Await

We all have our favorite campgrounds including those that we never talk about because we want to keep them all to ourselves. Here, in alphabetical order by state or province, is just a thin sampling of the wonderful places that wait for you Out There. An effort has been made to present the widest possible variety of camping styles, from the most inaccessible wilderness to drive-in campgrounds that offer karaoke, fine dining, golf, an activities director, and perhaps even a masseuse!

Camping spreads a wide enough tent for us all, from those who wouldn't be caught dead in a commercial campground to those who wouldn't think of tenting without hot showers and flush toilets. Rates range from under $10 for a primitive tent site to $50 or more for a camping cabin in a resort-style park.

Tent packed? Provisions tucked away? Let's head 'er on out!

Alaska

Denali National Park and Preserve, *P.O. Box 9, McKinley Park, AK 99755, (907) 683-2294, www.nps.gov/aplic/center. The Web site has information on all public lands in the state. Also Alaska Division of*

Gordon Groene

There is no other experience quite like camping Alaska.

Gordon Groene

Tourism, P.O. Box 11081, Juneau, AK 99811, (907) 465-2010, www.alaskan.com. Alaska State Parks, 550 West 7th Ave., Suite 1380, Anchorage, AK 99501, www.dnr.state.ak.us/parks.

Of all Alaska's awesome visits, none is more striking than the sight of Mount McKinley. It is so mammoth, it creates its own weather system, usually shrouding itself in dense cloud cover. Flying in, you may see its top from above the clouds; from a campsite on the ground you'll be blessed indeed if you're granted a full view of this majestic mountain. Camping here is a four-season delight. Of course, it's cold in winter, but the cold keeps crowds away and winter campers never forget the lights, sights, and silences of the Alaskan winter.

Whatever the season, a camping trip to Denali requires months of planning–especially if you're aiming for the brief, crowded summer season. If you're coming from afar, getting here involves time and expense, so you'll also want to plan an itinerary that includes other Alaska cities, glaciers, forests, parks, and sightseeing gems.

All of the park's seven campgrounds have tent sites; half of them can also accommodate wheeled campers. About half have pit toilets; half flush toilets. Water may be from a tap, from a river, or none at all. For back country camping, you'll need a permit and must pack everything in and out. Write ahead for maps and information, then zero in on dates, a campground, and activities. Advance reservations aren't accepted but, once registered, you can sign up for up to 14 days at your campsite.

Ride free buses to view the park and its wildlife. Take a ride in an airplane or helicopter for an overview. Fish. Mush. Get a state permit and you can hunt in the preserve (but not in wilderness or park areas). Join a naturalist for a nature hike, dog sled demonstration, or a campfire lecture.

California

Mount San Jacinto State Wilderness, *25905 Highway 243, Idyllwild, CA 92549, (909) 659-2607 or the San Jacinto Ranger District, U.S. Forest Service, (909) 659-2117. A wilderness permit must be requested before entering the area. Day-trippers can get permits from any ranger district or enter the park by road or the aero tram. Camping permits should be obtained in advance by mail or in person. For tram information, call (888) 515-TRAM or (760) 325-1449, www.pstramway.com.*

The views on the tram ride are eye-popping. As they climb through five unique life zones, from desert to Alpine wilderness, the cars rotate, giving you panoramic views galore. Write ahead, well in advance, for information and select one of the campgrounds. Round Valley has water and pit toilets; Little Round Valley has limited water and a pit toilet, and Strawberry Junction has no water but one pit toilet for three campsites. The campsites are hikes of 2.1-10.3 miles from the tramway. Other campgrounds in the wilderness, but in

Getting there is half the fun when you ride the tramway to camp Mount San Jacinto.

Kayak Newport Back Bay for spectacular sightings of bird life while you camp in a luxurious resort.

the San Bernadino National Forest, are about six miles from the tram at elevations of about 8,000 feet. Everything must be packed in and packed out, not buried, and no smoking is permitted. No campers under 18 are permitted without an adult. This is highly fragile country, with many hazards both for humans and for the wilderness; don't go if you're not a conservation-savvy camper who is accustomed to primitive camping and high-altitude exertion.

Newport Dunes Waterfront Resort, *1131 Back Bay Drive, Newport Beach, CA 92660, (949) 729-3800 or (800) 765-7661. Easily accessible from I-405 and the Pacific Coast Highway is an upscale resort, a rare chance to tent-camp on the exclusive California Riviera. Tents must be freestanding and require no stakes. Tarps cannot be used as tents. Two tents or one tent and one RV are permitted per site.*

The only difference between this campground and any other resort is that you bring your own housing. Sleep in a tent, RV, or boat, or bring a combination of toys and sleep on shore, then launch your boat, canoe or kayak by day. Swim off a private, 10-acre beach. Rent watersports equipment, rollerblades or a bicycle. Dine in the restaurant. Have a massage in the spa, work out in the fitness center, or join a class or activity in the clubhouse.

In the Village Center, find a big swimming pool, a well-stocked grocery store, laundry machines, and a rec room with big-screen TV. A full-time activities staff puts on volleyball tournaments, cooking classes, dance lessons, guided kayak tours (the area is known for its bird life), and group tours to Hollywood studios. Nearby, visit Disneyland, Knott's Berry Farm, Balboa Pier, Upper Newport Ecological Reserve, Magic Mountain, Movieland Wax Museum; fine restaurants, and shopping plazas.

Yosemite National Park, P.O. Box 578, Yosemite National Park, CA 95389, (559) 252-4848 or www.YosemitePark.com for reservations at Curry Village. You'll pay only about $50 a night for a canvas tent cabin for two and a few dollars more for a Housekeeping Camp that has a canvas room and a covered cooking-dining area. Children under age 12 stay free. The Visitor Information Line for the park is 209-372-1000.

The majesty of Yosemite, where hotel rooms start at more that $300 and suites go to almost $1,000, is yours for tent-camping prices. A mile east of Yosemite

Even the earliest settlers recognized the importance of setting aside Yosemite, which was established as a park in 1864.

Gordon Groene

Village, nestled in the shadow of Glacier Point and Half Dome, is a city of tents and cabins, shower and toilet facilities, food service stations, a tour desk, bicycle and raft rentals, a swimming pool, amphitheater that is used nightly in summer for ranger programs, an ice rink, and a mountaineering school. Nearby is horseback riding, hiking, fishing, skiing, rock climbing, rafting, and tennis. A free shuttle bus goes to various locations in Yosemite Valley depending on the season; facilities are also open seasonally, so check ahead and reserve well in advance.

Colorado

Weminuche Wilderness Area, *Durango Area Chamber Resort Association, 111 South Camino Del Rio, Durango, CO 81302, (970) 247-0312, www.durango.org. Request information about tent camping in the Durango area in the San Juan and La Plata mountain ranges. A wide choice of primitive, backcountry and developed sites are available.*

Choose a drive-in campsite or take off on foot with your backpack to explore the rugged mountains, meadows carpeted with wildflowers, and babbling streams. This is mountain biking country, idea for hiking, fishing, wildlife watching, rock climbing, and much more. Ice climbing is one of the area's winter sports as well as cross-country skiing, downhill skiing and snowshoeing. Campers can also pack in on horseback or with llamas. Take a ride on the Durango-Silverton Narrow Gauge Railroad for good views of the Animas River, then see it again on a rafting trip.

Connecticut

Litchfield Hills, *Litchfield Hills Visitors Bureau, P.O. Box 968, Litchfield, CT 06759, (860) 567-4506, www.litchfieldhills.com. Camping is at Point Folly Campground, which has tent sites on a finger of land surrounded by Bantam Lake, (860) 567-0089, and Windmill Hill in the woods, (860) 567-0857. Request a full list of area campgrounds from the Visitors Bureau.*

Durango Area Chamber

Durango Area Chamber

Drive in, hike in, or bike into a campsite in the mountains around Durango.

Litchfield Hills Visitor Bureau

Walk a boardwalk through wetlands filled with wildlife in the Litchfield Hills of Connecticut.

The camping season here is generally mid-April through late October. The season is short and intense, so reservations are a must.

Only 100 miles from New York City is this area of 26 towns and villages, vineyards, bicycle and hiking trails, canoeing the Housatonic and Farmington rivers, antique shops, and museums. History goes back to 1703, when the site for New Milford was purchased from Chief Waramaug. Wander country roads, cross covered bridges, photograph stone fences and white-steepled churches, and climb to the top of Bear Mountain for the awesome views.

Unwind as you roam the countyside by car, bicycle, and on foot. Bus service comes in from New York, so this is a superb destination for city folks who can bring their gear on their backs. Start with a mailing from the Visitors Bureau so you can plan your weekend around paddling, wine tasting, browsing old book shops, rafting, history hunting, or just reading in a shady campsite. Then reserve well in advance and start packing.

Florida

Disney's Fort Wilderness, *Walt Disney World Resort, 4401 Floridian Way, Lake Buena Vista, FL 32830, (407) 824-3000, www.disneyworld.com. Reserve well in advance and expect to pay more than you've paid at any other campground ($65 or more per night) but you'll get your money's worth. While this is a developed campground, it's possible to get a tent site with a lot of greenery and privacy.*

Gordon Groene

Fall color brings new splendor to woods and rivers of the Litchfield Hills.

©The Walt Disney Company

From your campsite at Disney's Fort Wilderness, take the free World-wide transportation to a new theme park each day.

Take a tent site, an RV site or a fully-furnished lodge that sleeps up to six people. Fort Wilderness is a complete theme park in itself, with a petting zoo, pony rides, in-line skating, an animated dinner show, nightly Disney movies, a homestyle restaurant, shops, playgrounds, lakes, fishing, swimming pools, hot tub, fishing, planned activities, and every other camping pleasure under the sun–plus the free Disney transportation system that whisks you to the theme park of your choice.

Some people come back year after year to see what's new at Epcot, the Magic Kingdom, Animal Kingdom, the water parks, and Disney-MGM Studios. Others come just for Fort Wilderness on its own merits. Reserve well in advance, and ask about combination and multi-day tickets that include admission to the theme parks and water parks. If you dream of "doing" Walt Disney World, camping is the most affordable way to have it all, including an on-property place to sleep. Everything, including the shower rooms, is sparkling clean.

Everglades National Park, *write South Florida National Parks & Preserves, 40001 State Road 9336, Homestead, FL 33034, (305) 247-3034, fax (305) 247-1225, or (305) 242-7700. www.nps.gov/ever/fnpma.htm. Big Cypress National Preserve, HCCCCR 61, Box 110, Ochopee, FL 33141, recorded information, (941) 695-4111, www.Nps.gov/bicy. Everglades National Park Information, (205) 242-7700; campground reservations, (800) 365-CAMP. Look in campground guides under Everglades City, Miami, and Naples for listings*

©The Walt Disney Company

In addition to the pools at Disney's Fort Wilderness, you can swim Disney's water parks.

The Everglades are home to many tropical birds and animals.

Visit Florida

of private campgrounds. Rates and admissions: Cars and RVs pay a $10 entrance fee at the main entrance and $8 at Shark Valley. Passes are good for a week. For $50 per year, a Parks Pass admits everyone in one car or RV to all national park areas where a fee is charged. Contact (888) GO-PARKS or www.nationalparks.org. Camping in Flamingo Campground and Long Pine Key Campground is $14 nightly; wilderness camping is by permit, which costs $10 for 1-6 people, $20 for groups of 7-12 and $30 for larger groups.

Florida's massive "River of Grass" covers millions of acres, of which 1.5 million acres are Everglades National Park. What Florida lacks in mountains and whitewater, it makes up for in fabulous beaches from stem to stern, miles of meandering streams, and the wonder of nature that is the Everglades. To camp here and at Fort Wilderness at Walt Disney World is to sample the two extremes of camping, from the most primitive to the most luxurious.

Plan your adventure well in advance, choosing your season and campsite carefully. It's hottest in July and August, wettest in May, June, and September. For wheeled campers, the best bet is Everglades National Park's Flamingo Campground, which has about 230 drive-in campsites. Located near the visitor center, the campground has rest rooms with showers, a restaurant, laundry, telephones, and a camp store well stocked with basic staples. Walk-in and boat-in campers have far more choices of campsites throughout the park including backcountry sites where you won't see another soul for days.

To most people, "national park" means dramatic canyons and peaks, but the drama of the Everglades is far more subtle–a fast flatness with dazzling sunrises and sunsets, swamps buzzing with life and the sudden death dealt by one creature to another. Hike miles of trails and canoe miles of other trails. See alligators galore, wading birds, soaring raptors, leaping fish. Take part in ranger-guided activities and campfire talks. Take a two-hour tram tour of Shark Valley and a boat tour out of Everglades City. Rent a bicycle and pedal the 15-mile Shark Valley loop. Start early in the day; there are no shortcuts back to camp.) Don't forget to request a Junior Ranger booklet for the kids.

Georgia

Bellaire Woods Campground, *805 Fort Argyle Road, Highway 204, Savannah, GA 31419, (800) 851-0717 reservations only or, for information, (912) 748-4000. Camp a full-service campground that welcomes everyone from tent campers to big rigs. Reservations are recommended; credit cards are accepted.*

Few states offer the diversity of Georgia, with its mountains, plains, the sprawling metropolitan engine that is Atlanta, and the golden marshes and endless beaches of the Low Country. Launch your boat on the Ogeechee River. Enjoy bountiful bass fishing. Camp under a spreading live oak tree that has been here for centuries. This is a commercial campground with all the bells and whistles including a camp store, telephone, firewood, and a fishing pier. It's a place to escape city

Among national parks, the Everglades are unique.

Visit Florida

life in a beautiful, Low Country setting but it's also a good place to overnight while visiting Savannah.

Take a tour to get inside mansions built by cotton barons. See the setting for *Midnight in the Garden of Good and Evil*. Walk the historic district where old homes face on stately squares that look much like London did when early English settlers planned the city. See the old railroad roundhouse. Take a carriage ride and a riverboat tour. Shop unique boutiques along the river. Choose from dozens of legendary restaurants. See historic plantations and take excursions to offshore islands teeming with bird life. Then end each day with a Low Country feast of Brunswick stew, oysters, she-crab soup, softshell crabs, and benne cakes.

Hawaiian Islands

Sand Island State Recreation Area, *Sand Island Access Road, Honolulu, Oahu, (808) 587-0300, has 32 tent sites, cold water showers, tables, fire rings, and grills on a picturebook beach. Reservations are required.*

Fly into Honolulu with your camping gear and rent a car to sightsee, starting with Pearl Harbor. Then explore the island while camping at this tents-only park. Pick up supplies along the way. Supermarkets are plentiful.

Illinois

KOA Chicago Northwest, *8404 South Union Road, Union IL 60180, (800) KOA-2827. It's off the Marengo*

The most popular sightseeing attraction on the island of Oahu is the Arizona Memorial, seen here from the decks of the U.S.S. Missouri on which the Japanese surrender was signed at the end of World War

Chicago, the City of Big Shoulders, is an easy bus or train ride away from more than a dozen country-side campgrounds.

exit of I-90. This is the closest campground to Chicago O'Hare Airport, where you can catch the train into the city. It's near the Illinois Railroad Museum, Six Flags, Magic Waters, and the Woodfield Mall. Campsites with and without hookups are available; reservations are highly recommended. It's open mid-April through mid-October. For tourist information, contact the Illinois Bureau of Tourism, 100 West Randolph St., Chicago, IL 60602, tel. (800) 2-CONNECT, www.enjoyillinois.com. Also the Chicago Office of Tourism, 77 East Randolph St., Chicago, IL 60602, tel. (312) 744-2400, www.city-ofchicago.org/tourism.

The best of city life is only a short ride away while you camp in a quiet, shady, countryside campground. Play miniature golf. Let the children run off steam in the playground and swimming pool. Rent a bicycle, see free movies on weekends, play horseshoes, and spend evenings around the fire built in your own fire ring.

Illinois, the Land of Lincoln, offers rivers and plains, cities and miles of farmland, but we focus on its great city, Chicago, the queen of America's heartland, for its unequaled sightseeing. Here's a chance to introduce the family to fine arts, history, superb science museums, and much more while enjoying the great outdoors at campground prices. Take the train into the city to spend all day at Navy Pier with its parks, six-story botanical garden, merry-go-round, and Ferris wheel. Save another day for the Field Museum, one of the nation's great natural history museums. At the Museum of Science and Industry, see a World War II German submarine and take a simulated ride on the space shuttle.

Chicago, offers the best in city life just miles from rural campgrounds.

Indiana

Yellowwood State Forest, *772 Yellowwood Lake Road, Nashville, IN 47448, (812) 988-7945. For information on Brown County, call (800) 753-3255, www.browncounty.com. Camp in a 23,326-acre old-growth forest filled with hiking and horse trails, and quiet, end-of-the-world campsites.*

Camping is pioneer style with pit toilets, but there are water spigots, a picnic area with a shelter, and a camp store that is open on State Road 46 on weekends. No wheeled campers can overnight here, so it's a dream for tenters who don't want to mingle with RVers. Simply pick out a tent site, set up camp, then go pay for your spot. (Reservations aren't taken.) Rangers patrol the campgrounds, which are kept in excellent condition.

Fish, hike trails that range from half a mile to five miles, hunt in season for deer, ruffed grouse, turkey and squirrel, and seek out the yellowwood trees. They're common further south but are rare in Indiana. Every third spring or so, the trees are covered with snowy flowers, seeds are like those of black locust, and the heartwood is dense and yellow. You'll find them on north-facing slopes and in deep ravines facing Crooked Creek Lake.

Brown County State Park is far better known, so discover this hideaway and have it all to yourself. Spring green-up and fall color are especially spectacular. A horse camp is also open for tenting for those who bring their own horses to ride the miles of trails here. (A horse permit is required). During hunting season, hikers and riders are advised to wear hunter orange clothing.

Kansas

Kanopolis Lake, U.S. Army Corps of Engineers, *105 Riverside Drive, Marquette, KS 67464, (785) 546-2294. Also Ellsworth/Kanolpolis Chamber of Commercie, 114 North Douglas, Ellsworth, KS, (785) 472-4071. No Web site or e-mail are available at press time.*

Ohio

Country Stage Campground, *40-C Township Road 1031, Nova, OH 44859, (419) 652-2267 or (888) 216-7260, www.ohioparks.net/countrystage. Camp in the heart of Mohican Country at a camping resort that offers plenty of options for the tent camper. Reservations are accepted.*

Camp by the night, week, month, season or year at this commercial campground southeast of Sandusky and southwest of Cleveland. Tent sites are available with water or water and electric hookups. Something is going on almost all the time at this switched-on resort, where live bands play on special evenings, and campers get together often for bingo, karaoke, holiday celebrations, educational programs, and potluck dinners. There s playground for the kids, a shady and primitive area for tenters who want to get away from RVs, a swimming pool, hot showers, flush toilets, and much more.

Idaho

See Wyoming

Fall color in Brown County, Indiana, is spectacular. Come for the apple butter stirrings, sweet autumn air, and camping at a little-known state forest.

Massachusetts

Pine Acres Family Camping Resort, *203 Bechan Road, Oakham, MA 01068, (508) 882-9509, e-mail* <u>*camp@pineacresresort.com.*</u>

In the heart of the state, 20 miles from historic Sturbridge and 15 miles from Worcester, find waterfront camping on the shores of Lake Dean. Tent sites with or without electricity and water hookups are found in a secluded area near bathrooms. RVers will find full-hookup sites. Boat, fish, water ski, play volleyball or sightsee, and enjoy planned activities such as a pig roast, competitions, entertainers, "junk yard wars," and family karaoke. The resort has a laundry video arcade, snack bar, and an adult lounge.

Minnesota

Boundary Waters Canoe Area, *Ely Chamber of Commerce, 1600 East Sheridan St., Ely, MN 55731, (218) 365-6123 or (800) 777-7281,* <u>*www.ely.org.*</u> *Also Minnesota Office of Tourism, 100 Metro Square, 121 Seventh Place East, St. Paul, MN 55101, (800) 657-3638, (800) 657-3700 or (651) 297-3291,* <u>*www.explorerminnesota.com.*</u> *Although this is a year-round area, facilities vary depending on the time of year. The area's tourist information center is open every day June through Labor Day, and weekdays, 9 a.m. to 5 p.m., other times. A permit is required to enter the BWCAW. Write ahead for information, then make arrangements with the campground or outfitter of your choice.*

According to locals, *National Geographic* named the Boundary Waters Canoe Area as one of the 50

Minnesota waters cast a magic spell, and offering some of the best canoe camping on the planet.

places everyone should visit in their lifetime. These waters have such a magic magnetism, some campers never go anywhere else on vacation. The late Dorothy Molter, the legendary "Root Beer lady" who died in 1986, lived all of her 79 years here on the shores of Knife Lake, often welcoming visitors with her home-made root beer. Her home is now a museum.

Fishing is hottest early in the season, starting in mid-May; in summer black flies and mosquitoes are thick, so bring plenty of repellent. Black bears are also common. To avoid problems, pack every crumb of food in waterproof bags and hang them between two trees where bears can't reach them. Never take food into your tent. Good maps are a must and, while it's permit-ted to build a fire from windfall wood, you'll need a campstove for rainy days and times of high fire danger.

Picture an enormous area of woods and waters with 1,500 miles of water trails through wilderness lakes and rivers. Fish for your breakfast, then break camp and paddle to the next tent site. Or, just pitch your tent in one of the full-service campgrounds and make it your home base for hiking, fishing, paddlesports, and trips into town for shopping and restaurants. Camping and paddling are best spring through fall but winter brings X-country skiing, dog sledding, ice fishing, and nature watching.

Missouri

KOA Kampground, *11020 East State Highway 76, Forsyth, MO 65354, reservations (800) 562-7560, information (417) 546-7560 is central to all the fun of Branson as well as nature's fireworks in the Ozarks. Bring your RV or tent or rent a Kamping Kabin. It's open March 1 to Dec. 1. For additional information see www.koa.org and* www.fantasticcaverns.com.

Although another KOA is closer to Branson's enter-tainments, this one is a good choice for fishing Bull Shoals Lake, sightseeing the area around Lake of the Ozarks, taking in a Branson show, and exploring the Springfield area. While you're here, spend a day at Fantastic Caverns to see rare species including cave crayfish, the grotto salamander, and the Ozarks blind Cavefish. The cave was discovered by a farmer and his dog in 1862. Ride trams on a mile-long tour through unworldly cathedrals of glistening rock while a guide explains the natural formations.

Other caves in the area include Bridal Cave in Thunder Mountain Park, Devil's Icebox and Ozark Caverns. Marvel Cave near Branson is the third largest cave in the United States. A museum at Fort Leonard Wood honors the Army Engineer Corps, Chemical Corps and Military Police Corps. Fish Lake of the Ozarks for black bass, stripers, and crappie. Lastly, spend a day at Silver Dollar City, a theme park built to resemble a mining town of the 1880s.

Montana

Glacier National Park, *(406) 888-7800, www.nps.gov/glac/home.htm, reservations, (800) 365-CAMP. For area information contact the Flathead*

Fantastic Caverns

While you're in the area, see caves and cave creatures found in few other spots on earth.

Gordon Groene

Mountain goats aren't at all afraid of visitors to Glacier National Park.

Sleep in the country and tour New York City.

NY Convention & Visitors Bureau

Convention & Visitor Center, 15 Depot Park, Kalispell, MT 59901, (800) 543-3105, e-mail fcvb@fcvb.org. Backcountry permits are available at park stations; make reservations well in advance. Fees vary according to the site.

If you've always dreamed of riding the Going-to-the-Sun Road, this is the place to camp. The valley has more than 60 backcountry campgrounds, each with no more than 10 tent sites plus pit toilet, food cache, and food preparation areas. Each site is limited to no more than four persons and two tents. Water may be available but it should be treated before use.

Think sunsets on shining lakes, snow-capped mountains, secluded trails, wild huckleberries for the picking, swimming and boating in mountain lakes, mountain biking, bird watching, horseback riding, and always the crisp air of an unsoiled outdoors. Fish for Dolly Varden, perch and whitefish. Photograph wildflowers. Straddle the Continental Divide, and visit an Indian pow wow. This is Big Sky country at its wildest and best, yet you can get here by train–from Manhattan if you like! Bring your backpack on the airlines, landing at Glacier Park International Airport, or take the bus into Missoula. By car or RV, take I-90 to Highway 93.

New York

Newburgh/New York City North KOA, *on the Freetown Highway, mail address P.O. Box 134, Plattekill, NY 12568, (845) 564-2836 or (800) 562-*

Cold mountain lakes and miles of pristine wilderness add up to the camping adventure of a lifetime.

Gordon Groene

7220, www.koa.com is in the heart of the historic Hudson Valley, the place to stay when you want to tour the Big Apple.

While others are paying $200 a night for a hotel room in Manhattan, you'll sleep in a wooded campground for under $40 a night. A city tour bus picks you up at the campground and takes you into the city to hit all the beloved sights from the Statue of Liberty and Rockefeller Center to the memorial to the twin towers tragedy. Close by are West Point, the home of Franklin D. Roosevelt, the Old Rhinebeck Aerodrome, and Hudson River sightseeing cruises.

This is a full-service campground with spots for everyone from the largest RVs to tenters, with or without hookups. Toilets and hot showers are provided. The campground has planned activities such as fire truck rides and hayrides, movies, a snack bar, gift shop, groceries and supplies, two swimming pools, a fish pond, miniature golf, hiking trails, and much more. For facilities and recreation, it carries *Woodall's* highest rating of five stars.

North Carolina

Colington Island Park, *1608 Colington Road, Kill Devil Hills, NC 27948, (252) 441-6128. From the U.S. 158 bypass at Colington Road, go 2.5 miles west. Camp any time of the year here; the bathhouse is heated and the park is open around the calendar.*

Although this wooded park has a number of seasonal and year-round RV residents, there's plenty here for tent campers including those who love the off season on these windswept sands. Sunsets on the sound are spectacular. Take a site with no hook-ups or a tent site with water and electric; use an electric heater for a small additional fee. This is one of the closest campgrounds to the Wright Brothers Memorial, so it's a good base for sightseeing, hang gliding the dunes, photographing lighthouses, and history hunting in the area where Virginia Dare was born and the Lost Colony vanished. The Outer Banks are a summer wonderland for every wind and water sport from kite flying to surf fishing. Area restaurants provide some of the best seafood dining on the coast. Many offer carry-out crab by the bucket or bushel.

In season, scuba divers visit wrecks in the area known as the graveyard of the Atlantic. Be sure to see the long-running musical drama The Lost Colony, performed in a waterfront amphitheater that takes you back to the days of Sir Walter Raleigh. Spend at least a day in Manteo for the shopping, dining, and living museums. This is one of those camping destinations that offer a top natural experience with superb history and culture as well.

The park offers kayaking, canoeing, salt-water fishing, basic supplies including foods and ice, and an interdenominational church service on Sunday. Rates start at under $25 for two; major credit cards are accepted.

Oregon

Oswald West State Park, *U.S. 101, 10 miles south of Cannon Beach, (503) 368-5154 or, for all Oregon State Park information, (800) 551-6949, www.oregonstateparks.org. The campground is open mid-March through October and has 30 tent sites, each with picnic table and fire ring. Water and flush toilets are nearby.*

Park your car in the spacious lot provided on the highway, and load your camping gear into a wheelbarrow for a trip into a green cathedral along the Oregon coastline. Giant Sitka spruce and Douglas fir watch

NC Division of Tourism

Camp year-round on the shining sands of North Carolina's Outer Banks.

Oregon Parks & Recreation Dept.

Park your car and load your camping gear onto a cart for the final leg of the trip into the wooded campground in Oregon.

your progress as you look for your campsite along the trail. You'll walk about a third of a mile to your site and another 1/3 mile to the beach.

The park lies along the Oregon Coast Trail, which you can hike for miles. Explore the 2,500-acre park, climb to the top of Neahkahnie Mountain for an awe-inspiring view of the Pacific, kayak in the sea, dig for clams, or try the trails of Ecola State Park next door. The area is a vast wildlife refuge and one of the best beach playgrounds in the West.

Tennessee/ North Carolina

Great Smoky Mountains National Park, *107 Park Headquarters Road, Gatlinburg, TN 37738, camp-ground reservations, (865) 429-5704, loconte-lodge.com. Also (800) 365-2267, http://reservations.nps.gov. Reservations are accepted only for some campgrounds at some times of the year. The park has 10 campgrounds, of which the best bets for tenting are Big Creek (tents only; open March 16 to Nov. 1) and Abrams Creek, (tents and small RVs, March 16 to Nov. 1). For updated park weather information, call (865) 436-1200.*

Camp the wildly beautiful mountains and hardwood forests of the East's first major national park. When lands were set aside, historic communities were stranded and abandoned, frozen in time. To visit Cataloochee and Cades Cove is to see hamlets that were once filled with townfolk, most of them living off the land almost completely.

The park is so close to so many eastern population centers, some visitors come back weekends and vacations, year in and year out, and never see it all. Start planning your campout months in advance, not just because some campsites are reserved a year or more

ahead but because there is so much to choose from. Request a wildflower brochure and plan to hike the wildflower trails according to the blooming calendar. Focus one trip on the forests and teach the children tree identification. Fish for brookies, brown trout, rainbow trout, rock bass, and smallmouth bass year-round.

Another special booklet describes the park's geology; another the waterfalls; another a galaxy of day hikes. Request the booklet/map on auto touring and do driving tours in all seasons. Ask for the Historic Areas map and brochure, seek out pioneer homes and villages, and learn the language of the mountaineers. A beegum was a bee hive, a blind house a cabin without windows, a granny woman the midwife. The park may be only a two-hour drive from cities such as Greenville or Chattanooga, but you will see bears and other wildlife, and must observe rules about food storage and personal safety.

Vermont

Underhill State Park, *mail address P.O. Box 249, Underhill Center, VT 05490, summer phone (802) 899-3022; January through May, (800) 252-2363. Web site, www.vtstateparks.com. The park is open mid-May to mid-October. Reservations are accepted and, because campsites are few, are recommended. The park is east of Burlington at the headwaters of Brown's River in the 34,000-acre Mt. Mansfield State Forest. Bring all supplies. The nearest shopping is within five miles.*

You're surrounded by some of Vermont's most spectacular mountain scenery including Mt. Mansfield, where you can hike to the summit on your choice of trails including the scenic Sunset Ridge Trail. Please stay on the trails. The alpine tundra near the summit, very rare in New England, is more typical of Arctic tun-

Vermont offers matchless mountain camping as well as island and lakefront camping on Lake Champlain.

VT Agency of Natural Resources

dra found hundreds of miles north of here. At the summit, serious hikers can connect with the Long Trail. The oldest long-distance trail in the United States, it follows the main ridge of the Green Mountains from the Massachusetts-Vermont line to the Canadian border.

The small campground's rest rooms have only cold water and flush toilets, no showers. Open tent sites and lean–to's are available. You can't park at your campsite, so this park isn't recommended for wheeled campers and RVs, but tenters can carry their gear in with one or two easy trips.

Take side trips to Smuggler's Notch (including the resort with its fine dining). Ride the Mt. Mansfield gondola, skate the in-line skating park, shop and dine Stowe Village, and walk the Stowe Recreation Path. Check out the park's log picnic shelter, which dates to the 1930s when it was built by the Civilian Conservation Corps.

South Carolina

Andrew Jackson State Park, *196 Andrew Jackson Park Road, Lancaster, SC 29720. For information write the South Carolina Department of Parks & Tourism, 1205 Pendleton St., Columbia, SC 29201, www.discoversouthcarolina.com. The park is open all year, (803) 285-3344. Reservations aren't available, so arrive early.*

Fish, rent a row boat, hike the trails of this 360-acre park, and tent camp or bring a small RV. Five pull-through sites are available; 25 sites have water and electric hook-up. Tenters will find toilets and hot showers. Many people visit the park just to see the equestrian statute of Andrew Jackson, who began his military career as a teen-ager during the Revolution. The park has an herb garden, orchard, nature trails, and a replica of an old schoolhouse. Ranger programs and crafts

SC Division of Tourism & Parks

Andrew Jackson State Park offers tent sites, some hookups, fishing, and nature study.

VT Agency of Natural Resources

Vermont offers matchless mountain camping as well as island and lakefront camping on Lake Champlain.

Stunning scenery greets campers at Palo Duro Canyon State Park.

Amarillo CVB

instruction are offered regularly in season. In town, nine miles north of the park, see the Old Waxhaw Church and Cemetery.

Texas

Palo Duro Canyon State Park, *11450 Park Road 5, Canyon, TX 79015, (806) 488-2227, www.tpwd.state.ts.us/park/paloduro/paloduro.htm, e-mail pdc@paloducanyon.com. More than 16,000 acres of state park range through two counties in the Panhandle and offer tent sites with water and backpack sites, with water available at the trailhead. Equestrian and RV sites with water and electricity are also available. For information on touring the region, contact the Amarillo Convention & Visitor Center, P.O. Box 9480, Amarillo, TX 79105, tel. (806) 374-1497 or (800) 692-1338, www.amarillo-cvb.org.*

Camp here to sight a large variety of wildlife including the rare Texas horned lizard and Palo Duro mouse. See cottontail rabbits, roadrunners, mule deer, barbary sheep, longhorn steers, and worlds of wildflowers in a picturebook canyon where photographers delight in the colors and changing shadows. Hike, mountain bike, take a scenic drive or a horseback ride, tour by covered wagon, or study nature. When you're tired of your own grub, eat at the Chuckwagon, which is open daily in summer breakfast through dinner. The park has a massive amphitheater that is the home of the Texas Musical Drama, a thrilling, theater spectacle that plays from early June to mid-August. Advance reservations are recommended.

Nearby, see the Storyland Zoo, museums, Wildcat Bluff Nature Center, Lake Meredith and Buffalo Lake National Wildlife Refuge.

Village Creek State Park, *P.O. Box 8575, Lumberton, TX 77657, (409) 755-7322, www.tpwd.state.tx.us. Reservations (512) 389-8900 and information only, (800) 792-1112. The park is part of Big Thicket National Preserve, a dozen land and water areas in southeast Texas. For more information about the area, contact the Beaumont Convention & Visitors Bureau, 801 Main St., Beaumont, TX 77701, (800) 392-4401 or (409) 880-3749.*

Camp in the park's developed campgrounds, which have special areas for tenting, or in one of the Preserve's hike-in, backcountry camping areas. Fish, flyfish, ride horseback, hike, bicycle, or birdwatch in the remnants of what was once known as The Big Thicket of Southeast Texas. Start your visit at the park's information station, seven miles north of Kountze off U.S. 69-287. It's open daily 9 a.m. to 5 p.m. except Christmas and New Year's.

The state park allows swimming at a sandbar, reached after a mile-long hike. You can also canoe 40 miles of trails, hike 10 miles of marked trails through bayberries along the creek bed, and shop the park's store for unique gifts. Picnic sites with grills are provided.

Utah

Moab KOA, *3225 South Highway 191, Moab, UT 84532, (435) 259-6683, koa@lasal.net, www.moab-utah.com/koa. Campsites and Kamping Kabins are available by reservation in a full-service campground where pets are welcome and wheelchairs can access.*

"Tenters welcome" are music to the ears of campers who like the activities and conveniences of a full-service campground but who also need clean, private bath-

Tillicum Village

rooms. This KOA has RV sites too, of course, but tent sites are spacious and shady. Swim in the heated pool, use the guest laundry, play mini-golf, let the children romp in a choice of two playgrounds, and shop the gift shop. Teens love the video game room. Horseback riding, biking, 4WD touring, and river rafting are nearby. The campground is handy to Arches and Canyonland National Parks, the Colorado River, and Dead Horse Point State Park. If you don't have a tent, bring everything else and rent a heated, air-conditioned, one- or two-room Kamping Kabin.

Washington

Blake Island Marine State Park, *mail address P.O. Box 277, Manchester, WA 98353, (360) 731-8330, www.parks.wa.gov. The park is open all year, with a 10-day camping limit May 1 through Sept. 30 and 15 days the rest of the year. It has 32 standard tent sites and 19 primitive sites, three of them on the Cascadia Marine Trail. You can bring a pet if it's kept on a leash eight feet or shorter. Campers are expected to take all their trash with them, for proper disposal on the mainland.*

Take the public ferry to this island in Puget Sound, or arrive in your own boat. A trail circles the entire, 473-acre island, giving campers easy access to five miles of beaches and many miles more of interior trails that thread throughout the native trees and shrubs. Every day is different at a unique village where authentic, Native American dining and culture are celebrated and preserved. Suquamish Indians camped the island in ancient times, and is thought to the birthplace of Chief

Tillicum Village

Camp on an island and relive early Native American ways at a salmon bake.

A resort campground just outside the District of Columbia offers tent sites and all the features of a resort.

Seattle. Today, Tillicum Village is a living history attraction representing 12 tribes native to Canada, Alaska, Idaho, Washington, and Oklahoma.

Allow plenty of time for the village, as well as for island birdwatching, wildlife and wildflower photography, hiking, and paddling the marine trail as well as enjoying the sweet quiet of a campsite.

Washington, D.C.

Cherry Hill Park, *9800 Cherry Hill Road, College Park, MD 20740, (301) 937-7116, www.cherryhill park.com, is one of the closest campgrounds of the capital with easy transportation into the district on tour buses or public transportation. Let them give you a list of all the free things that can be done in the nation's capital.*

Suitable for tenters and RVers, this is a resort campground. While it's not the place for hero hiking and wide open spaces, it is the best place to headquarter when you want to go into the District of Columbia each day and sightsee. (We could spend every day for two weeks in the Smithsonian alone).

Although RVs greatly outnumber tenters, there are clean, modern restrooms with hot showers, a playground, firewood for sale, and such resort luxuries as a restaurant, hot tub with sauna, a TV lounge, laundromat, and two big swimming pools, one of them heated. April-October, certified RV technicians are on hand so, if you're having technical problems, let them work on your rig while you're in the city. Grey Line offers day or evening tours or take Metro Rail, which is three miles away.

Wyoming

Grand Teton National Park, *P.O. Drawer 170, Moose, WY 83012, (307) 739-3399. Camping here is on a first-come basis, so it can be dodgy to find a site at the height of the season. Some campgrounds are full by 8 a.m., especially in July and August. The park has five campgrounds, one of them for tenters only. Backcountry camping is allowed with a permit in designated campsites and in camping "zones." For campground information, (307) 739-3603; cabins and dining, (800) 628-9988 or www.GTLC.com; park visitor information, (307) 739-3600, www.nps.gov/grte. Tent cabins can be reserved June 1 through early September, (800) 628-9988.*

This enormous park, mostly in Wyoming but partly in Idaho, has two main visitor centers, miles of roads and trails, an Indian Arts Museum, and an Information Center. Its gateway communities are Jackson, Teton Village, Victor, and Wilson. It's important to start planning well ahead and decide on what gateway to use, what campground to target, and what activities you plan to participate in. They include a scenic float trip, lunch or dinner floats, scenic tours, wagon and horseback trips, lake cruises, guided fishing, boat rental, and much more. Dining at Jackson Lake Lodge is a reward for the weary camp cook. Try the Pioneer Grill or the Blue Heron Lounge with its live entertainment and spectacular mountain views. For steak and pasta, stop at the Chuckwagon at Colter Bay Village; homestyle meals are served at Jenny Lake Lodge; patio luncheons at Strutting Grouse at the Jackson Hole Golf and Tennis Club overlook awesome, snow-topped mountains.

The good thing about Grand Teton is that you can rough it entirely in the backcountry, camp for a week and then take a week in the lodge, or live in your own tent (or in a rented tent cabin), giving the cook an occasional break by visiting the park's fine restaurants.

United States Virgin Islands

Approximately two-thirds of the entire island of St. John is national park, a national treasure in the tropics where temperatures differ very little winter and summer. Fly into bustling St. Thomas, which is as different from St. John as city from country, and take the ferry. Bring your own gear or rent a campsite that provides shelter, an ice chest,

Snorkel, ride horseback, explore old plantation ruins. Sun on powder-white beaches.

CANADA

British Columbia

Glacier National Park, *Box 350, Revelstoke, BC, V0E 2S0, (250) 837-7500. Also get information from Canadian Heritage, Pacific & Yukon Region Office, Room 300, 300 West Georgia St., Vancouver, British Columbia, Canada, V6B 6C6, (604) 666-0176.*

Established in 1886, this park on the Trans-Canada Highway has more than 100 glaciers in a setting of towering hemlock and cedar forests. This is one case where getting here, on a highway that offers one jaw-dropping view after another, is a highlight of the trip. The park, spread over 1,349 square kilometres, has two campgrounds. Loop Brook has 20 sites and Illecillewaet has 58 sites. Write ahead for information about backcountry camping with no facilities.

The majesty of the Grand Tetons towers over Colter Bay Village.

Grand Teton Lodge Company

Grand Teton Lodge Company

Tourists spend $1,000 a night or more at resorts of the island of St. John, but campers can romp the same beaches and swim the same waters.

Don Hebert/USVI Tourism

The famous rock formations at Hopewell Cape are known as the Flower Pots.

The summer season here is brief and can be crowded. Many people dream about beauties like these; only the lucky ones get here. Even better, in some opinions, are the off-seasons when nature can be at its best and the campgrounds and trails almost deserted. Off-season camping also requires extra planning, precautions and permissions, so begin your search as much as a year in advance.

New Brunswick

Ponderosa Pines Camground, *4325 Route 114, Hopewell Cape, NB E4H 4W7, (800) 822-8800, e-mail* pondrosa@nbnet.nb.ca. *Tent and RV sites are available; the campground has flush toilets, showers, hookups, boat rental, a swimming pool, miniature golf, and a snack bar. It's open May 15 through October.*

Explore the famous "flower pots," the huge rock formations of the Hopewell Cape on Chignetco Bay at the east end of the Bay of Fundy, and all the tunnels and caves that reveal themselves when the tide is out. Observe massive tides in the "reversing river" from Bore Park in Moncton. Fish for trout. Visit local museums. Go whale watching. Visit bird sanctuaries. When the lupines bloom, New Brunswick is one big garden.

Prince Edward Island, *Tourist Information Board, Box 2000, Charlottetown, PEI, Canada C1E 2B7, tel. 800-463-4734,* www.peiplay.com. *The entire island is a storybook, the home of the beloved Anne of Green Gables, and its scenes are a picturebook too. About 15 of the island's 29 provincial parks offer camping, and camping is also allowed in portions of Prince Edward Island National Park.*

A generation ago, this windswept island could not be reached by road, but today's tent campers have a choice of driving across the bridge, taking the ferry, or making a round trip that includes both. PEI has something for everyone–folk festivals, shopping, bicycling, sandy beaches, dunes with their unique ecosystem, pubs, seal watching, deep-sea fishing, city and country, summer theater, historic sites, and enough charm to win over thousands of vacationers year after year.

Discover the storybook charms of Prince Edward Island.

PART

4

Wisconsin Dept. of Tourism

Camping catalog

Wisconsin Department of Tourism

- Catalog Equipment
- Camping Apparel
- Campers and RVs
- Food and Cooking Gear
- Hiking Equipment
- Sleeping Bags
- Tents
- Travel Services
- Other

Camping Equipment

A.G. Russell Knives Inc.

1920 N. 26th St.

Lowell, AR 72745

(479) 631-0130

(800) 255-9034

Fax: (479) 631-8493

ag@agrussell.com

www.agrussell.com

A.G. Russell is the oldest mail order knife company, specializing in hunting knives and accessories. It sells its own brand, plus William Henry, Boker, Marble's, Ka-Bar, SOG, and other brands.

■ **Brand Name(s):** Many leading knife brands.

✔ Brochure

■ **Products:** • Knives

A.G. Russell's FeatherLite One Hand Knife weighs 1.5 ounces and features a general purpose or clip point blade.

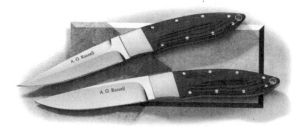

The A.G. Russell Hunters Carved Cocobolo Handles knives were created by Japanese makers using the wood that's rich in natural oils.

Abnet Inc.

28562 Oso Parkway, Suite D144

Rancho Santa Margarita, CA 92688

(949) 713-4034

(800) 731-7714

Fax: (949) 459-7054

abnet@ix.netcom.com

www.4abnet.com

Abnet is an authorized dealer for Swiss Army Brands, Wenger, Seiko, Victorinox, Suunto, and other brands of timepieces, compasses, knives, and tools. Sales are by Internet and phone.

✔ Online shop

■ **Products:** • Watches • Tools

Academy Broadway Corp.

1224 Fern Ridge Parkway

St. Louis, MO 63141

(314) 576-8044

(800) 338-7000

Fax: (314) 576-8010

Academy Broadway produces a variety of camping products, including tents, screen houses, sleeping bags, stuff bags, rainwear, and air mattresses.

■ **Brand Name(s):** Academy Broadway.

✔ Brochure

■ **Products:** • Tents • Sleeping bags • Rainwear • Air mattresses

The Hex Screen House from Academy Broadway is fire retardant polyester with UV and mildew resistant mesh, measuring 12 feet by 14 feet by 84 inches.

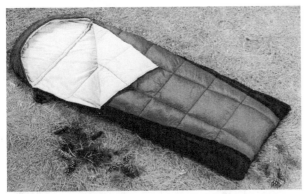

Academy Broadway's Adult Conversion Sleeping Bag is filled with four pounds of Thermal Fill II polyester with a temperature rating of 20 degrees and converts to four ways to sleep.

The Two Party Aluminum Cook Set from Academy Broadway has two plates, two cups, a fry pan, a sauce pan, grip handle, and leather strap.

ACAP of New York Inc.

51 Canon Drive

Staten Island, NY 10314

(718) 698-7926

tourmastr@aol.com

members.aol.com/tourmastr

ACAP produces the Tourmaster rolling luggage compartment, which can be used for camping, hiking, or biking.

■ **Brand Name(s):** Tourmaster

✔ Online shop

■ **Products:** • Luggage

Adventure Medical Kits

P.O. Box 43309

Oakland, CA 94624

(800) 324-3517

Fax: (510) 261-7419

www.adventuremedicalkits.com

Adventure makes medical kits that include treatments for fractures, stings, wounds, burns, and bleeding. It also has sports medicine and herbal medicine kits. Kits are available in stores or online.

■ **Brand Name(s):** Adventure Medical Kits.

✔ Online shop

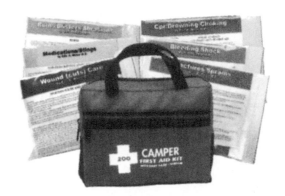

The Camper 200 medical kit from Adventure Medical Kit has emergency supplies for 1-4 people for up to four days. Several sizes and types are available.

Adventure-Camping.com

4425 Cherry Lane

Traverse City, MI 49684

(800) 718-3514

Fax: (231) 941-0333

sales@adventure-camping.com

www.adventure-camping.com

Adventure-Camping.com offers online shopping for a large selection of discount outdoors gear including tents, backpacks, sleeping bags, stoves, lanterns, and other camping equipment.

✔ Online shop

■ **Products:** • Tents • Sleeping bags • Backpacks • Camping equipment • Binoculars • Lanterns • GPS units

Altrec.com

135 Lake St. South #1000

Kirkland, WA 98033

(800) 369-3949

www.altrec.com

Altrec.com offers online shopping for camping, hiking, skiing, and outdoors equipment including clothing, backpacks, books, cooking supplies, tents, lights, and sleeping bags.

■ **Brand Name(s):** Many brand names are sold.

✔ Online shop

■ **Products:** • Tents • Clothing • Backpacks • Books • Stoves • Sleeping bags

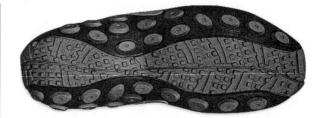

Altrec.com features Merrell Jungle Moc, a slip-on after-sport moc.

Nalgene colored wide-mouth Lexan water bottles are made of tough plastic that won't impart any added flavors to beverages.

Bridgedale Trail Socks are lightweight for trail and daily use, available on Altrec.com.

The Simms GuideVest is long cut, with maximum carrying capacity, comfort and fit.

Arkatents Outdoor Gear

3856 Highway 88 East
Mena, AR 71953
(479) 394-7893
helpdesk@arkatents.com
www.arkatents.com

Arkatents is an outdoor sporting goods retailer featuring Eureka, Camp Trails, Wenzel, Slumberjack and other leading brands. Sales are by phone, fax, mail, Internet, and at the company's retail store in Mena.

■ **Brand Name(s):** Leading camping brands are sold.

✔ Brochure ✔ Online shop ✔ Retail shop

■ **Products:** • Tents • Camping equipment

The Eureka! All Vehicle Tent is sold by Arkatents.

Atsko Inc.

2664 Russell SE
Orangeburg, SC 29115
(803) 531-1820
(800) 845-2728
Fax: (803) 531-2139
info@atsko.com
www.atsko.com

Atsko makes Sno-Seal waterproofer, plus products for laundry care, sun protection, skin care, odor control, and pet products.

■ **Brand Name(s):** Sno-Seal

✔ Brochure ✔ Online shop

■ **Products:** • Waterproofers • Odor control • Sun protection

Sno-Seal beeswax waterproofing protects leather from rain, sun, snow, and salt.

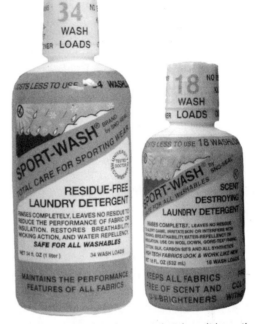

Sport-Wash from Atsko is a detergent that doesn't leave the residue that stops features like wicking, breathing, and water repellants from working.

Backcountry Experience

1205 Camino del Rio
Durango, CO 81301
(800) 648-8519
fungear@bcexp.com
www.bcexp.com

Backcountry Experience sells many types of camping equipment, including packs, tents, water filters, sleeping bags, clothing, cookwear, and climbing gear. Sales are made online and in the Durango store.

■ **Brand Name(s):** Name brand camping gear.

✔ Online shop ✔ Retail shop

■ **Products:** • Clothing • Tents • Cookwear • Climbing gear • Footwear • Packs

BackcountryStore.com

2210 S. U.S. Highway 40, Suite C

Heber City, UT 84032

(435) 657-2468

(800) 409-4502

Fax: (810) 958-4734

questions@bcstore.com

www.backcountrystore.com

BackcountryStore.com sells many camping, climbing, and skiing products in its online store, including tents, backpacks, clothing, footwear, eyewear, maps, and stoves.

■ **Brand Name(s)**: Several name brands are sold.

✔ Online shop

■ **Products:** • Backpacks • Tents • Sleeping bags • Stoves • Lights

Bass Pro Shops

2500 E. Kearney

Springfield, MO 65898

(800) 227-7776

Fax: (800) 566-4600

www.basspro-shops.com

Bass Pro Shops sells a wide variety of fishing and camping equipment through its online store, catalog, and Outdoor World retail stores. Camping gear includes tents, sleeping bags, lighting, outdoor furniture, and cookware.

■ **Brand Name(s):** Many leading brands are sold.

✔ Brochure ✔ Online shop ✔ Retail shop

■ **Products:** • Tents • Sleeping bags • Lights • Furniture • Cookware

The new RedHead 2-Room Dome Tent, measuring 10-feet by 12-feet, is available through Bass Pro Shops.

Coleman's Xcursion lantern, available through Bass Pro Shops, is 10 times brighter than conventional lanterns.

Bear Cutlery Inc.

1111 Bear Blvd. SW

Jacksonville, AL 36265

(256) 435-2227

(800) 844-3034

Fax: (256) 435-9348

Bear Cutlery, a division of Swiss Army Brands, makes a wide range of knives and tools that can be used for camping and other outdoors pursuits.

■ **Brand Name(s):** Bear MGC.

✔ Brochure

■ **Products:** • Knives • Tools

Super Bear Jaws is a 19-function tool that includes pliers, screwdrivers, ruler, and others that allows access to its components without first having to open the plier jaws.

The Bear MGC Camp Saw is 6 1/2 inches with Zytel handles and folds for storage.

Bobkatz Limited

Unit 75, Deerfield Place

Delta, BC V4M 2X3

(604) 943-7568

info@bobkatz.com
www.bobkatz.com

Bobkatz features tents, including a line of hand-painted tents, sleeping gear, and other camping equipment. Sales are online and through a catalog.

■ **Brand Name(s):** Bobkatz.

✔ Brochure ✔ Online shop

■ **Products:** • Tents • Sleeping bags • Camping equipment

BobWards.com

1600 North Ave. W #5

Missoula, MT 59801

(800) 800-5083

sales@bobwards.com

www.bobwards.com

BobWards.com started as Bob Ward & Sons, a sporting goods retailer in Montana. It offers online shopping for camping, fishing and hunting, and winter sports equipment and clothing.

■ **Brand Name(s):** Authorized Internet dealer for Columbia Sportswear Co., The North Face, Kelty, and others.

✔ Online shop

■ **Products:** • Outdoor clothing • Camping gear • Winter sports gear

Buck Knives

1900 Weld Blvd.

El Cajon, CA 92020

800-215BUCK

Fax: (619) 562-5774

www.buckknives.com

Buck Knives, more than a century old, makes a wide range of knives and tools for outdoors use.

Brand Name(s): Buck Knives.

✔ Brochure

Products: • Knives • Tools

The Buck Knives Camp Axe features an ergonomic handle and a head weighted for improved performance.

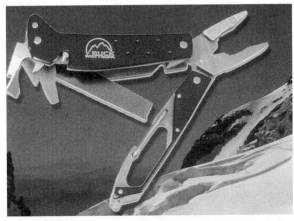

New from Buck Knives is the Navigator, a multi-purpose knife with an integral clipping mechanism, pliers, can opener, screwdrivers, and other tools.

Byer Manufacturing Co.

74 Mill St.
P.O. Box 100
Orono, ME 04473
(207) 866-2171
(800) 338-0580
Fax: (207) 866-3529
Byer@byerofmaine.com
www.byerofmaine.com

Byer has been making camping furniture for more than a century, including tables, cots, folding chairs, and hammocks.

■ **Brand Name(s):** Byer, Amazonas.
✔ Brochure ✔ Online shop
■ **Products:** • Tables • Cots • Hammocks • Folding Tables

The Penobscot Glider is a full-size sling chair with all-weather polyester cover and poly-filled pillow.

The Traveller Hammock from Byer of Maine is made of parachute nylon, weighs 10 ounces, and fits into a small bag.

C.C. Filson Co.

P.O. Box 34020
Seattle, WA 98124
(800) 624-0201
www.filson.com

Filson has been making outdoor clothing and luggage for more than a century, including footwear, shirts, gloves, outerwear, and caps. Sales are made by catalog, phone, or online.

■ **Brand Name(s):** Filson.
✔ Brochure ✔ Online shop
■ **Products:** • Clothing • Luggage

Filson is known for heavy-duty outdoors clothing, including Macinaw wool coats, vests, pants, bibs, hats, and blankets.

The Outfitter Sweater from Filson is durable worsted wool for wet and cold conditions.

Cabela's

812 13th Ave.

Sidney, NE 69160

(800) 237-4444

Fax: (800) 496-6329

www.cabelas.com

Cabela's sells a wide variety of camping equipment, including tents, sleeping bags, cooking gear, backpacks, lights, knives, tools, and survival gear. It has a large catalog, online shopping and several retail stores in the Midwest.

■ **Brand Name(s):** Cabela's as well as a variety of brand name equipment.

✔ Brochure. ✔ Online shop ✔ Retail shop

■ **Products:** • Sleeping bags • Tents • Lights • Backpacks • Camping gear

Camper's Choice Inc.

P.O. Box 1546

502 4th St. NW

Red Bay, AL 35582

(800) 833-6713

www.camperschoice.com

Camper's Choice sells a wide variety of camping and RV supplies and accessories by catalog, by phone, online, and in its Alabama retail store.

■ **Brand Name(s):** Leading brands.

✔ Brochure ✔ Online shop

■ **Products:** • Camping equipment

Camping R Corp.

1628 Jefferson Ave.

Ridgewood, NY 11385

(718) 418-2622

(877) 664-8444

Fax: (718) 497-2168

Support@CampingRus.com

www.campingrus.com

CampingRus.com offers online shopping for a wide variety of camping and outdoors products from many manufacturers.

■ **Brand Name(s):** CampingRus.com

✔ Online shop

Camping World

P.O. Box 90017

Bowling Green, KY 42102

(800) 626-3636

(800) 616-2267

Fax: (800) 334-3359

info@campingworld.com

www.campingworld.com

Camping World has 30 retail stores across the U.S. as well as telephone, catalog, and online shopping. It carries a wide range of products for RVs and camping, from grills and awnings to bedding, lighting, and books about camping.

✔ Brochure ✔ Online shop

■ **Products:** • RV products • Grills • Bedding • Lights • Storage products

A coupon book with discounts on camping products is included with a membership at Camping World.

Campmor.com

P.O. Box 997N

Paramus, NJ 07653

888CAMPMOR

(888) 226-7667

www.campmor.com

Campmor.com offers a wide variety of camping equipment in its catalog, online shop and its retail shop in Paramus, N.J. Products include tents, backpacks, clothing, sleeping gear, furniture and tools.

■ **Brand Name(s):** Various retail brands.

✔ Brochure ✔ Online shop ✔ Retail shop

■ **Products:** • Tents • Clothing • Furniture • Tools • Backpacks

Canvas Replacements

W2299 Highway 98
Loyal, WI 54446
(715) 255-9332
(800) 232-2079
Fax: (715) 255-9332
www.canvasreplacements.com

Canvas Replacements specializes in repairing and replacing canvas in tents and in pop-up travel trailers.

■ **Products:** • Tent repair

Caribou Mountaineering

400 Commerce Road
Alice, TX 78332
(361) 668-3766
(800) 824-4153
Fax: (361) 668-3769
caribou@vsta.com
www.caribou.com

Caribou Mountaineering is a manufacturer of outdoor equipment, including backpacks, sleeping bags, travel packs, and accessories. It sells through dealers and online.

■ **Brand Name(s):** Caribou, Primaloft.
■ **Products:** • Backpacks • Sleeping bags

Carlisle Paddles Inc.

P.O. Box 488
4562 North Down River Road
Grayling, MI 49738
(989) 348-9886
(800) 258-0290
Fax: (989) 348-8242
reply@carlislepaddles.com
www.carlislepaddles.com

Carlisle Paddles, a division of Johnson Outdoors, makes paddles for canoes and kayaks.

■ **Brand Name(s):** Carlisle
✔ Brochure ✔ Online shop
■ **Products:** • Paddles

Carson Optical

175A E. 2nd St.
Huntington Station, NY 11746
(631) 547-5000
8009-OPTICS
Fax: (631) 427-6749
info@carson-optical.com
www.carson-optical.com

Carson Optical makes several types of binoculars and telescopes, night vision instruments, and optical toys.

■ **Brand Name(s):** Carson Optical.
✔ Brochure
■ **Products:** • Binoculars • Telescopes

Cascade Designs Inc.

3800 First Ave. South
Seattle, WA 98134
(206) 505-9500
(800) 531-9531
Fax: (206) 505-9525
info@cascadedesigns.com
www.cascadedesigns.com

Cascade Designs manufactures outdoor and travel equipment under the brand names of Therm-a-Rest, Platypus, Sweetwater, Packtowl, SealLine, Tracks, and Mountain Safety Research. (See separate listings for details on these brands.)

■ **Brand Name(s):** Therm-a-Rest, Platypus, Sweetwater, Packtowl, SealLine, Tracks, MSR.
✔ Brochure
■ **Products:** • Outdoors products

Century Tool & Manufacturing Co. Inc.

1462 U.S. Route 20 Bypass
P.O. Box 188
Cherry Valley, IL 61016
(800) 435-4525
Fax: (815) 332-2090
www.centurytoolmfg.com

Century manufactures several camping products, including propane stoves, propane lanterns and heaters, and portable toilets. It also makes a line of bird feeders. Products are available at retail stores.

■ **Brand Name(s):** Century Camping Products.
■ **Products:** • Propane heaters • Lanterns • Stoves • Portable toilets

Double Mantle Lanterns by Century Tool: feature unbreakable mesh globes.

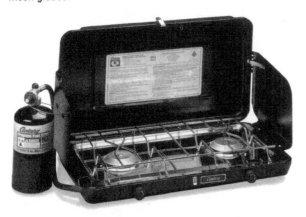

Century Tool's model 4665 Deluxe 2-Burner Stove has two 10,000 BTU burners and a chrome-plated drip tray for easy cleanup.

Cerf Bros. Bag Co.

2827 S. Brentwood Blvd.

Box 6816

St. Louis, MO 63144

800-CERFBAG

Fax: (314) 961-4903

www.campinn.com

Cerf Bros. Bag Co. produces the Camp Inn line of rugged outdoor gear, including duffles, cargo bags, totes, pouches, tent accessories, tarps, and waterproofing agents.

■ **Brand Name(s):** Camp Inn.

✔ Brochure

■ **Products:** • Bags • Tent accessories

A Padded Footlocker of waterproof urethane-coated nylon is one of many bags produced by Camp Inn.

A Dog Pack and a Dog Bowl, both made of waterproof urethane coated Cordura, are from Camp Inn's provisions for pets.

CheaperThanDirt.com

2524 NE Loop 820

Fort Worth, TX 76106

(800) 421-8047

Fax: (800) 596-5655

www.cheaperthandirt.com

CheaperThanDirt.com is an online store for sporting goods, including a wide variety of camping equipment. Gear includes grills, hammocks, coolers, blankets, packs, lanterns, and more. There is also a retail store in Fort Worth and a catalog.

■ **Brand Name(s):** Many camping brands.

✔ Brochure ✔ Online shop ✔ Retail shop

■ **Products:** • Backpacks • Lights • Emergency • Sleeping bags • Tents

Cherokee Electronics

1092 National Parkway
Schaumburg, IL 60173
(847) 839-0015
Fax: (847) 839-0016

Wireless Marketing Corp. is the home of Cherokee Electronics, Coleman Electronics, and First Alert Weather Radios. Besides weather radios, products include family radios, Citizen Band radios, two-way radios, and power converters.

■ **Brand Name(s):** Cherokee, Coleman Electronics, First Alert Weather Radios.

■ **Products:** • Radios

CMG Equipment

811 W. Evergreen, Suite 400
Chicago, IL 60622
(312) 932-0622
(888) 699-0622
Fax: (312) 932-0626
info@cmgequipment.com
www.cmgequipment.com

CMG makes flashlights and various portable lighting products, including the Bonfire tent light, Phoenix motion-sensing lantern, Infinity task light. Products are available at retail outlets.

■ **Brand Name(s):** Infinity, Bonfire, Phoenix.

■ **Products:** • Flashlights • Lighting products

Coalition for Portable Propane Product Safety

P.O. Box 45002
Cleveland, OH 44145
(216) 875-8860
(888) 226-7487
Fax: (216) 875-8870
www.propaneproducts.org

The Coalition is a safety organization set up to educate the public about safe use of portable propane products. The coalition is supported by Century Products, BP/ Paulin, Coleman Co. Inc., Mr. Heater Corp., and Worthington Cylinders.

Coghlan's

121 Irene St.
Winnipeg, MB R3T 4C7
(204) 284-9550
877-COGHLAN
Fax: (204) 475-4127
coghlans@coghlans.mb.ca

Canadian-based Coghlan's offers a long list of outdoor accessories, including firestarters, kitchen utensils, rainwear, knives and tools, tent pegs, compasses, first aid kits, storage bags, and water carriers.

■ **Brand Name(s):** Coghlan's.

✔ Brochure

■ **Products:** • Camping accessories • Utensils • Tools • Compasses • Rainwear

The Camp Grill from Coghlan's is of heavy duty steel with nickel plating and features a compact folding design.

When that rain shower pops up out of nowhere, Coghlan's Emergency Poncho can save the day.

A Folding Shovel is one of the handy tools available from Coghlan's.

Coleman has added a line of aluminum flashlights, taking AAA, AA, and D batteries.

Coleman Company Inc.

P.O. Box 2931

Wichita, KS 67201

(800) 835-3278

consumerservice@coleman.com

www.coleman.com

Coleman makes a huge variety of camping equipment, including tents, coolers, lighting products, cooking gear, backpacks and sleeping bags, raingear and clothing, grills, outdoor furniture, heaters, and stoves. Besides retail outlets, Coleman products are sold online.

■ **Brand Name(s):** Coleman.

✔ Brochure ✔ Online shop ✔ Retail shop

■ **Products:** • Tents • Cooking gear • Stove • Coolers • Clothing • Sleeping bags • Furniture • Heaters

The Coleman Exponent Backpacker's Table and Gear System conveniently mounts on a tree trunk to provide an instant table.

The Coleman RoadTrip Grill, with its cooking stand and side tables, folds easily and compactly for transporting or storing.

The Coleman Mosquito Deleto Inhibitor, which uses a scent cartridge, is portable and safe around pets and children.

Crazy Creek Products Inc.

1401 S. Broadway
P.O. Box 1050
Red Lodge, MT 59068
(406) 446-3446
(800) 331-0304
Fax: (406) 446-1411
carol@crazycreek.com
www.crazycreek.com

■ **Brand Name(s):** Crazy Creek chairs, Thermalounger, Power Lounger, Crazy Crib, CoolerRest, Crazy ThermaBand, Crazy HotPads.

✔ Brochure ✔ Online shop

■ **Products:** • Portable chairs • Tarps

Dana Design

19215 Vashon Highway SW
Vashon, WA 98070
(888) 357-3262
www.danadesign.com

Dana Design makes multiple styles and sizes of packs and tents. It has added wallets and satchels. Sales are through dealers.

■ **Brand Name(s):** Dana Design.

■ **Products:** • Packs • Tents

Dom's Outdoor Outfitters

1870 First St.
Livermore, CA 94550
(925) 447-9629
(800) 447-9629
domsinfo@domsoutdoor.com
www.domsoutdoor.com

Dom's stocks a wide variety of camping equipment, including clothing, footwear, furniture, lighting, cookwear, sleeping bags, stoves, and tents. Shopping is available online or at the store in Livermore.

■ **Brand Name(s):** Various brands.

✔ Brochure ✔ Online shop ✔ Retail shop.

■ **Products:** • Tents • Stove • Clothing • Sleeping bags • Packs

Duluth Pack

1610 W. Superior St.
Duluth, MN 55806
(800) 777-4439
orders@duluthpack.com
www.duluthpack.com

Duluth Packs, dating back to 1870, makes Duluth backpacks as well as luggage, totes, and camping gear. It stocks tents, clothing, books, and hunting and fishing gear. It has a retail store in Duluth.

■ **Brand Name(s):** Duluth Pack.

✔ Brochure ✔ Online shop ✔ Retail shop.

■ **Products:** • Packs • Bags • Tents • Clothing • Books

For the tired camper, Duluth Packs makes the Canvasback Hanging Chair, complete with footrest.

Duluth Packs' Camp Kitchen Pack has space for food, pockets for utensils, and enough room left over for a cook kit, stove, and fuel bottle.

Dunham's Sports

Customer Service

5000 Dixie Highway

Waterford, MI 48329

(248) 674-4991

Fax: (248) 674-4980

customersupport@dunhamssports.com

www.dunhamssports.com

Dunham's has more than 100 retail stores as well as online shopping for a broad selection of outdoors gear, including camping equipment. Camping gear includes tents, backpacks, kitchenware, lighting, clothing, and much more.

■ **Brand Name(s):** Many leading brands.

✔ Online shop ✔ Retail shop

■ **Products:** • Tents • Clothing • Furniture • Packs • Stove • Sleeping bags

Dura-Bilt Products Inc.

P.O. Box 188

Wellsburg, NY 14894

(570) 596-2000

info@durabilt.com

www.durabilt.com

Dura-Bilt makes screen rooms, awnings, and portable awnings for RVs.

■ **Brand Name(s):** Dura-Fold, Dura-Breeze.

✔ Brochure

■ **Products:** • Awnings

E-Z Sales & Mfg. Inc.

1432 W. 166th St.

Gardena, CA 90247

(310) 327-0343

(800) 767-0346

Fax: (310) 327-1159

ezhammocks@msn.com

www.ezsalesinc.com

E-Z Sales are "creators of outdoor comfort," producing hammocks, cots, chairs, folding tables, lanterns, tools, emergency equipment, and outdoor accessories.

■ **Brand Name(s):** E-Z Products.

✔ Brochure

■ **Products:** • Hammocks • Outdoor furniture • Lanterns

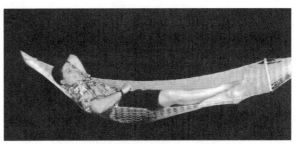

The Camper's Compact Hammock from E-Z Sales is hand-made from polyester with a hardwood spreader bar and weighs one pound.

The Tablebar from E-Z Sales fits all picnic tables and includes a multi-purpose utility rack that frees up table space.

Eagle Creek Inc.

3055 Enterprise Court

Vista, CA 92083

(760) 599-6500

(800) 874-1048

www.eaglecreek.com

Eagle Creek has a number of travel products, including packs, luggage, duffel bags, and travel accessories. Purchases can be made online, by catalog, or in stores.

■ **Brand Name(s):** Eagle Creek, Pack-It, Protect-It.

✔ Online shop

■ **Products:** • Packs • Luggage • Travel accessories

Eagle Creek's Ultimate Journey offers a combined 6,050 cubic inches of storage space, including a daypack, lumbar pack, and marsupial pocket.

The Latitude Wheeled Wide Body duffel bag has 5,900 cubic inches of space, with wheels to help carry the load.

Eastern Mountain Sports

327 Jaffrey Road

Peterborough, NH 03458

(888) 463-6367

Fax: (603) 924-7253

customerservice@ems.com

www.ems.com

Eastern Mountain Sports operates more than 80 retail stores, with equipment and apparel for camping, hiking, climbing, and cycling, including its own EMS brand. It also offers online shopping.

■ **Brand Name(s):** EMS

✔ Online shop ✔ Retail shop

■ **Products:** • Camping gear • Backpacks • Climbing gear • Hiking gear • Apparel

Eastman Outdoors

P.O. Box 380

Flushing, MI 48433

(810) 733-6360

www.eastmanoutdoors.com

Eastman Outdoors offers a complete line of outdoor products for camping and leisure. Included is cookware, utensils, propane stoves and spices, knives and tools, and camp chairs, tables, and gazebos.

■ **Brand Name(s):** Safari System, Eastman Outdoors.

✔ Brochure ✔ Online shop

■ **Products:** • Outdoor furniture • Cookware • Stoves • Tools

The Gourmet Stainless Steel Double Burner from Eastman Outdoors has restaurant grade construction.

The Surgeon General Replacement Blade Knife is always surgically sharp without having to resharpen the blade.

A Comprehensive 72-Hour Kit from Emergency Essentials provides supplies of food, warmth, light, and other basics to survive in a disaster or emergency.

The Ultimate Outdoor Cooking Kit includes a deep fry pot, fish fry pot, propane burner, thermometer, Eastman Outdoors Monster Marinade Injector, and a cookbook.

The Hand Axe/Saw Combination from Eastman Outdoors is a handy tool for the campfire.

A pair of Dietz 21st Century oil lamps, one in brass and one in gloss white, provide emergency or campground lighting.

Emergency Essentials

362 S. Commerce Loop, Suite B

Orem, UT 84058

(800) 999-1863

webmaster@beprepared.com

www.beprepared.com

Emergency Essentials sells survival and camping equipment, including food, water, shelter, first aid, and sanitation gear. Online shopping and a catalog are available, and the Web site has information about survival tactics.

■ **Brand Name(s):** Several brands are stocked.

✔ Brochure ✔ Online shop

■ **Products:** • Survival gear

Energizer

533 Maryville University

St. Louis, MO 63141

(800) 383-7323

www.energizer.com

Energizer makes dozens of types of batteries as well as a line of Eveready flashlights. Products are available in stores.

■ **Brand Name(s):** Energizer, Eveready.

■ **Products:** • Batteries • Flashlights

Exped Expedition Equipment

1402 20th St. NW, Suite 7
Auburn, WA 98001
(253) 735-6200
Fax: (253) 735-6228
www.exped.com

Exped, based in the U.S. and Switzerland, makes a variety of outdoor gear, including tents, tarps, sleeping bags and mats, ponchos, bivy bags, and accessories.

■ **Brand Name(s):** Exped.
✔ Brochure
■ **Products:** • Tents • Sleeping bags • Mats

Waterproof Pack Liners from Exped keep clothes dry in a storm and come in three sizes.

The Auriga Tent by Exped is a two-person dome tent that's lightweight, versatile and with quick set-up.

Ferrino USA

P.O. Box 3271
Staunton, VA 24402
(888) 219-8641
Fax: (540) 213-2102
info@ferrino-usa.com
www.ferrino-usa.com

Ferrino has been creating mountaineering equipment since 1870. It has an extensive selection of tents, sleeping bags, and backpacks.

■ **Brand Name(s):** Ferrino
✔ Brochure ✔ Online shop
■ **Products:** • Tents • Backpacks • Sleeping bags

FlagHouse Inc.

601 FlagHouse Drive
Hasbrouck Heights, NJ 07604
(201) 288-7600
(800) 793-7900
Fax: (201) 288-7887
sales@flaghouse.com
www.flaghouse.com

FlagHouse sells camping and recreation equipment found in its catalogs by telephone.

✔ Brochure
■ **Products:** • Recreation gear

Gander Mountain

4567 W. 80th St.
Minneapolis, MN 55437
(952) 830-8700
Fax: (952) 832-8642
www.gandermountain.com

Gander Mountain has more than 50 stores in seven midwestern states, selling equipment for camping, fishing, and hunting. Camping gear includes tents, sleeping bags, backpacks, cooking equipment, and other camping gear.

■ **Brand Name(s):** Stores sell leading brands of camping equipment.
✔ Retail shop.
■ **Products:** • Sleeping bags • Tents • Cooking gear • Backpacks

Gearout Outdoor GearStore

100 E. Corsicana St., Suite 200

Athens, TX 75751

(866) 443-2768

Fax: (903) 675-8179

info@Gearout.com

www.gearout.com

Gearout offers online shopping for a variety of camping equipment, including backpacks, coolers, heaters, sleeping bags, insect repellant, tents, trailer accessories, clothing, cooking gear, and lights.

■ **Brand Name(s):** Leading brands of camping equipment.

✔ Online shop

■ **Products:** • Tents • Sleeping bags • Heaters • Coolers • Backpacks • Cooking gear

GearPro.com

P.O. Box 11047

Knoxville, TN 37939

fulfillment@gearpro.com

www.gearpro.com

GearPro.com has been selling outdoors equipment online since 1996. It offers a variety of camping gear, including backpacks, tents, sleeping bags, stoves, cookware, and clothing, as well as paddling, cycling, and climbing gear.

■ **Brand Name(s):** Many brand names are sold.

✔ Online shop

■ **Products:** • Tents • Backpacks • Sleeping bags • Stoves • Cookware

Gerber Manufacturing Ltd.

2917 Latham Drive

Madison, WI 53713

(800) 393-9923

www.gerbertables.com

Gerber makes picnic tables, grills, park benches, and patio and poolside equipment.

■ **Brand Name(s):** Gerber.

✔ Brochure ✔ Online shop

■ **Products:** • Tables • Benches • Grills

Gerber Legendary Blades/Fiskars Inc.

14200 SWS 72nd Ave.

Portland, OR 97224

(530) 639-6161

(800) 950-6161

Fax: (503) 684-7008

www.fiskars.com

Gerber Legendary Blades is a division of Fiskars, headquartered in Helsinki and dating back to 1649. It produces knives and tools for hunting, camping, fishing, and outdoors use.

■ **Products:** • Knives • Tools

Gerber's Multi-Plier 800 Legend is a multi-function tool that includes wire cutter, knife, scissors, saw coupler, three screwdrivers, bottle opener, and a file.

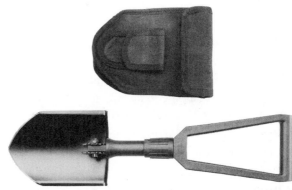

The Fiskars Folding Spade is a combination of nylon and steel that creates a light and strong spade.

Gerber's Camp Axes have forged steel heads for durability and a handle of Polymid Fiberglass that is virtually indestructible.

Get Organized

600 Cedar Hollow Road
Paoli, PA 19301
(800) 803-9400
www.getorginc.com

Get Organized sells an assortment of storage and carrying containers as well as a portable shower and other camping items. Orders are by catalog, phone, and online.

✔ Brochure ✔ Online shop

■ **Products:** • Organizers • Portable showers

Granite Gear

2312 10th St.
Two Harbors, MN 55616
(218) 834-6157
Fax: (218) 834-5545
info@granitegear.com
www.granitegear.com

Granite Gear provides a variety of hiking, climbing, and canoeing equipment, including backpacks, winter clothing, gear sacks, and even dog gear.

■ **Brand Name(s):** Cirrus, Stratus, Nimbus, Aquatherm.

✔ Brochure ✔ Online shop

■ **Products:** • Backpacks • Clothing • Dog equipment • Sacks

Gregory Mountain Products

27969 Jefferson Ave.
P.O. Box 9015
Temecula, CA 92589
(909) 676-5621
(800) 477-3420
Fax: (909) 676-6777
www.gregorypacks.com

Gregory produces a full line of packs for hiking, mountaineering, ski touring, and expedition, as well as other types of packs and accessories.

■ **Brand Name(s):** Gregory

■ **Products:** • Packs

The Inertia pack by Gregory Mountain Products combines storage space with an insulated reservoir sleeve to keep fluids cool.

Gregory's Denali Pro is its largest expedition pack, offering as much as 7,000 cubic inches of storage space.

Human Nature

12307 Nevada City Highway
Grass Valley, CA 95945
(530) 477-2427
www.humannaturegear.com

Human Nature makes several lines of backpacks
and climbing gear, tents, duffels, and other
camping and biking equipment.

■ **Brand Name(s):** Human Nature

■ **Products:** • Backpacks • Tents • Bags

Imperial Schrade Corp.

7 Schrade Court
P.O. Box 7000
Ellenville, NY 12428
(845) 647-6700
(800) 272-4723
Fax: (845) 210-8670
info@schradeknives.com
www.schradeknives.com

For nearly a century, Imperial Schrade has been
making knives and tools for outdoors use.
Among its offerings is a line of Ducks
Unlimited products.

■ **Brand Name(s):** Cliphanger, i-Quip, Old
Timer, Uncle Henry.

✔ Brochure

■ **Products:** • Knives • Tools

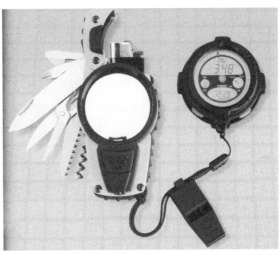

The new Schrade i-Quip tool combines a computer module
with altimeter, barometer, digital compass, and digital clock,
with survival tools including an LED flashlight, signal mirror,
survival whistle, screwdriver, blade, scissors, and can opener.

Insect-Out Inc.

P.O. Box 49643
Colorado Springs, CO 80949
(719) 532-0285
(888) 488-0285
www.insectout.com

Insect-Out provides clothing and equipment to
prevent insect bites, including hoods, shirts,
pants, and gloves. Orders are taken by Internet,
phone, or mail.

■ **Brand Name(s):** Insect-Out.

✔ Brochure

■ **Products:** • Protective clothing

The Tradesman TMT1 Multi-Tool includes 11 functions, with
pliers, wire cutter, two blades, four screwdrivers, can opener,
and cap lifter.

When the bugs are really bugging you, Insect-Out has shirts
with attached hoods of polyester no-see-um mesh.

Integral Designs

5516 Third St. S.E.

Calgary, AL T2H 1J9

(403) 640-1445

Fax: (403) 640-1444

info@integraldesigns.com

www.integraldesigns.com

Integral Designs, based in Canada, manufactures
tents, bivy shelters, sleeping bags, and clothing.
Sales are through dealers or by mail.

■ **Brand Name(s):** Primaloft, XPD.

■ **Products:** • Tents • Sleeping bags • Bivy •
Clothing

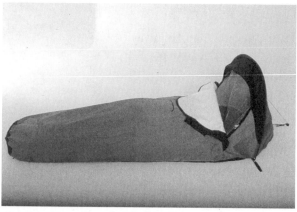

The Unishelter Bivy by Integral Designs is the easiest shelter
to get in and out of, with a single hoop pole providing clear
space around the head and shoulders.

Integral Designs' MK1 Lite is a no frills tent for moving fast
and light through the mountains, weighing less than four
pounds with a floor measuring 82 inches by 46 inches.

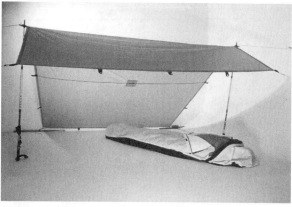

The South Col year-round bivy by Integral Designs combines
with the 8-foot by 10-foot SilTarp 2 to shelter a camper or
climber.

Interactive Outdoors Inc.

500 W. Main St.

Aspen, CO 81621

(970) 920-7097

(800) 741-1717

Fax: (970) 920-9680

www.wildernet.com

Wildernet.com is an online guide to outdoor recreation. It features a Gear Store, Book Store, Gift
Center, and general information about outdoor
products and activities.

■ **Brand Name(s):** Wildernet.

✔ Online shop

■ **Products:** • Camping equipment

J.R. Liggett Ltd.

Rt. 2, Box 911

Cornish, NH 03745

(603) 675-2055

www.jrliggett.com

J.R. Liggett makes personal care products, including shampoo, bath products, and body washes.

■ **Brand Name(s):** J.R. Liggett.

✔ Online shop

■ **Products:** • Shampoo • Bath products

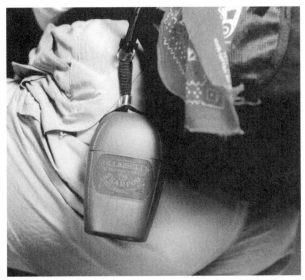

The Natural Traveler carrying system for J.R. Liggett's Old Fashioned Bar Shampoo goes anywhere and weighs six ounces.

Jamestown Advanced Products Corp.

2855 Girts Road

Jamestown, NY 14701

(716) 483-3406

(800) 452-0639

Fax: (716) 483-5398

www.jamestownadvanced.com

Jamestown makes campground equipment, including picnic tables, campfire rings, grills, and benches.

✔ Brochure ✔ Online shop

Jax Outdoors

1200 N. College Ave.

Fort Collins, CO 80524

(800) 336-8314

Fax: (970) 493-1013

information@jaxoutdoor.com

www.jaxoutdoor.com

Jax Outdoors stocks camping equipment, clothing, footwear, kitchenware, and hardware.

✔ Online shop ✔ Retail shop

■ **Products:** • Camping gear • Clothing

K&R Adventure Gear

1128 Boise Ave.

Idaho Falls, ID 83402

(208) 522-5279

(877) 369-7407

knrgear@srv.net

www.knradventuregear.com

K&R Adventure Gear has an online catalog featuring camping and mountaineering equipment as well as a retail store in Idaho Falls.

✔ Online shop ✔ Retail shop

■ **Products:** • Clothing • Sleeping bags • Tents • Climbing gear • Stoves • Lanterns • Packs

Knife Outlet

66400 Oak Road

Lakeville, IN 46536

(219) 656-4127

(800) 607-9948

info@knifeoutlet.com

www.knifeoutlet.com

Knife Outlet provides online shopping for knives, sharpeners, and flashlights.

■ **Brand Name(s):** Brands sold include Cold Steel, Gerber, Kershaw, SOG, and Spyderco.

✔ Online shop

■ **Products:** • Knives • Flashlights

Kondos Outdoors

626 Kawishiwi Trail

Ely, MN 55731

(218) 365-4189

(218) 365-3535

Fax: (218) 365-4189

kondos@kondosoutdoors.com

www.kondosoutdoors.com

Kondos Outdoors manufactures outdoor equipment including camping gear, tarps, canoe packs, stuff sacks, utensil pouches, and anchor bags. It also makes dog harnesses and collars for sled dogs.

■ **Brand Name(s):** Kondos Outdoors.

✔ Brochure ✔ Online shop

■ **Products:** • Canoe packs • Tarps • Stuff sacks • Dog equipment

Lansky Sharpeners

P.O. Box 800
Buffalo, NY 14231
(716) 877-7511
(800) 825-2675
www.lansky.com

Lansky makes sharpeners for knives, sportsmen's equipment, and the Crock Stick line of kitchen sharpeners.
■ **Brand Name(s):** Lansky, Crock Stick.
✔ Brochure
■ **Products:** • Knife sharpeners

The Easy Grip Knife Sharpener is one of more than 60 products in the Lansky Sharpeners lineup.

Lawson Hammock Co.

P.O. Box 12602
Raleigh, NC 27605
(919) 829-7076
Fax: (919) 829-9527
info@lawsonhammockco.com
www.lawsonhammock.com

Lawson Hammock makes several styles of hammocks, including the Blue Ridge Camping Hammock.
■ **Brand Name(s):** Blue Ridge Camping Hammock, Big Daddy Hammock.
✔ Online shop
■ **Products:** • Hammocks

LCN Outdoors

P.O. Box 864
Windsor Locks, CT 06096
(800) 552-2267
Fax: (800) 952-6329
lcnoutdoors@snet.net
www.lcnoutdoors.com

LCN Outdoors is a wholesale provider of outdoors equipment to stores.

Leatherman Tool Group Inc.

P.O. Box 20595
12106 NE Ainsworth Circle
Portland, OR 97294
(503) 253-7826
(800) 847-8665
Fax: (503) 253-7830
mktg@leatherman.com
www.leatherman.com

Leatherman manufactures several multi-tools that are useful in camping.
■ **Brand Name(s):** Leatherman.
✔ Brochure
■ **Products:** • Tools

The Flair is a typical Leatherman tool for all-purpose camping use, including two pliers, wire cutters, corkscrew, knife blades, scissors, can opener, bottle opener, and four screwdrivers.

Lehman's

P.O. Box 41
One Lehman Circle
Kidron, OH 44636
(330) 857-5757
(888) 438-5346
Fax: (330) 857-5785
info@lehmans.com
www.lehmans.com

Lehman's offers the largest collection of old-fashioned, non-electric appliances, tools, kitchenware, toys, and more in the world. Campers will find tools, stoves, lanterns, portable showers, cookware, and more in the Lehman's catalog and online store.

■ **Brand Name(s):** Lehman's.
✔ Brochure ✔ Online shop ✔ Retail shop
■ **Products:** • Tools • Stoves • Lanterns

A freezer from Lehman's cranks out homemade ice cream.

A portable shower has a hand pump and propane bottle.

An Amish double-wick lamp from Lehman's offers twice the light.

Dietz lanterns stay lit in any weather.

Let's Go Aero Inc.

3116 Century St.
Colorado Springs, CO 80907
(719) 630-3800
877-GO4AERO
Fax: (719) 447-9735
info@letsgoaero.com
www.letsgoaero.com

Let's Go Aero makes Herman Sport Performance Trailers and Remora Sport Performance Carriers that provide storage space for travelers.
■ **Brand Name(s):** Herman, Remora.
■ **Products:** • Cargo trailers • Travel carrier

Liberty Mountain

4375 W. 1980 South, Suite 100
Salt Lake City, UT 84104
(800) 366-2666
Fax: (801) 954-0766
sales@libertymountain.com
www.libertymountain.com

Liberty Mountain is a distributor of camping equipment, including packs, tents, bags, compasses, knives, stoves, cookware, and lights.
■ **Brand Name(s):** Major brands.
✔ Brochure
■ **Products:** • Camping equipment

MAC Sports

1736 Wright Ave.
LaVerne, CA 91750
(800) 938-9886
Fax: (909) 392-8283
service@maccabeesports.com
www.maccabeesports.com

MAC Sports makes a variety of portable outdoor furniture (MAC stands for Mobile And Collapsible). Included are chairs, stools, stadium seats, cots, tables, and umbrellas. Online shopping is available.

■ **Brand Name(s):** MAC Sports.
✔ Brochure ✔ Online shop
Products: • Portable furniture

The MAC La Jolla Love Chair with Table features two comfortable chairs separated by a table.

The Bazaar Captain Chair for Junior, by MAC Sports, is made of denier polyester with steel tubes and weighs about four pounds.

Madden Mountaineering

2400 Central Ave.
Boulder, CO 80301
(303) 442-5828
www.maddenusa.com

Madden makes a variety of packs and bags, including expedition packs, day packs, travel packs, and accessories. It offers online shopping and products are available in retail stores.

■ **Brand Name(s):** Madden
✔ Brochure ✔ Online shop
■ **Products:** • Packs

Mag Instrument Inc.

1721 E. Locust St.
Ontario, CA 91761
(909) 947-1006
Fax: (909) 947-5041
warranty@magmail.com
www.maglite.com

Mag Instrument makes a line of Maglite flashlights for a variety of uses.

■ **Brand Name(s):** Maglite.
✔ Brochure
■ **Products:** • Flashlights

The Mini Maglite AA flashlight features a high-intensity beam, durability, and dependability.

Magellan's International

110 W. Sola St.
Santa Barbara, CA 93101
(800) 962-4943
Fax: (800) 962-4940
www.magellans.com

Magellan's sells travel supplies, including binoculars, maps, picnic gear, packs, clothing, and health equipment. Shopping is available by catalog or online.

■ **Brand Name(s):** Several brands are available.

✔ Brochure ✔ Online shop

■ **Products:** • Travel aids • Clothing • Packs

Marmot Mountain Works

3049 Adeline St.
Berkeley, CA 94703
(510) 849-0735
(800) 627-6689
Fax: (510) 849-3312
info@marmotmountain.com
www.marmotmountain.com

Marmot stocks a variety of camping equipment, including clothing, footwear, packs, tents, sleeping bags, and accessories, as well as climbing and paddling gear. Shopping is available online as well as in several West Coast Marmot Mountain stores.

■ **Brand Name(s):** Several brands are sold.

✔ Online shop ✔ Retail shop

■ **Products:** • Tents • Boots • Clothing • Sleeping bags

McNett Corp.

1411 Meador Ave.
Bellingham, WA 98226
(360) 671-2227
Fax: (360) 671-4521
customerservice@mcnett.com
www.mcnett.com

McNett makes more than 170 products for outdoor and sporting enthusiasts, including camping equipment. Camping gear includes water filters, water and stain repellant, repair tape, sleeping bag cleaner, and seam repair material.

■ **Brand Name(s):** Seam Grip, Thunder Shield, Quick Fresh, Megathane, Aquamira.

■ **Products:** • Water repellant • Cleaners • Deodorizers • Repair kits

Seam Sure Water Based Seam Sealer, a fast-drying urethane formula, from McNett works for tents, packs, rainwear, and tarps.

Tenacious Brand Sealing & Repair Tape from McNett provides instant repairs to tents, tarps, and raingear.

Meyerco USA/Camp USA

4481 Exchange Service Drive
Dallas, TX 75236
(214) 467-8949
Fax: (241) 467-9241
meyerco@bnfusa.com
www.meyercousa.com

Meyerco USA makes a wide range of knives as well as camping tools and fishing fillet sets under the Meyerco USA and Camp USA brands.

■ **Brand Name(s):** Meyerco USA, Camp USA.

✔ Brochure

■ **Products:** • Knives • Camping equipment

The Camp USA Folding Camp Shovel is all steel, and folds down for storage. It comes with a carrying case that can be worn on a belt.

Camp USA designed and built the Camp 20 and Camp 21 knives for heavy duty use, with a 1/8-inch blade, serrated or regular, with a glass-filled nylon handle and heavy duty sheath.

Moonbow

P.O. Box 25

Glencliff, NH 03238

(603) 898-0040

Fax: (801) 912-7311

info@moonbowgear.com

www.moonbowgear.com

Moonbow offers custom sewing and manufacturing of camping equipment in addition to its line of camping gear and clothing, climbing gear and pet gear. It also has a shop in Glencliff, N.H.

■ **Brand Name(s):** Moonbow

✔ Retail shop

■ **Products:** • Camping gear • Tents • Backpacks • Clothing

Moosineer Outdoor Gear

2702 S. 3600 West, Suite H

Salt Lake City, UT 84119

(800) 896-3060

Fax: (801) 966-4177

gear@moosineer.com

www.moosineer.com

Moosineer is a camping equipment Internet dealer and retailer. It stocks Apache Tents, Coleman products, Rokk, Slumberjack, Nebo Sleeping Bags, Zodi tent heaters and showers, Mountain

House foods, first aid kits, portable toilets, and other outdoors products.

■ **Brand Name(s):** Many camping brands.

✔ Brochure ✔ Online shop

■ **Products:** • Tents • Sleeping bags • Foods • Heaters

The Hot Vent SC Tent Heater, sold by Moosineer, provides instant heat for a cold tent.

A Cooksack Solar Oven Kit heats water to 190 degrees, weighs 12 ounces, and uses no fuel.

The Apache Star-Lite Instant AL Tent, available from Moosineer, accommodates two campers and weighs about seven pounds.

Mountain Safety Research

3800 1st Ave. South

Seattle, WA 98134

(800) 531-9531

Fax: (206) 224-6492

info@cascadedesigns.com

www.msrcorp.com

Mountain Safety Research manufactures a broad range of camping equipment, including backpacking stoves, water filters, hydration reservoirs, tents, cookware, Mountain Gourmet foods, trekking/snowshoe poles, and snowshoes.

■ **Brand Name(s):** MSR, Mountain Gourmet

■ **Products:** • Stoves • Water • Tents • Cookware • Snowshoes

The Fusion 3 is a three-person convertible MSR tent designed for all seasons

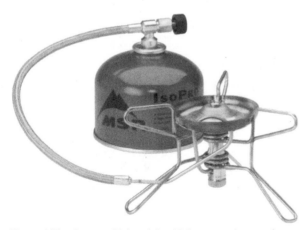

The rapidFire Stove, which weighs 12.5 ounces, is one of MSR's canister camping stoves.

MPI Outdoors

10 Industrial Drive

Windham, NH 03087

(603) 890-0455

(800) 343-5827

Fax: (603) 890-0477

info@mpioutdoors.com

www.mpioutdoors.com

MPI products, including the Space emergency blankets and bags, are sold in major retail stores. Outdoors survival information is available on its Web site.

■ **Brand Name(s):** Space All Weather and Space Emergency Blankets and Emergency Bag. Safe Signal Mirror. Esbit Solid Fuel and Pocket Stove.

✔ Brochure

■ **Products:** • Camping gear • Survival gear

The MPI Outdoors Focusing Headlamp leaves the hands free while doing camping chores.

Grasshopper is a multi-functioning pop-up camp light with a built-in stand, allowing light in a 360-degree arc.

New from MPI Outdoors is the Pathfinder non-glare LED pocket penlight, with a bulb that will last 100,000 hours.

The Space Emergency Blanket and Emergency Bag have become outdoor staples as shelter and protection in critical situations.

Mr. Heater Corp.

4560 W. 160th St.

Cleveland, OH 44135

(216) 881-5500

(800) 251-0001

Fax: (216) 881-5870

www.mrheater.com

Mr. Heater is America's leading manufacturer of propane heaters. Sales are through dealers.

■ **Brand Name(s):** Mr. Heater, Hot Stuff.

■ **Products:** • Propane heaters

A tent camper is kept warm by Mr. Heater's Portable Buddy indoor safe propane heater.

Nalgene Outdoor Products Division

Nalge Nunc International Corp.

75 Panorama Creek Drive

Rochester, NY 14625

(800) 625-4327

Fax: (716) 586-8987

nnics@nalgenunc.com

www.nalgene-outdoor.com

Nalgene makes a selection of bottles and jars, including travel mugs, water bottles, travel kits, fuel bottles, and accessories. Online shopping is available and products are found in stores.

✔ Online shop

■ **Products:** • Bottles • Containers

NEBO Sports

12382 Gateway Parkplace #300

Draper, UT 84020

(888) 526-1295

Fax: (801) 495-2151

service@neboproducts.com

www.neboproducts.com

NEBO Sports produces a number of camping products, including tents, sleeping bags, backpacks, and sunglasses.

■ **Brand Name(s):** NEBO Sports.

✔ Brochure

■ **Products:** • Tents • Sleeping bags • Packs • Sunglasses

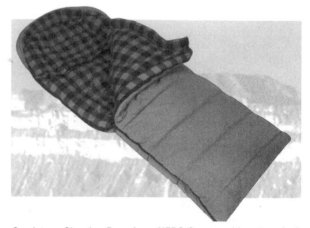

Sandstone Sleeping Bags from NEBO Sports, with cotton duck canvas shell and cotton flannel lining, are rated at 0 and −30 degrees.

NEBO Rocky 75 and Wilderness 55 Backpacks are lightweight and durable, with an aluminum reinforced frame.

Newell International Inc. USA

1750 S. 500 West, Suite 900

Salt Lake City, UT 84115

(801) 908-6836

Fax: (801) 908-6841

info@newellinternational.com

www.newellinternational.com

Newell International makes The Backside line of tents, sleeping bags and pads, and packs. It also makes the Black Pine Sports line of packs, travel gear, and sleeping bags.

■ **Brand Name(s):** The Backside, Black Pine Sports.

✔ Brochure

■ **Products:** • Tents • Sleeping bags • Mats • Packs

The T-3 Tent from The Backside is a two-pole free-standing tent for two or three people for camping in three seasons.

Versions of Black Pine Sports' Hyperloft sleeping bags keep sleepers warm from zero to 35 degrees.

Nikon USA

1300 Walt Whitman Rd.

Melville, NY 11747

800NIKONUS

www.nikonusa.com

Nikon produces a line of sporting optics, including binoculars and scopes, as well as cameras.

■ **Brand Name(s):** Nikon, StabilEyes.

✔ Brochure ✔ Online shop

■ **Products:** • Binoculars • Scopes • Cameras

Nikon's Mountaineer II binoculars come in 8x25 and 10x25 styles that are waterproof, fogproof and shockproof.

Nikon's new StabilEyes VR is a 14x40 binoculars that eliminates movement from waves and vibration from hand shake.

Nikwax

P.O. Box 1572

Everett, WA 98206

(425) 303-1410

Fax: (425) 303-1242

nikwax@watershedusa.com

www.nikwax-usa.com

Nikwax makes waterproofing products for camping, hiking, backpacking, climbing, and other outdoors activities. It is used for tents, sleeping bags, outerwear, and footwear.

✔ Brochure

■ **Products:** • Waterproofing products

Oregon Scientific Inc.

19861 SW 95th Place

Tualatin, OR 97062

(503) 639-8883

Fax: (503) 684-8883

info@oscientific.com

ww.osi.com

Oregon Scientific's products include a portable NOAA/ FRS emergency weather radio, Exactset travel clocks, and weather instruments.

■ **Brand Name(s):** Exactset, Cable Free.

✔ Brochure ✔ Online shop

■ **Products:** • Weather radios • Travel clocks

Orion Safety Products

Route 6, Box 542

Peru, IN 46970

(765) 472-4375

(800) 851-5260

Fax: (765) 473-3254

mcustomerservice@orionsignals.com

www.orionsignals.com

Orion has acquired Skyblazer to add to its line of emergency signal devices and survival products for outdoors enthusiasts. Products include signal flares, survival kits, and camp fire starters.

■ **Brand Name(s):** Orion.

■ **Products:** • Survival kits • Signal flares • Fire starters

The Ultimate Signal and Survival Kit from Orion includes flares, fire starters, a survival blanket, whistles, flashlight, candles, matches, mirror, and other handy devices.

Camp Fire Starters by Orion burn hotter than wax-based fire starters in rain and wind, and can also be used as distress signals.

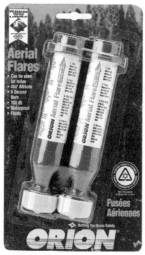

Aerial Signal Flares from Orion provide an effective day or night signal for attracting attention.

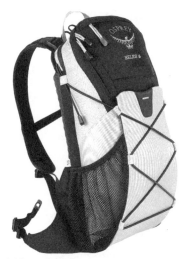

The Helios 14 from Osprey can carry hydration and basic necessities for trail-running, mountain biking, or other back-country fun.

Oshman's SuperSports USA

1050 W. Hampden Ave.
Englewood, CO 80110
president@gartsports.com
www.oshmans.com

Oshman's, which began in Texas in 1919, has spread to include 42 SuperSports stores and 15 regular stores, as well as an online store. Camping equipment includes a full range of supplies, from cots and tents to tools and clothing.

■ **Brand Name(s):** Many name brands are sold.
✔ Online shop ✔ Retail shop
■ **Products:** • Tents • Tools • Clothing • Sleeping bags • Lights • Survival gear

The Crescent 110 from Osprey Packs is the expedition load monster, with three sizes from 6,500 cubic inches to 6,900 cubic inches.

Osprey Packs Inc.

115 W. Progress Circle
Cortez, CO 81321
(970) 564-5900
Fax: (970) 565-2120
info@ospreypacks.com
www.ospreypacks.com

Osprey makes a complete line of packs, including custom-fit backpacks, day packs, lightweight packs, and travel and hunting gear. Products are available in stores.

■ **Brand Name(s):** Osprey Packs.
■ **Products:** • Backpacks

Outbound Products

8585 Fraser St.
Vancouver, BC V5X 3Y1
(604) 321-5464
Fax: (604) 321-8525
custserv@outbound.ca
www.outbound.ca

Outbound makes camping, hiking, and mountaineering gear including tents, packs, sleeping bags, and outdoor accessories. Sales are by catalog and through retailers.

■ **Brand Name(s):** Outbound.
✔ Brochure

Outdoor Edge Cutlery Corp.

6395 Gunpark Drive, Suite Q

Boulder, CO 80301

(303) 530-7667

(800) 447-3343

Fax: (303) 530-7020

info@outdooredge.com

www.outdooredge.com

Outdoor Edge manufactures knives, axes, and saws that can be used for various outdoors activities, including camping.

■ **Brand Name(s):** Outdoor Edge.

✔ Brochure

■ **Products:** • Knives • Saws • Axes

Outdoor Edge's Pack-Axe has an extra-wide splitting head and a rubberized Kraton handle for non-slip grip and control.

Outdoor Edge has two versions of the Wedge quick access knife that can be used for outdoors activities including camping, backpacking, climbing, and fishing.

The Pack-Saw from Outdoor Edge Cutlery includes three blades for wood, bone and metal, and a nylon storage case for easy packing.

Outdoor Products

1919 Vineburn Ave.

Los Angeles, CA 90032

(800) 438-3353

packsforlife@outdoorproducts.com

www.outdoorproducts.com

Outdoor Products makes "packs for life" including packs, fannies, duffles, camping backpacks, and travel bags. Retailers handle the products.

■ **Brand Name(s):** Outdoor Products.

■ **Products:** • Packs

Outdoor Research

2203 First Ave. South

Seattle, WA 98134

8884-ORGEAR

Fax: (206) 467-0374

info@orgear.com

www.orgear.com

Outdoor Research makes many camping and hiking products, including apparel, footwear, sacks, kitchen kits, water toters, medical kits, and travel pouches. Products are available online, through catalog or phone sales, and through dealers.

■ **Brand Name(s):** Outdoor Research.

✔ Brochure ✔ Online shop

■ **Products:** • Clothing • Footwear • Sacks • Medical Supplies

Outdoor Research makes several kitchen kits, including this Camper Kitchen Kit for trailside cooking, weighing 17.6 ounces.

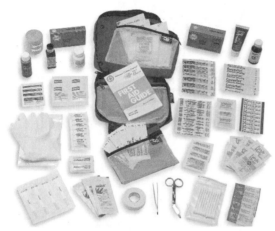

The Family Camping Medical Kit stocks such essentials as bandages and first aid equipment.

The Bombay Duffel Bag is built from "bombproof" Hydroseal-1000 fabric for rugged use.

The Deluxe Bivy Sack from Outdoor Research has a single pole and a forward roof section that can be pulled back to leave the netting uncovered.

Oware

10670 Somerset Drive

Truckee, CA 96161

(888) 292-4534

Fax: (530) 587-7294

backpacking@owareusa.com

www.owareusa.com

Oware makes camping products, including tents, tarps, sleep systems, stuff sacks, and outerware, as well as custom products.

■ **Brand Name(s):** Oware.

✔ Online shop

■ **Products:** • Tents • Tarps • Sacks

Patagonia Inc.

8550 White Fir St.

P.O. Box 32050

Reno, NV 89523

(800) 638-6464

Fax: (800) 543-5522

www.patagonia.com

Patagonia has a variety of outdoor clothing, climbing gear, packs and travel gear, paddling and fishing gear. Purchases can be made online, by catalog or in stores.

■ **Brand Name(s):** Patagonia.

✔ Brochure ✔ Online shop

■ **Products:** • Clothing • Canoeing • Climbing gear

Insulation is the key to warmth for Patagonia's Regulator R1 Flash pullovers and pants, made of Polartec Power Dry plyester.

Warm weather campers can combine comfort and style with Patagonia's tropical flats pants, and shorts.

Pelican Products

23215 Early Ave.

Torrance, CA 90505

(310) 326-4700

Fax: (310) 326-3311

www.pelican.com

Pelican Products makes an extensive line of flashlights and larger lights. It also makes watertight protector cases.

■ **Brand Name(s):** Pelican

■ **Products:** • Flashlights

Pelican makes 25 different sized heavy-duty cases for sports, computer, and other equipment, including this model 1450.

Pelican's MityLite 2AA is water resistant, operates on two AA alkaline batteries and has a beam 600 percent brighter than other personal lights.

The Tracker Pocket Flashlight includes a hat and clothing clip, and a key ring.

Black Knight Series flashlights by Pelican Products are rechargeable.

Peregrine Outfitters

25 Omega Drive
P.O. Box 1500
Williston, VT 05495
(800) 222-3088
Fax: (800) 645-5002
www.peregrineoutfitters.com

Peregrine Outfitters is a wholesale distributor supplying outdoors retailers with more than 6,000 products, including clothing, books, tools, backpacks, sleeping bags, and tents. It is the exclusive distributor of Nesters Cookware.

✔ Brochure ✔ Online shop

PhotonLight.com

200 W. 38th Ave.
Eugene, OR 97405
(541) 927-3552
(877) 584-6898
Fax: (541) 484-6898
bryan@photonlight.com
www.photonlight.com

PhotonLight makes several small flashlights, many of which will fit on keychains, as well as batteries and accessories. Orders are taken online, by phone, or by fax.

■ **Brand Name(s):** Photon, Rav'n Party Light.
✔ Brochure ✔ Online shop
■ **Products:** • Flashlights

Piggy Pack

301 Piper Cub
Scotts Valley, CA 95066
(888) 723-1208
Fax: (831) 461-1187
dave@piggypack.com
www.piggypack.com

Piggy Pack makes travel equipment and containers, including the Piggy Pack car top carrier, bike racks, cargo boxes, truck tents and a pet barrier. Shopping is online, by phone, or in stores.

■ **Brand Name(s):** Piggy Pack
✔ Online shop
■ **Products:** • Car top carriers • Truck tents • Cargo boxes

Pilot Rock Park Equipment

P.O. Box 946
Cherokee, IA 51012
(712) 225-5115
(800) 762-5002
Fax: (712) 225-5796
www.pilotrock.com

R.J. Thomas Manufacturing Co. makes Pilot Rock Park Equipment, which includes campfire rings, grills, picnic tables, and park benches.

■ **Brand Name(s):** Pilot Rock.
✔ Brochure ✔ Online shop
■ **Products:** • Picnic tables • Benches • Grills • Campfire ring

Pit-2-Go

844 Holly Oak Court
Hollister, CA 95023
800-PIT2GO4
www.pit2go.com

Pit-2-Go makes a portable campfire pit that folds up to less than four inches and burns wood, charcoal, or pressed logs. It comes with a tote bag and accessories available include a spark shield, grate grabber, and pit scoop.

Brand Name(s): Pit-2-Go.
Products: • Portable firepit

The Pit-2-Go firepit creates an instant campfire using wood, charcoal or pressed logs, and folds down to four inches.

Platypus

4000 1st Ave. South
Seattle, WA 98134
(800) 531-9531
Fax: (206) 531-9531
info@cascadedesigns.com
www.cascadedesigns.com/platypus

Platypus makes flexible hydration systems, including bottles and holsters; hydration reservoirs; carriers; hydration packs, and paddlesport hydration packs.

■ **Brand Name(s):** Platypus.
■ **Products:** • Hydration packs

Hosers, in several sizes, are one of the hydration systems offered by Platypus to be carried in backpacks or daypacks.

Roadrunner is one of the Platypus hydration packs, with this model carrying 70 ounces of water.

Plow & Hearth

P.O. Box 6000
Madison, VA 22727
(800) 494-7544
www.plowhearth.com

Plow & Hearth has a variety of outdoors products that could be useful to campers, including furniture, umbrellas, weather instruments, snowshoes, lights, apparel, and footwear. Sales are by catalog and online, as well as at four Virginia stores.

■ **Brand Name(s):** Several name brands available.
✔ Brochure ✔ Online shop ✔ Retail shop

Primus AB

Box 1366
171 26 Solna
Sweden
info@primus.se
www.primus.se

Primus, a Swedish company, makes LP gas appliances, including stoves and lanterns for camping.

■ **Brand Name(s):** Primus.
■ **Products:** • Stoves • Lanterns

Princeton Tec Sport Lights

P.O. Box 8057
Trenton, NJ 08650
(609) 298-9331
Fax: (609) 298-9601
info@princetontec.com
www.princetontec.com

Princeton Tec produces a variety of headlamps and flashlights for outdoors use, as well as diving gear.

■ **Brand Name(s):** Matrix, Pulsar, Tec, Predator, Quest, Sport Flare.
✔ Brochure ✔ Online shop
■ **Products:** • Headlamps • Flashlights

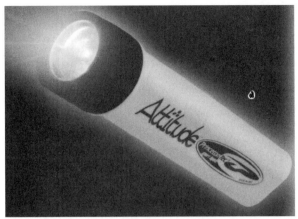

Princeton Tec's new Attitude flashlight features the triangular configuration of three high-output LEDs.

The Predator headlamp can burn for eight hours and is water-proofed to 2,000 feet.

Recreational Equipment Inc. (REI)

6750 S. 228th St.
Kent, WA 98032
(800) 426-4840
Fax: (253) 891-2523
www.rei.com

REI is a consumer cooperative that sells a variety of camping equipment online and in its more than 60 retail stores across the U.S. Equipment includes backpacks, tents, sleeping gear, lighting, stoves, furniture, cookware, and many other outdoor products.

■ **Brand Name(s):** REI stocks most major brands.
✔ Online shop ✔ Retail shop

■ **Products:** • Tents • Cookware • Stoves • Sleeping bags • Lights • Furniture

REI's OKT Shell features a water-repellent finish and breathable nylon microfiber.

The REI Valahalla is a minimalist weekender/climber pack with side zipper access and front shovel pocket.

A popular shelter is REI's Half Dome Plus 2 tent, with two doors, rainfly window, and Featherlite poles, weighing five pounds.

Reliance Products

1093 Sherwin Road

Winnipeg, MB R3H 1A4

(204) 633-4403

(800) 665-0258

Fax: (204) 694-5132

sales@relianceproducts.mb.ca

www.relianceproducts.com

Reliance Products, based in Canada, makes a variety of camping products, including coolers, jugs, water bottles, organizer boxes, portable showers, tent stakes, and portable toilets.

■ **Brand Name(s):** Reliance.

✔ Brochure

■ **Products:** • Coolers • Containers • Toilets • Showers

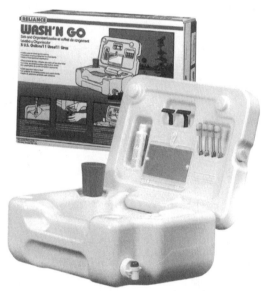

The Wash'n Go Compact Sink/Organizer from Reliance Products provides a portable sink, room for three gallons of water, and holders for basic toiletries.

Reliance's Quench-Mates with insulated covers and Pristine Water Treatment keep water safe and cool.

River Sports Outfitters Inc.

2918 Sutherland Ave.

P.O.Box 11047

Knoxville, TN 37919

Other addresses: 73 White Bridge Road, 4G
    Paddock Place, Nashville, TN 37205

(865) 523-0066

(615) 356-5230

Fax: (865) 552-5921

rivsport@usit.net

www.GearPro.com

■ **Products:** Specialty retail and rental camping products, all major brands. Guide services also available.

■ **Brand Name(s):** GearPro

✔ Brochure ✔ Online shop ✔ Retail shop.

Rokk

1224 Fern Ridge Parkway

St. Louis, MO 63141

877-765ROKK

www.rokkgear.com

Rokk makes a full line of backpacks and a line of tents. Products are available at retail stores.

■ **Brand Name(s):** Rokk.

■ **Products:** • Tents • Backpacks

Russell's For Men

1920 N. 26th St.

Lowell, AR 72745

(479) 631-0130

(800) 255-9034

Fax: (479) 631-8493

www.russellsformen.com

Russell's For Men is a mail order catalog of fine gifts for men. Included are camping accessories, watches, tools, luggage, knives, and collectibles. Sales are by catalog or online.

■ **Brand Name(s):** Leading brand names.

✔ Brochure ✔ Online shop

■ **Products:** • Camping gear • Knives • Luggage • Tools

Compact folding lawn furniture by Shakespeare is among the camping items offered by Russell's For Men.

Campers and hikers will have a tough time getting lost if they use the Brunton Multi-Navigator GPS unit sold by Russell's For Men.

S. King Company Inc.

8519 Fox Haven Chase

Sturtevant, WI 53177

(262) 884-9240

(888) 892-2547

Fax: (262) 884-9774

www.skingcompany.com

S. King sells "mobile living" products including kitchenware, electronics, portable power generators and rechargers, and cooling and heating products.

■ **Brand Name(s):** Igloo, Road Pro, Cherokee.

✔ Brochure ✔ Online shop

■ **Products:** • Rechargers • Kitchenware • Cooling and Heating Products • Generators • Spotlights

Sea to Summit

601 Jade Cliffs Lane

Las Vegas, NV 89144

(702) 240-1600

Fax: (801) 838-6382

info@seatosummitusa.com

www.seatosummitusa.com

Sea to Summit produces several camping products, including stuff sacks and dry sacks, sleeping bag liners, umbrellas, and towels.

■ **Brand Name(s):** Sea to Summit.

✔ Brochure

■ **Products:** • Sacks • Bag liners

Sea to Summit offers Lightweight Dry Sacks in seven sizes to keep critical items dry while camping.

Sherpa Mountain Products

145 W. Broadway

Vancouver, BC V5Y 1P4

(604) 872-2504

(800) 321-3423

Fax: (604) 874-0674

service@sherpa-mtn.com

www.sherpa-mtn.com

Sherpa Mountain Products is a Canadian distributor of outdoor gear, including boots, tents, packs, and sleeping pads by Meindl, Tatonka, Wechsel, and others.

■ **Products:** • Boots • Packs • Tents

Sierra Designs

1255 Powell St.

Emeryville, CA 94608

(800) 635-0461

www.sierradesigns.com

Sierra Designs makes tents, sleeping bags, and men's and women's outdoor clothing. A catalog is available and products are in stores.

■ **Brand Name(s):** Sierra Designs.

✔ Brochure

■ **Products:** • Tents • Sleeping bags • Clothing

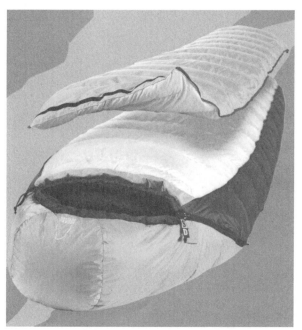

ThermoSpectrum DryDown expedition bags from Sierra Designs are sleeping bags that feature goose down and a water resistant and breathable DryDown shell, with a zip-off layer.

The Omega CD is Sierra Designs' lightest two-person convertible tent; simple to pitch and easy to live in.

Slumberjack Products

P.O. Box 7048A

St. Louis, MO 63117

(800) 233-6283

Fax: (314) 576-8054

info@slumberjack.com

www.slumberjack.com

Slumberjack makes a full line of outdoor sleep systems, including sleeping bags, self-inflating mats, bivouac shelters, and accessories, as well as camping furniture. Products are available in retail stores.

■ **Brand Name(s):** Slumberjack.

✔ Brochure

■ **Products:** • Sleeping bags • Camping furniture • Sleeping mats

The Bonnie & Clyde sleeping bag, in Slumberjack's Basecamp Series, keeps a couple comfortable to 30 degrees and includes a 100 percent cotton plaid flannel liner.

Slumberjack's outdoor furniture includes the Big Mesh Quad chair with an aluminum frame and poly/mesh fabric.

The Cataclysm sleeping bag, part of Slumberjack's Denali Series, keeps a sleeper warm at temperatures to 30 below zero but weighs just 4 pounds, 10 ounces.

The Casita Grande Two-Room Tent from StanSport has a detachable privacy divider.

Snow Peak USA Inc.

15790 SE Piazza Ave. #101

Clackamas, OR 97015

(503) 697-3330

Fax: (503) 699-1396

info@snowpeak.com

www.snowpeak.com

Snow Peak produces compact camping equipment, lightweight backpacks, lanterns, cookware, and other outdoor supplies. Dealers sell the products throughout the U.S. and Canada.

■ **Brand Name(s):** Snow Peak.

■ **Products:** • Backpacks • Cookware • Lanterns • Outdoor furniture

StanSport

2801 E. 12th St.

Los Angeles, CA 90023

(323) 269-0510

(800) 421-6131

Fax: (323) 269-2761

stansport@stansport.com

www.stansport.com

StanSport is a distributor that doesn't sell to the general public. It offers a wide variety of camping gear, including tents, sleeping bags, furniture, cookware, tools, and clothing.

■ **Products:** • Tents • Furniture • Cookware • Tools • Clothing

A picnic in a backpack is available in the Deluxe Two Person Picnic Set from StanSport.

Stephensons Warmlite

22 Hook Road

Gilford, NH 03249

(603) 293-7016

Fax: (603) 293-8526

inquiries@warmlite.com

www.warmlite.com

Warmlite, produced by Stephensons since 1956, makes sleeping bags and tents for extreme weather. Orders are by catalog only.

■ **Brand Name(s):** Warmlite.

✔ Brochure

■ **Products:** • Tents • Sleeping bags

Stephensons Warmlite tents are designed to protect campers in extreme conditions.

StoneCreek Designs Inc.

3003 Arapahoe St.
Denver, CO 80205
(303) 382-1105
Fax: (303) 382-1237
www.stonecreekdesigns.com

StoneCreek Designs produces a line of backpacks, the Sport Boomerang bag, and MuttHutt pet carriers.

■ **Brand Name(s):** StoneCreek, MuttHutt.
✔ Brochure
■ **Products:** • Backpacks • Bags • Pet carriers

The MuttHutt, in varying sizes, by StoneCreek Designs doubles as a carrier and protection for pets.

StoneCreek's Sport Boomerang is a stylish bag for travel, bike riding, or wearing around town, made of cordura and mesh with pockets for wallet, keys, and water bottle.

Summit Hut

5045 E. Speedway Blvd.
Tucson, AZ 85712
(520) 325-1554
(800) 499-8696
Fax: (520) 795-7350
summit@summithut.com
www.summithut.com

Summit Hut offers gear and clothing for camping, hiking, and climbing, including tents, packs, travel gear, clothing, and books. Products are sold online, by phone, and in a Tucson store.

■ **Brand Name(s):** Many brands are available.
✔ Online shop ✔ Retail shop.
■ **Products:** • Tents • Packs • Clothing • Sleeping bags

Survival Inc.

2633 Eastlake Ave. East, Suite 103
Seattle, WA 98102
(206) 726-9363
888-BEREADY
Fax: (206) 726-0130
www.ultimatesurvival.com

Survival Inc. produces the Ultimate Survival Outdoors Tools line, including fire starters, whistles, mirrors, saws, and an all-weather carrying case. Online shopping is available.

✔ Brochure ✔ Online shop
■ **Products:** • Survival tools

The Ultimate Survival Tool Kits from Survivor Inc. include fire starters, a whistle, mirror, saw, and case.

Suunto

2151 Las Palmas Drive, Suite F
Carlsbad, CA 92009
(760) 931-6788
(800) 543-9124
Fax: (760) 931-9875
info@suuntousa.com
www.suuntousa.com

Suunto, headquartered in Finland, makes high-quality compasses and wristwatch-style computers. Other outdoor products include Primus stoves and lanterns, and CEBE eyewear.

■ **Brand Name(s):** Suunto, Primus, CEBE.

■ **Products:** • Compasses • Stoves • Lanterns • Eyewear

Swift Instruments Inc.

952 Dorchester Ave.
Boston, MA 02125
(617) 436-2960
Fax: (716) 436-3232
www.swift-optics.com

Swift Instruments makes a variety of binoculars and telescopes.

■ **Brand Name(s):** Swift.

✔ Brochure

■ **Products:** • Binoculars • Telescopes

Swiss Army Brands Inc.

P.O. Box 874
Shelton, CT 06484
(888) 658-0717
86699swiss
travelgear@swissarmybrands.com
www.swissarmy.com

Besides its famous knives, Swiss Army sells camping tools and travel gear, and has launched a line of outdoors apparel.

■ **Brand Name(s):** Swiss Army, Victorinox® Apparel.

✔ Brochure ✔ Online shop

■ **Products:** • Knives • Apparel • Tools • Backpacks

Tecfen Corp.

5860-C Hollister Ave.
Santa Barbara, CA 93117
(805) 967-1153
Fax: (805) 967-1295
tecfen@tecfen.com
www.tecfen.com

Tecfen makes wilderness survival gear, including all-weather and emergency blankets and the FireMate Flint Fire Starter. It also has a line of medical emergency products.

■ **Brand Name(s):** Tecfen.

✔ Brochure

■ **Products:** • Survival gear • Medical emergency kits

The Camping Gear Store

Armitage Hardware
925 W. Armitage
Chicago, IL 60614
(773) 348-3267
Fax: (773) 348-8246
cascor@xsite.net
www.colemanoutdoors.com

The Camping Gear Store by Armitage Hardware carries Coleman Camping Products and is an authorized reseller of Coleman Products. It offers online shopping as well as a retail store.

■ **Brand Name(s):** Coleman Camping Products.
✔ Online shop ✔ Retail shop.
■ **Products:** • Coleman camping gear

The Escape Co.

P.O. Box 520867
Independence, MO 64052
(816) 353-5596
Fax: (816) 353-1554
escape@escape-co.com
www.escape-co.com

ESCAPE stands for Emergency, Survival, Camping, and Preparedness Equipment. Gear includes lights, security items, solar equipment, water products, tools, and first aid kits. Shopping is available online and at a retail store in Independence, Mo.

■ **Brand Name(s):** Several brands are available.
✔ Online shop ✔ Retail shop.
■ **Products:** • Emergency gear • Lighting • Water products • Solar items • First aid kits

The Outdoor World of California

2720 S. Rodeo Gulch Road
Soquel, CA 95073
(888) 344-9500
Fax: (831) 462-0576
info@theoutdoorworld.com
www.theoutdoorworld.com

The Outdoor World carries a wide variety of outdoor equipment, including camping gear, packs, boots, sleeping bags, and tents. Purchases can be made online and in several retail stores in California.

■ **Brand Name(s):** Many name brands.
✔ Online shop ✔ Retail shop.
■ **Products:** • Tents • Packs • Clothing • Boots

The Wenzel Company

1224 Fern Ridge Parkway
St. Louis, MO 63141
(800) 325-8368
Fax: (314) 576-8010
www.wenzelco.com

The Wenzel Company, founded in 1887, makes a wide variety of camping equipment, including tents, screenhouses, sleeping bags, mats, airbeds, stoves, lanterns, and lighting.

■ **Brand Name(s):** Wenzel.
✔ Brochure
■ **Products:** • Tents • Sleeping bags • Stoves • Lanterns

The Panorama II screen house provides room for campground or backyard gatherings with a 17-foot by 15-foot base and 93-inch center height.

The Oasis from Wenzel is a spacious and open sun shade, 14-foot by 12-foot with a 96-inch center height.

Therm-a-Rest

4000 1st Ave. South
Seattle, WA 98134
(800) 531-9531
Fax: (206) 224-6492
info@cascadedesigns.com
www.cascadedesigns.com/thermarest

Therma-a-Rest specializes in making self-inflating camping mattresses, closed cell foam pads, camp chairs, pillows, and accessories.

■ **Brand Name(s):** Therm-a-Rest.

■ **Products:** • Mattresses • Camp chair • Pillows

CampLite is a camping mattress from Therm-a-Rest that's light enough for backpacking.

Lite Chairs by Therm-a-Rest are camp chairs that are light enough to be used for backpacking or mountaineering.

Therm-a-Rest pillows are available in a variety of colors and sizes.

Timberline Group

4040 Heeb Road
Manhattan, MT 49741
(800) 405-5516
timber1@avicom.net
www.timberlinefurniture.com

Timberline's Outdoor Supply offers outdoor adventure gear including tents, backpacks, sleeping bags, and other camping gear.

■ **Brand Name(s):** Leading brand names are offered.

✔ Online shop

■ **Products:** • Tents • Backpacks • Stoves • Binoculars • Snowshoes

ToolLogic

2290 Eastman Ave., Suite 109
Ventura, CA 93003
(805) 339-9725
(800) 483-8422
Fax: (805) 339-9712
sales@toollogic.com
www.toollogic.com

ToolLogic features credit card compact multi-tool kits with features such as knife, bottle opener, screwdrivers, nail file, toothpick, compass, ruler, and LED light. Other products include survival kits and tools. Internet shopping is available.

■ **Brand Name(s):** ToolLogic.

✔ Brochure ✔ Online shop

■ **Products:** • Survival tools • Credit card tool kits

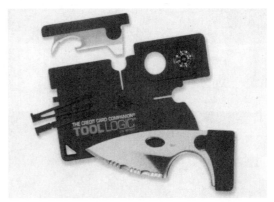

The Credit Card Companion and ICE Companion, from Toollogic, features a knife, lens, compass, can opener, screwdriver, tweezers, toothpick, and ruler.

Tough Traveler Ltd.

1012 State St.

Schenectady, NY 12307

(518) 393-0168

800GOTOUGH

Fax: (518) 377-5434

service@toughtraveler.com

www.toughtraveler.com

Tough Traveler makes a variety of backpacks, child carriers, pet carriers, sleeping bags, and luggage. It has a retail store in Schenectady in addition to online and retail sales.

■ **Brand Name(s):** Tough Traveler, Tough Traveler KidSystems.

✔ Brochure ✔ Online shop ✔ Retail shop

■ **Products:** • Luggage • Backpacks • Child care • Sleeping bags

The Tough Traveler Stallion is recommended in *Outside Magazine* as the best carrier backpack for use by tall parents.

Trail Blazer

100 Ilsley Ave., Unit G

Dartmouth, NS B3B 1L3

(902) 481-0267

(800) 565-6564

Fax: (902) 481-0263

info@trailblazerproducts.com

www.trailblazerproducts.com

Trail Blazer is a Canadian-based manufacturer of hunting knives, camping and pruning saws, and extension poles. Online shopping is available.

■ **Brand Name(s):** Trail Blazer

✔ Brochure ✔ Online shop

■ **Products:** • Saws • Knives

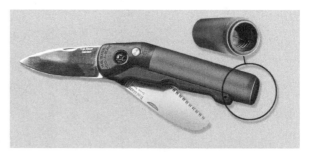

The Camper's Edge has a high-carbon stainless steel knife blade and a saw blade that makes short work of branches.

Tough Traveler's Kid Carrier includes a rain/sun hood for a child's extra comfort.

TravelChair Co.

5709 34th Ave. NW
P.O. Box 1757
Gig Harbor, WA 98335
(253) 851-7519
Fax: (253) 851-5359
trvelchair@aol.com

TravelChair makes outdoor and travel furniture, including chairs, folding picnic tables, stools, and cushions.

■ **Brand Name(s):** TravelChair.
✔ Brochure
■ **Products:** • Outdoor furniture

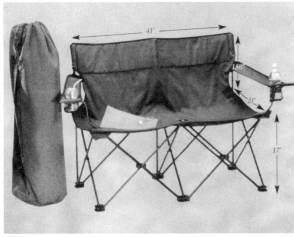

TravelChair's Portable Loveseat with Armrests folds with one easy squeeze and includes a matching storage/carrying bag.

The Ultimate TCC Recliner from TravelChair includes an adjustable pillow headrest, padded armrests, adjustable reclining positions, and PVC coated polyester mesh fabric.

Trondak Inc.

11710 Airport Road, #300
Everett, WA 98204
(425) 290-7530
Fax: (425) 355-9101
info@aquaseal.com
www.aquaseal.com

Trondak makes Aquaseal brand waterproofing products, including seam sealers, map and fabric sealers, and footwear conditioner.

■ **Brand Name(s):** Aquaseal.
■ **Products:** • Waterproofing products

Tubbs Snowshoe Co.

52 River Road
Stowe, VT 05672
(802) 253-7398
(800) 882-2748
Fax: (802) 253-9982
info@tubbssnowshoes.com
www.tubbssnowshoes.com

Tubbs makes snowshoes that could be used by winter campers. They are available in sporting goods stores.

■ **Brand Name(s):** Tubbs Snowshoes.
✔ Brochure
■ **Products:** • Snowshoes

A Snowshoe Starter Kit from Tubbs Snowshoe Co. includes a pair of Discovery Series snowshoes, a pair of snowshoe poles, and a Tubbs Trailnet CD.

UCO Corp.

9225 151st Ave. NE

Redmond, WA 98052

(425) 883-6600

(888) 297-6062

Fax: (425) 883-0035

www.ucocorp.com

UCO makes candle lanterns and accessories to provide campground lighting. Sales are through retailers.

■ **Brand Name(s):** UCO.

■ **Products:** • Lanterns

The new UCO Duo, an LED light for UCO candle lanterns, can be attached to a lantern as a flashlight or used as a headlamp.

The Value Pack includes the Original Candle Lantern by UCO and a pack of three candles along with a protective fleece bag.

Variety International Inc.

525 Aldo Ave.

Santa Clara, CA 95054

(408) 988-1988

(800) 700-1666

Fax: (408) 988-1989

sales@varietyintl.com

www.varietyintl.com

Variety International produces a variety of lightweight portable furniture, including chairs, tables, stools, and cots, in aluminum and polyester fabric.

■ **Brand Name(s):** Variety International.

✔ Brochure

■ **Products:** • Portable furniture

Variety International's Aluminum-A-Cot is a lightweight cot with reinforced aluminum frame and 600-denier fabric with carry bag.

The Majestic Rest Chair from Variety International has an aluminum frame, 600-denier polyester RealTree Hardwoods pattern fabric, and plenty of room for beverages.

Vaude Sports Inc.

P.O. Box 3413

Tavern Road

Mammoth Lakes, CA 93546

(800) 447-1539

Vaude Sports makes a variety of camping equipment, including tents, packs, stoves, and cycling gear. A catalog is available.

■ **Brand Name(s):** Vaude

✔ Brochure

■ **Products:** • Tents • Stove • Packs

The Galaxy 3 tent by Vaude Sports is year-round, with room for three, and has two entrances and two vestibules.

The Hot Rod Titanium Stove weighs only three ounces and measures 2 1/2 inches by 2 inches. It features electric ignition.

Vaude Sports' Siena 40 features a built-in rain cover and will hold two 100-ounce reservoirs.

Vermont Country Store

P.O. Box 3000
Manchester Center, VT 05255
(802) 362-8460
Fax: (802) 362-0285
customerservice@vermontcountrystore.com
www.vermontcountrystore.com
The Vermont Country Store is a catalog and online store that sells a variety of practical and hard-to-find items, including outdoor products and clothing. Retail stores are in Weston and Rockingham, Vt.
■ **Brand Name(s):** Many brands are sold.
✔ Brochure ✔ Online shop ✔ Retail shop
■ **Products:** • Outdoor equipment • Clothing

A baseball cap for women, featuring a three-inch bill, is one of many clothing items at Vermont Country Store.

Vermont Country Store says its outdoor furniture is made to last a lifetime.

W.R. Case & Sons Cutlery Co.

P.O. Box 4000
Owens Way
Bradford, PA 16701
(800) 523-6350
Fax: (814) 368-1736
casesales.com
W.R. Case makes a wide variety of pocket knives and sporting knives, including campers' knives.
■ **Brand Name(s):** W.R. Case
✔ Brochure
■ **Products:** • Knives

The Camper's Knife with Pliers by W.R. Case includes a spear blade, punch, pliers, and screwdriver/cap lifter.

Watchful Eye Designs

173 N. 300 W

Midway, UT 84049

(435) 657-9655

(800) 355-1126

Fax: (435) 657-9694

info@watchfuleyedesigns.com

www.watchfuleyedesigns.com

Watchful Eye Designs makes the Aloksak Element Proof Storage bags to protect valuables against the weather. Included are Splash Caddy nylon waist packs and shoulder bags, and map cases lined with Aloksak bags.

■ **Brand Name(s):** Aloksak.

✔ Brochure

■ **Products:** • Waterproof bags

Aloksak waterproof bags come in several sizes and provide linings for Splash Caddy products.

WeatherRite Outdoor

602 Fountain Parkway

Grand Prairie, TX 75050

(800) 255-6061

www.weatherrite.com

WeatherRite Outdoor makes an assortment of camping equipment, including tents, lanterns, stoves, heaters, portable furniture, tent accessories, and cookware.

■ **Brand Name(s):** WeatherRite Outdoor.

✔ Brochure

■ **Products:** • Tents • Stoves • Portable furniture • Cookware

New to the WeatherRite Outdoor line is a series of Speed Dome tents, including this 4-Peak Dome Tent that sets up in 40 seconds and sleeps five.

The Single Propane Heater from WeatherRite has a seven-inch reflector and kicks out 2,890 BTU of heat.

WeatherRite's Folding Picnic Table measures 34 inches wide by 54 inches long and folds compactly for storage.

WelCom Products Inc.

4455 Torrance Blvd., #1000

Torrance, CA 90503

(310) 792-7712

Fax: (310) 792-7719

www.welcomproducts.com

WelCom Products makes a line of outdoor furniture, including backpack chairs and sport chairs. Online shopping is available.

■ **Brand Name(s):** WelCom.

✔ Brochure ✔ Online shop

■ **Products:** • Outdoor chairs

The Winston Churchill Full-Length Lounger from WelCom Products features an adjustable pillow and dual drink holders.

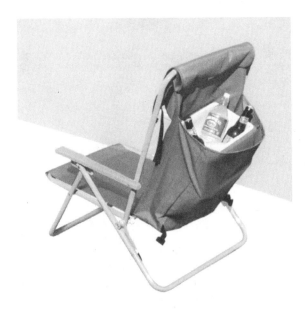

The WearEver Hi-Back Chair from WelCom Products offers instant comfort and can be folded into a backpack.

Wiggy's Inc.

P.O. Box 2124

Grand Junction, CO 81505

(800) 748-1827

Fax: (970) 241-5921

wiggys@wiggys.com

www.wiggys.com

Wiggy's produces clothing, backpacks, sleeping bags, footwear, shelters, and camping accessories. Products are sold online as well as in stores.

■ **Brand Name(s):** Wiggy's.

✔ Brochure ✔ Online shop

■ **Products:** • Clothing • Sleeping bags • Packs • Shelters • Footwear

The Ultima Thule sleeping bag by Wiggy's weighs 5.1 pounds and carries a –20 degree rating.

Wiggy's Expedition 1 features a large, self-compressing back pocket that is weather-proof.

Wilcor International

700 Broad St.

Utica, NY 13501

(315) 733-3542

■ **Products:** • Camping supplies

Wild Mountain Outfitters

541 W. Cordova Road

Santa Fe, NM 87501

(505) 986-1152

(800) 988-1152

Fax: (505) 982-5369

fungear@wildmountainoutfitters.com

www.bcexp.com

Wild Mountain Outfitters offers a variety of camping equipment, including packs, tents, boots, sleeping bags, clothing, cookwear, and climbing gear. Sales are made online as well as in the Santa Fe store.

■ **Brand Name(s):** Various equipment brands.
✔ Online shop ✔ Retail shop.

■ **Products:** • Tents • Clothing • Cookware • Footwear • Packs

Wild Things

64 Hobbs St.

Conway, NH 03818

(603) 447-6907

info@wildthingsgear.com

www.wildthingsgear.com

Wild Things has made climbing equipment since 1981.

■ **Brand Name(s):** Icesac, Rocsac, Rock Raptor, Predator, Spandura
✔ Brochure ✔ Online shop

■ **Products:** • Climbing gear • Packs • Apparel

Wisemen Trading and Supply

8971 Lentzville Road

Athens, AL 35614

(256) 729-8868

(888) 891-8411

Fax: (256) 729-6788

contact@wisementrading.com

www.wisementrading.com

Wisemen Trading offers a wide range of camping and survival equipment, including cookware, can-dles and lanterns, tools, camp stoves, bedding, and food products. Sales are online or by phone.

■ **Brand Name(s):** Many brands are sold.
✔ Online shop

■ **Products:** • Stoves • Bedding • Lighting • Cookware

Woods Canada Ltd.

1430 Birchmount Road

Toronto, ON M1P 2E8

(416) 465-2403

(877) 537-3002

Fax: (416) 465-2310

custserv@woodscanada.com

www.woodscanada.com

Operating since 1885, Woods makes tents, sleeping bags, packs, outerwear, and accessories.

■ **Brand Name(s):** Woods.

■ **Products:** • Tents • Sleeping bags • Clothing • Packs

Woods Canada's Adventure pack, with 2,135 cubic inches of space, has one large compartment and a removable fanny pack.

The Ultimate Parka features a down lining, a water-repellent shell and oversized hand-warmer pockets with Velcro closures.

WPC Brands Inc.

1 Repel Road
Jackson, WI 53037
(800) 558-6614
Fax: (262) 677-9006
info@wpcbrands.com
www.destinationoutdoors.com

WPC Brands makes Repel insect repellant, StingEze insect bite relief, Reflect Suncare, Baitmate fish attractant, Atwater Carey first aid kits, and Potable Aqua water treatment kits. The company's Web site also offers advice on insect protection, sun protection.

■ **Brand Name(s):** Repel, StingEze, Baitmate, Reflect Suncare, Atwater Carey, Potable Aqua.
✔ Brochure
■ **Products:** • Insect repellants • Insect bite relief • Sun lotion • First aid kits

Repel's insect repellant products include this mosquito netting that can be used at a campsite.

Reflect Sport Sunscreen comes ready to attach to clothing or a backpack.

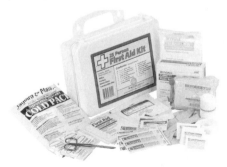

Atwater Carey first aid kits come in various sizes and contain essentials, from bandages to scissors and forceps.

Zodi Outback Gear

P.O. Box 4687
Park City, UT 84060
(800) 589-2849
Fax: (800) 861-8228
www.zodi.com

Zodi's products include portable showers, outdoor hot water heaters, and tent heaters. Sales are by catalog or in stores.
■ **Brand Name(s):** Zodi.
✔ Brochure
■ **Products:** • Hot water heaters • Portable showers • Tent heaters

The Hot Camp Shower from Zodi Outback Gear includes a four-gallon plastic case and battery-operated pump.

The Zodi Hot Vent quickly warms up a tent on cool nights with clean fresh hot air.

Camping Apparel

Boreal

S.W. Partners Inc. (U.S. distributor)

P.O. Box 7116

Capistrano Beach, CA 92624

(949) 498-1011

Fax: (949) 498-9798

info@borealusa.com

www.borealusa.com

Boreal makes footwear and apparel for hiking, trekking, mountain climbing, and outdoors wear. Sales are made online, by phone, and in stores.

■ **Brand Name(s):** Boreal.

✔ Online shop.

■ **Products:** • Footwear • Apparel

Cordura/DuPont

P.O. Box 80711

Wilmington, DE 19880

cordura-na@usa.dupont.com

www.dupont.com/cordura

DuPont's Cordura is used in a variety of outdoors equipment, including packs and bags, footwear, and luggage, as well as clothing.

■ **Brand Name(s)**: Cordura

■ **Products:** • Packs • Luggage • Footwear • Apparel

Danner Shoe Mfg. Co.

18550 NE Riverside Parkway

Portland, OR 97230

(503) 251-1100

(800) 345-0430

Fax: (503) 251-1119

info@danner.com

www.danner.com

Danner makes lines of boots for hiking, hunting, fishing, and outdoors wear. Sales are through dealers and an outlet store in Portland.

■ **Brand Name(s):** Danner.

✔ Retail shop.

■ **Products:** • Boots

Danner's Radical 45 GTX is part of the line of redesigned outdoor cross training shoes.

Design Salt USA

P.O. Box 1220

Redway, CA 95560

(800) 254-7258

Fax: (707) 923-4605

support@designsalt.com

www.designsalt.com

Design Salt makes light sleep gear for travelers and backpackers. Products include sleeping bag liners, sheets, outdoor blankets, and sleepwear. Products are available online or in stores.

■ **Brand Name(s):** DesignSalt, Cocoon.

✔ Online shop.

■ **Products:** Sleeping products

Duofold

25 Liberty St.

Tamaqua, PA 18252

www.duofold.com

Duofold makes thermal underwear for outdoors use while camping, hiking or skiing. Products are available in stores.

■ **Brand Name(s):** Duofold.

■ **Products:** • Thermal underwear

Eddie Bauer

P.O. Box 97000

Redmond, WA 98073

(800) 625-7935

Fax: (425) 869-4629

www.eddiebauer.com

From a single store in Seattle in 1920, Eddie Bauer has grown to more than 550 stores across the U.S. as well as an online and catalog merchant. Eddie Bauer sells clothing for outdoor wear as well as luggage and duffels.

■ **Brand Name(s):** Eddie Bauer.

✔ Brochure, ✔ Online shop, ✔ Retail shop

■ **Products:** • Clothing • Luggage

frogg toggs

517 Gunter Ave.

P.O. Box 428

Guntersville, AL 35976

(256) 505-0075

(800) 349-1835

Fax: (256) 505-0307

froggtoggs@localaccess.net

www.froggtoggs.com

frogg toggs makes waterproof, breathable, lightweight rainwear. Purchases can be made online, by catalog, or in stores.

■ **Brand Name(s):** frogg toggs.

✔ Brochure ✔ Online shop

■ **Products:** • Rainwear

The man wears the PA102 Pro Action Suit while the woman wears the FT-102 frogg toggs original suit.

Georgia Boot Co.

408 Rudolph Ave.

Nashville, TN 37206

(888) 262-7717

Fax: (615) 258-3338

www.georgiabootcompany.com

Georgia Boot, a division of Breyer International, produces boots for sport and trail.

■ **Brand Name(s):** Georgia Boot.

✔ Online shop.

GoLite LLC

5785 Arapahoe Ave., Suite D

Boulder, CO 80303

(888) 546-5483

www.golite.com

GoLite designs, maunfactures, and sells lightweight hiking and climbing gear and clothing, including raingear, packs, shelters, and sleep systems. Sales are through dealers and on the Internet.

✔ Brochure, Online shop

The Squall storm shell, for men and women, from GoLite. provides for fast packing and lightweight hiking or ski touring.

Izeo 2 Design

P.O. Box 3852
San Rafael, CA 94912
(415) 459-3800
Fax: (415) 455-9599
www.hatinabag.com

Izeo 2 Design has created the Hat in a Bag, a line of foldable sunproof hats with a UPF50 sun protection rating in several styles.

■ **Brand Name(s):** Hat in a Bag.

✔ Brochure.

■ **Products:** • Hats

The Hat in a Bag by Izeo 2 Designs is a portable hat that can be stored in a pocket or purse, ready for sun or rain, and has a lifetime guarantee and UPF50 sun protection rating.

L.L. Bean

11 Casco St.
Freeport, ME 04033
(800) 648-7024
www.llbean.com

In addition to its extensive line of clothing, L.L. Bean offers a large inventory of camping equipment, including tents, sleeping bags, backpacks, kitchen and water treatment gear, and camping and hiking accessories.

■ **Brand Name(s):** L.L. Bean

Brochure, Online shop

■ **Products:** • Apparel • Tents • Sleeping bags • Backpacks • Camping equipment

Lands' End

Lands' End Lane
Dodgeville, WI 53595
(800) 963-4816
www.landsend.com

Lands' End offers catalog and online shopping for a variety of apparel, including outerwear, hiking boots, and clothing for camping. It also stocks backpacks and products such as outdoor dinnerwear and furniture, coolers, and Polartec blankets.

■ **Brand Name(s):** Lands' End.

✔ Brochure ✔ Online shop ✔ Retail shop.

■ **Products:** • Clothing • Boots • Outdoor clothing • Blankets

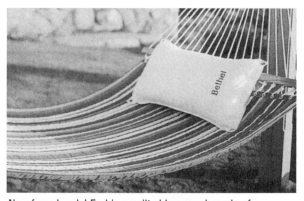

New from Lands' End is a quilted hammock made of Sunbrella fabric that holds two adults.

A set of enamelware dinnerware from Lands' End is designed for camping, tailgating, or dinner on the patio.

Manzella Productions Inc.

80 Sonwil Drive
Buffalo, NY 14225
(800) 645-6837
Fax: (715) 618-6888
www.manzella.com

Manzella makes gloves for cold, windy, and wet weather. The gloves are available in stores.

■ **Brand Name(s):** Manzella.

■ **Products:** • Gloves

Merrell Footwear

9341 Courtland Drive
Rockford, MI 49351
(888) 637-7001
www.merrellboot.com

Merrell makes boots and shoes, primarily for outdoor wear.

■ **Brand Name(s):** Merrell

■ **Products:** • Footwear

Mountain Hard Wear

4911 Central Ave.
Richmond, CA 94804
(510) 558-3000
Fax: (510) 559-6709
www.mountainhardwear.com

Mountain Hard Wear produces all-weather clothing designed for camping, hiking, and climbing, including windbreakers, fleece shirts, hats, and footwear. It also sells lightweight mountaineering tents, and sleeping bags and pads.

■ **Brand Name(s):** Mountain Hard Wear.

✔ Brochure

■ **Products:** • Clothing • Tents • Sleeping bags

The Ethereal Ice Parka, the lightest of the Gore-Tex XCR shells, is part of Mountain Hard Wear's clothing lineup.

The Micro Chill Zip T from Mountain Hard Wear is made of soft microfleece and is "sinfully soft."

Navarro Weather Gear

201-975 Vernon Drive
Vancouver, BC V6A 3P2
(604) 251-1756
Fax: (604) 251-9862
info@navarro.ca
www.navarrogear.com

Navarro produces a wide range of clothing for the outdoors, including paddle jackets and pants, fleece outerwear, and insulated clothing for winter wear. Sales are by catalog and through stores.

■ **Brand Name(s):** Navarro.

✔ Brochure

■ **Products:** • Outerwear • Insulated clothing

The Go-Lite Jacket and Pants from Navarro Weather Gear is water resistant and breathable for hiking, running, or cycling.

Oakley

1 Icon
Foothill Ranch, CA 92610
(800) 431-1439
(800) 733-6255
info@oakley.com
www.oakley.com

Oakley makes a variety of outdoor attire, including sports clothing, footwear, eyewear, goggles, and watches.

■ **Brand Name(s):** Oakley

■ **Products:** • Clothing • Eyewear • Footwear

Packtowl

4000 1st Ave. South
Seattle, WA 98134
(800) 531-9531
Fax: (206) 224-6492
info@cascadedesigns.com
www.cascadedesigns.com/packtowl

Packtowl makes camp towels and accessories.

■ **Products:** • Towels

New to the lineup of Packtowls is the Packtowl Personal, a lightweight, compact, and fast drying towel for camping and traveling.

R.U. Outside Inc.

455 S. Main St.

Driggs, ID 83422

(800) 279-7123

Fax: (800) 704-8909

tetons@ruoutside.com

www.ruoutside.com

R.U. Outside sells a variety of outdoor clothing, footwear, and winterwear, including performance clothing, hats, socks, and boots. Sales are online and through a catalog.

■ **Brand Name(s):** Clothing name brands.

✔ Brochure ✔ Online shop

■ **Products:** • Clothing • Footwear

The Renegade Winter Boot, which includes a waterproof leather upper, quick-lock lacing, ankle support strap and buckle, and four-layer liner, is rated to –40 degrees.

R.U. Outside's midweight EC2 Performance Long Johns are designed to transport moisture from the skin while providing warmth.

SmartWool

P.O. Box 774928

Steamboat Springs, CO 80477

(970) 879-2913

Fax: (970) 879-0937

www.smartwool.com

Smartwool specializes in wool socks for hiking, walking, running, cycling, and skiing. It also makes long underwear, headwear, and gloves.

■ **Brand Name(s):** Smartwool

✔ Brochure

■ **Products:** • Socks • Underwear

Rodeo Socks by R.U. Outside are made of merino wool, which wicks away moisture and helps regulate temperature.

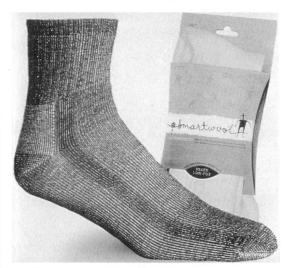

The hiking low-cut sock from SmartWool.

Sportif USA

1415 Greg St., Suite 101

Sparks, NV 89431

(775) 359-6400

800-SPORTIF

Fax: (775) 353-3400

www.sportif.com

Sportif sells clothing "for the everyday extremist," specializing in clothing for outdoors and travel. Sales are made online, by phone, by catalog, and through stores.

■ **Brand Name(s):** Sportif USA.

✔ Brochure, ✔ Online shop

■ **Products:** • Clothing

Teva Sport Sandals

2420 N. Third St., Suite B

P.O. Box 968

Flagstaff, AZ 86002

(800) 367-8382

Fax: (928) 779-6004

www.teva.com

Teva makes sandals and footwear for outdoors pursuits, including hiking, running, and water sports as well as clothing. Online and catalog shopping is available and products are sold in stores.

■ **Brand Name(s):** Teva Sport Sandals.

✔ Brochure, ✔ Online shop

■ **Products:** • Footwear • Clothing

The Women's Pretty Rugged Nylon sandals are part of Teva's Original Series of footwear.

The Women's Rodium is a breathable, quick-draining shoe in Teva's Hydro Series for performance in the water.

Thor-Lo Inc.

2210 Newton Drive

Statesville, NC 28677

(800) 438-0209

Fax: (704) 838-6323

JT@thorlo.com

www.thorlo.com

Thor-Lo makes Thorlo socks for sports and outdoors wear, including hiking, backpacking, climbing, and skiing. Products are available in stores.

■ **Brand Name(s):** Thorlos.

■ **Products:** • Socks

Travelsmith

60 Leveroni Court

Novato, CA 94949

(800) 950-1600

Fax: (800) 950-1656

service@travelsmith.com

www.travelsmith.com

Travelsmith stocks many travel supplies, including clothing, footwear, hats, and luggage. Sales are by catalog and online.

✔ Brochure, ✔ Online shop

■ **Products:** • Clothing • Luggage

Teva's Terrain Series of lightweight, rugged footwear includes the Men's Quest waterproof shoe.

Turtle Fur

P.O. Box 1010
146 Industrial Park Drive
Morrisville, VT 05661
(802) 888-6400
(800) 526-3257
Fax: (802) 888-3025
cust_service@turtlefur.com
www.turtlefur.com

Turtle Fur makes warm hats, mittens, and clothing from acrylic fleece and wool for winter wear. Products are available online as well as in stores.

■ **Brand Name(s):** Turtle Fur.
✔ Online shop
■ **Products:** • Hats • Mittens

W.L. Gore & Associates

551 Paper Mill Road
Newark, DE 19711
(888) 914-4673
info@wlgore.com
www.gore.com

W.L. Gore makes Gore-Tex and Windstopper fabrics for outdoor wear. It also makes ReviveX Water and Stain Repellant.

■ **Brand Name(s):** Gore-Tex, Windstopper, ReviveX.
■ **Products:** • Fabrics • Water repellant

Wickers America

20 Wickers Drive
Wolfboro, NH 03894
(800) 648-7024
www.wickers.com

Wickers specializes in high-performance underwear for active people.

■ **Brand Name(s):** Wickers
✔ Online shop
■ **Products:** • Apparel

Wickers Performance Underwear featured Akwatek, a fabric that wicks away moisture from the body.

Wild Roses

2203 First Ave. South
Seattle, WA 98134
877WLDROSE
Fax: (206) 467-0374
info@wrgear.com
www.wrgear.com

Wild Roses, a partner of Outdoor Research, is an outdoor clothing line created for women. Sales are online, by catalog, and through dealers.

■ **Brand Name(s):** Wild Roses.
✔ Brochure, ✔ Online shop
■ **Products:** • Outdoor clothing

Will B. Free Travel Store

1605 D Chapel Hill Road
Columbia, MO 65203
(573) 447-3733
info@willbfree.com
www.willbfree.com

Will B. Free sells luggage, travel clothing, and travel accessories on its Web site as well as in its retail store in Columbia. Brands offered include Ex Officio, The North Face, Eagle Creek, Travel Pro, Royal Robbins, and Swiss Army.

■ **Brand Name(s):** Various travel item brands.
✔ Online shop, ✔ Retail shop
■ **Products:** • Clothing • Luggage

Wintergreen Designs

205 E. Sheridan St.
Ely, MN 55731
(218) 365-6602
(800) 584-9425
info@wintergreendesigns.com
www.wintergreendesigns.com

Wintergreen Designs specializes in hand-made
clothing for outdoors, especially in layering for
warmth and wind protection. Sales are by catalog, online, and in a store in Ely.

■ **Brand Name(s):** Wintergreen.

✔ Brochure, ✔ Online shop

■ **Products:** • Clothing

A girl wearing the Kid's Wind Pro Vest from Wintergreen
gives a pat to her favorite horse.

Keeping ears warm in the winter is one of the functions of the Wintergreen Shell Hat, featuring a water-repellent Supplex shell with
shearling pile lining.

Campers and RVs

Aero Coach

1018 W. Brooklyn St.
Syracuse, NY 46567
(574) 534-1224
Fax: (574) 533-3807
www.thorindustries.com

Aero Coach manufactures trailers, RVs, and campers in many sizes and styles under the brand names Aerostar, Aerolite, and Skamper.

■ **Brand Name(s):** Aerostar, Aerolite, Skamper.

■ **Products:** • Campers • Trailers

One of the staples in the Aero Coach Recreational Vehicles lineup is the Skamper Sport pop-up camper trailer.

Aliner/Columbia Northwest Inc.

One Main St.
Mammoth, PA 15664
(724) 423-7440
Fax: (724) 423-8485
aliner@wpa.net
www.aliner.com

Aliner makes a line of campers, including pop-up and truck-mounted models.

■ **Brand Name(s):** Aliner

■ **Products:** • Campers

All Tent Trailer Rentals & Sales

6660 Leland Ave.
Ventura, CA 93003
(805) 644-2450
Fax: (805) 650-1637
www.alltents.com

All Tent is a dealer for Coleman Trailers by Fleetwood and sells and rents other tent trailers.

■ **Brand Name(s):** All Tent.
✔ Retail shop
■ **Products:** • Tent trailers

BackTrek

19104 Obsidian Road
Bend, OR 97702
(541) 389-8497
www.backtrek.com

BackTrek makes trailers designed to haul recreation equipment such as camping gear, bicycles, and kayaks.

■ **Brand Name(s):** BackTrek

■ **Products:** • Trailers

BackTrek's Deluxe Sport Trailer has an aluminum body with plastic liner and a frame of tubular steel, shown with an optional high rack.

The Sport Trailer by BackTrek has room inside to carry camping equipment, plus space outside to carry bicycles.

Coachmen Clipper folding camping trailers are available in 12 floor plans, including three Sport, three Sport Plus, and six Classic models.

Chalet RV Inc.

725 First Ave. SE
Albany, OR 97321
(541) 791-4610
Fax: (541) 791-4618
sales@chaletrv.com
www.chaletrv.com
Chalet makes a line of folding camping trailers.

■ **Brand Name(s):** Chalet.

■ **Products:** • Campers

Coachmen Recreational Vehicle Co., LLC

P.O. Box 30
423 N. Main St.
Middlebury, IN 46540
(219) 825-5821
Fax: (219) 825-7868
www.coachmenrv.com
Coachmen manufactures several lines of camper trailers and RVs, ranging from Coachmen folding trailers to full-size Coachmen and Shasta RVs.

■ **Brand Name(s):** Coachmen, Shasta, GBM.
✔ Brochure

■ **Products:** • Campers • RVs

Coleman Trailers

258 Beacon St.
Somerset, PA 15501
www.foldingtrailers.com
Coleman Folding Trailers by Fleetwood offers a lineup of folding and pop-up type campers.

■ **Brand Name(s):** Fleetwood Folding Trailers.
✔ Brochure

■ **Products:** • Campers

The Grand Tour Series Westlake model features easy setup, BackSaver bed supports, galley, and two stoves.

Coleman Folding Trailers by Fleetwood fold up for towing and provide extra storage on top for a canoe or bicycles.

Jayco Inc.

P.O. Box 460

Middlebury, IN 46540

(574) 825-5861

Fax: (574) 825-7354

www.jayco.com

Jayco makes many models of campers, trailers, and RVs, starting with fold-down camping trailers.

■ **Brand Name(s):** Jayco.

■ **Products:** • Campers • RVs

Jayco's Heritage fold-down camping trailer includes such amenities as a galley, shower, oak cabinets, vinyl flooring, and bunk mattresses.

The roomy interior of an Eagle camping trailer includes a stainless steel sink, oak cabinets, dinette cushions, window shades, and a shower.

Eagle campers by Jayco range from 10 feet to 14 feet, and include double-wall construction, crank-down stabilizer jacks, and electric brakes.

Lance Camper Manufacturing Corp.

43120 Venture St.

Lancaster, CA 93535

(661) 949-3322

www.lancecamper.com

Lance makes several models of truck-mounted campers. They are available through dealers.

■ **Brand Name(s):** Lance.

✔ Brochure.

■ **Products:** • Campers

Lance Campers, mounted atop a pickup truck, are called the "SUVs of RVs."

Lance Slideout Campers expand for extra living space and can include a rollout side awning.

Napier Enterprises

2315 Whirlpool St., Suite 161

Niagara Falls, NY 14305

(905) 935-0427

(800) 567-2434

Fax: (905) 935-2918

sportz@niagara.com

www.sportztrucktent.com

Napier makes the Sportz Truck Tent, which fits in the bed of a pickup, in several models.

- **Brand Name(s):** Sportz.

- **Products:** • Truck tents

The Sportz SUV Tent by Napier Enterprises is designed to wrap around an SUV or mini van to provide tent camping space.

Napier Enterprises' Sportz Truck Tent II fits in a pickup truck and includes the tailgate and a 6-foot canopy.

Scamp

P.O. Box 2

Backus, MN 56435

(800) 346-4962

www.scamptrailers.com

Scamp makes compact travel trailers in 13-foot, 16-foot, and 19-foot sizes.

- **Brand Name(s):** Scamp

- **Products:** • Trailers

Starcraft RV Inc.

P.O. Box 458

Topeka, IN 46571

(800) 945-4787

www.starcraftrv.com

Starcraft makes various sizes of campers, trailers, and RVs, including folding camping trailers and truck campers.

- **Brand Name(s):** Starcraft

- **Products:** • Campers

Viking Recreational Vehicles LLC

P.O. Box 549

580 W. Burr Oak St.

Centreville, MN 49032

(616) 467-6321

www.vikingrv.com

Viking produces fold-down camping trailers.

- **Brand Name(s):** Viking.

- **Products:** • Campers

The Epic fold-down camping trailer from Viking can be towed by most cars and can sleep six people.

The Viking Legend camping trailer sleeps six to eight people, with six floor plans ranging from 20 feet to 23 feet.

Food and Cooking Gear

Adventure Foods

481 Banjo Lane

Whittier, NC 28789

(828) 497-4113

Fax: (828) 497-7529

customerservice@AdventureFoods.com

www.AdventureFoods.com

Adventure Foods has a variety of entrees, desserts, side dishes, and ready-to-eat dinners that can be prepared at a campsite. It also has developed BakePacker, which bakes, poaches, and cooks foods over a camp stove.

■ **Brand Name(s):** Adventure Foods

✔ Brochure, ✔ Online shop

■ **Products:** • Prepared foods

AlpineAire Foods

4031 Alvis Court

Rocklin, CA 95677

(800) 322-6325

Fax: (916) 824-5020

cgrant@alpineairefoods.com

www.alpineairefoods.com

AlpineAire makes outdoor recreational foods and shelf-stable food products. Included are pouch products and Gourmet Reserves designed for camping, fishing, and backpacking.

■ **Brand Name(s):** AlpineAire

■ **Products:** • Food products

Athena International Inc.

1100 Mark Circle

Gardnerville, NV 89410

(775) 783-3110

(800) 272-8603

Fax: (775) 782-5687

mailbox@athenainternational.com

www.athenainternational.com

Athena International makes a line of gas and electrical appliances under the Athena and Max Burton brands, including burners, stoves, heaters, lanterns, fuels, gourmet cookware, and 12-volt appliances. It also makes E-Z-Est cleaners and polishes.

■ **Brand Name(s):** Athena, Max Burton, Glowmaster, E-Z-Est.

✔ Brochure, ✔ Online shop.

■ **Products:** • Portable gas appliances • 12-volt appliances • Lanterns • Cookware

BlueSkyKitchen.com

The Glowmaster Butane Heater from Athena International offers adjustable heat control with auto ignition.

The Athena Coffee To Go 12-volt coffeemaker brews four cups and plugs into a car's cigarette lighter.

Backpacker's Pantry

635 Gunpark Drive

Boulder, CO 80301

(303) 581-0518

info@backpackerspantry.com

www.backpackerspantry.com

Backpacker's Pantry is a family-owned business that provides camping food, Outback ovens and Evolution cookware.

■ **Products:** • Food, • Ovens, • Cookware

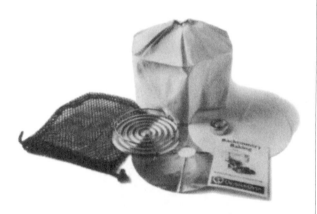

The Outback Oven Ultralight from Backpacker's Pantry weighs 9.5 ounces and works with most cooksets.

Cache Lake

506 Beltrami Ave.

Bemidji, MN 56601

(800) 442-0852

Fax: (218) 444-9414

npopt@npoptical.com

www.cachelake.com

Cache Lake Quality Camping Food offers "camping food so good, you'll want to eat it at home." Included are soups, frying pan bread, pancakes, and entrees that can be prepared in 20 minutes or less. Online shopping is available.

■ **Brand Name(s):** Cache Lake.

✔ Brochure, ✔ Online shop.

■ **Products:** • Camping food

Camelbak Products Inc.

1310 Redwood Way, Suite 200

Petaluma, CA 94954

(707) 792-9700

(800) 767-8725

Fax: (707) 665-9231

webmaster@camelbak.com

www.camelbak.com

Camelbak makes water-carrying gear for hiking, biking, winter sports, and general outdoors use.

■ **Brand Name(s):** Camelbak.

■ **Products:** • Water carriers

Camp Chef

675 N. 600 West

Logan, UT 84321

(435) 752-3922

800-650CHEF

Fax: (435) 752-1592

www.campchef.com

Camp Chef makes a variety of cooking stoves and grills, both gas and charcoal, as well as cookware, roasters, and accessories. Sales are available online as well as through dealers.

■ **Brand Name(s):** Camp Chef, Crown Chef, Sport Grill.

✔ Brochure

■ **Products:** • Grills • Cookware

Universal output two-burner cooker.

Ultimate Roasting System for turkey, ribs, lamb or seafood.

Deluxe two-burner cooker, DB-60D.

Chuckwagon Supply

1230 Fern St.
Pocatello, ID 83201
(208) 234-2580
(877) 388-2468
info@chuckwagonsupply.com
www.chuckwagonsupply.com

Chuckwagon Supply is a Dutch oven and camp cooking specialist, offering griddles, Dutch ovens, utensils, trivets, even dinner bells. Purchases can be made online or by catalog.

■ **Brand Name(s):** Chuckwagon Supply.

✔ Brochure, ✔ Online shop

■ **Products:** • Dutch ovens • Cooking gear

Cooks' Nook Inc.

2391 SW Buckman Road
West Linn, OR 97068
(888) 557-8761
info@cooksnook.com
www.cooksnook.com

Cooks' Nook offers cookware, including many barbecue items, cutlery, foods, coffee and tea, and condiments for online shoppers or by phone or fax.

■ **Brand Name(s):** Many brands are available.

✔ Brochure, ✔ Online shop

■ **Products:** • Cookware • Cutlery • Food

Exstream Water Technologies Inc.

1035 W. Bruce St.
Milwaukee, WI 53204
(800) 563-6968
www.exstreamwater.com

Exstream makes water purification units and water filters. Sales are online and in retail stores.

■ **Brand Name(s):** Exstream.

✔ Online shop

■ **Products:** • Water purification units

Fox Hill Corp.

P.O. Box 259
13970 E. Highway 51
Rozet, WY 82727
(307) 682-5358
(800) 533-7883
Fax: (307) 682-3061
www.foxhill.net

Fox Hill makes portable camping ovens in single and double models, as well as other cooking equipment. They can be purchased online or in stores.

■ **Brand Name(s):** Fox Hill.

✔ Online shop

■ **Products:** • Camping ovens

The Fox Hill single oven offers a way to bake on a camp stove.

The double oven from Fox Hill holds two non-stick baking pans and has a temperature gauge.

Garcia Machine

14097 Ave. 272
Visalia, CA 93292
(559) 732-3785
Fax: (559) 732-5010

Garcia Machine makes the Backpacker's Cache, a bear resistant food container, as well as a carrying case and liner bags. The containers are used by Denali, Glacier Bay and Yosemite National Parks.

■ **Brand Name(s):** Backpacker's Cache.

✔ Brochure

■ **Products:** • Bear-resistant food containers

Garcia Machine makes the Backpacker's Cache food container, tested by grizzlies and used by national parks.

General Ecology Inc.

151 Sheree Blvd.
Exton, PA 19341
(610) 363-7900
(800) 441-8166
Fax: (610) 363-0412
info@generalecology.com
www.generalecology.com

General Ecology produces chemical-free water purifiers and micro water filters.

■ **Brand Name(s):** First Need Water Purifiers.
Brochure, Online shop.

■ **Products:** • Water purifiers

GSI Outdoors

1023 S. Pines Road
Spokane, WA 99206
(509) 928-9611
Fax: (509) 928-8339
info@gsioutdoors.com
www.gsioutdoors.com

GSI Outdoors specializes in camp cookware, including dutch ovens, fry pans, enamelware, tableware, and campfire grills. Sales are through sporting goods and outdoor stores.

■ **Brand Name(s):** GSI Outdoors.

■ **Products:** • Cookware • Tableware • Utensils

A Dutch Oven set from GSI Outdoors is rustproof, easy to clean, and good for stewing, boiling, steaming, baking, roasting, and frying.

A rugged steel Tri-Pod Stand is handy for hanging coffee pots or kettles for trouble-free cooking.

GSI Outdoors' Camp Gourmet Extreme Non-Stick Frypans range from 8 inches to 14 inches.

Harvest Foodworks

445 Highway 29
Route 1
Toledo, ON K0E 1Y0
(613) 275-2218
(800) 268-4268
Fax: (613) 275-1359
thefolks@harvestfoodworks.com
www.harvestfoodworks.com

Harvest Foodworks provides packaged foods for camping, including entrees, salads, soups, desserts, and snacks. Orders are taken by mail and online.

■ **Brand Name(s):** Harvest Foodworks.
✔ Online shop
■ **Products:** • Packaged foods

Harvest Foodworks offers a full range of camping foods, including breakfasts, dinners, soups, side dishes, desserts, and drinks.

Hawgeyes BBQ

1313 SW Ordnance Road
Ankeny, IA 50021
(515) 965-1206
(877) 841-7192
Fax: (515) 965-8338
sales@tntlandscaping.com
www.hawgeyesbbq.com

Hawgeyes BBQ sells barbecue smokers and gas grills, barbecue wood, accessories, and sauces. There is a retail shop in Ankeny.

✔Online shop, ✔Retail shop
■ **Products:** • Grills • Barbecues

Hi Mountain Jerky Inc.

1000 College View Drive
Riverton, WY 82501
(800) 829-2285
Fax: (307) 856-6657
sales@himtnjerky.com
www.himtnjerky.com

Hi Mountain Jerky Cures & Seasonings are Wyoming recipes that add flavor to jerky, sausages, bologna, or bratwurst. Sales are through an online store and a catalog.

■ **Brand Name(s):** Hi Mountain Jerky.

✔ Brochure, ✔ Online shop

■ **Products:** • Seasonings

Hi Mountain's Western Legends seasonings include the Original Mountain Man Blend Breakfast Sausage Seasoning.

Wild River Trout Brine Mix is made with honey to add flavor to smoked fish.

Hydro-Photon Inc.

P.O. Box 675
Blue Hill, ME 04614
(207) 374-5800
(888) 826-6234
www.hydro-photon.com

Hydro-Photon has developed the Steri-Pen, a small, battery-powered water purification system that treats up to 16 ounces of clear water at a time. The product can be purchased online or in stores.

■ **Brand Name(s):** Steri-Pen.

✔ Online shop

■ **Products:** • Water purification

Hickory flavor is one of a dozen flavors of Jerky Cure & Seasoning from Hi Mountain Seasonings.

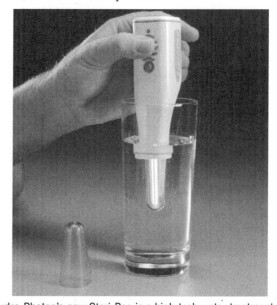

Hydro-Photon's new Steri-Pen is a high-tech water treatment device that uses ultraviolet light to purify water in less than one minute.

Katadyn Products Inc.

Black Mountain Stores

1721 N. Texas

Odessa, TX 79761

(800) 670-7942

Fax: (915) 332-1053

www.katadyn.net

Katadyn Products, based in Switzerland, is a worldwide supplier of water treatment equipment, including filters and purifiers.

■ **Brand Name(s):** Katadyn.

■ **Products:** • Water filters

Lawry's Foods Inc.

222 E. Huntington Drive

Monrovia, CA 91016

8009-LAWRYS

www.lawrys.com

Lawry's produces a line of seasonings, spices, and marinades. Grilling tips are one of the features on its Web site.

■ **Brand Name(s):** Lawry's.

■ **Products:** • Spices • Recipes

Lodge Manufacturing Co.

Box 380

204 E. Fifth St.

South Pittsburg, TN 37380

(423) 837-7181

Fax: (423) 837-8279

lodgesl@cdc.net

www.lodgemfg.com

Lodge makes a variety of cast iron camp cookware, including Dutch ovens, griddles, skillets, hibachis, deep fryers, and tripods.

■ **Brand Name(s):** Lodge

✔ Brochure

■ **Products:** • Cast iron cookware

Lodge's slogan is "America's Original Cookware."

The undersides of Lodge's iron covers are designed with self-basting tips.

Lodge makes the "Official Camp Oven" of the Boy Scouts of America.

Long Life Food Depot

P.O. Box 8081

Richmond, IN 47374

(765) 939-0110

(800) 601-2833

Fax: (765) 939-0065

sales@longlifefood.com

www.longlifefood.com

Long Life Food makes meals ready to eat (MREs), ranging from jambalaya to stew to cookies. They come in individual-serving pouches for quick preparation and will keep for months. Sales are by catalog, phone, and the Internet.

✔ Brochure, ✔ Online shop

■ **Products:** • Ready to eat meals

Long Life Food Depot's meal ready to eat (MRE) case contains 12 poly bags with ingredients.

Market Gap

P.O. Box 3842

Flagstaff, AZ 86003

(800) 821-8478

grubbox@infomagic.net

ww.blueskykitchen.com

BlueSky Kitchen has outdoor kitchen work areas, including the "chuck box" or "grub box," to provide storage and work surfaces for camp kitchens. A catalog and online ordering are available.

✔ Brochure, ✔ Online shop

■ **Products:** • Outdoor cooking gear

Mountain House

525 25th Ave. SW

Albany, OR 97321

(800) 547-0244

www.mountainhouse.com

Mountain House freeze-dried foods have been produced for backpackers, hikers, campers, and outdoors enthusiasts for more than 30 years. Food ranges from macaroni and cheese to desserts. Sales are available online, by phone or mail, or in stores.

■ **Brand Name(s):** Mountain House.

✔ Online shop

■ **Products:** • Freeze-dried foods

Freeze dried vegetable lasagna is one of many entrees for camping made by Mountain House.

Nesco/American Harvest

P.O. Box 237

1700 Monroe St.

Two Rivers, WI 54241

(800) 288-4545

www.nesco.com

Nesco/American Harvest, divisions of Metal Ware Corp., make cooking products, including grills, dehydrators, coffee makers, travel items, and spices. Sales are online as well as through stores.

■ **Brand Name(s):** Nesco, American Harvest.

✔ Brochure, ✔ Online shop

■ **Products:** • Cookware • Spices

Snackmaster Elite is a four-tray dehydrator made by American Harvest.

"Kar 'n Home" 6-cup perk from Nesco runs on 12/120V.

NPO Foods

506 Beltrami Ave.
Bemidji, MN 56601
(218) 751-0115
(800) 442-0852
Fax: (218) 751-7559
npopt@npoptical.com
www.cachelake.com

NPO Foods is the manufacturer and exclusive distributor of Cache Lake Quality Camping Foods. Soups, breakfast items, frying pan breads, salads, and meats are among the packaged foods available.

■ **Brand Name(s):** Cache Lake Quality Camping Foods.

✔ Brochure, ✔ Online shop

■ **Products:** • Soups • Bread • Salad • Meats

Open Country

P.O. Box 237
Two Rivers, WI 54241
(920) 793-1368
(800) 624-2949
Fax: (920) 793-1086
www.nesco.com

Open Country Adventure Campware is made by Metal Ware Corp., which also makes Nesco /American Harvest. Included are aluminum mess kits, cooking sets, boilers, and pots and pans. Sales are through retail stores.

■ **Brand Name(s):** Open Country.

✔ Brochure

■ **Products:** • Cookware

Deluxe six-person non-stick camp set.

Camp perks and camp boilers from Open Country.

Open Country deluxe 50-piece organizer bag set.

Pacific Cornetta Inc.

25999 SW Canyon Creek Road, Suite C
Wilsonville, OR 97070
(503) 582-8787
Fax: (503) 570-8585
www.pacific-cornetta.com

Pacific Cornetta makes a variety of vacuum bottles, cups, mugs, and tumblers, as well as picnic sets and lamps.

■ **Brand Name(s):** Pacific Cornetta.

✔ Brochure

■ **Products:** • Picnic sets • Vacuum bottles • Cups, mugs • Lamps

The Liquid Solution Bullet Series of vacuum bottles from Pacific Cornetta comes in four sizes from 12 ounces to 30 ounces.

Pacific Cornetta's Ever Glow Table Lamp features a Xenon light bulb, runs on four D batteries, and collapses to a storage position.

The 26-Piece Picnic Set from Pacific Cornetta includes a setting for four plus a carving knife, grill brush, spatula, tongs, and serving bowl.

PUR

9300 N. 75th Ave.
Minneapolis, MN 55428
(800) 787-5463
www.purwater.com

PUR makes a variety of water filtration products.

■ **Brand Name(s):** PUR.

■ **Products:** • Water filters

Richmoor Corp.

P.O. Box 8092
Van Nuys, CA 91409
(800) 423-3170
www.richmoor.com

Richmoor, family owned and operated since the 1950s, produces Richmoor Camping Foods, including entrees and complete dinners. It also produces the Natural High all natural gourmet line of lightweight camping foods, including no-cook entrees, breakfasts

- **Brand Name(s):** Natural High.
- ✔ Brochure
- **Products:** • Camping foods

Rome Industries Inc.

1703 W. Detweiller Drive

Peoria, IL 61615

(800) 818-7603

Fax: (800) 936-7663

www.pieirons.com

Rome Industries has been a manufacturer of family camping cookware since 1964, making Pie Iron sandwich cookers, hot dog and marshmallow forks, grill baskets, folding camp grills, and open fire cookware accessories.

- **Brand Name(s):** Pie Iron.
- ✔ Brochure
- **Products:** • Cookware • Pie Iron • Hot dog forks

Rome Industry's Pioneer Popcorn Popper is a hit around the evening campfire.

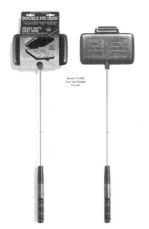

The double pie iron, made of cast iron, can cook two grilled sandwiches at one time or cook calzone, fish, chops, or breads.

Soft Path Cuisine Inc.

P.O. Box 65004

Calgary, AL T2N 4T6

(403) 282-8080

softpath@cadvision.com

www.organiccampingfood.com

Soft Path Cuisine manufactures camping meals, including dried vegetarian dinners, breakfasts, and desserts.

- **Brand Name(s):** Soft Path Cuisine.
- ✔ Brochure
- **Products:** • Camping food

Sun Ovens International Inc.

39W835 Midan Drive

Elburn, IL 60119

(630) 208-7273

(800) 408-7919

Fax: (630) 208-7386

sunovens@execpc.com

www.sunoven.com

Sun Ovens produces solar ovens that can be used for camping, using the sun for fuel. They can be purchased online or in stores.

- **Brand Name(s):** Sun Ovens.
- ✔ Online shop
- **Products:** • Solar ovens

Sunbeam Corp.

P.O. Box 948389

Maitland, FL 32794

(800) 200-2300

www.sunbeam.com

Sunbeam makes a variety of outdoor and kitchen cooking products, including Grillmaster grills, Sunbeam and Oster appliances.

- **Brand Name(s):** Sunbeam, Oster, Grillmaster.
- **Products:** • Grills • Kitchen cooking products

Sweetwater

4000 1st Ave. South

Seattle, WA 98134

(800) 531-9531

Fax: (206) 224-6492

info@cascadedesigns.com

www.cascadedesigns.com

Sweetwater makes water filter and purification devices.

- **Products:** • Water purifiers

The WalkAbout Microfilter by Sweetwater weighs nine ounces and uses replaceable filter cartridges.

Thermos Co.

300 N. Martingale Road, Suite 200
Schaumburg, IL 60173
(800) 831-9242
www.thermos.com

Thermos makes coolers, vacuum and insulated containers, mugs, food containers, and cookware. Products are available in stores.

■ **Brand Name(s):** Thermos, Thermos Nissan.

■ **Products:** • Coolers • Vacuum • Cookware

A Multi-Course Lunch Tote by Nissan Stainless tucks four microwavable containers inside one vacuum insulated container.

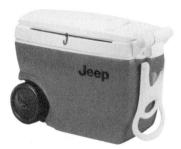

The Thermos Ice Chest Express 60 quart cooler includes a foldout table and wheels for easy handling.

Ursack

P.O. Box 5002
Mill Valley, CA 94942
866-BEARBAG
www.ursack.com

Ursa produces a bear safe food storage bag of "bullet proof" fabric. The bags, of various sizes, are designed to protect food.

■ **Products:** • Bear-proof food bags

A bear tries to rip food out of the Ursack bear-proof food storage bag.

ZZ Manufacturing Inc.

P.O. Box 1798
Glendora, CA 91740
(800) 594-9046
Fax: (626) 852-9690
zzmfg@aol.com
www.zzstove.com

ZZ Manufacturing makes Sierra stoves and related equipment for campers and backpackers, and Eagle portable fire pits for camping. Products are sold online, by catalog, and through dealers.

■ **Brand Name(s):** Sierra, Eagle.

■ **Products:** • Stoves

Hiking Equipment

Adventure GPS Products Inc.

1629 4th Ave. SE
Decatur, AL 35601
(256) 351-2151
(888) 477-4386
Fax: (256) 351-2325
info@gps4fun.com
www.gps4fun.com

Adventure GPS sells global positioning equipment for navigation and outdoor recreation through online and telephone sales.

■ **Brand Name(s):** Dealer for Garmin, Magellan, and others.

✔ Brochure, ✔ Online shop

■ **Products:** • GPS equipment

ArcTeryx Equipment Inc.

4250 Manor St.
Burnaby, BC V5G 1B2
(604) 451-7755
(800) 985-6681
Fax: (604) 451-7705
bird@arcteryx.com
www.arcteryx.com

ArcTeryx makes mountain climbing and hiking equipment, including outerwear, packs and hardware.

■ **Brand Name(s):** ArcTeryx.

✔ Brochure

■ **Products:** • Climbing gear • Clothing • Packs

Black Diamond Equipment

2092 E. 3900 South
Salt Lake City, UT 84124
(801) 278-0233
Fax: (801) 278-5544
bdstore@bdel.com
www.bdel.com

Black Diamond handles a variety of climbing and backcountry equipment, including packs, clothing, shelters, skis, boots, lamps, and accessories. It can be purchased online and in stores.

■ **Brand Name(s):** Black Diamond

✔ Online shop, ✔ Retail shop

■ **Products:** • Packs • Shelters • Clothing • Ski equipment

A variety of high-performance trekking poles is one of the hiking and climbing lines from Black Diamond.

Black Diamond's Ice Pack features heavily padded shoulder straps and hip belt, with room for climbing tools and gear.

Brule Mountain Gear - PanPack

P.O. Box 12

Aylmer, QU J9H 5E4

(819) 685-9163

888-430PACK

www.panpack.com

Brule Mountain makes backpacks and convertible panniers for hiking, biking, trekking, and touring. Products can be purchased online or in stores.

■ **Brand Name(s):** Brule Mountain Gear.

✔ Brochure, ✔ Online shop

■ **Products:** • Packs

Brunton Co.

620 E. Monroe Ave.

Riverton, WY 82501

(307) 856-6559

www.brunton.com

Brunton makes a line of compasses as well as binoculars.

■ **Brand Name(s):** Brunton.

■ **Products:** • Compasses • Binoculars

Camp Trails

P.O. Box 966

Binghamton, NY 13902

(800) 572-8822

www.camptrails.com

Camp Trails, a division of Johnson Outdoors, manufactures many types of packs as well as accessories.

■ **Brand Name(s):** Camp Trails.

✔ Brochure

■ **Products:** • Packs

The McKinley pack from Camp Trails has five pockets and a capacity of 2,880 cubic inches to 3,880 cubic inches, along with six height and three width adjustments.

The Paragon pack by Camp Trails features large capacity with three-way access, including a bottom sleeping bag compartment and seven pockets.

CampMan Inc.

17812 SE 12th Drive

Vancouver, WA 98683

(360) 883-5507

Fax: (360) 883-0072

www.campman.com

CampMan offers equipment for backpacking, climbing, and paddling on its Web site. Included are packs, two-way radios, books, clothing, and cookware.

■ **Brand Name(s):** Several leading brands are sold.

✔ Online shop

■ **Products:** • Backpacks • Furniture • Stoves • Clothing • Tools

Deuter USA Inc.

P.O. Box 606

Niwot, CO 80544

(303) 652-3102

Fax: (303) 652-3125

www.deuterusa.com

Deuter makes several styles and sizes of packs for hiking, alpine, biking, and travel. Packs are available in stores.

■ **Brand Name(s):** Deuter.

■ **Products:** • Packs

Forty Below Ltd.

P.O. Box 39

Graham, WA 98338

(253) 846-2081

warmfeet@40below.com

www.40below.com

Forty Below manufactures high-altitude extreme cold weather insulated boot covers and insulated bottle covers and related items. Sales are through dealers.

■ **Brand Name(s):** Forty Below

✔ Brochure

■ **Products:** • Insulated boot covers

Garmin International Inc.

1200 E. 151st St.

Olathe, KS 66062

(913) 397-8200

Fax: (913) 397-8282

www.garmin.com

Garmin makes several models of global positioning systems (GPS) and mapping equipment.

■ **Brand Name(s):** Garmin, eTrex.

✔ Brochure

■ **Products:** • GPS units • Map gear

The Garmin eMap combines the global positioning system with mapping capabilities.

Garmin's eTrex is a 12 parallel channel GPS receiver that weighs six ounces and measures four inches by two inches. It runs 18 hours on two batteries.

Gregory Mountain Products

27969 Jefferson Ave.

P.O. Box 9015

Temecula, CA 92589

(909) 676-5621

(800) 477-3420

Fax: (909) 676-6777

www.gregorypacks.com

Gregory produces a full line of packs for hiking, mountaineering, ski touring, and expeditions, as well as other types of packs and accessories.

■ **Brand Name(s):** Gregory.

■ **Products:** • Packs

The Inertia pack by Gregory Mountain Products combines storage space with an insulated reservoir sleeve to keep fluids cool.

The Wind River is a large capacity pack by Gregory that includes a huge front "mondo" pocket to stow a tent body, rain gear, or sleeping pad.

Gregory's Denali Pro is its largest expedition pack, offering as much as 7,000 cubic inches of storage space.

Hembree Enterprises Inc. (HEI)

P.O. Box 2036
Bowie, MD 20718
Fax: (301) 262-4049
newinfo@h-e-i-com
www.h-e-i.com

HEI offers backpacking products, including The Equalizer, a device for leveling and supporting backpacking stoves.

■ **Brand Name(s):** The Equalizer
✔ Online shop

James Kits

P.O. Box 933
164 E. Deloney
Jackson, WY 83001
800-396KITS
Fax: (307) 733-0216
jkits@sharplink.com
www.sharplink.com/jkits/

James Kits contain survival equipment and come in three models. They can be purchased online and in stores.

■ **Brand Name(s):** James Kits.
✔ Online shop
■ **Products:** • Survival gear

JanSport USA

P.O. Box 1817
Appleton, WI 54912
(800) 346-8239
www.jansport.com

JanSport makes backpacks and hiking products as well as duffel bags and travel luggage. It is a wholesaler and has no direct sales, but products can be found in retail stores.

■ **Brand Name(s):** JanSport.
■ **Products:** • Backpacks • Luggage

Jansport's Nebula 25 combines comfortable suspension and organizational features to make it a crossover pack for trails and everyday use.

The Supernova Lady multi-purpose trail shoe is one of many mountaineering and hiking shoes and sandals by La Sportiva.

Travel packs from Jansport include the Wheeled Daypack with 1,700 cubic inches of space and a telescoping handle.

The Stretch Short is among several comfortable, yet rugged shorts, pants, and tops from La Sportiva designed for climbing or hiking.

La Sportiva NA

3850 Frontier Ave., Suite 100

Boulder, CO 80301

(303) 443-8710

Fax: (303) 442-7541

custserv@sportiva.com

www.sportiva.com

La Sportiva makes a variety of shoes and boots for hiking, climbing, and mountaineering.

■ **Brand Name(s):** La Sportiva.

✔ Brochure

■ **Products:** • Hiking boots

Montrail

2505 Airport Way South

Seattle, WA 98134

(206) 621-9303

Fax: (206) 621-0230

goodfit@montrail.com

www.montrail.com

Montrail makes outdoor footwear for hiking including Vitesse, Java GTX, Storm GTX, Sandia Peak, and Torre GTX.

■ **Brand Name(s):** Montrail.

✔ Brochure

■ **Products:** • Hiking footwear

Kinetic is a weatherproof hiking shoe that features a durable Schoeller fabric upper.

Escapegoat is Montrail's new low-cut leather hiking shoe.

Escelerace XCR is an all-synthetic over-the-ankle light hiker lined with Gore-Tex XCR.

Moonstone Mountain Equipment

1700 Westlake Ave. N, Suite 200

Seattle, WA 98109

(800) 390-3312

info@moonstone.com

www.moonstone.com

Moonstone Mountain makes a variety of sleeping bags and mountaineering clothing. Products are sold in camping and mountaineering stores.

■ **Brand Name(s):** Moonstone.

■ **Products:** • Sleeping bags • Clothing

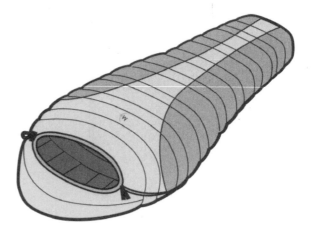

The 650 Red Rock sleeping bag from Moonstone is filled with 650 Power Goose Down and has a temperature rating of −32 degrees.

The Women's Ridge Line Jacket is part of Moonstone's 3-layer Reflex stretch fabric line.

Mountain Tools

P.O. Box 222295

Carmel, CA 93922

(831) 620-0911

(800) 510-2514

Fax: (831) 620-0977

www.mtntools.com

Mountain Tools has a wide variety of camping and mountaineering equipment, including attire, footwear, tents, rescue gear, and climbing equipment. Products are available on the Internet, in a catalog, and through dealers.

■ **Brand Name(s):** Mountain Tools.

✔ Brochure , ✔ Online shop

■ **Products:** • Apparel • Climbing gear • Footwear

Mountainsmith

18301 W. Colfax Ave., Building P
Golden, CO 80401
(800) 551-5889
www.mountainsmith.com

Mountainsmith produces a variety of backpacks as well as sleeping bags and other outdoors gear. Sales are by catalog as well as through stores.

■ **Brand Name(s):** Mountainsmith.

✔ Brochure

■ **Products:** • Packs • Sleeping bags

Mountainsmith's Altitude Series packs are big enough for expedition-sized loads.

Ortlieb USA LLC

1402 20th St. NW, Suite 7
Auburn, WA 98001
(253) 833-3939
www.ortliebusa.com

Ortlieb USA is the distributor of Ortlieb Outdoor Gear, including a line of waterproof packs as well as biking equipment. Retail and online camping stores handle the products.

■ **Brand Name(s):** Ortlieb Outdoor Gear.

■ **Products:** • Packs

Overland Equipment

2145 Park Ave. #4
Chico, CA 95928
(530) 894-5605
(800) 487-8851
Fax: (530) 894-1460
info@overlandequipment.com
www.overlandequipment.com

Overland makes several styles and sizes of backpacks, shoulder bags, outdoor lifestyle accessories, waist packs, and daypacks. A catalog is available and sales are through dealers.

■ **Brand Name(s):** Overland Equipment.

✔ Brochure

■ **Products:** • Backpacks • Bags

Overland Equipment's Modoc is ready for an expedition and is available in three sizes.

The Mendocino fanny pack is a travel companion featuring easy access storage.

Petzl America

Freeport Center Building M-7

P.O. Box 160447

Clearfield, UT 84016

info@petzl.com

www.petzl.com

Petzl makes equipment for climbing, caving, and trekking, including headlamps, sacks, harnesses, and climbing gear.

■ **Brand Name(s):** Petzl.

■ **Products:** • Headlamps • Climbing gear

Silva

P.O. Box 966

Binghamton, NY 13902

(800) 572-8822

www.silvacompass.com

Silva makes a line of compasses that are guaranteed accurate for life as well as accessories.

■ **Brand Name(s):** Silva.

✔ Brochure

■ **Products:** • Compasses

The Trekker lightweight compass from Silva is designed for backpacking, camping, or fishing.

The North Face Inc.

2013 Farallon Drive

San Leandro, CA 94577

(800) 447-2333

www.thenorthface.com

The North Face makes clothing, footwear, and equipment for rugged outdoors use, primarily climbing and hiking, including tents, packs, sleeping bags, and duffel bags. Sales are through 2,500 dealers.

■ **Brand Name(s):** The North Face.

■ **Products:** • Tents • Sleeping bags • Footwear • Apparel

Tracks

4000 1st Ave. South

Seattle, WA 98134

(800) 531-9531

Fax: (206) 224-6492

info@cascadedesigns.com

www.cascadedesigns.com/tracks

Tracks manufactures walking staffs and trekking poles.

■ **Brand Name(s):** Tracks.

■ **Products:** • Walking staffs

The Compact Travel Staff, which collapses for compact storage, is one of several walking staffs and trekking poles made by Tracks.

Ultimate Direction

1255 Powell St.

Emeryville, CA 94608

(800) 426-7229

Fax: (510) 601-5518

www.ultimatedirection.com

Ultimate Direction makes hydration equipment "for the insanely athletic (and sensibly active)," including water bottles, tanks, and packs for hiking, running, paddling, or other sports. Sales are through dealers.

■ **Brand Name(s):** Ultimate Direction.

✔ Brochure

■ **Products:** • Water bottles

Vasque

314 Main St.

Red Wing, MN 55066

800224HIKE

www.vasque.com

Vasque makes high performance backpacking and hiking footwear.

■ **Brand Name(s):** Vasque

✔ Brochure, ✔ Online shop

■ **Products:** • Boots

Whistle Creek

P.O. Box 580

Monument, CO 80132

(719) 488-1999

Fax: (719) 488-1950

george@whistlecreek.com

www.whistlecreek.com

Whistle Creek is the largest maker of rustic walking and hiking sticks in the U.S. It offers online shopping and its products are found at retail stores.

■ **Brand Name(s):** Whistle Creek

✔ Brochure, ✔ Online shop

■ **Products:** • Walking sticks

Whistle Creek has added a line of Field & Stream walking and hiking sticks to its inventory.

Sleeping Bags

Big Agnes Inc.

P.O. Box 773072

735 Oak St.

Steamboat Springs, CO 80477

(970) 871-1480

(877) 554-8975

Fax: (970) 879-8038

info@bigagnes.com

www.bigagnes.com

Big Agnes manufactures a variety of sleeping bags and sleeping pads. Sales are online, by catalog, and by phone.

■ **Brand Name(s):** Big Agnes.

✔ Brochure, ✔ Online shop, ✔ Retail shop

■ **Products:** • Sleeping bags

The Encampment sleeping bag by Big Agnes has a Polarguard 3D fill and is rated to 15 degrees.

The BA Layering System sleeping bag by Big Agnes provides comfortable sleeping from –25 degrees to 70 degrees.

DreamSacks Inc.

271 Morton St.

Ashland, OR 97520

(541) 482-0601

(800) 670-7661

info@dreamsack.com

www.dreamsack.com

DreamSacks has several styles and sizes of sleeping bags as well as sheets and comforters. Sales are by Internet, catalog, or in stores.

■ **Brand Name(s):** DreamSacks.

✔ Brochure, ✔ Online shop

■ **Products:** • Sleeping bags

The DreamSack, at 7 feet, 9 inches, provides plenty of space and the comfort of silk, but weighs six ounces.

Feathered Friends

1119 Mercer St.

Seattle, WA 98109

(206) 292-6292

Fax: (206) 292-6403

www.featheredfriends.com

Feathered Friends produces a line of down sleeping bags as well as down outerwear, bivy sacks, and bag liners. Sales are by catalog and phone as well as a Seattle retail store.

■ **Brand Name(s):** Feathered Friends, Pangaea.

✔ Brochure, ✔ Retail shop

■ **Products:** • Sleeping bags • Down outerwear

Kelty

6235 Lookout Road

Boulder, CO 80301

(303) 530-7670

(800) 423-2320

Fax: (303) 504-2745

www.kelty.com

Kelty makes a wide variety of sleeping bags, liners, tents, shelters, backpacks, and apparel for camping.

■ **Brand Name(s):** Kelty, Kelty K.I.D.S.

✔ Brochure

■ **Products:** • Sleeping bags • Backpacks • Tents • Travel daypac • Kelty K.I.D.S

Kelty's Cyclone 2/3 Tent has a strong three-pole, free-standing design with two large mesh door panels and a full-coverage rainfly.

Kelty's Big Thunder Jacket is a full-featured parka-length jacket offering full rain protection, made of nylon with waterproof PU coating.

The Light Year 3D sleeping bag from Kelty is made of Polarguard 3D and keeps a sleeper warm to 30 degrees.

Western Mountain Sports

1025 S. 5th St.

San Jose, CA 95112

(408) 287-8944

Fax: (408) 287-8946

www.westernmountaineering.com

Western Mountaineering makes more than 30 models of sleeping bags, as well as down jackets and vests. Products are available in stores.

■ **Brand Name(s):** Extremelite.

■ **Products:** • Sleeping bags

Cloud packs from Kelty are light, tough mountaineering backpacks of white spectra fabric assembled with kevlar and PTFE thread and weighing just over one pound.

The Ponderosa sleeping bag from Western Mountaineering is a large bag that weighs 2 pounds, 14 ounces, and is comfortable to 15 degrees.

Tents

AirZone Recreation Inc.

240 Clifton Road North
Kelowna, BC V1V 1N3
(250) 860-6167
(877) 767-9663
Fax: (250) 860-6198
info@airzonerecreation.com
www.airzonerecreation.com

AirZone Recreation has developed pneumatic tent pole tents that can be set up and taken down in just seven seconds, using a CO2 cartridge, air tank, bicycle pump or spare tire. Online shopping is available.

■ **Brand Name(s):** AirZone Recreation.

✔ Online shop

■ **Products:** • Tents

AirZone's tents, with air-filled poles, are strong enough to support a kayak.

Pneumatic tent poles that can be pumped with a bicycle pump, spare tire, or CO2 cartridge are the key to the AirZone tents that can be erected in seconds

Anchor Industries Inc.

P.O. Box 3477
Evansville, IN 47733
(812) 867-2421
www.anchorinc.com

Anchor, founded in 1892, makes camp tents and canopies of various sizes and styles.

■ **Brand Name(s):** Anchor

✔ Brochure, ✔ Online shop

■ **Products:** • Tents

Arctic Canvas

1928 Main St. West
North Bay, ON P1B 8G5
(705) 472-5005
Fax: (705) 472-6301
www.on-biz.com/arcticcanvas/

Arctic Canvas makes tents and repairs canvas products, including tents, teepees, cots, and duffel bags.

✔ Retail shop

■ **Products:** • Tents

Bibler Tents

2084 E. 3900 South
Salt Lake City, UT 84124
(801) 278-5533
tents@bdel.com
www.biblertents.com

Bibler Tents, a division of Black Diamond Equipment, makes a line of tents, bivys, and accessories. Purchases can be made online, by catalog, or in stores.

✔ Brochure, ✔ Online shop

■ **Products:** • Tents

The Tempest, from Bibler Tents, is a sturdy shelter for two against howling winds, with two vestibules and 44 square feet of space.

ENEL Co.

1330 Orange Ave., Suite 300

Coronado, CA 92118

(800) 757-0505

Fax: (619) 522-0028

www.enelcompany.com

ENEL Co. makes truck tents and vehicle awnings. Several models are available.

■ **Brand Name(s):** ENEL.

■ **Products:** • Truck tents.

The Original Adventure Truck Tent from ENEL Co. fits in most pickups and sleeps two to three persons.

Eureka!

625 Conklin Road

P.O. Box 966

Binghamton, NY 13902

(607) 779-2200

Fax: (607) 779-2293

www.eurekatent.com

Eureka! has been making tents since 1895. A division of Johnson Outdoors, Eureka! makes a variety of tents, from lightweight backpacking tents and camping tents to large tents and canopies. Rentals are also available through dealers.

■ **Brand Name(s):** Eureka!

✔ Brochure

■ **Products:** • Tents

A Eureka! tent, with rainflap open, rests on a campground site.

A hiker rests next to a lightweight Eureka! tent.

Campers enjoy a traditional campground setup, including a Eureka! tent.

Hilleberg the Tentmaker

14685 NE 95th St.

Redmond, WA 98052

(425) 883-0101

(866) 848-8368

Fax: (425) 869-6632

tentmaker@hilleberg.com

www.hilleberg.com

Hilleberg is a family-owned company with 30 years of experience in making lightweight, four-season tents. Orders are taken online, by catalog, and through dealers.

■ **Brand Name(s):** Hilleberg the Tentmaker.

✔ Brochure, ✔ Online shop

■ **Products:** • Tents

Winter camping is more pleasant with Tarra by Hilleberg the Tentmaker.

The Nammatj GT tent by Hilleberg stands up to a bicycle trip through Pakistan's Karakorum range.

Infinity Sports Imports Inc.

E101-19720-94A Ave.

Langley, BC V1M 3B7

(604) 888-3430

Fax: (604) 888-2540

www.infinity-outdoor.com

Infinity makes a line of Infinity tents as well as Asolo packs, sleeping bags, and travel luggage. Sales are through dealers.

■ **Brand Name(s):** Infinity, Asolo.

■ **Products:** • Tents • Packs

Ken's Custom Tent & Canvas

Route 1, Box 1079A

Homedale, ID 83628

(208) 337-5104

888-WALTENT

Fax: (208) 337-3746

www.idfishnhunt.com/kens.html

Ken's makes custom, rugged, outdoor equipment, specializing in tents.

✔ Retail shop

■ **Products:** • Tents

Paha Que Wilderness Inc.

13670 Danielson St.,Suite D

Poway, CA 92064

888700-TENT

Fax: (858) 748-3764

happytrails@pahaque.com

www.pahaque.com

Paha Que Wilderness makes several styles of tents for backpacking and camping, including a shower and restroom tent, and a screenroom.

■ **Brand Name(s):** Paha Que.

■ **Products:** • Tents

The Paha Que ScreenRoom gives campers a 10-foot by 12-foot space free of bugs and out of the rain.

The Pamo Valley tent from Paha Que is a three-seasons tent that comes in its own nylon carrying bag and weighs 35 pounds.

A new addition to the Paha Que line is the Wilderness Blind, which promises to become a favorite of birdwatchers.

TentOnSale.com

131 Chatsworth Circle
Schaumburg, IL 60194
Fax: (847) 519-0356
customerservice@tentonsale.com
www.tentonsale.com

TentOnSale is a group of outdoor equipment manufacturers that sells directly to online customers. Featured equipment is family tents, backpacking tents, sleeping bags, packs, vacuum bottles, and accessories.

■ **Brand Name(s):** Unipen, Newest.
✔ Online shop
■ **Products:** • Tents • Sleeping bags • Packs • Vacuum

Thunder Mountain Tent & Canvas

107 McClure Ave.
Nampa, ID 83651
(208) 467-3109
(800) 925-9175
Fax: (208) 463-9952
thundermtntent@msn.com
www.idfishnhunt.com/thunder.html

Thunder Mountain makes canvas and synthetic fabric products, including tents, teepees, and canopies.
✔ Retail shop
Products: • Tents

Wechsel/Equinox Ltd.

1307 Park Ave.
Williamsport, PA 17701
(800) 326-9241
Fax: (570) 322-0746
explore@equinoxltd.com
www.equinoxltd.com

Equinox is the U.S. wholesaler of German-based Wechsel, which makes a variety of tents and shelters.
■ **Brand Name(s):** Wechsel.
✔ Brochure
■ **Products:** • Tents

The Challenger RP tent from Wechsel has a geodesic three-pole design to offer stability against the wind.

The Polaris is a lightweight four-seasons tent with a side vestibule large enough for two backpacks and two APEX ventilation flaps.

Travel Services

Anderson's Campground Directory

Drawer 467
Lewisburg, WV 24901
(304) 645-1897
(888) 645-1897
Fax: (304) 645-1697
camping@mountain.net
www.andersonsdirectory.com

Anderson's prints a directory of more than 400
private, federal, state, and county campgrounds
along the East Coast, from upstate New York to
the Florida Keys.

■ **Products:** • Campground directory

Camp Florida

1340 Vickers Road
Tallahassee, FL 32303
(850) 562-7151
Fax: (850) 562-7179
flaarvc@aol.com
www.floridacamping.com

Camp Florida is a free camping directory with
more than 330 Florida campgrounds and RV
parks, featuring details listings and maps. It also
provides the Florida Camper Club, which provides discounts, coupons, and newsletters.

✔ Brochure

■ **Products:** • Camping information

Camper Clubs of America

P.O. Box 25286
Tempe, AZ 85282
(800) 369-2267
Fax: (480) 731-9014
www.camperclubs.com

Camper Clubs of America offers $10 per night RV
camping rates at member campgrounds, insurance, InTouch voice mail, and an online campground directory.

■ **Products:** • Travel information

Campground Owners of New York

P.O. Box 497
Dansville, NY 14437
www.rvdestinations.com/cony

Campground Owners of New York prints a
Camping Guide with information about more
than 200 campgrounds in New York State, as
well as providing information online.

✔ Brochure

Coast to Coast Resorts

64 Inverness Drive
Englewood, CO 80112
(800) 368-5721
www.coastresorts.com

Coast to Coast Resorts has about 1,000 member
RV resorts and campgrounds across the U.S. It
offers travel information, including an online
directory of campgrounds.

Coleman Campground & RV Park Directory

10305 U.S. 1
Sebastian, FL 32958
866-RVDIRECT
Fax: (863) 424-8316
robert@colemandirectory.com
www.colemandirectory.com

The Coleman Campground & RV Park Directory
is a travel guide for campers.

■ **Brand Name(s):** Coleman.

✔ Brochure

■ **Products:** • Campground information

DeLorme Mapping Co.

2 DeLorme Drive
P.O. Box 298
Yarmouth, ME 04096
(800) 511-2459
Fax: (800) 575-2244
sales@delorme.com
www.delorme.com

DeLorme has a variety of map-related products, including atlases, software, and GPS receivers and equipment. DeLorme products are sold in many retail stores.

■ **Brand Name(s):** Street Atlas USA, Earthmate GPS Receiver, Topo USA 4.0.

✔ Online shop

■ **Products:** • Maps • GPS

Florida Association of RV Parks and Campgrounds

1340 Vickers Road
Tallahassee, FL 32303
(850) 562-7151
Fax: (850) 562-7179
flaarvc@aol.com
www.floridacamping.com

The Florida campground association represents more than 330 Florida campgrounds and RV parks. The group publishes the official Florida camping directory which is free to campers who call.

✔ Brochure

■ **Products:** • Campground information

Good Sam Club

2575 Vista Del Mar Drive
Ventura, CA 93001
(805) 667-4100
(800) 293-5177
www.goodsamclub.com

The Good Sam Club is one of the oldest camping clubs and has more than 1 million members. It offers a subscription to its Highways Magazine and discounts on campground fees and other benefits. Campers can join the group by enrolling online.

✔ Brochure, ✔ Online shop

■ **Products:** • Travel information

Members of the Good Sam Club receive discounts on camping fees and Highways Magazine.

Indiana Campground Owners Association

P.O. Box 17
Gas City, IN 46933
www.rvdestinations.com/icoa/

This group produces a Travel Guide to Indiana campgrounds and also has an online directory.

Kampgrounds of America Inc.

P.O. Box 30558
Billings, MT 59114
(406) 248-7444
Fax: (406) 248-7414
www.koakampgrounds.com

KOA Kampgrounds own or franchise about 500 campgrounds in North America. It offers toll-free reservations, clean restrooms, playgrounds and pools, and a variety of lodging options from RV sites to cabins. Online information is available, as well as a directory of campgounds.

■ **Brand Name(s):** KOA Kampgrounds.

✔ Brochure

■ **Products:** • Campgrounds

Family members play Frisbee outside their Kamping Kabin at a KOA Kampgrounds.

A family enjoys a KOA Kamprounds site while traveling with their truck camper.

Bicycling is one of many outdoor activities available at KOA Kampgrounds.

Lee Island Coast Visitor & Convention Bureau

2180 W. First St., Suite 100
Fort Myers, FL 33901
(239) 338-3500
(800) 237-6444
Fax: (239) 334-1106
www.leeislandcoast.com

Lee Island Coast publishes a brochure on Florida's Gulf Coast destinations, including Fort Myers, Cape Coral, Bonita Springs, and Sanibel Island.

✔ Brochure

■ **Products:** • Travel information

LoveTheOutdoors.com

P.O. Box 1004
North Wales, PA 19454
kim@lovetheoutdoors.com
www.lovetheoutdoors.com

LoveTheOutdoors provides information about camping and campgrounds as well as providing links to online camping equipment stores.

✔ Online shop

■ **Products:** • Camping information

Maine Campground Owners Association

655 Maine St.
Lewiston, ME 04240
(207) 782-5874
Fax: (207) 782-4497
www.campmaine.com

The Maine Campground Owners Association has a Maine Camping Guide as well as an online campground directory and information about Maine on its Web site.

✔ Brochure

■ **Products:** • Campground information

Maptech

10 Industrial Way

Amesbury, MA 01913

(978) 792-1000

(888) 839-5551

www.maptech.com

Maptech features topographic maps, a national park digital guide, Appalachian Trail guide, GPS equipment, and marine charts and guides.

■ **Brand Name(s):** Maptech

✔ Online shop

■ **Products:** • Maps • Navi • Mari • GPS

Mississippi Division of Tourism

P.O. Box 849

Jackson, MS 39205

(800) 927-6378

Fax: (601) 359-5757

www.visitmississippi.org

The Division of Tourism provides information on resorts and outfitters. It publishes the Mississippi Outfitters Guide and Mississippi Hunting, Fishing and Outdoor Recreation Guide.

✔ Brochure

■ **Products:** • Travel information

New Hampshire Campground Owners' Association

P.O. Box 320

#427 Route 115

Twin Mountain, NH 03595

(800) 822-6764

Fax: (603) 846-2151

info@ucampnh.com

www.ucampnh.com

The New Hampshire campground trade group produces an 80-page camping guide listing private and public campgrounds, updated annually.

■ **Products:** • Camping information

New Jersey Campground Owners Association

29 Cook's Beach Road

Cape May Courthouse, NJ 08210

(609) 465-8444

800-2CAMPNJ

Fax: (609) 463-8484

njcoa@campnj.com

www.newjerseycampgrounds.com

The group is a trade association for the private campgrounds in New Jersey. It provides the New Jersey Campground & RV Park Guide.

■ **Products:** • Travel information

North Carolina Association of RV Parks and Campgrounds

893 U.S. Highway 70 W

Garner, NC 27529

(919) 779-5709

Fax: (919) 779-5642

www.kiz.com/campnet/html/cluborgs/nccoa

This group has an online listing of North Carolina's campgrounds. A camping guide is also available.

■ **Products:** • Campground guide

North Carolina Division of Tourism, Film, Sports Division

4324 Mail Service Center

Raleigh, NC 27699

800-VISITNC

www.visitnc.com

This office provides information about camping in North Carolina.

■ **Products:** • Travel information

Ohio Division of Travel and Tourism

P.O. Box 1001
Columbus, OH 43216
800-BUCKEYE
Fax: (614) 466-6744
www.ohiotourism.com

The Ohio tourism office provides a variety of travel information about the state, including a free travel planner and calendar of events.

✔ Brochure

■ **Products:** • Travel information

Pennsylvania Campground Owners Association

P.O. Box 5
New Tripoli, PA 18066
(610) 767-5026
Fax: (610) 767-5034
www.pacamping.com

The Pennsylvania Campground Owners Association offers a 52-page directory of the nearly 200 campground members in Pennsylvania as well as online information.

✔ Brochure

Resort Parks International

P.O. Box 7738
3711 Long Beach Blvd., Suite 110
Long Beach, CA 90807
(800) 635-8498
(800) 456-7774
Fax: (562) 490-0669
mail@resortparks.com
www.resortparks.com

RPI has about 100,000 members who camp at RV parks across the country. It includes an online campground directory.

■ **Products:** • Travel information

Southeast Publications USA

4360 Peters Road
Ft. Lauderdale, FL 33317
(800) 832-3292
webmaster@sepub.com
www.rvingusa.com

Southeast Publications publishes an online guide to RV parks and campgrounds across the United States.

■ **Brand Name(s):** RVingUSA.com
✔ Online shop
■ **Products:** • Travel guide

Tennessee Association of RV Parks and Campgrounds

P.O. Box 39
Townsend, TN 37882
www.rvnetlinx.com/dba/dba.php3?id=2668

This Web site provide an online listing of Tennessee campgrounds.

Texas Assocation of Campground Owners

P.O. Box 14055
Austin, TX 78761
(800) 657-6555
Fax: (512) 707-9171
www.texascampgrounds.com

The Texas campground owners offer a free RV Travel & Camping Guide to Texas and New Mexico as well as an online directory of campgrounds.

✔ Brochure, ✔ Online shop

Trailer Life -- TL Enterprises

2575 Vista Del Mar
Ventura, CA 93001
(800) 825-6861
info@trailerlife.com
www.trailerlife.com

Trailer Life publishes a magazine for RV owners and offers online, CD, and print guides to RV parks and campgrounds.

■ **Brand Name(s):** Trailer Life

✔ Brochure, ✔ Online shop

■ **Products:** • Travel information

Visit Florida

P.O. Box 1100

Tallahassee, FL 32302

(850) 488-5607

888-7FLAUSA

Fax: (850) 224-2938

www.flausa.com

Visit Florida is the official tourism marketing agency for the state of Florida. It promotes campgrounds, attractions, and entertainment in Florida. Consumers can find discounts on Visit Florida's Web site under "Florida's Hot Vacation Deals."

■ **Products:** • Travel information

West Virginia Division of Tourism

90 MacCorkle Ave. SW

South Charleston, WV 25303

800CALLWVA

www.callwva.com

Division of Tourism promotes camping, parks and tourism in West Virginia and offers a variety of information on facilities, activities, parks, lodging.

✔ Brochure

Wheelers Guides, Print Media Services

1310 Jarvis Ave.

Elk Grove Village, IL 60007

(847) 981-0100

Fax: (847) 981-0106

gwheelers@yahoo.com

www.wheelersguides.com

Wheelers Guides prints Wheelers RV Resort & Campgrounds Guide as well as Wheelers Road Atlas.

■ **Brand Name(s):** Wheelers Guides.

✔ Brochure

■ **Products:** • Travel information

Wheelers Road Atlas and Wheelers RV Resort & Camprounds Guide are printed by Wheelers Guides.

Women's Wilderness Institute

1628 Walnut St., Suite A

Boulder, CO 80302

(303) 938-9191

moreinfo@womenswilderness.org

www.womenswilderness.org

The Women's Wilderness Institute is a non-profit organization that offers instruction in wilderness living and outdoor skills to women and girls.

Wyoming Companion

Box 1111

Laramie, WY 82073

(877) 441-4711

editor@wyomingcompanion.com

www.wyomingcompanion.com

Wyoming Companion is a tourism guide to Wyoming, including its campgrounds. Print and online campground directories are available.

✔ Brochure

■ **Products:** • Tourism information

Other

Cherry Hill Park

9800 Cherry Hill Road
College Park, MD 20740
12 miles from Washington, D.C.
(301) 937-7116
(800) 801-6449
Fax: (301) 937-3110
dccamping@aol.com
www.cherryhillpark.com

Cherry Hill Park is the 2002 Campground of the
Year. It features bus service to Washington, two
pools, sauna, lounge and cafe, and phone-ready
campsites.
✔ Brochure
■ **Products:** • Campground

Cherry Hill Park in College Park, Md., is just 12 miles from
Washington, D.C.

Dagger Canoes

111 Kayaker Way
Easley, SC 29642
(800) 433-1969
webmaster@dagger.com
www.dagger.com

Dagger makes several styles of canoes and kayaks
in whitewater, touring, recreational, and racing
categories.

■ **Brand Name(s):** Dagger
✔ Brochure, ✔ Online shop
■ **Products:** • Canoes • Kayaks

The Bayou is a Dagger recreational kayak for all occasions,
including fishing and sporting use on lakes and streams.

At 9 feet, 10 inches, the Phantom is the shortest and most
maneuverable of Dagger's Royalex canoes.

Feathercraft Folding Kayaks Ltd.

4-1244 Cartwright St.
Granville Island
Vancouver, BC V6H 3R8
(604) 681-8437
Fax: (604) 681-7282
Feathercraft makes folding kayaks.

■ **Brand Name(s):** Feathercraft.
■ **Products:** • Kayaks

Kidstuff Playsystems Inc.

5400 Miller Ave.

Gary, IN 46403

(800) 255-0153

Fax: (219) 938-3340

rhagelberg@earthlink.net

www.fun-zone.com

Kidstuff is a manufacturer of playground equipment for commercial and residential use. It also sells picnic tables, benches, and other campground equipment. Installation is available.

■ **Brand Name(s):** Fun Zone, Healthtrek Fitness Courses.

✔ Brochure, ✔ Online shop

■ **Products:** • Playground equipment

Lee Enterprises Manufacturing Co. Inc.

25583 North Park

Elkhart, IN 46514

(800) 353-7705

Fax: (574) 262-1545

Lee Enterprises is a custom builder of resort cabins and park model cabins.

■ **Products:** • Cabins

Natrapel Inc.

P.O. Box 290

106 Burndy Road

Littleton, NH 03561

(800) 258-4696

Fax: (603) 444-6735

www.tendercorp.com

Natrapel specializes in making insect bite protection and suncreen without chemical repellents such as DEET.

■ **Brand Name(s):** Natrapel.

✔ Brochure

■ **Products:** • Insect repellents • Sunscreen

Natrapel insect repellents and sun block are DEET-free, relying on a patented natural Citronella formula.

Pet Pouch

PMB #224

369 Montezuma Ave.

Santa Fe, NM 87501

(505) 986-9970

Fax: (505) 983-1070

www.petpouch.com

Pet Pouch offers a hands-free way to carry your pet, in several sizes and colors. Purchases can be made online or in stores.

■ **Brand Name(s):** Pet Pouch.

✔ Online shop

■ **Products:** • Pet equipment

Porta-Bote International

1074 Independence Ave.

Mountain View, CA 94043

(800) 227-8882

info@porta-bote.com

www.porta-bote.com

Porta-Bote makes folding, portable boats in 8-foot, 10-foot, and 12-foot models that can be folded to four inches flat.

■ **Brand Name(s):** Porta-Bote.

✔ Brochure

■ **Products:** • Portable boats

The Porta-Bote comes in sizes from 8-feet to 12-feet, weighing 49 to 69 pounds.

RV owners can tuck a Porta-Bote, which folds to four inches flat, on the side of their trailer.

Baja Deck Bags are made of durable 20 ounce PVC and feature Zip Lips closure and detachable shoulder straps.

Black Canyon Bags, coming in four sizes, by SealLine keep kayaking gear dry.

Salamander Paddle Gear

6350 Gunpark Drive

Boulder, CO 80301

(303) 581-0518

(800) 641-0500

info@salamanderpaddlegear.com

www.salamanderpaddlegear.com

Salamander makes a variety of products for canoeing and kayaking, including rescue gear, clothing, duffel bags, and gear bags. It's also known as PlanetaryGEAR. Products can be purchased online or in stores.

■ **Brand Name(s):** Salamander Paddle Gear, PlanetaryGEAR.

✔ Brochure, ✔ Online shop

■ **Products:** • Kayaking gear • Clothing

SealLine

4000 1st Ave. South

Seattle, WA 98134

(800) 531-9531

Fax: (206) 224-6492

info@cascadedesigns.com

www.cascadedesigns.com

SealLine makes a variety of kayaking products, including control systems, kayak deck bags, paddling cushions, submersible and protective cases, nylon dry bags, vinyl dry bags, waterproof packs, and waist packs and duffels.

■ **Brand Name(s):** SealLine.

■ **Products:** • Kayak products • Packs and bags

Stearns Inc.

P.O. Box 1498

St. Cloud, MN 56302

(320) 252-1642

(800) 328-3208

Fax: (320) 252-4425

www.stearnsinc.com

Stearns makes a variety of outdoors and watersports equipment, including sleeping pads, showers, water filters, and camping accessories as well as kayaks, waders, and lifejackets.

■ **Brand Name(s):** Stearns, Stearns Outdoors.

✔ Brochure

■ **Products:** • Sleeping pads • Portable showers • Kayaks • Lifejackets

The Ripstop Portable Awning, offers a six-foot or seven-foot canopy, is one of Stearns' camping products.

The Sunshower from Stearns has a four-gallon capacity for three or four showers, and features a soap and shampoo pocket.

The Soflex Rainsuit from Stearns is made of PVC/Polyester Rayon, and features pockets and bib pants with suspenders.

Tender Corp.

P.O. Box 290

Littleton, NH 03561

(603) 444-5464

(800) 258-4696

Fax: (603) 444-6735

sales@tendercorp.com

www.tendercorp.com

Tender Corp. makes a variety of outdoor skin care products, including After Bite and After Sting insect bite treatments, Family Medic lotions, Dry Hands lotion, Natrapel insect repellent, Bug Dots repellent, and Ben's insect repellent. Sales are online.

■ **Brand Name(s):** Ben's, Natrapel, Bug Dots, After Bite, After Sting, Dry Hands, Family Medic.

Brochure. ˌ Online shop.

■ **Products:** • Insect repellents • Sunburn treatment • Insect bite treatment.

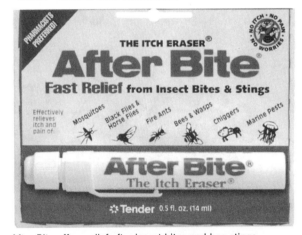

After Bite offers relief after insect bites and bee stings.

Bug Dots repel bugs without the mess of sprays or lotions.

Trailmate Inc.

2359 Trailmate Drive
Sarasota, FL 34243
(800) 777-1034
Fax: (800) 477-5141
jonathan@trailmate.com
www.trailmate.com

Trailmate is a manufacturer of specialty cycles, including the Fun Cycle, Banana Peel, Mini Peel, and Low Rider, that are offered as rentals at many campgrounds. Sales are made through dealers.

■ **Brand Name(s):** Trailmate.

■ **Products:** • Cycles

The Low Rider is one of the unusual bicycle designs offered by Trailmate.

We-no-nah Canoes

P.O. Box 247
Winona, MN 55987
(507) 454-5430
Fax: (507) 454-5448
info@wenonah.com
www.wenonah.com

We-no-nah makes canoes in 23 hull designs and also offers accessories including paddles, life jackets, seat pads, storage bags, and books and videos.

■ **Brand Name(s):** We-no-nah.
Brochure.

■ **Products:** • Canoes

Wilderness Press

1200 5th St.
Berkeley, CA 94710
(510) 558-1666
(800) 443-7227
Fax: (510) 558-1696
mail@wildernesspress.com
www.wildernesspress.com

For more than 35 years, Wilderness Press has been producing books on hiking, biking, kayaking, fishing, snow sports, and the wilderness. Orders are taken direct by phone or mail and books are in stores.

■ **Brand Name(s):** Wilderness Press.
✔ Brochure
■ **Products:** • Books

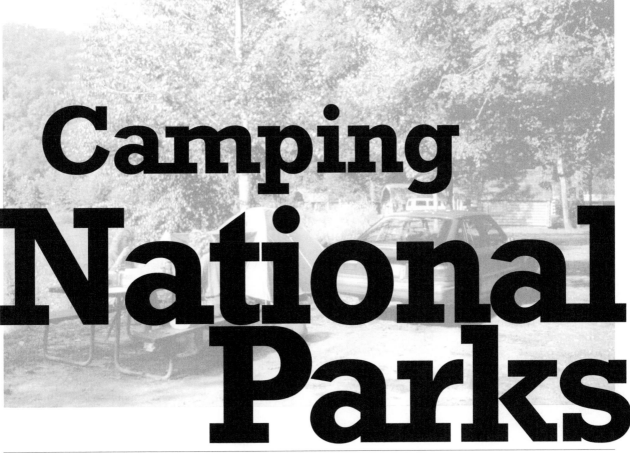

Camping National Parks

Campers will find a wide variety of opportunities in nearly 150 of the national parks, monuments and recreation areas scattered from Alaska to the Virgin Islands. The scenery ranges from magnificent mountains to the Everglades to rugged spots along mighty rivers.

Campers can choose from truly roughing it in backcountry, wilderness areas to setting up tents or driving in RVs or trailers in scenic but developed campgrounds. While many parks have first come-first served policies, quite a few accept reservations through local ranger stations or via the (800) 365-CAMP reservation line. Reservations for some campgrounds are also accepted online at reservations.nps.gov. And the National Park Service's Web site at www.nps.gov is searchable by parks or by areas of interest such as camping.

In addition to the camping fees listed, many parks and national monuments charge entrance or usage fees. National Park Passes are available for $50 that will allow entry into any site in the system for one year. Golden Age Passports for U.S. citizens aged 62 and older provide lifetime access.

Appalachian National Scenic Trail, 2,167 miles from Maine to Georgia

Information available from Appalachian Trail Conference, PO Box 807, Harpers Ferry, WV 25425-0807, Phone: (304) 535-6331.

ALASKA

Alagnak Wild River, King Salmon, Alaska
Primitive camping only, permits available at no charge at King Salmon Visitor Center.

Aniakchak National Monument & Preserve, King Salmon, Alaska. Primitive camping only.

Bering Land Bridge National Preserve, Nome, Alaska
Six cabins available for emergency winter use, Serpentine Hot Springs cabin with small bathhouse sleeps 15-20 people, no formal campsites but unrestricted primitive camping.

Denali National Park & Preserve, Denali Park, Alaska
Igloo Creek Campground: Open mid-May to mid-September, 7 tent sites, no vehicles, no water, $6 per night, reserve at Visitor Center.
Morino Backpacker: Open mid-May to mid-September, for backpackers only, $6 per night.
Riley Creek Campground: Year-round, 100 sites for RVs and tents, flush toilets, $4 reservation fee, information (800) 622-7275.
Sanctuary River Campground: Open mid-May through mid-September, seven sites for tents only, $6 per night, reserve at Visitor Center.
Savage River Campground: Open mid-May through mid-September, 53 sites for RVs and tents, flush toilets, $12 per night, reservations (800) 622-7275.
Wonder Lake Campground: Open June through mid-September, 28 sites for tents only, flush toilets, $12 per night, reservations (800) 622-7275.

Gates of the Arctic National Park & Preserve, Bettles, Alaska. Wilderness area with no established campgrounds.

Glacier Bay National Park & Preserve, Gustavus, Alaska
Bartlett Cove: Open May 1-Sept. 30, free, reservations not taken but permit required.

Katmai National Park & Preserve, King Salmon, Alaska
Brooks Camp Campground: Open June 1-early September, $10 user fee plus $5 camping fee, reservations required (800) 365-CAMP.

Kenai Fjords National Park, Seward, Alaska
Glacier Campground and Back Country Cabins: Open in summer, 12 walk-in sites and three cabins, accessible by boat or plane, reservations and permits needed in advance, information (907) 224-3175.

Klondike Gold Rush National Historical Park, Skagway, Alaska
Dyea Campground: Open May 15-Sept. 30, 22 rustic sites, 10 miles from Skagway, information (907) 983-9224.

Wrangell-St. Elias National Park & Preserve, Copper Center, Alaska
Glacier View Campground: Open May-September, scenic sites, information (907) 554 4490.
Nabesna District Camping Areas: Year-round, sites available on roadside pullouts, no reservations taken, backcountry camping also available.

ARIZONA

Canyon De Chelly National Monument, Chinle, Ariz.
Year-round, campsites at no charge, backcountry camping allowed with a guide.

Chiricahua National Monument, Willcox, Ariz.

Bonita Canyon Campground: Year-round, 25 sites for tents and RVs less than 26 feet, restrooms but no hookups or showers, $12 per night, no reservations taken, group site available for 8-24 people in tents.

Glen Canyon National Recreation Area, Arizona and Utah
Bullfrog Campgrounds: Year-round, 78 sites, 24 RV sites, restrooms, reservations not taken, $18 per night; fees vary for RV sites; also primitive camping area for $6 per night, information (435) 684-3000.
Halls Crossing Campground: Year-round, 64 sites, $18 per night; also 32 RV sites with varying fees, information (435) 684-7000.
Hite Camping: Year-round, several primitive sites, no reservations, $6 per night.
Lake Powell Shoreline Camping: Year-round, no facilities, no fees.
Lees Ferry Campground: Year-round, 30 primitive sites, $10 per night.
Wahweap Campground: Year-round, water and restrooms, $18 per night; also RV sites with varying fees.

Grand Canyon National Park, Grand Canyon, Ariz.
Backcountry camping: Year-round, permit required from the Backcountry Information Center, fee is $10 for a permit plus $5 per night per person.

Desert View Campground, South Rim: Open mid-May through mid-October, $10 per site per night, no hookups, reservations not taken.

Mather Campground, South Rim: Year-round, tent and RV sites, $15 per night, reservations taken (800) 365-2267, group sites available; reservations not taken, from December through March with $10 per night fee.

North Rim Campground: Open mid-May through mid-October, $15 per night, no hookups, reservations taken (800) 365-2267; limited sites available after mid-October with limited services until snow closes Highway 67.

Trailer Village, South Rim: Year-round, RV sites with hookups, $24 per site per night for two people, $2 for each extra person over age 16, reservations taken (800) 365-2267.

Lake Mead National Recreation Area, Mojave Desert, Arizona and Nevada. Eight campgrounds, all year-round with restrooms, water, all offered for tents, trailers or RVs, all with 15-day or 30-day limits. Boulder Beach, 154 sites; Callville Bay, 80 sites; Cottonwood Cove lower, 49 sites; Cottonwood Cove upper, 100 sites; Echo Bay, 166 sites; Katherine Landing, 173 sites; Las Vegas Bay, 89 sites; Temple Bar, 153 sites.

Lake Mead

Navajo National Monument, Black Mesa, Ariz.
Year-round, 31 sites, water and restrooms, no campfires, no hookups, RVs less than 27 feet, no reservations taken.

Organ Pipe Cactus National Monument, Ajo, Ariz.
Alamo Campground: Year-round, four sites, tents only, primitive, $6 per night, no reservations taken but permit required.

Twin Peaks Campground: Year-round, 208 sites, RVs up to 35 feet, water, restrooms, $10 per night, no reservations taken.

Petrified Forest National Park, Ariz.
Wilderness area backpacking only, free permit required.

Organ Pipe

All U.S. Park Service Photos

Petrified Forest

Sunset Crater Volcano National Monument, Flagstaff, Ariz.
Bonito Campground: Open late May through mid-October, maximum vehicle size 35 feet, no hookups, information (520) 526-0866.

ARKANSAS

Buffalo National River, Harrison, Ark.
Buffalo Point: Year-round, 83 drive-in sites at $15 per night and 20 walk-in sites at $10 per night, five group sites, with showers, flush toilets and hookups, no reservations taken, information (870) 741-5443.

Carver: Year-round, eight primitive sites, no fees.
Erbie: Year-round, 14 drive-in sites, 16 walk-in sites and 10 group sites, water, no fees. Hasty: Year-round, two primitive sites, no fees.
Highway 14 Bridge: Year-round, primitive with open camping, no fees.

Kyles Landing: Year-round, 33 primitive sites, water, no fees.

Lost Valley: Year-round, 15 primitive sites, water and flush toilets, no fees.

Maumee South: Year-round, primitive with open camping, no fees.

Mt. Hersey: Year-round, primitive with open camping, no fees.

Ozark: Year-round, 35 primitive sites with water and flush toilets, no fees.

Ozark

Rush: Year-round, primitive with open camping, water, no fees.

Steel Creek: Year-round, 26 primitive sites, water, no fees.

Tyler Bend: Year-round, 28 drive-in sites and 10 walk-in sites at $10 per night, five group sites by reservation, showers, flush toilets available, information (870) 741-5443.

Woolum: Year-round, primitive with open camping, no fees.

Hot Springs National Park, Hot Springs, Ark.

Gulpha Gorge: Year-round, water and restrooms but no hookups or showers, $10 per night, no reservations taken.

CALIFORNIA

Channel Islands National Park, Ventura, Calif.

Camping allowed on Anacapa Island, San Miguel Island, Santa Barbara Island, Santa Cruz Island and Santa Rosa Island. Year-round, accessible by boat, primitive sites, $10 fee, reservations (800) 365-CAMP.

Death Valley National Park, Death Valley, Calif.

Emigrant: Year-round, 10 sites, tents-only, water and flush toilets, no fees.

Furnace Creek: Year-round, 136 sites, water, flush toilets, $16 per night during winter and $10 during summer, reservations (800) 365-CAMP.

Mahogany Flat: Open March 1-Nov. 30, 10 sites, free.

Mesquite Spring: Year-round, 30 sites, water, flush toilets, $10 per night.

Stovepipe Wells: Open Oct. 15-April 15, 190 sites, water, flush toilets, $10 per night.

Sunset: Open Oct. 15-April 15, 1,000 sites, water, flush toilets, $10 per night.

Texas Spring: Open Oct. 15-April 15, 92 sites for tents with limited RV space, water, flush toilets, $12 per night.

Thorndike: Open March 1-Nov. 30, six sites, free.

Wildrose: Year-round, 23 sites, free.

Devils Postpile National Monument, Sierra Nevada near Mammoth Lake, Calif.

Six campgrounds available with 180 sites, closed in winter, no reservations taken.

Golden Gate National Recreation Area, San Francisco, Calif.

Bicentennial Campground: Year-round, three tent sites, water, no fees, maximum three nights per year, information (415) 331-1540.

Hawkcamp Campground: Year-round, three tent sites, no fees, maximum three nights per year, reservations taken, information (415) 331-1540.

Haypress Campground: Year-round, five tent sites, no fees, maximum three nights per year, reservations taken, information (415) 331-1540.

Kirby Cove: Open April 1-Oct. 31, four tent sites, no fees, maximum three nights per year, reservations taken, information (415) 331-1540.

Joshua Tree National Park, Palm Springs, Calif.

Belle: Year-round, 18 sites, no water, no fees.

Black Rock: Year-round, 100 sites, water, flush toilets, $10 per night, reservations (800) 365-CAMP.

Cottonwood: Year-round, 62 sites, water, flush toilets, $10 per night, three group sites, $25 per night.

Hidden Valley: Year-round, 39 sites, no water, no fees.

Indian Cove: Year-round, 101 sites, no water, $10 per night, 13 group sites at $20-$35, reservations (800) 365-CAMP.

Jumbo Rocks: Year-round, 125 sites, no water, no fees.

Ryan: Year-round, 31 sites, no water, no fees.

Sheep Pass: Year-round, six group sites, $20-$35, no water, reservations (800) 365-CAMP.

White Tank: Year-round, 15 sites, no water, no fees.

Lassen Volcanic National Park, Mineral, Calif.

Butte Lake: Open late May to late September, 42 sites, trailers to 35 feet, water, boat launch, $10 per night.

Crags: Open late June to early September, 45 sites, trailers to 35 feet, water, $8 per night.

Juniper Lake: Open late June to early October, 18 sites, not recommended for trailers, $10 per night, also

Lassen

group site and stock corral by reservation only, information (530) 595-4444 ext. 5184.

Lost Creek: Open late June to late September, nine group sites by reservation only, tents only, $45 per night, information (530) 595-4444 ext. 5184.

Manzanita Lake: Open late May until snow falls, 179 sites, trailers to 35 feet, showers, store, boat launch, $14 per night during summer, $8 per night from late September until snow.

Southwest Walk-in: Year-round, 21 sites, flush toilets, store nearby, $12 in summer, $8 after late September.

Summit Lake North: Open late June to early September, 46 sites, trailers to 35 feet, water, swimming, $14 per night.

Summit Lake South: Open late June to early September, 48 sites, trailers to 35 feet, water, swimming, $12 per night.

Warner Valley: Open late May until snow falls, 18 sites, trailers not recommended, water, $12 in summer, $8 after early October.

Lava Beds National Monument, Tulelake, Calif.
Indian Wells Campground: Year-round, 40 sites for tents to small RVs, water, flush toilets, $10 per night, information (530) 667-2282, Ext. 230.

Mojave National Preserve, Barstow, Calif.
Black Canyon Equestrian & Group Campground: Year-round, $25 per night, information (760) 326-6322.

Hole in the Wall Campground: Year-round, 35 sites for tents or trailers, water, no hookups, no reservations taken, $12 per night.

Mid-Hills Campground: Year-round, 26 sites, not recommended for RVs or trailers, water, no reservations taken, $12 per night.

Point Reyes National Seashore, Point Reyes, Calif.
Coast Camp, Glen Camp, Sky Camp and Wildcat Camp are backpacking camps with designated sites, no cars, no dogs, $10 per night, group sites at $20 and $30, permits required, reservations (415) 663-8054.

Boat-in beach camping available on Tomales Bay, $10 per night, group sites at $20 and $30.

Presidio of San Francisco
Rob Hill Campground: Year-round, two group campgrounds up to 30 people each, reservations (415) 561-5444.

Redwood National and State Parks, Del Norte and Humboldt counties, Calif
Del Norte Redwoods State Park: Open April 1-Sept. 30, 145 tent or RV sites, RVs up to 31 feet, showers, restrooms, no hookups, $12 per night, reservations (800) 444-7275.

Freshwater Lagoon Spit Overnight Area: Year-round, tent and vehicle areas, $10 vehicle fee per night, $3 per bicyclist or hiker.

Jedediah Smith Redwoods State Park: Year-round, 106 tent or RV sites, RVs to 36 feet, showers, restrooms, nature center, no hookups, $12 per night, one group site for 50 people, information (800) 444-7275.

Prairie Creek Redwoods State Park: Year-round, 25 RV sites, 29 tent sites, no trailers, second park area has 75 sites and does allow trailers, showers, restrooms, $12 per night, no reservations taken.

Santa Monica Mountains National Recreation Area, Thousand Oaks, Calif.
California State Parks Campgrounds: Year-round, four campgrounds, fees vary, reservations taken, information (818) 880-0350.

Circle X Group Campground: Year-round, sites for 10-75 people, reservations required, information (805) 370-2300, Ext. 1702.

Sequoia and Kings Canyon National Parks, Three Rivers, Calif.
Atwell Mill Campground (Sequoia): Open late May-Oct. 31, 21 sites, trailers and RVs not permitted, $8 per night.

Azalea (Kings Canyon): Year-round, 113 sites, flush toilets, showers, restaurant and gift shop nearby, $14 per night.

Buckeye Flat (Sequoia): Seasonal, 28 sites, tents only, flush toilets, $14 per night.

Canyon View (Kings Canyon): Open May to October, 37 sites, flush toilets, near restaurant and market, $14 per night.

Cold Springs (Sequoia): Open late May-Oct. 31, 40 sites, RVs and trailers not permitted, near resort, $8 per night.

Dorst (Sequoia): Open late May to Labor Day, 204 sites, flush toilets, $16 per night, reservations (800) 365-CAMP.

Lodgepole (Sequoia): Year-round, 214 sites, flush toilets, $16 during summer then $14, reservations (800) 365-CAMP.

Moraine (Kings Canyon): Open May to October, 120 sites, flush toilets, near restaurant and gift shop, $14 per night.

Potwisha (Sequoia): Seasonal, 42 sites, flush toilets, $14 per night.

Sentinel (Kings Canyon): Open late April to mid-November, 82 sites, flush toilets, near restaurant and market, $14 per night.

Sheep Creek (Kings Canyon): Open May to October, 111 sites, flush toilets, near restaurant and market, $14 per night.

South Fork (Sequoia): Year-round, 10 sites, no water, unpaved road.

Sunset (Kings Canyon: Open late May to mid-September, 200 sites, flush toilets, near restaurant and market, $14 per night.

Whiskeytown National Recreation Area, Whiskeytown, Calif.

Brandy Creek RV Campground: Year-round, $14 per night in summer, $7 per night winter, no reservations taken, information (530) 242-3400.

Dry Creek Group Tent Campground: Year-round, two group sites for tents only, reservations required from April 1-Sept. 30, reservations (800) 365-CAMP.

Oak Bottom Campground: Year-round, lakeside sites are $18 per night with other tent sites $16 per night, RV sites are $14, winter rates are $8 per night for tents and $7 for RVs, reservations taken for May 15-Sept. 15 at (800) 365-CAMP.

Primitive Tent Campsites: Year-round, $10 per night summer, $5 winter, no reservations taken.

Whiskey Creek Group Picnic Area: Open April 1-Sept. 30, three day use picnic areas available.

Yosemite National Park, Sierra Nevada, Calif.

Park has 13 campgrounds, reservations for up to seven are available five months in advance, reservations (800) 436-PARK. Wawona, Hodgdon Meadow, and two campgrounds in Yosemite Valley are open all year.

High Sierrra Camps: Five camps available, canvas tent cabins, showers, restrooms, reservations taken and campers selected on lottery basis, information (559) 253-5674.

COLORADO

Black Canyon of the Gunnison National Park, Montrose, Colo.

North Rim: April-October, 13 sites in forest, water but no hookups, $10 per night.

South Rim: April-October, 88 sites, water and electricity, $10 per night or $15 per night with hookup.

Colorado National Monument, Fruita, Colo.
Saddlehorn Campground: Year-round, 80 sites, restrooms, no showers, $10 per night.
Curecanti National Recreation Area, Gunnison, Colo.

Cimarron: Open April-December, 20 miles east of Montrose, 22 sites, water, flush toilets, $10 per night.

Dry Gulch: Open May-November, 17 miles west of Gunnison, 10 sites, water, $10 per night.

East Elk Creek: Open mid-May through September, 16 miles west of Gunnison, group campsite for up to 50 people, $2 per person with $30 minimum.

East Portal: Open mid-April through mid-November, bottom of Black Canyon, no trailers or large RVs, water, $10 per night.

Elk Creek: Year-round, 16 miles west of Gunnison on Highway 50, 179 sites, flush toilets, showers, restaurant, $10 per night.

Gateview: Open mid-May to mid-November, on Lake Fork of Gunnison River, seven sites, water.

Lake Fork: Open mid-April through September, 27 miles west of Gunnison on Highway 50, 87 sites, flush toilets, showers, marina, $10 per night.

Ponderosa: Open late-April through November, nine walk-in and 20 drive-in sites, water, boat ramp, $10 per night.

Red Creek: Open mid-May to mid-November, near Blue Mesa Reservoir, two sites at $10 per night, one group site at $2 per person with $20 minumum.

Stevens Creek: Open May-October, 12 miles west of Gunnison, 54 sites, water, boat ramp, $10 per night.

Great Sand Dunes National Monument & Preserve, Mosca, Colo.

Pinyon Flats: Year-round, 88 sites in forest, flush toilets, water, $10 per night, reservations not taken.

Mesa Verde National Park, Cortez and Mancos, Colo.

Morefield Campground: Open late April to late October, 400 sites for tents and trailers, restrooms, showers, store, $19 per night, $25 with hookups, information (800) 449-2288.

Rocky Mountain National Park, Estes Park and Grand Lake, Colo.

Rocky Mountain National Park

Aspenglen: Open mid-May to late September, 54 sites along Fall River, $18 per night, information (970) 586-1206.

Glacier Basin: Open mid-May to late September, sites in pine forest by Glacier Creek, $18 per night, reservations (800) 365-CAMP.

Longs Peak: Year-round, 26 site for tents only, near Longs Peak Trail, $18 per night, $10 per night in winter when water is turned off, no reservations taken.

Moraine Park: Year-round, sites in pine forest, reservations accepted May 23-Sept. 23 for $18 per night, $10 per night in winter, reservations (800) 365-CAMP, group camping in winter.

Timber Creek: Year-round, 100 sites overlooking Kawuneeche Valley, $18 per night, $10 during winter months.

FLORIDA

Big Cypress National Preserve, Ochopee, Fla.
Bear Island: Year-round, primitive with no water or restrooms.

Midway: Open as needed during visitor season, primitive with no water or restrooms, call (941) 695-4111 for information.

Mitchell's Landing: Year-round, primitive with no water or restrooms.

Monument: Year-round, flush toilets and water but no hookups, $14 per night.

Pinecrest: Year-round, primitive with no water or restrooms.

Biscayne National Park, Miami, Key Biscayne and Homestead, Fla.
Boca Chita Key Campground: Year-round, no running water, accessible by boat only (call 305-230-1100), $10 per night or $15 if bringing a boat to the harbor.

Elliott Key Campground: Year-round, waterfront and forested sites on seven-mile long island, restrooms and water, accessible by boat only (call 305-230-1100), $10 per night or $15 if bringing a boat to the harbor, information (305) 230-7275.

Canaveral National Seashore, Titusville and New Smyrna Beach, Fla.
Beach camping: Open Nov. 1-April 30, no RVs or trailers, permit required, information (386) 428-3384 Ext. 10.

Island camping: Year-round, no RVs or trailers, permit required, accessible only by water, information (386) 428-3384 Ext. 10.

Dry Tortugas National Park, Key West, Fla.
Garden Key: Year-round, 13-site primitive, $3 per night, group sites available, information (305) 242-7700.

Everglades National Park, Miami, Naples and Homestead, Fla.
Flamingo Campground: Year-round, 234 drive-in sites, 64 walk-in sites, showers, store, $14 per night, reservations (800) 365-CAMP.

Long Pine Key Campground: Year-round, 108 sites for tents and RVs, restrooms but no showers or hookups, $14 per night, reservations (800) 365-CAMP.

Gulf Islands National Seashore, Florida and Mississippi
Davis Bayou Campground: Year-round, 51 sites with hookups, bathhouse, $14 per night or $16 with electricity, no reservations taken, information (228) 875-9057.

Fort Pickens Campground: Year-round, south of Pensacola, hookups available, $15 per night or $20 with electricity, also group area, information (850) 934-2621.

Naval Live Oaks Youth Group Tent Area: Year-round, limited to youth groups.

GEORGIA

Cumberland Island National Seashore, St. Marys, Ga.
Sea Camp: Year-round, restrooms, showers, water, $4 per person, reservations required.

Backcountry Camping: Year-round, four sites, $2 per person, reservations required.

HAWAII

Haleakala National Park, Kula, Maui, Hawaii
Hosmer Grove: Year-round, small campground near summit, space available without permit, water, no reservations taken.

Kipahulu Campground: Year-round, primitive campground near ocean, space available without permit, no reservations taken.

Wilderness cabins and wilderness camping available, information (808) 572-4400.

Hawaii Volcanoes National Park, Hilo, Hawaii
Namakani Paio: Year-round, water and restrooms available, no fees, no reservations taken.

Kulanaokuaiki: Year-round, three sites, no fees, no reservations taken.

IDAHO

City of Rocks National Reserve, Almo, Idaho
Year-round, 75 sites and three group sites, primitive, $7 per night, $59 for 17 minimum at group sites, reservations taken (208) 824-5519.

Craters of the Moon National Monument, Arco, Idaho

Craters of the Moon Lava Flow Campground: Open dependent on snow conditions, 52 sites, water, restrooms, no hookups or showers, limited number of RVs and trailers permitted, no reservations taken, group camp available by reservation only, information (208) 527-3257.

ILLINOIS

Illinois & Michigan Canal National Heritage Corridor, Illinois

Des Plaines Fish and Wildlife Area: Open Jan. 1-Oct. 31, sites have gravel pads, water, $7 per night, information (815) 423-5326.

I&M Canal State Trail: Year-round, backpack carry-in along 61-mile trail, $6 per night, information (815) 942-0796.

I&M Canal State Trail, Channahon Access: Year-round, limited tent or primitive sites, $6 per night, also youth camping areas, permits required, information (815) 467-4271.

I&M Canal State Trail, Gebhard Woods Access: Year-round, limited tent or primitive sites, toilets, water, $6 per night, also youth camping areas, permits required, information (815) 942-0796.

Illini State Park Campground: Year-round, overlooking Illinois River, sites with showers and electricity, $8 plus $3 utility fee, sites with electricity, $7 plus $3 utility fee, youth group area available, information (815) 795-2448.

Starved Rock State Park Campground: Year-round, 133 sites with water, electricity and showers, toilets, $8 per night plus $3 utility fee, information (815) 667-4726.

INDIANA

Indiana Dunes National Lakeshore, Porter, Ind.

Dunewood Campground: Open April 1-Oct. 31, 79 sites, showers, reservations not accepted.

Indiana Dunes

KENTUCKY

Big South Fork River & Recreation Area, Oneida, Ky., and Tenn.

Alum Ford: Year-round, eight primitive sites, $5 per night.

Bandy Creek Campground: Year-round, 100 sites with water and electric for $18 per night, 50 tent sites at $15 per night, two group areas, showers, restrooms and swimming pool, reservations taken April 1-Oct. 31 at (800) 365-CAMP.

Blue Heron Campground: Open April 1-Nov. 15, 45 sites with water, electricity, restrooms, showers, $15 per night, reservations taken at (800) 365-CAMP.

Cumberland Gap National Historical Park, Middlesboro, Ky.

Wilderness Road Campground: Year-round, 160 woodland sites, restrooms, showers, electricity, $10 per night or $15 with electricity, no reservations taken, backcountry camping free with permit, group camping $20 with reservation, information (606) 248-2817.

Mammoth Cave National Park, Mammoth Cave, Ky.

Headquarters Campground: Open March 1-Nov. 30, 109 sites, no hookups, $13 per night, reservations taken, information (800) 967-2283.

Houchins Ferry Campground: Year-round, 12 primitive sites, water, boat launch.

Maple Springs Group Campground: Open March 1-Nov. 30, water, horses allowed, reservations (800) 365-CAMP.

MAINE

Acadia National Park, Bar Harbour, Maine

Blackwoods Campground: Year-round, five miles south of Bar Harbour on Route 3, in woods within 10 minute walk of ocean, reservations accepted, $20 a day, restrooms, showers nearby.

Seawall Campground: Open late May through Sept. 30, four miles south of Southwest Harbor on Route 102A, in woods within 10 minute walk of ocean, reservations accepted, $14-$20 a day, restrooms, showers nearby.

MARYLAND

Antietam National Battlefield, Sharpsburg, Md.

Rorhbach Campground: Open March 1-Nov. 30, 10 sites, primitive camping for Scouts and organized groups, $25 for one- or two-night stay, reservations by mail only.

Assateague National Seashore, Berlin, Md., and Chintoteague, Va.

Year-round camping in oceanside and bayside campgrounds, reservations recommended at 800-365-CAMP from April 15-Oct. 15, $12 per night winter and $16 April 15-Oct. 15, more information is available at (410) 641-3030.

Catoctin Mountain Park, Thurmond, Md.

Camp Misty Mount: Open mid-April through October, rustic cabins in 30-acre camp, cots, flush toilets, showers, $40-$110 per night per cabin, information (301) 271-3140.

Owens Creek Campground: Open mid-April through mid-November, 51 wooded sites at $14 per night, tents and RVs, flush toilets, showers but no hookups, no reservations taken.

Poplar Grove Youth Tent Camping Area: Year-round, three sites for 25 each, $20 per night per site, reservations required (301) 663-9388.

Chesapeake & Ohio Canal National Historic Park, Washington, D.C., Maryland, West Virginia

Camping at Antietam Creek, Fifteen Mile Creek, Marsden Tract Group Campground, McCoys Ferry, Paw Paw, Spring Gap as well as 31 hiker-biker campgrounds along the canal. Year-round, fees charged, information (301) 299-3613.

Greenbelt Park, Greenbelt, Md.

Year-round, 174 sites, flush toilets and showers, no hookups, $13 per night, reservations (800) 365-CAMP.

MASSACHUSETTS

Boston Harbor Islands National Recreation Area, Boston, Mass.

Camping from early May through mid-October, primitive camping with access only by boat on four islands, information (617) 223-8666.

MICHIGAN

Isle Royale National Park, Houghton, Mich.

Camping in 36 areas of the island park: Open mid-April to Oct. 31, tents or shelters, group sites available, minimum impact, no reservations taken, $4 per day user fee, information (906) 282-0984.

Pictured Rock National Lakeshore, Munising, Mich.

Hurricane River Campground: Open May 10-Oct. 31, 21 sites, $10 per night, no reservations taken.

Little Beaver Lake Campground: Open May 10-Oct. 31, eight sites on lake, boat ramp, $10 per night, no reservations taken.

Pictured Rock

Twelvemile Beach Campground: Open May 10-Oct. 31, 37 sites, $10 per night, no reservations taken.

Sleeping Bear Dunes National Lakeshore, Empire, Mich.

D.H. Day Campground: Open early April through November, 88 rustic sites, near Lake Michigan beach, $10 per night, reservations not taken.

North Manitou Island or South Manitou Island Backcountry Campsites: Open Memorial Day to early October, no designated sites, accessible by boat or ferry, permits $5 per night or $10 for groups up to 10 people, information (231) 326-5134.

Platte River Campground: Year-round, 179 sites, water, restrooms, showers, group sites available, reservations (800) 365-CAMP.

Valley View Backcountry Campground: Year-round, five sites, $5 per night permit required.

White Pine Backcountry Campground: Year-round, six sites, $5 per night permit required.

MINNESOTA

Grand Portage National Monument, Grand Marais, Minn.

Fort Charlotte: Year-round, two primitive sites for up to 10 people each, no fee but a permit is required, information (218) 387-2788.

Voyageurs National Park, International Falls, Minn.

Year-round, 215 tent, houseboat or day use sites on

Voyageurs

four lakes, also overnight sites accessible by boat, information (218) 283-9821.

MISSISSIPPI

Natchez Trace Parkway, Tupelo, Miss.
Jeff Busby Campground: Year-round, 18 sites, no hookups, no fees, reservations not taken.
Meriwether Lewis Campground: Year-round, 32 sites, located in Tennessee, no hookups, no fees, reservations not taken.
Rocky Springs: Year-round, 22 sites, no hookups, no fees, reservations not taken.

MISSOURI

Ozark National Scenic Riverways, Van Buren, Mo.
Alley Spring: Year-round, 162 sites, no hookups, $12 per night, no reservations taken, group sites available by reservation (573) 323-4236.
Big Spring: Year-round, 123 sites, no hookups, $12 per night, no reservations taken, group sites available by reservation (573) 323-4236.
Pulltite: Year-round, 55 sites, no hookups, $12 per night, no reservations taken, group sites available by reservation (573) 323-4236.
Round Spring: Year-round, 60 sites, no hookups, $12 per night, no reservations taken, group sites available by reservation (573) 323-4236.
Two Rivers: Year-round, 12 sites, no hookups, $12 per night, no reservations taken, group sites available by reservation (573) 323-4236.

MONTANA

Bighorn Canyon National Recreation Area, Fort Smith, Mont., Wyo.

Glacier National Park, northwest Montana
Park has 13 campgrounds with about 1,000 sites. Fish Creek and St. Mary Campgrounds accept reservations at (800) 365-CAMP; others have no reservations.

NEVADA

Great Basin National Park, Baker, Nev.
Grey Cliffs Group Campground: Open Memorial Day to Labor Day, $25 per night for up to 25 people, $10 non-refundable deposit, RVs not recommended, information (775) 234-7331 ext. 213.

Baker Creek Campground: Open mid-May to mid-October, 32 primitive sites, $10 per night.
Lower Lehman Creek Campground: Year-round, 11 sites, open to small RVs and trailers, water in summer only, $10 per night.
Upper Lehman Creek Campground: Open mid-May to Oct. 31, 24 sites, water in summer only, $10 per night.
Wheeler Peak Campground: Open from late May to Oct. 1, 37 sites, RVs and trailers not recommended, no water, $10 per night.

NEW JERSEY

Delaware National Scenic River and Delaware Water Gap National Recreation Area, New Jersey and Pennsylvania
Appalachian Trail: Year-round, camping permitted only for hikers on extended trips, limited to 100 feet of the trail.
River Camping: Year-round, primitive camping areas for boaters, limited to one-night stay, no permits and no fees.
Worthington State Forest Campground: April 1-Dec. 31, information (908) 841-9575.

NEW MEXICO

Bandelier National Monument, Los Alamos, N.M.
Juniper Campground: Year-round except for some bad-weather winter days, 94 sites, water and flush toilets, $10 per night, no reservations taken.
Ponderosa Group Campground: Year-round, located on State Route 4, two sites for 50 people each, $35 per night, water but no hook-ups or showers, call (505) 672-3861 ex 534 for reservations.

Chaco Culture National Historic Park, Nageezi, N.M.
Gallo Campground: Year-round, 47 sites, trailers up to 30 feet, $10 per night, no reservations accepted. Group sites available for 10 or more, reservations required, information: (505) 786-7014.

El Malpais National Monument, Grants, N.M.
The Narrows: Year-round, primitive campground, check-in with Bureau of Land Management Ranger Station, information (505) 240-0300.

El Moro National Monument, Ramah, N.M.
Year-round, nine sites, fees charged during summer, reservations not taken.

Gila Cliff Dwellings National Monument, Silver City, N.M.

Forks Campground: Year-round, primitive sites along the West Fork of the Gila River, no fees, reservations not taken.

Grapevine Campground: Year-round, primitive sites, no fees, reservations not taken.

Lower Scorpion Campground: Year-round, developed sites with water and flush toilets, no fees, reservations not taken.

Upper Scorpion Campground: Year-round, developed sites with water and flush toilets, no fees, reservations not taken.

NEW YORK

Fire Island National Seashore, Patchogue, N.Y.
Watch Hill Campground: Open May 15-Oct. 15, 26 tent sites, one group site, near marina and concessions, reservations (631) 597-6633.

Gateway National Recreation Area, New York and New Jersey
Floyd Bennett Field Campgrounds: Seasonal, reservations required (718) 338-4306.
Sandy Hook Campground: Limited to organized groups, reservations required (732) 872-5970.

NORTH CAROLINA

Blue Ridge Parkway, Asheville, N.C.
Linville Falls and Otter Creek areas open year-round; Crabtree Meadows, Doughton Park, Mt. Pisgah, Peaks of Otter, Price Park, Roanoke Mountain and Rocky Knob are seasonal, opening about May 1.

Cape Hatteras National Seashore, Manteo, N.C.
Cape Point: Open late May-Labor Day, near Cape Hatteras Lighthouse Historical District, tents and RVs, showers, flush toilets, $17 per night.
Frisco: Open mid-April to early October, ocean views, tents and RVs, showers, flush toilets, $17 per night.
Ocracoke Campground: Open mid-April to early October, near ocean on Ocracoke Island, tents and RVs, showers, flush toilets, $17 per night.
Oregon Inlet Campground: Open mid-April to early October, near Bodie Island Lighthouse, tents and RVs, showers, flush toilets, $17 per night.

Cape Lookout National Seashore, Harkers Island, N.C.
Year-round, primitive camping on Core Banks and Shackleford Banks, permit required but no fee.

NORTH DAKOTA

Theodore Roosevelt National Park, Medora and Watford City, N.D.
Cottonwood Campground: Year-round, 70 sites, water, flush toilets, no hookups, $10 per night, group sites available, no reservations taken, information (701) 623-4466.
Juniper Campground: Year-round, 50 sites, no water during winter, no hookups, $10 per night, $5 per night in winter, information (701) 842-2333.
Roundup Group Camp: Open early May to mid-October, horse use permitted, information (701) 623-4466.

OKLAHOMA

Chickasaw National Recreation Area, Sulphur, Okla.
Camping available at Buckhorn, Central, Cold Springs, Guy Sandy, Rock Creek and The Point. Open Memorial Day to Labor Day, no reservations taken except for group sites at Central, some sites have electricity, $8 per night, $14 for sites with utilities, $16 for group sites.

OREGON

Crater Lake National Park, Crater Lake, Ore.
Lost Creek Campground: Open mid-July to early October, 16 tent sites.
Mazama Campground: Open early June through early October, 200 sites, water, flush toilets, reservations not taken.

SOUTH CAROLINA

Congaree Swamp National Monument, Hopkins, S.C.
Bluff campsite and backcountry camping available year-round, primitive, free permit available at Ranger Station.

Kings Mountain National Military Park, Blacksburg, S.C.
Garner Creek Campsite: Year-round, one backcountry site holds up to 10 people, permit required, no advance registration.

SOUTH DAKOTA

Badlands National Park, southwestern South Dakota
Cedar Pass Campground: Year-round, $10 per night

Theodore Roosevelt National Park

during summer with 10-day limit and $8 per night during winter months, no reservations taken, four group sites available for $25 with reservations taken at (605) 433-5235.

Sage Creek Campground: Year-round, free, primitive camping only, no water, no reservations taken.

Missouri National Recreational River, Yankton, S.D.

Niobrara State Park: Open mid-April to mid-October, year-round for primitive camping, information (402) 857-3373.

Ponca State Park: Open mid-April to mid-November, year-round for primitive camping, information (402) 755-2284.

Wind Cave National Park, Hot Springs, S.D.

Elk Mountain Campground: Open April 1 to mid-September, 75 sites, water, flush toilets, no showers or hookups, no reservations taken, $10 per day.

TENNESSEE

Great Smoky Mountains National Park, Tennessee and North Carolina

Abrams Creek Campground: Open mid-March to Nov. 1, 16 sites, water but no hookups or showers, $12 per night, reservations not taken.

Balsam Mountain Campground: Open mid-May to mid-October, 26 sites, water but no hookups or showers, $14 per night, reservations not taken.

Big Creek Campground: Open mid-March to Nov. 1, 12 sites for tents only, water but no showers, $12 per night, group sites available, reservations (800) 365-CAMP.

Cades Cove Campground: Open May 1-Oct. 31, 159 sites, water but no hookups or showers, store, $14-$17 per night, reservations (800) 365-CAMP.

Cataloochee Campground: Open mid-March to Nov.

1, 27 sites, water but no hookups or showers, $12 per night, reservations (800) 365-CAMP.

Cosby Campground: Open mid-March to Nov. 1, 175 sites, water but no hookups or showers, $14 per night, reservations (800) 365-CAMP.

Deep Creek Campground: Open mid-April to Nov. 1, 92 sites, water but no hookups or showers, $14 per night, reservations (800) 365-CAMP.

Elkmont Campground: Open mid-March to late November, 220 sites, water but no hookups or showers, $14-$20 per night, group sites available, reservations (800) 365-CAMP.

Look Rock Campground: Open late May to Nov. 1, 92 sites, water but no hookups or showers, $14 per night, reservations (800) 365-CAMP.

Smokemont Campground: Year-round, 142 sites, water but no hookups or showers, $14-$17 per night, group sites available, reservations (800) 365-CAMP.

Obed Wild & Scenic River, Wartburg, Tenn.

Rock Creek Campground: Year-round, 12 undeveloped sites, $7 per night, no reservations taken.

TEXAS

Amistad National Recreation Area, Del Rio, Texas

277 North: Year-round, 17 sites with primitive camping only, tents and RVs permitted, no reservations taken.

Governors Landing: Year-round, 15 sites with primitive camping only, water available, tents and RVs less than 28 feet, no reservations taken.

San Pedro: Year-round, 35 sites, primitive camping only, tents and RVs, no reservations taken.

Spur 406: Year-round, eight sites with primitive camping only, tents and RVs, no reservations taken.

Big Bend National Park, Rio Grande, Texas

Chisos Basin Campground: Year-round, 65 sites with flush toilets and water but no hookups, $8 per night, trailers over 20 feet and RVs over 24 feet not recommended, no reservations taken.

Cottonwood Campground: Year-round, 31 campsites with water but no hookups, $8 per night, no reservations taken.

Rio Grande Village Campground: Year-round, 100 sites with flush toilets and water, $8 per night, no reservations taken.

Rio Grande Village RV Park: Year-round, 25 sites with hookups, register at Rio Grande Village Store.

Big Thicket National Preserve, Beaumont, Texas

Year-round, backcountry camping only with permit, call (409) 246-2337.

Guadalupe Mountains National Park, Salt Flat, Texas

Backcountry: Year-round, 10 campgrounds available, free but permit required.

Dog Canyon: Year-round, tent and RV sites, water and restrooms, $8 per night, group sites available.

Pine Springs: Year-round, tent and RV sites, water and restrooms, $8 per night, group sites available.

Lake Meredith National Recreation Area, Fritch, Texas

Blue Creek Bridge: Year-round, no designated sites, off-road vehicle use area, no water or hookups, no fees.

Blue West: Year-round, no water or hookups, no fees, boat launch nearby.

Bugbee: Year-round, semi-developed with no individual sites, no water or hookups, no fees.

Cedar Canyon: Year-round, small campground with no designated sites, restrooms open seasonally, no hookups, no fees, boat launch nearby.

Fritch Fortress: Year-round, water and flush toilets seasonally, no hookups, no fees, boat launch nearby.

Harbor Bay: Year-round, located just outside Fritch, no individual sites, no hookups, no fees.

McBride Canyon: Year-round, no designated sites, no water, no hookups, no fees.

Mullinaw: Year-round, undeveloped sites, no water, no hookups, horseback riding allowed, no fees.

Plum Creek: Year-round, no designated sites, no water, no hookups, horseback riding allowed, no fees.

Rosita: Year-round, no designated sites, no hookups, off-road vehicles and horseback riding allowed, no fees.

Sanford-Yake: Year-round, on a bluff near marina, water and flush toilets, no hookups, no fees, boat ramp nearby.

Spring Canyon: Year-round, designated sites, no hookups, swimming with no lifeguard service, no fees.

Padre Island National Seashore, Corpus Christi, Texas

Bird Island Basin: Year-round, primitive, tents and RVs, free permit required and $5 day user fee, windsurfing, boat launch, information (361) 949-8068.

Malaquite: Year-round, 50 semi-primitive sites for tents and RVs, $8 per night, no reservations accepted.

Padre Island

North Beach: Year-round, primitive, permit required with no fee, open to tents or RVs.

South Beach: Year-round, primitive, permit required with no fee, no roads but driving permitted on beach.

Yarborough Pass: Year-round, primitive, permit required with no fee, accessible by four-wheel drive vehicles.

UTAH

Arches National Park, Moab, Utah

Devils Garden Campground: Year-round, 18 miles from park entrance, 52 sites with water and flush toilets but no showers, some RV sites, $10 per night, no advance registration but daily preregistration starts at 7:30 a.m.

Bryce Canyon National Park, Bryce Canyon, Utah

North Campground: Year-round, tent and trailer sites, restrooms and showers but no hookups, $10 per night.

Sunset Campground: May 1-Oct. 10, tent and trailer sites, restrooms and showers but no hookups, $10 per night.

Sunset Group Campsite: One group site available by reservation only, information (435) 834-4801.

Canyonlands National Park, Moab, Utah

Squaw Flat Campground: Year-round, 26 sites with water and bathrooms, maximum RV size is 28 feet, $10 per night, no reservations taken.

Willow Flat Campground: Year-round, 12 sites, no water, maximum RV size is 28 feet, $5 per night, no reservations taken.

Group sites and background areas available.

Capitol Reef National Park, Torrey, Utah

Cathedral Valley Campground: Year-round, primitive sites, no water, no fees.

Cedar Mesa Campground: Year-round, primitive sites, no water, no fees.

Fruita Campground: Year-round, 71 sites, restrooms and water, $10 per night, information (435) 425-3791.

Dinosaur National Monument, Vernal, Utah, and Dinosaur, Colo.

Deerlodge: Year-round, eight sites for tents, primitive, no fees.

Echo Park: Closed by snow in winter, 17 sites for tents, water, $6 per night.

Gates of Lodore: Year-round, sites for tents and RVs, water, $5 per night.

Green River: Open from April-October, 88 sites for tents and RVs, restrooms, $12 per night.

Rainbow Park: Year-round, two tent sites, primitive, no fees.

Split Mountain: Year-round, four group sites, water, restrooms, information (435) 781-7759.

Natural Bridges National Monument, Blanding, Utah
Year-round, 13 sites, vehicles less than 26 feet, $10 per night, no reservations taken.

Zion National Park, Springdale, Utah
Lava Point Campground: Open May 1-Oct. 15, six primitive sites, reservations not accepted.
South Campground: Open April 1 to Oct. 31, primitive sites, no showers, no hookups, $14 per night, no reservations taken, information (435) 772-3256.
Watchman Campground: Year-round, no showers, tents $14 per night, electricity access $16 per night, group sites $3 per person, reservations (800) 365-CAMP.

VIRGINIA

Prince William Forest Park, Triangle, Va.
Chopawamsic Backcountry: Open March 1-Oct. 15, hike-in campsites, permit required, no fees.
Oak Ridge Campground: Year-round, wooded sites for tents or small RVs, showers, flush toilets, $10 per night, no reservations taken.
Travel Trailer Village: Year-round, RV sites with hookups, showers, pool, reservations (703) 221-2474.
Turkey Run Ridge Group Campground: Year-round, for groups of seven or more, $40 per night, reservations required (703) 221-7181.

Shenandoah National Park, Luray, Va.
Mathews Arm Campground: Open spring through October, near Overall Run Falls, 179 sites, $14 per night.
Big Meadows Campground: Open mid-May through November, 217 sites, $17 per night, reservations

required during summer (800) 365-CAMP.
Lewis Mountain Campground: Open spring through October, 32 sites, $14 per night.
Loft Mountain Campground: Open spring through October, 219 sites, $14 per night.
Dundo Group Campground: Open spring through November, seven group sites, $30 per night, reservations required (540) 298-9625.

VIRGIN ISLANDS

Virgin Islands National Park, St. John, Virgin Islands
Cinnamon Bay Campground: Year-round, bare sites, tents and cottages available, store and restaurant, reservations (340) 776-6330.

WASHINGTON

Ebey's Landing National Historical Reserve, Coupeville, Wash.
Fort Casey State Park: Year-round, trailer camping, no reservations taken.
Fort Ebey State Park: May 1-Dec. 1, tent and trailer camping.

Lake Roosevelt National Recreation Area, Columbia River, Wash.
Evans Campground: Year-round, 34 sites for tents and RVs, water and restrooms, no hookups, no reservations taken, $10 per night.
Fort Spokane Campground: Year-round, 67 sites for tents and RVs, no hookups, water and restrooms, Fort Spokane museum open in summer, no reservations taken, $10 per night.
Gifford Campground: Year-round, 47 sites for tents and RVs, no hookups, restrooms, no reservations taken, $10 per night.

Shenandoah National Park

Lake Roosevelt

Hunters Campground: Year-round, 39 sites for tents and most RVs, no hookups, water and restrooms, no reservations taken, $10 per night.

Keller Ferry: Year-round, 55 sites, no hookups, water and restrooms, no reservations taken, $10 per night.

Kettle Falls Campground: Year-round, 89 sites, tents and RVs, no hookups, no reservations taken, adjacent to marina and boat launch, $10 per night.

Porcupine Bay: Year-round, 31 sites, no hookups, water and restrooms, no reservations taken, $10 per night.

Spring Canyon: Year-round, 87 sites, no hookups, water and restrooms, no reservations taken, $10 per night.

Mount Rainier National Park, Ashford, Wash.

Cougar Rock: Seasonal, 173 sites for tents and RVs, water, flush toilets, five group sites, reservations (800) 365-CAMP.

Ipsut Creek: Year-round, 31 sites for tents and RVs, no water, two group sites, road subject to flooding.

Mowich Lake: Seasonal, 30 walk-in sites, no water, no fires.

Ohanapecosh: Seasonal, 188 sites for tents or RVs, water, flush toilets, one group site, reservations (800) 365-CAMP.

Sunshine Point: Year-round, 18 sites for tents or RVs, water.

White River: Seasonal, 112 sites for tents or RVs, water, flush toilets.

North Cascades National Park, Marblemount, Wash.

Colonial Creek Campground: Open mid-May through September, 162 sites in forest, boat ramp, $12 per night.

Goodell Creek Campground: Year-round, 21 sites in forest, water available in summer, $10 per night.

Newhalem Creek Campground: Open mid-May to early November, water, $12 per night, group camp available with reservations, information (360) 856-5700 ext. 515.

Olympic National Park, Port Angeles, Wash.

Park has 16 campgrounds with 910 sites, fees are $8-$12 per night, no reservations taken, seasonal, information (360) 565-3130.

Olympic

WEST VIRGINIA

Gauley River National Recreation Area, Summersville, W.Va.

Gauley Tailwaters: Year-round, 18 primitive sites, for tents or RVs, no water or hookups

New River Gorge National River, Fayetteville, W. Va.

Army Camp: Year-round, 11 primitive sites, self-contained RVs allowed, no fees.

Glade Creek: Year-round, five primitive sites, no large RVs, no fees.

Grandview Sandbar: Year-round, 16 primitive sites, no large RVs, no fees.

Stone Cliff: Year-round, 10 primitive sites, no large RVs, no fees, subject to flooding.

WISCONSIN

Apostle Islands National Lakeshore, Lake Superior, Wis.

Camping on remote islands, including developed sites near docks and wilderness sites, permits required with $15 administrative fee, reservations available at (715) 779-3398.

Saint Croix National Scenic River, Saint Croix Falls, Wis.

Year-round, primitive sites, most only accessible by water, some group sites, no fees or permits, no reservations accepted.

WYOMING

Devils Tower National Monument, Devils Tower, Wyo.

Belle Fourche Campground: Open mid-April to mid-September, 30 sites for tents or RVs, restrooms, $12 per night, reservations not taken.

Grand Teton National Park, Moose, Wyo.

Colter Bay Campground: Open mid-May to mid-September, 25 miles north of Moose, 350 sites for tents or RVs, wooded, showers.

Flagg Ranch Campground: Open dependent on weather, 11 miles southeast of Moose, 360 sites, mix of sites along Gros Ventre River, information (800) 443-2311.

Jenny Lake Campground: Open early May to mid-September, eight miles north of Moose, 49 sites for tents only, vehicles limited to 14 feet.

Lizard Creek Campground: Open early June to Labor Day, 32 miles north of Moose, 60 sites in forest, vehicles limited to 30 feet.

Signal Mountain Campground: Open mid-May to early October, 16 miles north of Jenny Lake, 86 sites

Yellowstone National Park

with forest, lake and mountain views, vehicles limited to 30 feet.

Yellowstone National Park, Wyoming, Idaho, Montana

Bridge Bay Campground: Open late May through mid-September, 430 sites, flush toilets, $15 per night, reservations (307) 344-7311.

Canyon Campground: Open late May through mid-September, 272 sites, flush toilets, showers, $15 per night, reservations (307) 344-7311.

Fishing Bridge RV Park: Open from mid-May through late September, 344 sites, hard-side vehicles only, flush toilets, showers, $29-plus per night, reservations (307) 344-7311.

Grant Village Campground: Open late June to late September, 425 sites, flush toilets, showers, $15 per night, reservations (307) 344-7311.

Indian Creek Campground: Open from mid-June to mid-September, 75 sites, primitive, $10 per night, no reservations taken.

Lewis Lake Campground: Open from mid-June to early November, 85 sites, primitive, $10 per night, no reservations taken.

Madison Campground: Open from early May to late October, 280 sites, flush toilets, $15 per night, reservations (307) 344-7311.

Mammoth Campground: Year-round, 85 sites, flush toilets, $12 per night, no reservations taken.

Norris Campground: Open from mid-May through September, 116 sites, flush toilets, $12 per night, no reservations taken.

Pebble Creek Campground: Open from late May through September, 32 sites, primitive, $10 per night, no reservations taken.

Slough Creek Campground: Open late May through October, 29 sites, primitive, $10 per night, no reservations taken.

Tower Fall Campground: Open late May through September, 32 sites, primitive, $10 per night, no reservations taken.

National Forest Campgrounds

There are thousands of opportunities for campers to enjoy the outdoors at national forests – 4,300 opportunities to be exact. That's the number of campgrounds maintained by the U.S. Forest Service across the country.

The Forest Service also has 23,000 recreation sites, including picnic areas, boat ramps, ski areas and resorts in its 177 sites, which include 192 million acres.

To make it easier for you to find these campgrounds, we've compiled a list of visitor centers in the national forests. There's more information at the Forest Service Web site, www.fs.fed.us, and its mailing address, USDA Forest Service, Recreation, Heritage and Wilderness Resources, Mail Stop 1125, 1400 Independence Ave. SW, Washington, D.C. 20090-1125.

Entrance fees are charged at many of the national forests, including the Golden Eagle Passport, the Golden Age Passport for those 62 and older, and the Golden Access Passport for blind and disabled visitors. User fees for camping are also charged in some areas.

Online reservations can be made at many of the national forests through the www.reserveusa.com Web site or at the toll-free number (877) 444-6777.

Visitor Centers

ALASKA

Chugach National Forest
Begich, Boggs Visitor Center, Glacier Ranger District, P.O. Box 129, Girdwood, AK 99587, (907) 783-2326.
Chubach Marine Highway Visitor Center, Glacier Ranger District, P.O. Box 129, Girdwood, AK 99587, (907) 783-3242.
Valdez and Crooked Creek Information Site, Cordova Ranger District, P.O. Box 1513, Valdez, AK 99686, (907) 835-4680.

Tongass National Forest
Forest Service Information Center, Juneau Ranger District, Centennial Hall, 101 Egan Drive, Juneau, AK 99801, (907) 586-8751 or 586-7894.
Forest Service Information Center, Admiralty National Monument, 8461 Old Dairy Road, Juneau, AK 99801, (907) 586-8790.
Mendenhall Glacier Visitor Center, Juneau Ranger District, 8465 Old Dairy Road, Juneau, AK 99801, (907) 586-8800.
Petersburg Information Center, Ketchikan Ranger District, First and Fram, P.O. Box 810, Petersburg, AK 99822, (907) 772-4636.
Southeast Alaska Discovery Center, 50 Main St., Ketchikan, AK 99901, (907) 228-6220 or 228-6237.
Tongass Marine Highway Visitor Center, Alaska Region, 8461 Old Dairy Road, Juneau, AK 99801, (907) 586-8790.

ARIZONA

Coronado National Forest
Columbine Visitor Center, Safford Ranger District, P.O. Box 709, Safford, AZ 85546, (520) 428-4150.
Palisades Visitor Center, Catalina Ranger District, Tuscon, AZ 85750, (520) 749-8700.
Portal Visitor Center, Douglas Ranger District, P.O. Box 16126, Tuscon, AZ 85750, (520) 558-2221.
Sabino Canyon Visitor Center, Santa-Catalina Ranger District, 5700 Sabino Canyon Road, Tuscon, AZ 85750, (520) 749-8700.

Kaibab National Forest
City of Williams/Forest Visitor Center, 200 W. Railroad Ave., Williams, AZ 86046, (800) 863-0546 or (520) 635-4707.
Kaibab Plateau Visitors Center, HC 64, Highways 67 and 89A, Jacob Lake, AZ 86022, (520) 643-7298

ARKANSAS

Ozark-St. Francis National Forest
Arkansas River Visitor Center, Old Post Road Park, Russellville, AR 72801, (501) 968-2452.
Blanchard Springs Caverns Visitor Center, Sylamore Ranger District, P.O. Box 2779, Mountain View, AR 62560, (501) 269-3229.

CALIFORNIA

Angeles National Forest
Big Pines Visitor Center, P.O. Box 1011, Wrightwood, CA 92397, (619) 249-3504.
Chilao Visitor Center, Star Route, La Canada, CA 91011, (626) 796-5541.
Grassy Hollow Visitor Center, Valyermo Ranger District, P.O. Box 1011, Wrightwood, CA 92397, (626) 821-6737 or (661) 994-2187.
Mount Baldy Schoolhouse Visitor Center, P.O. Box 592, Mount Baldy Road, Mount Baldy Village, CA 91759, (909) 982-2829.

Cleveland National Forest
Laguna Mountain Visitor Center, Descanso Ranger District, P.O. Box 250, Sunrise Highway, Mount Laguna Village, CA 91948, (619) 473-8547.

Eldorado National Forest
Eldorado National Forest Information Center, 3070 Camino Heights Drive, Camino, CA 95709, (530) 644-6048.

Inyo National Forest
Ancient Bristlecone National Forest Center, White Mountain Ranger Station, 798 N. Main St., Bishop, CA 93514, (760) 873-2500.

Interagency Visitor Center, P.O. Box R, Highway 395, Lane Pine, CA 93545, (760) 876-4252.

Lone Pine Interagency Visitor Center, Mount Whitney Ranger District, P.O. Box R, Lone Pine, CA 93545, (760) 876-6222.

Mammoth Visitor Center, Mammoth Lakes Ranger District, P.O. Box 148, Highway 203, Mammoth Lakes, CA 93546, (760) 924-5500.

Mono Basin National Scenic Area Visitor Center, Mono Lake Ranger District, P.O. Box 429, Highway 395, Lee Vining, CA 93541, (760) 647-3044 or (760) 647-3045.

Schulman Grove Visitor Center, White Mountain Ranger District, 798 N. Main St., Bishop, CA 93514, (619) 873-2500.

White Mountain Visitor Center, Highway 395, 798 N. Main St., Bishop, CA 93514, (760) 873-2500.

Lake Tahoe Basin Management Unit

Lake Tahoe Visitor Center, 870 Emerald Bay Road, Suite 1, South Lake Tahoe, CA 96150, (530) 573-2674.

Meyers Interagency Information Center, 870 Emerald Bay Road, Suite 1, South Lake Tahoe, CA 96150, (916) 573-2600.

San Bernardino National Forest

Barton Flat Visitor Center, Highway 38, Angelus Oaks, CA 92305, (909) 794-4861 or 794-1123.

Big Bear Discovery Center, Highway 38, P.O. Box 60, Fawnskin, CA 92333.

Children's Forest Visitor Information Center, Highway 18, P.O. Box 350, Sky Forest, CA 92385, (909) 337-5256.

Shasta-Trinity National Forest

Shasta Lake Visitor Center, Shasta Lake Ranger District, 14225 Holiday Road, Redding, CA 96003, (503) 275-1587.

Tahoe National Forest

Big Bend Visitor Center, I-80 at Rainbow, P.O. Box 830, Soda Springs, CA 95728, (530) 426-3609.

COLORADO

Arapaho-Roosevelt National Forest

Clear Creek Visitor Center, Clear Creek Ranger District, P.O. Box 3307, Idaho Springs, CO 80452, (303) 567-2901.

Forest Visitor Information Center, 1311 S. College Ave., Fort Collins, CO 80524, (907) 498-2700 or 498-2707.

Rio Grande National Forest

Creede Underground Mining Museum, 407 N. Loma, Creede, CO 81130, (719) 658-0811.

FLORIDA

Ocala National Forest

Ocala National Forest Visitor Center, Lake George Ranger District, 10863 E. Highway 40, Silver Springs, FL 34488, (352) 625-7470.

Pittmann Visitor Center, Seminole Ranger District, 45621 State Highway 19, Altoona, FL 32702, (352) 669-7495.

Salt Springs Visitor Center, 14100 N. Highway 19, Salt Springs, FL 32134, (352) 685-3070.

GEORGIA

Chattahoochee-Oconee National Forests

Anna Ruby Falls Visitor Center, Anna Ruby Falls Road, Helen, GA 30545, (706) 878-3574 or 878-1448.

Brasstown Bald Visitor Center, Brasstown Ranger District, P.O. Box 9, 1881 Highway 515, Blairsville, GA 30512, (404) 745-6928.

IDAHO

Boise National Forest

Idaho City Visitor Center, P.O. Box 129, Highway 21 and Main Street, Idaho City, ID 83631, (208) 392-6040.

Clearwater National Forest

Lochsa Visitor Center, Lochsa Ranger District, Kooskia, ID 83539, (208) 926-4275.

Nez Perce National Forest

Slate Creek Ranger Station Museum, Salmon River Ranger District, White Bird, ID 83554, (208) 839-2211.

Salmon-Challis National Forest

Land of the Yankee Fork Historic Area, P.O. Box 1086, Junction Highway 7593, Challis, ID 83226, (208) 879-5244.

Sawtooth National Forest

Redfish Lake Visitor Center, Star Route Highway 75, Ketchum, ID 83340, (208) 726-5000.

Sawtooth National Recreation Area Headquarters Visitor Center, Star Route Highway 75, Ketchum, ID 83340, (208) 726-5000.

Targhee National Forest

Eastern Idaho Visitors Information Center, 505 Lindsay Blvd., Idaho Falls, ID 83451, (208) 523-3278.

KENTUCKY

Daniel Boone National Forest
Gladie Historic Site, Stanton Ranger District, Highway 715, Red River Gorge Geologic Area, KY, (606) 663-2852.

Morehead Visitor Center, Morehead Ranger District, 2375 Kentucky 801, South Morehead, KY 40351, (606) 784-6428.

MAINE

White Mountain National Forest
Evans Notch Visitor Center, 18 Mayville Road, Bethel, ME 04217, (207) 824-2134 or 824-3312.

MICHIGAN

Huron-Manistee National Forest
Lumberman's Monument Visitor Center, Tawas Ranger District, 329 Newman St., East Tawas, MI 48730, (517) 362-4477.

Ottawa National Forest
Watersmeet Visitor Center, Watersmeet Ranger District, U.S. 45, P.O. Box 276, Watersmeet, MI 49969, (906) 358-4724.

MINNESOTA

Chippewa National Forest
Cut Foot Visitor Center, Deer River Ranger District, P.O. Box 188, Deer River, MN 56636, (218) 246-8233.

Norway Beach Visitor Center, U.S. Highway 2, 200 Ash Ave., Cass Lake, MN 56633, (218) 335-2544.

Superior National Forest
Voyageur Visitor Center, Ely Ranger District, P.O. Box 149, Ely, MN 55731, (218) 365-6226.

All U.S. Park Forest Service Photos

Camping Minnesota

Beach Michigan

Fishing Minnesota

MONTANA

Bitterroot National Forest
Darby Road Historical Visitor Center and Museum, Darby Ranger District, Darby, MT 59829, (406) 821-3913.
Clearwater National Forest
Lolo Pass Visitor Center, Powell Ranger District, Lolo, MT 59847, (208) 942-3113.

Flathead National Forest
Big Mountain Environmental Education Center, Tally Lake Ranger District, Whitefish, MT 59937, (406) 862-2508.
Hungry Horse Visitor Center, Hungry Horse Ranger District, Hungry Horse, MT 59919, (406) 387-5241.

Gallatin National Forest
Madison River Earthquake Area Visitor Center, Hebgen Lake Ranger District, West Yellowstone, MT 59758, (406) 646-7369.

Lewis and Clark National Forest
Lewis and Clark Interpretive Center, 4201 Giant Springs Road, P.O. Box 1806, Great Falls, MT 59403, (406) 727-8733.
Augusta Information Station, 405 Manix Street, Augusta, MT 59401, (406) 562-3247.
Belt Creek Information Station, 4234 Highway 89 North, Neihart, MT 59465, (406) 236-5511.

Lolo National Forest
Nine-Mile Remount Area, Nine-Mile Ranger District, P.O. Box 616, Nine-Mile Road, Huson, MT 59846, (406) 626-5201.
Smokejumper Visitor Center, Missoula Ranger District, Missoula, MT 59801, (406) 329-3814.

NEW HAMPSHIRE

White Mountain National Forest
New Hampton Information Center, P.O. Box 2, Exit 23 Plaza, Route 104, New Hampton, NH 03256, (603) 744-9165.
Pinkham Notch Visitor Center, P.O. Box 298, Gorham, NH 03581, (603) 466-2721.

NEW MEXICO

Carson National Forest
Ghost Ranch Living Museum Visitor Center, Canjilon Ranger District, Canjilon, NM 87510, (505) 684-2486.

Cibola National Forest
Four Seasons Visitor Center, Sandia Ranger District, 11776 Highway 337, Tijeras, NM 87059, (505) 242-4177.
Sandia Crest Visitor Center, Sandia Ranger District, 11776 Highway 337, Tijeras, NM 87059, (505) 248-0190.
Gila National Forest
Gila Cliff Dwellings National Monument, Wilderness Ranger District, Mimbres, NM 88049, (505) 536-2250.
Gila Cliff Dwellings Visitor Center, Silver City Ranger District, Silver City, NM 88061, (505) 538-2771.

Santa Fe National Forest
Public Lands Information Center, 1474 Rodeo Road, Santa Fe, NM 87505, (505) 438-7542.

NORTH CAROLINA

Nantahala National Forest
Highlands Visitor Center, Highlands Ranger District, 2010 Flat Mountain Road, Highlands, NC 28741, (828) 526-4765.

Pisgah National Forest
Cradle of Forestry Discovery Center, Pisgah Ranger District, 1001 Pisgah Highway, Brevard, NC 28768, (828) 877-3130.
Grandfather Visitor Center, Grandfather Ranger District, Route 1, P.O. Box 110A, Nebo, NC 28761, (828) 652-2144.
Linville Gorge Visitor Center, Highway 105, Route 1, P.O. Box 110, Nebo, NC 28761, (828) 652-2144.
Pisgah Visitor Center, Pisgah Ranger District, 101 Pisgah Highway, Pisgah Forest, NC 28768, (828) 877-3350.
Roan Mountain Information Cabin, Appalachia Ranger District, P.O. Box 128, U.S. Highway 19 East Bypass, Burnsville, NC 28714, (828) 682-6146.

OREGON

Columbia River Gorge National Scenic Area
Bonneville Lock and Dam Visitor Center, U.S. Army Corps of Engineers, Cascade Locks, OR 97014, (541) 374-8820.
Cascade Locks Marine Park Visitor Center and Sternwheeler, P.O. Box 307, Cascade Locks, OR 97014, (541) 374-8619.
Columbia Gorge Discovery Area, I 84, 5000 Discovery Drive, The Dalles, OR 97058, (541) 296-8600.

The Dalles Lock and Dam Visitor Center, U.S. Army Corps of Engineers, P.O. Box 564, The Dalles, OR 97058, (541) 296-9778.

The Gorge Discovery Center and Wasco County Historical Museum, 5000 Discovery Drive, The Dalles, OR 97058, (541) 296-8600.

Deschutes National Forest

Lava Lands Visitor Center, Fort Rock Ranger District, 1230 Southeast Third #A-262, Bend, OR 97707, (541) 593-2421.

Redmond Air Center, 1740 SE Ochooa Way, Redmond, OR 97756, (541) 504-7200.

Mount Hood National Forest

Clackamas Lake Historic Ranger Station, Zig Zag Ranger District, Forest Road 42, 70220 East Highway 26, Zig Zag, OR (503) 622-5622.

Mount Hood Information Center, 65000 East Highway 26, Welches, OR 97067, (503) 622-7674.

Multnomah Falls Visitor Center, Columbia Gorge National Scenic Area, 902 Wasco Ave., Hood River, OR 97031, (541) 695-2372.

Timberline Lodge Visitor Center, Zig Zag Ranger District, 70220 East Highway 26, Zig Zag, OR 97049, (503) 622-3191.

Siskiyou National Forest

Gold Beach Visitor Center, Gold Beach Ranger District, 29279 Ellensburg, Gold Beach, OR 97444, (541) 247-3600.

Illinois River Valley Visitor Center, 200 Caves Highway, Cave Junction, OR 97523, (541) 592-4076.

Rand Information Center, 14335 Galice Road, Merlin, OR 97532, (541) 479-3735.

Cape Perpetua Visitor Center, Waldport Ranger District, 1049 Southwest Pacific Highway, P.O. Box 400, Waldport, OR 97394, (503) 547-3289.

Oregon Dunes National Recreation Visitor Center, 855 Pacific Highway, Reedsport, OR 97467, (503) 271-3611.

Umatilla National Forest

Tollgate Visitor Center, (541) 271-3611.

Umpqua National Forest

Colliding Rivers Information Center, North Umpqua Ranger District, 18782 N. Umpqua Highway, Glide, OR 97443, (541) 496-0157.

Diamond Lake Visitor Center, Diamond Lake Ranger District, 2020 Toketee Ranger Station Road, Idlewyld Park, OR 97447, (541) 793-3310.

Wallowa-Whitman National Forest

Hells Canyon Launch Site, P.O. Box 99, Oxbow, OR 97840, (541) 785-3395.

Wallowa Mountains Visitor Center, 88401 Highway 82, Enterprise, OR 97828, (541) 426-5546.

PENNSYLVANIA

Allegheny National Forest

Grey Towers National Historic Landmark, Pinchot Institute, P.O. Box 188, Milford, PA 18337, (570) 296-9230.

PUERTO RICO

Caribbean National Forest

El Portal Tropical Forest Center, P.O. Box 490, Road 191 K-4, Palmer, Puerto Rico 00721, (787) 888-1880.

Palo Colorado Visitor Center, same address and phone.

Sierra Palma Visitor Center, same address and phone.

Yokahu Tower Visitor Center, same address and phone.

SOUTH DAKOTA

Black Hills National Forest

Black Hills National Forest Visitor Center, Mystic Ranger District, Highway 385, 800 Soo San Drive, Rapid City, SD 57701, (605) 343-8755.

Pactola Visitor Center, Mystic Ranger District, Rapid City, SD 57701, (605) 343-1567.

TENNESSEE

Cherokee National Forest

Cherokee Tennessee Overhill Heritage Association, P.O. Box 143, Etowah, TN 37331, (423) 263-7232.

Coker Creek Visitor Center, Tellico River Ranger District, 12528 Highway 68, Coker Creek, TN 37314, (423) 261-2310.

Hiwassee Visitor Center, Tanasi Ranger District, 727 Tennessee Ave., L and N Depot, Etowah, TN 37331, (423) 263-5486.

Ocoee White Water Center, Tanasi Ranger District, Route 1, P.O. Box 285, Highway 64 West, Copper Hill, TN 37317, (423) 496-5197.

UTAH

Ashley National Forest

Flaming Gorge Visitor Center, P.O. Box 279, Dutch John, UT 84046, (435) 781-5242.

Red Canyon Visitor Center, same address and phone.

Rock Creek Visitor Center, Duchesne Ranger District, P.O. Box 981, Upper Stillwater, Rock Creek Road, Duchesne, UT 84021, (435) 454-3024.

Dixie National Forest
Interagency Visitor Center, Pine Valley Ranger District, 196 E. Tabernacle, St. George, UT 84770, (435) 652-3100.

Manti La Sal National Forest
Interagency Information Center, Moab Ranger District, P.O. Box 386, Moab, UT 84532, (435) 259-7155 or 259-6111.

Uinta National Forest
Herber Valley Visitor Center, 2460 S. Highway 40, Heber, UT 84032, (435) 654-0470.
Strawberry Visitor Center, Heber Ranger District, P.O. Box 190, Heber City, UT 84032, (435) 654-0470 or 548-2321.

VIRGINIA

George Washington and Jefferson National Forests
Damascus Caboose Visitor Center, Mount Rogers National Recreation Area, 104 S. Beaver Dam Ave., Damascus, VA 24236, (800) 628-7202.
Forest Place Visitor Center, Warmsprings Ranger District, Route 2, P.O. Box 30, Hotsprings, VA 24445, (540) 839-5281.
Gathright Dam and Lake Moomaw Visitor Center Corps of Engineers, James River District, Gathright Lane off Coles Mountain Road, Covington, VA 24426, (540) 962-1138.
Green Cove Station, Mount Rogers National Recreation Area, 41259 Green Cove Road, Damascus, VA 24236, (540) 388-3386.
Highlands Gateway Visitor Center, Factory Merchant Mall, 731 Factory Outlet Drive, Suite D8, Max Meadows, VA 24360, (800) 446-9670.
Massanuttan Visitor Center, Lee Ranger District, 3220 Lee Highway, New Market, VA 22844, (540) 740-8310.
Mount Rogers Visitor Center, 3714 Highway 16, Marion, VA 24354, (800) 628-7202.
Sherando Lake Information Center, Glenwood-Pedlar Ranger District, 747 Sherando Lake Road, Lyndhurst, VA 22952, (540) 949-0918.
Natural Bridge Information Center, Glenwood Pedlar Ranger District, P.O. Box 100, Natural Bridge Station, VA 24579 (540) 291-1806.

WASHINGTON

Columbia River Gorge National Scenic Area
Multnomah Falls Visitor Center, I 84, 902 Wasco Ave., Suite 200, Hood River, OR 97031, (503) 695-2372.
Skamania Lodge Information Center, 1131 SW Skamania Lodge Drive, Stevenson, WA 98648, (509) 427-2528.

Colville National Forest
Spokane Information Office, 904 W. Riverside, Room 135, Spokane, WA 99201.

Gifford Pinchot National Forest
Coldwater Ridge Visitor Center, 3029 Spirit Lake Highway, Castle Rock, WA 98611, (360) 274-2131 or 274-2102.
Johnson Ridge Visitor Center, 3029 Spirit Lake Highway, Castle Rock, WA 98611, (360) 274-2140.
Mount St. Helens National Volcanic Monument, 42218 NE Yale Bridge Road, Amboy, WA 98601, (360) 274-3900 or 274-3902.
Mount St. Helens Visitor Center, 3029 Spirit Lake Highway, Castle Rock, WA 98611, (360) 274-2100 or 274-2102.
Silver Lake Visitor Center, Route 1, P.O. Box 369, Amboy, WA 98601, (206) 274-2120.
Wind River Information Center, 1262 Hemlock Road, Carson, WA 98610, (509) 427-3200 or 427-4541.

Mount Baker-Snoqualmie National Forest
Glacier Public Service Center, Mount Baker Ranger District, Glacier, WA 98244, (360) 599-2714.
Heather Meadows Visitor Center, same address and phone.
Outdoor Recreation Information Center, 222 Yale Ave. North, Seattle, WA 98109, (206) 470-4060.
Snoqualmie Pass Visitor Center, North Bend Ranger District, Snoqualmie Pass, WA 98068, (425) 434-6111.
Verlot Public Service Center, Darrington Ranger District, Verlot, WA 98252, (360) 691-7791.

Okanogan National Forest
Early Winters Visitor Center, Twisp Ranger District, 502 Glover, P.O. Box 188, Twisp, WA 98856, (503) 997-2131.
Methaw Valley Visitor Center, Building 49, Highway 20, 24 W. Chewuch Road, Winthrop, WA 98862, (509) 996-4000.
Winthrop Visitor Center, Twisp Ranger District, P.O. Box 579, Winthrop, WA 98862, (509) 996-4022.

WEST VIRGINIA

Monongahela National Forest
Cranberry Mountain Nature Center, Gauley Ranger District, P.O. Box 110, Richwood, WV 26261, (304) 846-2695.
Seneca Rocks Discovery Area, Potomac Ranger District, Route 3, P.O. Box 240, Petersburg, WV 27847, (304) 257-4488.

Deer in West Virginia

WISCONSIN

Chequamegon-Nicolet National Forests
Florence Natural Resource and Wild River Interpretive Center, Florence Ranger District, 8 HC1, P.O. Box 83, U.S. 2 and 101/70, Florence, WI 54121, (715) 528-4464.

Biker in Wisconsin

WYOMING

Ashley National Forest
Green River Chamber of Commerce, 1450 Uinta, Green River, WY 82939, (307) 875-5711.
Burgess Junction Visitor Center, Tongue Ranger District, U.S. Highway 14, Burgess Junction, WY, (307) 672-4451.
Shell Falls Interpretive Center, Medicine Wheel Ranger District, U.S. Highway 14, Burgess Junction, WY, (307) 272-0819.
Interagency Visitor Center, P.O. Box 1888, 340 N. Cache, Jackson, WY 83001, (307) 734-8760.
Togwatee Lodge Nature Center, Buffalo Ranger District, Highway 26/287, P.O. Box 91, Moran, WY 83013, (307) 543-2847.

Buffalo in Wyoming

Elk in Wyoming

Web Addresses

ALABAMA

Adventure GPS Products Inc. - www.gps4fun.com
Camper's Choice Inc. - www.camperschoice.com
frogg toggs - www.froggtoggs.com
Integral Designs - www.integraldesigns.com
Soft Path Cuisine Inc. -
   www.organiccampingfood.com
Wisemen Trading and Supply -
   www.wisementrading.com

ARKANSAS

A.G. Russell Knives Inc. - www.agrussell.com
Arkatents Outdoor Gear - www.arkatents.com
Russell's For Men - www.russellsformen.com

ARIZONA

BlueSkyKitchen.com - www.blueskykitchen.com
Camper Clubs of America -
   www.camperclubs.com
Summit Hut - www.summithut.com
Teva Sport Sandals - www.teva.com
AirZone Recreation Inc. -
   www.airzonerecreation.com
ArcTeryx Equipment Inc. - www.arcteryx.com
Bobkatz Limited - www.bobkatz.com
Infinity Sports Imports Inc. -
   www.infinity-outdoor.com
Navarro Weather Gear - www.navarrogear.com
Outbound Products - www.outbound.ca
Sherpa Mountain Products -
   www.sherpa-mtn.com

CALIFORNIA

Abnet Inc. - www.4abnet.com
Adventure Medical Kits -
   www.adventuremedicalkits.com
All Tent Trailer Rentals & Sales -
   www.alltents.com
AlpineAire Foods - www.alpineairefoods.com
Boreal - www.borealusa.com
Buck Knives - www.buckknives.com
Camelbak Products Inc. - www.camelbak.com
Design Salt USA - www.designsalt.com
Dom's Outdoor Outfitters -
   www.domsoutdoor.com
E-Z Sales & Mfg. Inc. - www.ezsalesinc.com
Eagle Creek Inc. - www.eaglecreek.com
ENEL Co. - www.enelcompany.com
Good Sam Club - www.goodsamclub.com
Gregory Mountain Products -
   www.gregorypacks.com

Human Nature - www.humannaturegear.com
Izeo 2 Design - www.hatinabag.com
Lance Camper Manufacturing Corp. -
   www.lancecamper.com
Lawry's Foods Inc. - www.lawrys.com
MAC Sports - www.maccabeesports.com
Mag Instrument Inc. - www.maglite.com
Magellan's International - www.magellans.com
Marmot Mountain Works -
   www.marmotmountain.com
Mountain Hard Wear -
   www.mountainhardwear.com
Mountain Tools - www.mtntools.com
Oakley - www.oakley.com
Outdoor Products - www.outdoorproducts.com
Overland Equipment -
   www.overlandequipment.com
Oware - www.owareusa.com
Paha Que Wilderness Inc. - www.pahaque.com
Pelican Products - www.pelican.com
Piggy Pack - www.piggypack.com
Pit-2-Go - www.pit2go.com
Porta-Bote International - www.porta-bote.com
Resort Parks International - www.resortparks.com
Richmoor Corp. - www.richmoor.com
Sierra Designs - www.sierradesigns.com
StanSport - www.stansport.com
Suunto - www.suuntousa.com
Tecfen Corp. - www.tecfen.com
The North Face Inc. - www.thenorthface.com
The Outdoor World of California -
   www.theoutdoorworld.com
ToolLogic - www.toollogic.com
Trailer Life -- TL Enterprises - www.trailerlife.com
Travelsmith - www.travelsmith.com
Ultimate Direction - www.ultimatedirection.com
Ursack - www.ursack.com
Variety International Inc. - www.varietyintl.com
WelCom Products Inc. -
   www.welcomproducts.com
Western Mountain Sports -
   www.westernmountaineering.com
Wilderness Press - www.wildernesspress.com
ZZ Manufacturing Inc. - www.zzstove.com

COLORADO

Backcountry Experience - www.bcexp.com
Big Agnes Inc. - www.bigagnes.com
Coast to Coast Resorts - www.coastresorts.com
Deuter USA Inc. - www.deuterusa.com
GoLite LLC - www.golite.com
Insect-Out Inc. - www.insectout.com

Interactive Outdoors Inc. - www.wildernet.com
Jax Outdoors - www.jaxoutdoor.com
Kelty - www.kelty.com
La Sportiva NA - www.sportiva.com
Let's Go Aero Inc. - www.letsgoaero.com
Madden Mountaineering - www.maddenusa.com
Mountainsmith - www.mountainsmith.com
Oshman's SuperSports USA - www.oshmans.com
Osprey Packs Inc. - www.ospreypacks.com
Outdoor Edge Cutlery Corp. -
    www.outdooredge.com
Salamander Paddle Gear -
    www.salamanderpaddlegear.com
SmartWool - www.smartwool.com
StoneCreek Designs Inc. -
    www.stonecreekdesigns.com
Whistle Creek - www.whistlecreek.com
Wiggy's Inc. - www.wiggys.com
Women's Wilderness Institute -
    www.womenswilderness.org

CONNECTICUT

LCN Outdoors - www.lcnoutdoors.com
Swiss Army Brands Inc. - www.swissarmy.com

DELAWARE

Cordura/DuPont - www.dupont.com/cordura
W.L. Gore & Associates - www.gore.com

FLORIDA

Camp Florida - www.floridacamping.com
Coleman Campground & RV Park Directory -
    www.colemandirectory.com
Florida Association of RV Parks and
    Campgrounds - www.floridacamping.com
Lee Island Coast Visitor & Convention Bureau -
    www.leeislandcoast.com
Southeast Publications USA - www.rvingusa.com
Sunbeam Corp. - www.sunbeam.com
Trailmate Inc. - www.trailmate.com
Visit Florida - www.flausa.com

IOWA

Bug-Out Outdoorwear Inc. -
    www.bug-out-outdoorwear.com
Hawgeyes BBQ - www.hawgeyesbbq.com
Pilot Rock Park Equipment - www.pilotrock.com

IDAHO

Chuckwagon Supply -
    www.chuckwagonsupply.com
K&R Adventure Gear -
    www.knradventuregear.com
Ken's Custom Tent & Canvas -
    www.idfishnhunt.com/kens.html
R.U. Outside Inc. - www.ruoutside.com
Thunder Mountain Tent & Canvas -
    www.idfishnhunt.com/thunder.html

ILLINOIS

Century Tool & Manufacturing Co. Inc. -
    www.centurytoolmfg.com
CMG Equipment - www.cmgequipment.com
Rome Industries Inc. - www.pieirons.com
Sun Ovens International Inc. - www.sunoven.com
TentOnSale.com - www.tentonsale.com
The Camping Gear Store -
    www.colemanoutdoors.com
Thermos Co. - www.thermos.com
Wheelers Guides, Print Media Services -
    www.wheelersguides.com

INDIANA

Anchor Industries Inc. - www.anchorinc.com
Coachmen Recreational Vehicle Co., LLC -
    www.coachmenrv.com
Indiana Campground Owners Association -
    www.rvdestinations.com/icoa/
Jayco Inc. - www.jayco.com
Kidstuff Playsystems Inc. - www.fun-zone.com
Knife Outlet - www.knifeoutlet.com
Long Life Food Depot - www.longlifefood.com
Orion Safety Products - www.orionsignals.com
Starcraft RV Inc. - www.starcraftrv.com

KANSAS

Coleman Company Inc. - www.coleman.com
Garmin International Inc. - www.garmin.com

KENTUCKY

Camping World - www.campingworld.com

MASSACHUSETTS

Maptech - www.maptech.com
Swift Instruments Inc. - www.swift-optics.com
Reliance Products - www.relianceproducts.com

MARYLAND

Cherry Hill Park - www.cherryhillpark.com
Hembree Enterprises Inc. (HEI) - www.h-e-i.com

MAINE

Byer Manufacturing Co. - www.byerofmaine.com
DeLorme Mapping Co. - www.delorme.com
Hydro-Photon Inc. - www.hydro-photon.com
L.L. Bean - www.llbean.com
Maine Campground Owners Association -
    www.campmaine.com

MICHIGAN

Adventure-Camping.com -
    www.adventure-camping.com
Carlisle Paddles Inc. - www.carlislepaddles.com
Dunham's Sports - www.dunhamssports.com
Eastman Outdoors - www.eastmanoutdoors.com
Merrell Footwear - www.merrellboot.com

MINNESOTA

Cache Lake - www.cachelake.com
Duluth Pack - www.duluthpack.com
Granite Gear - www.granitegear.com
Kondos Outdoors - www.kondosoutdoors.com
NPO Foods - www.cachelake.com
PUR - www.purwater.com
Scamp - www.scamptrailers.com
Stearns Inc. - www.stearnsinc.com
Vasque - www.vasque.com
Viking Recreational Vehicles LLC -
    www.vikingrv.com
We-no-nah Canoes - www.wenonah.com
Wintergreen Designs -
    www.wintergreendesigns.com

MISSOURI

Bass Pro Shops - www.basspro-shops.com
Cerf Bros. Bag Co. - www.campinn.com
Energizer - www.energizer.com
Rokk - www.rokkgear.com
Slumberjack Products - www.slumberjack.com
The Escape Co. - www.escape-co.com
The Wenzel Company - www.wenzelco.com
Will B. Free Travel Store - www.willbfree.com

MISSISSIPPI

Mississippi Division of Tourism -
    www.visitmississippi.org

MONTANA

BobWards.com - www.bobwards.com
Crazy Creek Products Inc. - www.crazycreek.com
Kampgrounds of America Inc. -
    www.koakampgrounds.com
Timberline Group - www.timberlinefurniture.com

NORTH CAROLINA

Adventure Foods - www.AdventureFoods.com
Lawson Hammock Co. -
    www.lawsonhammock.com
**North Carolina Association of RV Parks and
    Campgrounds** - www.kiz.com/campnet/
    html/cluborgs/nccoa
**North Carolina Division of Tourism, Film,
    Sports Division** - www.visitnc.com
Thor-Lo Inc. - www.thorlo.com

NEBRASKA

Cabela's - www.cabelas.com

NEW HAMPSHIRE

Eastern Mountain Sports - www.ems.com
J.R. Liggett Ltd. - www.jrliggett.com
Moonbow - www.moonbowgear.com
MPI Outdoors - www.mpioutdoors.com
Natrapel Inc. - www.tendercorp.com
**New Hampshire Campground Owners'
    Association** - www.ucampnh.com

Stephensons Warmlite - www.warmlite.com
Tender Corp. - www.tendercorp.com
Wickers America - www.wickers.com
Wild Things - www.wildthingsgear.com

NEW JERSEY

Campmor.com - www.campmor.com
FlagHouse Inc. - www.flaghouse.com
New Jersey Campground Owners Association -
    www.newjerseycampgrounds.com
Princeton Tec Sport Lights -
    www.princetontec.com

NEW MEXICO

Pet Pouch - www.petpouch.com
Wild Mountain Outfitters - www.bcexp.com
Trail Blazer - www.trailblazerproducts.com

NEVADA

Athena International Inc. -
    www.athenainternational.com
Patagonia Inc. - www.patagonia.com
Sea to Summit - www.seatosummitusa.com
Sportif USA - www.sportif.com

NEW YORK

ACAP of New York Inc. -
    members.aol.com/tourmastr
Aero Coach - www.thorindustries.com
Camp Trails - www.camptrails.com
Campground Owners of New York -
    www.rvdestinations.com/cony
Camping R Corp. - www.campingrus.com
Carson Optical - www.carson-optical.com
Dura-Bilt Products Inc. - www.durabilt.com
Eureka! - www.eurekatent.com
Imperial Schrade Corp. - www.schradeknives.com
Jamestown Advanced Products Corp. -
    www.jamestownadvanced.com
Lansky Sharpeners - www.lansky.com
Manzella Productions Inc. - www.manzella.com
Nalgene Outdoor Products Division - www.nal-
    gene-outdoor.com
Napier Enterprises - www.sportztrucktent.com
Nikon USA - www.nikonusa.com
Silva - www.silvacompass.com
Tough Traveler Ltd. - www.toughtraveler.com

OHIO

Coalition for Portable Propane Product Safety -
    www.propaneproducts.org
Lehman's - www.lehmans.com
Mr. Heater Corp. - www.mrheater.com
Ohio Division of Travel and Tourism -
    www.ohiotourism.com
Arctic Canvas - www.on-biz.com/arcticcanvas/
Harvest Foodworks - www.harvestfoodworks.com
Woods Canada Ltd. - www.woodscanada.com

OREGON

BackTrek - www.backtrek.com
Chalet RV Inc. - www.chaletrv.com
Cooks' Nook Inc. - www.cooksnook.com
Danner Shoe Mfg. Co. - www.danner.com
DreamSacks Inc. - www.dreamsack.com
Leatherman Tool Group Inc. -
    www.leatherman.com
Mountain House - www.mountainhouse.com
Oregon Scientific Inc. - ww.osi.com
Pacific Cornetta Inc. - www.pacific-cornetta.com
PhotonLight.com - www.photonlight.com
Snow Peak USA Inc. - www.snowpeak.com

PENNSYLVANIA

Aliner/Columbia Northwest Inc. - www.aliner.com
Coleman Trailers - foldingtrailers.com
Duofold - www.duofold.com
General Ecology Inc. - www.generalecology.com
Get Organized - www.getorginc.com
LoveTheOutdoors.com -
    www.lovetheoutdoors.com
Pennsylvania Campground Owners Association -
    www.pacamping.com
W.R. Case & Sons Cutlery Co. - casesales.com
Wechsel/Equinox Ltd. - www.equinoxltd.com
Brule Mountain Gear - PanPack -
    www.panpack.com

SOUTH CAROLINA

Atsko Inc. - www.atsko.com
Dagger Canoes - www.dagger.com

TENNESSEE

GearPro.com - www.gearpro.com
Georgia Boot Co. - www.georgiabootcompany.com
Lodge Manufacturing Co. - www.lodgemfg.com
River Sports Outfitters Inc. - www.GearPro.com
**Tennessee Association of RV Parks and
    Campgrounds** - www.rvnetlinx.com/
    dba/dba.php3?id=2668

TEXAS

Caribou Mountaineering - www.caribou.com
CheaperThanDirt.com - www.cheaperthandirt.com
Gearout Outdoor GearStore - www.gearout.com
Katadyn Products Inc. - www.katadyn.net
Meyerco USA/Camp USA - www.meyercousa.com
Texas Assocation of Campground Owners -
    www.texascampgrounds.com
WeatherRite Outdoor - www.weatherrite.com

UTAH

BackcountryStore.com -
    www.backcountrystore.com
Bibler Tents - www.biblertents.com
Black Diamond Equipment - www.bdel.com
Camp Chef - www.campchef.com
Emergency Essentials - www.beprepared.com

Liberty Mountain - www.libertymountain.com
Moosineer Outdoor Gear - www.moosineer.com
NEBO Sports - www.neboproducts.com
Newell International Inc. USA -
    www.newellinternational.com
Petzl America - www.petzl.com
Watchful Eye Designs -
    www.watchfuleyedesigns.com
Zodi Outback Gear - www.zodi.com

VIRGINIA

Ferrino USA - www.ferrino-usa.com
Plow & Hearth - www.plowhearth.com

VERMONT

Peregrine Outfitters - www.peregrineoutfitters.com
Tubbs Snowshoe Co. - www.tubbssnowshoes.com
Turtle Fur - www.turtlefur.com
Vermont Country Store -
    www.vermontcountrystore.com

WASHINGTON

Altrec.com - www.altrec.com
C.C. Filson Co. - www.filson.com
CampMan Inc. - www.campman.com
Cascade Designs Inc. - www.cascadedesigns.com
Dana Design - www.danadesign.com
Eddie Bauer - www.eddiebauer.com
Exped Expedition Equipment - www.exped.com
Feathered Friends - www.featheredfriends.com
Forty Below Ltd. - www.40below.com
GSI Outdoors - www.gsioutdoors.com
Hilleberg the Tentmaker - www.hilleberg.com
McNett Corp. - www.mcnett.com
Montrail - www.montrail.com
Moonstone Mountain Equipment -
    www.moonstone.com
Mountain Safety Research - www.msrcorp.com
Nikwax - www.nikwax-usa.com
Ortlieb USA LLC - www.ortliebusa.com
Outdoor Research - www.orgear.com
Packtowl - www.cascadedesigns.com/packtowl
Platypus - www.cascadedesigns.com/platypus
Recreational Equipment Inc. (REI) -
    www.rei.com
SealLine - www.cascadedesigns.com
Survival Inc. - www.ultimatesurvival.com
Sweetwater - www.cascadedesigns.com
Therm-a-Rest -
    www.cascadedesigns.com/thermarest
Tracks - www.cascadedesigns.com/tracks
Trondak Inc. - www.aquaseal.com
UCO Corp. - www.ucocorp.com
Wild Roses - www.wrgear.com

WISCONSIN

Canvas Replacements -
    www.canvasreplacements.com
Exstream Water Technologies Inc. -
    www.exstreamwater.com

Gander Mountain - www.gandermountain.com
Gerber Manufacturing Ltd. -
    www.gerbertables.com
JanSport USA - www.jansport.com
Lands' End - www.landsend.com
Nesco/American Harvest - www.nesco.com
Open Country - www.nesco.com
S. King Company Inc. - www.skingcompany.com
WPC Brands Inc. - www.destinationoutdoors.com

WEST VIRGINIA

Anderson's Campground Directory -
    www.andersonsdirectory.com

West Virginia Division of Tourism - www.callw-
va.com

WYOMING

Brunton Co. - www.brunton.com
Fox Hill Corp. - www.foxhill.net
Hi Mountain Jerky Inc. - www.himtnjerky.com
James Kits - www.sharplink.com/jkits/
Wyoming Companion -
    www.wyomingcompanion.com

SWEDEN

Primus AB - www.primus.se

State Tourism Offices

Alabama

Alabama Bureau of Tourism and Travel
401 Adams Ave.
P.O. Box 4927
Montgomery, AL 36103-4927
800-ALABAMA
www.touralabama.org

Alaska

Alaska Travel Industry Association
2600 Cordova Street, Ste. 201
Anchorage, AK 99503
www.travelalaska.com
info@alaskatia.org

Arkansas

Arkansas Department of Parks & Tourism
One Capitol Mall
Little Rock, AR 72201
800-NATURAL
www.arkansas.com
info@arkansas.com

Arizona

Arizona Office of Tourism
2702 North 3rd Street, Suite 4015
Phoenix, AZ 85004
Phone: 602-230-7733, Fax: 602-540-5432
Toll-Free visitor information: 888-520-3434
www.arizonavacationvalues.com

California

caltour@commerce.ca.gov
800-GOCALIF

Colorado

Colorado Tourism Office
1625 Broadway, Ste. 1700
Denver, CO 80202
800-COLORADO
www.colorado.com

Connecticut

Connecticut Office of Tourism
Department of Economic and Community
    Development
505 Hudson Street
Hartford, CT 06106
(860) 270-8080 Fax (860) 270-8077
www.tourism.state.ct.us

Delaware

Delaware Tourism Office
  99 Kings Highway
  Dover, DE 19901
(302) 739-4271
  (866) 2-VISITDE
Fax (302) 739-5749
www.visitdelaware.net

Florida

VISIT FLORIDA
661 East Jefferson Street, Suite 300
Tallahassee, FL 32301
(850) 488-5607 Fax (850) 224-2938
www.flausa.com

Georgia

Georgia Tourism
285 Peachtree Center Ave., Suite 1000
Atlanta, GA 30303
800-VISITGA (1-800-847-4842)
www.georgia.org/tourism

Hawaii

Hawaii Visitors and Convention Bureau
2270 Kalakaua Ave., 8th Floor
Honolulu, HI 96815
(808) 923-1811 Fax: (808) 924-0290
www.gohawaii.com

Idaho

Idaho Department of Commerce
700 W. State St.
P.O. Box 83720
Boise, ID 83720-0093
(208) 334-2470
(800) 842-5858
Fax: (208) 334-2631
www.visitid.org
tourism@idoc.state.id.us

Illinois

Illinois Bureau of Tourism
James R. Thompson Center
100 W. Randolph St., Suite 3-400
Chicago, IL 60601
800-2CONNECT
www.enjoyillinois.com
Tourism@commerce.state.il.us

Indiana

Indiana Tourism Division
Indiana Department of Commerce
One North Capitol, Suite 700
Indianapolis, IN 46204-2288
    888-ENJOY-IN fax: 317-233-6887
www.enjoyindiana.com
    webmaster@enjoyindiana.com

Iowa

Iowa Department of Economic Development
    Iowa Tourism Office
200 East Grand Ave.
    Des Moines, IA 50309
    (515) 242-4705
    (888) 472-6035
    Fax: 515-242-4718
www.traveliowa.com

Kansas

Kansas Department of Commerce & Housing
Travel & Tourism Development Division
1000 S.W. Jackson St., Suite 100
    Topeka, Kansas 66612-1354
(785) 296-8478, Fax: (785) 296-6988
www.kansas-travel.com
travtour@kdoch.state.ks.us

Kentucky

Kentucky Department of Travel
PO Box 2011, Dept WWW,
Frankfort, KY 40602
(800) 225-8747
www.kytourism.com

Louisiana

Louisiana Office of Tourism
P.O. Box 94291
Baton Rouge, LA 70804-9291
(225) 342-8100
Fax: (225) 342-8390
www.louisianatravel.com
free.info@crt.state.la.us

Maine

Maine Office of Tourism
59 State House Station
Augusta, ME 04330
(207) 287-5711
www.visitmaine.com

Maryland

Maryland Office of Tourism Development
217 East Redwood St., 9th Floor
Baltimore, MD 21202
800-MDISFUN
www.mdisfun.org

Massachusetts

Massachusetts Office of Travel & Tourism
10 Park Plaza, Suite 4510
Boston, MA 02116
Phone: (617) 973-8500
Toll-free: (800) 227-MASS
Fax: (617) 973-8525
www.massvacation.com

Michigan

Travel Michigan
Michigan Economic Development Corporation
 P.O. Box 30226
Lansing, MI 48909-7726
(800) 676-1743
travel.michigan.org

Minnesota

Minnesota Office of Tourism
100 Metro Square
121 7th Place East
St. Paul, MN 55101-2146
(800) 657-3700
(651) 296-5029
exploreminnesota.com
explore@state.mn.us

Mississippi

Mississippi Development Authority
Division of Tourism Development
P. O. Box 849
Jackson, MS 39205
(601) 359-3297
Fax (601) 359-5757
(800) 927-6378
www.visitmississippi.org
lturnage@mississippi.org

Missouri

Missouri Division of Tourism
P.O. Box 1055
Jefferson City, MO 65102
(573) 751-4133
Fax: (573) 751-5160
(800) 877-1234
www.missouritourism.org
tourism@mail.state.mo.us

Montana

Travel Montana
PO Box 7549
Missoula MT 59807-7549
1-800-VISITMT
(1-800-847-4868)
www.visitmt.com

Nebraska

Nebraska Department of Economic Development
P.O. Box 94666
301 Centennial Mall South
Lincoln, NE 68509-4666
(800) 228-4307 or (877) 632-7275
FAX: (402) 471-3778
www.visitnebraska.org

Nevada

Nevada Commission on Tourism
401 North Carson St.
Carson City, NV 89701
Telephone: 800-NEVADA-8, (775) 687-4322
Fax (775) 687-6779
www.travelnevada.com
ncot@travelnevada.com

New Hampshire

**New Hampshire Division of Travel and Tourism
Development**
172 Pembroke Road
P.O. Box 1856
Concord, NH 03302-1856
1-800-FUN-IN-NH (1-800-386-4664) -
FAX: 603-271-6870
www.visitnh.gov

New Jersey

**New Jersey Commerce & Economic Growth
Commission**
P.O. Box 820
20 W. State St.
Trenton, NJ 08625
(800) VISIT NJ
(609) 777-0885
/www.visitnj.org

New Mexico

New Mexico Tourism Department
491 Old Santa Fe Trail
The Lamy Building
Santa Fe, 87503
(800) 733-6396 ext 0643
www.newmexico.org

New York

New York State Division of Tourism
Empire State Development
30 S. Pearl St., 2nd Floor
Albany, NY 12245
800 CALL-NYS
(518) 474-4116
www.iloveny.com

North Carolina

North Carolina Division of Tourism, Film, and Sports Development
301 N. Wilmington St.
Raleigh, NC 27601
800 VISITNC
www.visitnc.com

North Dakota

North Dakota Tourism
Liberty Memorial Building
604 East Blvd.
Bismarck, N.D. 58505-0825
800-HELLO ND
www.ndtourism.com

Ohio

Ohio Department of Development-Travel&Tourism
77 S. High St.
P.O. BX 1001
Columbus, Ohio 43216-1001
800-BUCKEYE
www.ohiotourism.com
AskOhioTourism@CallTech.com

Oklahoma

Oklahoma Tourism and Recreation Department
Travel & Tourism Division
P.O. Box 60789
Oklahoma City, OK 73146-0789
(800) 652-6552
information@travelok.com

Oregon

Oregon Tourism Commission
775 Summer St. NE
Salem, OR 97301-1282
(800) 547-7842
www.traveloregon.com

Pennsylvania

Tourism, Film and Economic Development
Marketing Office
4th Floor, Commonwealth Keystone Building
400 North St.
Harrisburg, PA 17120-0225
(800) 237-4363
(717) 787-5453
Fax: 717-787-0687
www.experiencepa.com

Rhode Island

Rhode Island Tourism Division
One W. Exchange St.
Providence, RI 02903
(401) 222-2601
(800) 556-2484
Fax: (401) 273-8270
www.visitrhodeisland.com

South Carolina

South Carolina Department of Parks, Recreation & Tourism
1205 Pendleton St.
Columbia, SC 29201
888-SCSMILE
www.discoversouthcarolina.com

South Dakota

Department of Tourism
Capitol Lake Plaza
711 East Wells Ave.
c/o 500 East Capitol Ave.
Pierre, SD 57501-5070
(605) 773-3301
1-800-S-DAKOTA (1-800-732-5682)
www.travelsd.com
SDINFO@state.sd.us

Tennessee

Tennessee Department of Tourist Development
320 Sixth Avenue N., 5th Floor Rachel
Jackson Bldg.
Nashville, TN 37243
(615) 741-2159
www.tourism.state.tn.us

Texas

Texas Department of Transportation Travel Division
125 E. 11th Street
Austin, TX 78701
(512) 486-5900
800-8888-TEX
Fax: (512) 486-5909
www.traveltex.com

Utah

Utah Travel Council
P.O. Box 147420
Salt Lake City, UT 84114-7420
(801) 538-1030
www.utah.com
travel@utah.com

Vermont

Vermont Department of Tourism & Marketing
Vermont Dept. of Tourism and Marketing
6 Baldwin St., Drawer 33
Montpelier, VT 05633-1301
800-VERMONT
www.travel-vermont.com
vttravel@dca.state.vt.us

Virginia

Virginia Tourism Corp.
901 E. Byrd St.
Richmond, VA 23219
(800) 321-3244
www.virginia.org
VAinfo@virginia.org

Washington

Washington State Office of Trade and Economic
   Development
210-11th Ave SW, Room 101
PO Box 42500
Olympia, WA 98504-2500
(360) 725-5052.
tourism@cted.wa.gov

West Virginia

West Virginia Division of Tourism
90 MacCorkle Ave., SW
South Charleston, WV 25303
(304)558-2200
800-CALL WVA (800-225-5982)
www.callwva.com

Wisconsin

Wisconsin Department of Tourism
P.O. Box 7976
Madison, WI 53707-7976
(800) 432-TRIP
www.travelwisconsin.com

Wyoming

Wyoming Business Council
Travel & Tourism
I-25 at College Drive
Cheyenne, WY 82002
(307) 777-7777
Fax: (307) 777-2877
www.wyomingtourism.org

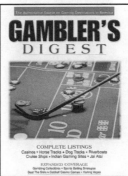
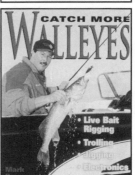